SEDBERGH LETTERS

LETTERS HOME, 1954–1960, FROM SCHOOL HOUSE, SEDBERGH

Jamie and Sandy 1959

SEDBERGH LETTERS

LETTERS HOME, 1954–1960, FROM SCHOOL HOUSE, SEDBERGH

THE LETTERS OF
JAMIE AND SANDY BRUCE LOCKHART
EDITED AND INTRODUCED BY

JAMIE BRUCE LOCKHART

for
Dugald and Andrew,
Mark, Natasha and Simon

ISBN 9781494360634

CONTENTS

INTRODUCTION

Sedbergh School

The School website (2013) provides a brief account of the school's history and provenance in the following terms:

> The school's founder, Roger Lupton, is thought to have been born at Cautley in the parish of Sedbergh in 1456 and he provided for a Chantry School in Sedbergh in 1525 while he was Provost of Eton. By 1528, land had been bought, a school built, probably on the site of the present School Library, and the foundation deed had been signed, binding the School to St John's College, Cambridge and giving the College power over the appointment of Headmasters. This link to St John's College probably saved Sedbergh in 1546-48 when most chantries were dissolved and their assets seized by Henry VIII's Commission.
>
> Sedbergh was re-established and re-endowed as a Grammar School in 1551 and the fortunes of the School in the coming centuries seem to have depended very much on the character and abilities of the Headmasters with pupil numbers fluctuating and reaching as low a total as 8 day boys in the early 19th century.
>
> One particularly successful period was during the Headship of John Harrison Evans (1838-1861) who restored the prestige and achievements of the School and also funded the building of the Market Hall and Reading Room in the town.
>
> A more independent Governing Body was established in 1874 in a successful bid to maintain Sedbergh's independence (amalgamation with Giggleswick had been suggested) and the first meeting took place in The Bull Inn in Sedbergh in December.
>
> In the 1870s there was a tremendous amount of development and building work at Sedbergh, under the careful eye of the Headmaster, Frederick Heppenstall. This included the Headmaster's House (now School House), classrooms, a chapel and four other boarding Houses.
>
> Henry George Hart took over as Headmaster in 1880 and his tenure saw the new Chapel built in 1897, the founding of the Old Sedberghians in 1897/98, the creation of the

prefectorial system, the inaugural Wilson Run and the
confirmation of the School motto "Dura Virum Nutrix" (Stern
Nurse of Men).

When Sandy and I were there in the mid-1950s the school had three main catchment areas. A good number of boys came from homes in Edinburgh and the Scottish borders – sons of sheep farmers and manufacturers of woollens and tweed;. The largest catchment area, however, were the business, professional and landowning classes of North and West Yorkshire, north and western Lancashire (not Cheshire) together with a strong contingent from the East coast from Tyne and Tees to Hull (for instance the Hudson and Boyd fishing fleet owners). Finally, around one quarter of the intake came from the south, Northern Ireland and abroad, usually with existing Sedberghian connections.

For all these groups the school offered a well-rounded education broadly in the Arnold-Vaughan mould of muscular Christianity. Its aims were to produce leaders and decision makers in British middle class society - future civil or colonial   servants, lawyers and soldiers, leaders of agricultural and industrial enterprises; solid, dependable, honest men to run the affairs of the country. In the 1950s the traditional industries of the north such as, cotton, wool, coal, steel and fishing were still alive and well, making Sedbergh not too cut off from the mainstreams of British industrial life at that period even in its remote mountain fastness. The school may not have been in the modern idiom by new liberal standards, and was certainly a bit parochial; nevertheless we were well taught and learnt to think straight by some outstanding staff who had been recruited to the hills for us.

By the 1950s Sedbergh School's reputation was far flung. It counted among the leading public schools in England, but probably in the second rather than in the premier division. It was at the top among the northern and Scottish schools. Its reputation for rugger was outstanding, with Old Sedberghians providing a large number of players at international as well as top club levels. It had a respectable academic record with half a dozen Oxbridge scholarships (of which a number were closed exhibitions) in both science and arts subjects) to its credit each year. It had, thanks in part to the enthusiasm of my grandfather J.H. Bruce Lockhart, acquired a fine reputation for music; and the school was known nationwide for the toughness of its Ten Mile cross country race and for its fell running. As well as rugger teams, the school produced some fine cricket teams in northern schools' competitions, and shooting (at both team and individual level) was frequently good, and average tennis teams.

More important for boarders were inter-house competitions at senior and junior levels in all games, sports and athletics too. The commonly wet weather favoured some emphasis on playing of fives (Rugby fives), at which Sedbergh again produced players at university and national championships levels, and squash was played as a hobby.

ii

Where Sedbergh perhaps fell behind a little was in wider, ancillary subjects. The programme of debate and civics lectures was not extensive. An active debating society included 'Sharps' practice (impromptu debates) and mock elections etc.; but school lectures and 'civics' lectures tended more towards entertainment or geographical interest than to issues of modern society and politics. Classroom training in socio-political-economic subjects was slim too; and emphasis on formal prizes was in the classic subjects, with awards for essays and recitation following older-fashioned traditions. Literature, philosophical, cultural societies were for the most part supported by the strong English-History VIth form, Clio. In School House we had a small literature society, and lectures on music, including jazz and art, informally organised by interested prefects. More successful, on the other hand, was a small natural history society named after the great Cambridge geologist Adam Sedgwick, born and bred in Dent valley and an Old Sedberghian.

As is evident from our letters the school's programme of music was very successful, thanks to the enthusiastic interest of Michael Thornely, bringing concerts (some on a subscription basis) and performances from visiting musicians of all kinds. The school produced a series of National Youth orchestra representatives (three from School House in my years alone), ran three orchestras and active chamber music at school level, and lively inter-house competitions which included unison and quartet singing. In other cultural fields, arts and crafts took off in the post-war period (under Van Gogh lookalike, A. Inglis, and Dave Alban, gifted potter as well as Clio master and tennis coach. Each house had its own magazine and boys were involved in production of School magazines, including a literary publication The Phoenix.

The main informal outdoor activities - from swimming to fishing and caving - were self-organised and self-propelled, with the help of one or two members of staff. In School House we were lucky to have 'Jake' Durran, keen walker and amateur geologist as House tutor. The day had not yet come for Duke of Edinburgh awards or organised school expeditions to distant and exotic regions. But we devoted time weekly to the CCF, with drill competitions on an inter-house basis and energetic field days, and house runs (when pitches were unplayable) got the fidgets out of teenage youth. In general the school lived up to its motto: *dura virum nutrix* and we benefited from that.

Two new boys at School House

We came to Sedbergh with strong personal links to the town, the school and especially School House (where indeed I was born) and to the surrounding countryside. This represented some advantages, and yet I went through an entirely normal development through my school years there. When I arrived my grandfather was no longer headmaster, so the direct link had gone, and I do not remember being conscious at the time that these personal connections were in any way peculiar. Nor do I think my peers saw me as being different or belonging to School House in a different way. But, much as I might have felt at home at Sedbergh when I arrived in September 1954, moving to one's second, big, school after prep school is a large and serious step; and so it was for me.

It probably took a year to overcome the demands of an entirely new environment and grow accustomed to life at the bottom of a hierarchy, but by the second year I felt I belonged at school and in the house. Representing one's house in games at Panters (Junior under 16) level, even if not the school, was a chance to mould tribal associations. By my third year I was aware of being quite a useful member of school society, and that if I did not excel at anything in particular, I could do a number of things as well as, and sometimes possibly better than, many other boys. My fourth and fifth years were great fun and enormously rewarding in every aspect.

At the time one is unlikely to be aware of the nature and inherent difficulties of passage through teenage years - and Sedbergh's full and hardy life helpfully left little time to brood on such matters – but the fact is we survived rather well. My grandfather, an experienced headmaster and housemaster, used to say that it was a source of constant surprise and pleasure for him to see how boys who arrived as troubled, difficult and sometimes unattractive teenagers, changed over five years into nice young men set to become responsible members of society, without a housemaster having done anything much about it except to provide a suitable framework. That is indeed how it seems to have been: we came through and somehow or other grew up.

Family background

As described in *Different Days*,[1] my direct ancestors on all sides were solidly rooted in the middle class that flourished in Britain and its imperial dependencies from the early nineteenth-century onwards. English private boarding school education was part of that world, and was in large measure created and developed for it. Recent generations also brought me a fair number of direct connections to the school-mastering in that environment. The English public school was my natural habitat.

The Lockharts had prospered in commerce in Glasgow in the late eighteenth century and in the nineteenth century were engaged in a wide range of commercial management or more adventurous enterprises in Canada and the USA. They were joined by the Bruces, and their connections, who had long been factors on the estates of aristocratic landowners in the Scottish Lowlands. On the other side of my father's

---

[1] Different Days Courseware4trainers, ..., 2012; an account of my upbringing in the 1940s and early 1950s,

family were the Macgregors, Highlanders from Tomintoul who had settled in the Spey valley in the 1820s where they established a large farm, a milling business and – rather more profitable – a distillery. Descendants travelled the world, with a number going into farming in New Zealand, and the solid returns from the distillery were invested in rubber plantations in Malaya. Fortunes were made and lost in many ventures and adventures, but it was my great-grandfather, Robert Bruce Lockhart, who was the first to take to a new and more solid middle-class road into the professions.

A good scholar and a skilled games-player, he became a preparatory school headmaster, starting as Headmaster of the Wade Academy at Anstruther in Fife and ending his career as head of Eagle House School in Berkshire. He was the founder of a dynasty of successful schoolmasters and sportsmen, and his offspring all went into the professions, diplomatic and military services and school teaching. My grandfather, the second son, was a schoolmaster, first at Rugby where he became a housemaster, then headmaster of Cargilfield, Edinburgh and finally of Sedbergh School itself. He had married Mona Brougham (known to us as Dear).

Her forebears were Anglican churchmen in Ireland from the end of the eighteenth century. Her grandfather was Dean of Lismore in County Waterford (as had been his father before him) but her father remained in England after Oxford to become a schoolmaster and later a housemaster at Wellington College. When the young schoolmaster at Rugby School and the daughter of the Wellington housemaster were married, a close friend in common was W.W. Vaughan, then headmaster of Wellington and later of Rugby, under whom my grandfather served, who did much to modernize the concept of education based on the principles of muscular Christianity as promoted by his famous predecessor, Thomas Arnold.

The schoolmastering connection continued down the generations. My father was a master at Rugby before the Second World War, recruited by Vaughan, and my uncles Rab and Logie both had distinguished careers as public school headmasters. Four first cousins of mine in the next generation likewise became schoolmasters.

On my mother's side, family traditions and background were clerical and medical. Her mother's family, descended from a wealthy Lancashire cotton mill owner, devoted themselves to philanthropy, and of course the daughters naturally taught in various local and Sunday schools. Her father, Campbell Hone, who became Bishop of Wakefield, was another family member to have been much involved in education, throughout his career in Yorkshire and in the House of Lords. My mother herself did a spell (rather reluctantly) as a mistress at Duncombe Park preparatory school for girls before the war, and her brother Robin Hone became head of classics at Clifton and then Headmaster of Exeter School. British private schools and schoolmastering was certainly in my blood.

* * *

During the war when my father was on service abroad, my mother lived first at School House Sedbergh for nearly two years, and then moved in 1943 with us and our nurse, Ada (former nanny to my uncles at Rugby in the 1920s) to Oxford. There she set up house first with her sister Katherine Mills and her two children and then, when my father took up a posting to the British Embassy in Paris at the end of 1945, she bought and moved into a house of her own in Summertown. In 1946 my grandfather Campbell Hone retired and came to live in Oxford too and my mother's brother Robin came to finish his degree at New College. She was thus surrounded by her family in Oxford, and there Sandy and I started our education at the excellent Greycotes Junior Schools (Miss Cunliffe).

In early 1948 my mother, with us, joined my father on a posting to Germany. For Sandy and me the upshot was a change of pace in our upbringing. We moved from the relatively laissez-faire regime under an effectively single mother in Oxford to the interventionist attentions and strong, if affectionate, educational direction from my father, keen to make up for lost time in introducing his children to the kind of education and upbringing he himself had had.

For a year-and-a-half I attended a well-run local British Forces Education Service School (Sandy for a further year); and we were treated to a rich and wonderful life in Germany, with every kind of games and leisure facilities available to us: riding and golf, private swimming pools (an unbelievable luxury at that period) in summer and skiing in the winter in the rather particular surroundings of post-war British military occupation of Germany. We were very spoilt – with my father's batman for company and guardian, and three or four staff around the house to keep an eye on and help us when our parents were otherwise occupied, as they very often were, on business and social rounds.

There followed an enjoyable interlude in my education when I spent a month in the summer of 1949, on the eve of going to the Dragon, with my Bruce Lockhart grandparents at School House, Sedbergh where I received a gentle introduction, not only to my family's traditions and Scottish roots, but also, as an observer, to life in a boarding school.

Other holidays were also formative, in particular a two months' summer holiday in 1952 in Canada and the USA. The last stage in my home life before Sedbergh was arrival at Herons March, Ockley in Surrey, where Sandy and I messed about, accompanied by Jeb, an adored Irish wolfhound, in a large garden surrounded by woodland, at the bottom of which was an eleven-acre lake for boating, fishing, sailing and exploring.

Thus, significant ingredients in my early upbringing were strong traditions in the background, family affection in the foreground, intriguing and pleasing surroundings with which I was able to identify and, finally, the special pleasure of sharing my upbringing with a brother to whom I was very close in age and outlook. Sandy and I were rarely separated, even though we led different lives at school, until the age of nineteen. At home we did everything together; indeed if I ever thought about it, I viewed him as being essentially of the same age and we were well-matched in nearly all games and activities. This close companionship perhaps allowed us to be detached observers of life and people around us. It may perhaps have prevented each us from exploring a wider world on our own separate terms, but I doubt it, and in any case the partnership at home provided a solid counterpart to our boarding school life.

Prep School days

I had had a calm and comfortable passage through my preparatory school, the Dragon School, Oxford[2]. Aged thirteen, I was of medium height and size, on the slight side, light in build and weight; freckled and smiling. My character was already largely formed, I think, by the time I arrived at Sedbergh. I was a conformist and a keen participator; eager to learn, biddable and anxious to please. Games, formal and informal, were a pleasure; I had a reasonably good eye and was nimble on my feet; I enjoyed reading and music. But I was somewhat sensitive and did not like crowds, roughness and too much noise. I was a natural tribal being, with a strong sense of loyalty and I was also accustomed to discipline.

Some key character traits had indeed already been identified at the end of my first term, aged three years and nine months, at my very first school, Greycotes Nursery School, Oxford, 'Charming character, anxious to please and not hurt others, lacks self-confidence, has plenty of intelligence'. In my last term (December 1947) at Greycotes Middle School, the headmistress reported, 'very intelligent and interested in all his lessons. Pleasing progress'. One year later the headmaster of the British Forces Education Service School in Bad Salzuflen echoes that opinion, 'Willing, and satisfying pupil to teach. Well ahead for his age in standards and keen participant in any class activity.'

At the Dragon, where I went in September 1949, it was much the same. I got off to a quick start in both school work and life - followed by some periods of acceleration (the fourth year in particular) and some points of stand-still - and the intelligent, eager and biddable pupil theme continued, with a few exceptions, through my school reports there too.

At the Dragon I received a good academic education and valuable extra-curricular experience. By the time I left I had begun to formulate notions of self-identity, and had some emerging ideas about preferences – social, intellectual, cultural and spiritual matters. In sum, I had arrived there as an able pupil but rather anxious little boy, but five years later I had gained in self-confidence and was ready for the next stage of my schooling.

The same was broadly true for Sandy, but he remained at the Dragon for two terms longer than the normal five years to allow him time to

---

[2] Dragon Days,

develop further in mind and body before going on to his second school. Sandy was behind in his learning and lessons, and suffered mild dyslexia. In those days few concessions were made for the condition and backwardness in class was not regarded as a matter for special concern or treatment. At the same time Sandy was also on the small size for his age and in his middle years at the Dragon had suffered more from illnesses than did most.

On arrival at Sedbergh, we had advantages compared to some new boys, there is no doubt. Boarding itself held no terror. Having already experienced being boarders with distant parents, Sandy and I had got over the worst of any negative feelings; and now at least our parents were in England. Nor was the proximity of adults who were official school staff not family a cause for worry. The Dragon had shown that it was possible to see masters as friends or as companions (or uncles). In addition, I was fit (not unimportant for embarking on a Sedberghian life) and enjoyed good health; and at home we enjoyed a solid base of family affection and supportive older relations.

For Sandy this was generally true too, but some aspects may have worked in a different way. I do not propose to try to comment for him; but I wonder whether, following a year or so behind an older brother who was doing reasonably well at work and in games when he himself was slower at learning and at that stage smaller in size and strength, Sandy might have felt under some additional pressure in ordinary walks of school life. If so, the disadvantage may have helped spur him on to major achievements in other, less mainstream, fields of activity at Sedbergh, from cross country running to fishing, tennis to fell walking, and to an adventurous spirit and lateral thinking which I did not bring in the same measure to my Sedbergh life. Another factor in his School House life (referred to in his letters) was the bad luck of arriving in the third term of an academic year, in the wake of a very large intake, with the result that he received only slow promotion from junior to senior status through the house and was unluckily denied the experience of being a prefect.

What sort of a boy was I then when I came to Sedbergh? I was a traditionalist in general outlook, and accepted the given structures and hierarchies of life. I was proud of my family. I was not a social 'snob' but I tended to see the structure of society as being preordained and fairly immutable. At the same time I was aware of a duty to help the less fortunate. Having no sisters or girl cousins around regularly – and there were only a dozen or so girls (daygirls) among the four hundred Dragon children – I did not have much understanding of girls. My attitude to religion was rather traditional – having something about it of an old-fashioned English churchgoer who liked to worship in a recognizable house of God with Gothic vaulting, stained glass and echoing music, whereas the Lynams preferred to minimize religion on the main Dragon agenda. And if the Dragon was yet another institution formed in the late nineteenth century to create and train rulers of Empire, I doubt that we thought about it very much at the school. For most of us, 'empire' meant exotic adventures or the glamorous world of exploration. Indeed, one of the problems our transitional generation of the 1950s faced was being left with aspirations that could no longer be fulfilled. As to public affairs, the Dragon encouraged us to read newspapers, observe our surroundings, ask intelligent questions and draw our own conclusions about the world we lived in. Sandy and I made a start but I do not think we got very far.

I identified with my country in a way typical of the times. The Dragon, like other boarding schools in the early 1950s, was moulded by the experiences of two world wars; in many ways its ethos went back to Edwardian precepts and to a world outlook of the heroes of Buchan or Henty. In a time of post-war anxiety and change, the school and parents probably shared a natural preference for education to be well embedded in the Victorian muscular Christian tradition as a solid foundation for both personal life and a public career. The new liberal mood only really took a hold in Britain one decade later and the upshot was that the Dragon sensibly concentrated its efforts on offering a first class, rounded, broad-based education.

In sum, when I reached Sedbergh School I was beginning to become aware of how I fitted in in the world; I was conscious of an identity and starting to carve out my own space – with small achievements in one sphere giving some confidence in others.

Some general remarks on our letters home

Home was so important in Sandy's and my letters that I have introduced sets of letters at different periods with descriptions of where our minds were drawn to when writing home. As the family lived in three different homes during our Sedbergh years, each having a notably different setting – namely, Ockley in the Surrey countryside, Vicarage Gate in Kensington, London and then Rye on the coast of East Sussex – the letters fall conveniently into three periods. These periods in turn coincide broadly with our early, middle and later years at school.

* * *

A number of aspects of these letters stand out to me today and are perhaps worth a note.

Striking is the combined effect of two sets of letters from brothers who were very close in age, sharing a common background but rather different in outlook. This double view of the same or similar events provides a richer documentation and more penetrating perspective than would one single account. The letters are marked too by our different temperaments (Sandy mercurial, I more conformist and conventional) and our quite different approaches to writing home (Sandy's accounts of a week's activities being more off the cuff, open and spontaneous; mine more considered and more guarded).

Also striking on reflection is the extent to which the letters do not need to explain background because we took for granted our parents' full acquaintance with the life and customs of boarding public schools in general and Sedbergh, and indeed School House in particular. Both had lived there themselves at different periods. My mother worked at School House during the war helping out as matron and in the kitchen and it was of course my father's home while he was at St Andrew's and then a master at Rugby School. They knew the score, so Sandy and I we were able to deploy safely a private shorthand. Even the destinations of our weekend outings – Keisley or Windermere – were all very familiar to them.

Looking back from a gap of some fifty five years since the letters were written, I am greatly struck by the extent of the changes in the style and even meaning of school life between those days and today. In the first place there is the closeness in time of my schooldays to two savage World Wars. Memories of wartime hardships were still fresh, acceptance of hard conditions and strict levels of discipline was much readier than it would be today. This is reflected in particular in the role played at Sedbergh in the 1950s of the Combined Cadet Force. National Service was in full play until my second last year. The CCF was not concerned with Outward Bound courses or experience entertainments such as; tall ship sail training. Its military aspect was taken seriously for historical reasons, which were, furthermore, an important justification for the school's general ethic at the period of muscular Christianity.

The remoteness of Sedbergh from the outside world is also apparent from the letters – rare buses, or taxis hired frim Braithwaite's garage, to take you over the fells to Oxenholme represented virtually the only way out of the mountain fastness in those days. Up to a point there was a tendency to metaphorical remoteness, and maybe it was harder for teenagers closeted in a school in that rural environment to focus on the reality of the social, political or economic issues of the day.

At Sedbergh we had considerable freedom, for instance to run free on the fells and in the environs of the school. We made our own fun, explored new grounds and constructed our own ways of life, from messing about on the hills, to training and coaching at games or practising or attending music, arts and literature. We did not expect to have things dished up for us on a plate; we were learning how to fend for ourselves and stood ready to be counted on. On the whole we rejected the option of whiling away every possible afternoon over a bottle of pop and a jam tart at the Grubber.

Also striking today is how Sandy's and my relationship at school worked. While our lives were closely intertwined at home, they were lived at a certain distance at school. The letters show how we occupied separate (albeit parallel) worlds, but keeping aware of the other, with a watchful,

x

kindly eye out. It happened that we played tennis and squash together at times, and we used to meet to talk about the affairs of home and holidays as necessary, but generally our paths did not cross very much. In School House, I kept an elder-brotherly eye on him – and indeed he kindly said many years later how much I had helped him through his first couple of years; and Sandy's attitude to me was always very positive – even if he jibbed occasionally at any prefectorial impositions.

One difference between us, however, which manifested itself at the end of our respective schooldays was that Sandy knew where he was heading – he wanted to train to be a farm manager – whereas I had no idea, and tumbled towards university without really knowing why. Sandy's strong ideas about where he wanted his education to take him was an advantage in the growing up process and added to the strength he found through cutting his own path his own way at school.

The letters also show very markedly the tribal nature of the life we led. With hindsight it is remarkable how closely we were thrown together, and how well, on the whole, we survived that tribal existence. In a house of 60 boys, we naturally fell into groups of roughly twelve boys who had started out at the same time and travelled our school and house careers together. The result was constant and intense communication with others through which individual identities emerged as we accepted, declined or denied common assumptions. In the late-1950s long weekends or extended half terms away from school were unknown, so Dayroom and dormitory life unremittingly constrained us to take a position (consciously or unconsciously), say, as a leader or follower, a sportsman or scholar, an extrovert or a loner, an accepter of tradition or a rebel, a keen participant or an observer. These self-identities gave rise to feelings of communality which in turn involved loyalties and responsibilities. This constant interface among peers is no doubt one of the things which make term times so tiring for a boarder, but arguably it gives them experience of processes which they will face on leaving school and leaving the nuclear family at home and which continue through life.

Finally, I am struck by how the world has changed since Sandy's and my days at Sedbergh. In the 1950s we were the first of the modern Elizabethans, as different from schoolboys today as we were ourselves from, say, the early Elizabethans and the very first days of 'public school' education in England.

***

Note:
Unless otherwise marked, the letters are addressed to both parents jointly, although sometimes a letter may contain passages, short or longer, explicitly or implicitly intended for the attention of one parent in particular.

The visual essay combines a handful photographs taken at school which still exist along with a fair number of photographs from our holiday periods – mostly taken and preserved by my mother. Together they give something of a feel for the stages of growing up of two young Sedberghians at school and at home in the second half of the 1950s.

LETTERS HOME FROM SEDBERGH SCHOOL, 1954-1960

Background: The early years at home, 1954-55

My parents returned from USA to England in 1953 and by 1954 my father had decided to embark on a commuting life from Surrey to his job in the FO in London. They bought Herons' March in Ockley, half way between Dorking and Horsham. At first our life revolved around the wooded grounds and the lake there, with Jeb the family's Irish wolfhound ever our companion, but as we moved on to schooling at Sedbergh, first myself and then Sandy, our range of interests began to widen.

In Herons March, aged thirteen to fourteen, the spheres of my life were not yet divided. Sandy and I lived life at home safe in the bosom of our family, although my father was absent a lot on account of frequent travel abroad in his work. Sandy and I were inseparable companions and preferred our own company to that of others. We rarely if ever had difficulty finding things to do. Daily life of the house was focussed around my baby sister, Sally, and my mother had her hands full, even when helped by au pair girls, of whom there were several – including a wonderful Danish girl, Kirsten, who was very good with Sally and spoilt us boys rotten and Jeb even more. She became bi-lingual and was often taken for a Scot.

The grounds at Herons March were large (some four acres) and the surrounds enticing, and most of the time we had our being outside. The formal garden itself was small, but Sandy and I had our own territories. We were allowed to use the lower lawn as we liked, for instance for deck quoits or badminton; and we played and camped (not often overnight) in our home woods and we shot with bows and arrows and a BB pellet gun at many and varied targets. Then there was boating on our lake - in our indestructible 10 foot aluminium rowing boat. We also had a little canvas sailing boat for fun and experiment. We tried coarse fishing but it did not hold our attention for long, and we preferred to spin or trawl for pike with a spinner. We timed ourselves in rowing races and explored with axes and saws the marshes at the head of the lake. It was a whole private, Swallows and Amazons, world of fun and games. We took Jeb for long walks in the surrounding woodland, and explored the lanes by bicycle, which included a mile and a half's run to the village shop for sweets and pop and occasional errands.

By 1955, however, we began to seek other forms entertainment, away from the house but still essentially in family care. We were able to

1

persuade my mother to take us to, or drop us off at, the cinema in Dorking, or the small hilly 9-hole Dorking golf course - sometimes with my father at a weekend. A favourite destination was Laughing Waters, a swimming pool club–cum–hotel. These were all places where we could be left safely while the grown-ups had other business to attend to. Steep Box Hill with its open grassland, and woody Leith Hill were popular spots for outings and walking Jeb. My mother liked driving and we regularly went visiting relatives and family friends throughout Surrey, West Kent and Sussex. Chessington Zoo was another destination we enjoyed for a change.

Indoors at home we had our own cosy playroom (about 10 ft square), with all our belongings and toys from way back. It was a perfect den for games and hobbies. It was warm in winter, being next door to the kitchen with its Aga; it had a sensible linoleum covered floor, a square pine table, three chairs, cupboard and shelves, and toy boxes; and it enjoyed a private escape route in to the world outside through the kitchen to a back passage and away, without needing to cross grown-ups' territory. At the same time we were expected to carry out certain traditional household duties such as filling up the anthracite hods for the Aga and emptying the ashes into dustbins, shoe cleaning and washing up, and looking after and feeding Jeb – all of which helped lighten my mother's load. In every sense, this was a life close to the family hearth.

Come 1956, however, our life began to change. We discovered the pleasure of the company of neighbours of our own age, mostly girls, who lived within bicycling range. Sexual awareness began to play a role in our lives and at the same time new friendships sparked a dawning consciousness of a possible life beyond the parents and home. A propos, I do not recall Sandy being out of step, he was growing and developing quickly by the time he moved to Sedbergh.

We found new entertainments: several of the girls played tennis or owned, or rode, ponies and we joined the many other Surrey youngsters who never missed the pony club dances in the Christmas holidays. Our first Junior Hunt Ball introduced us to a new life of socialising – complete with the mysteries of alcohol and evening dress - one in which parents did not figure or count except as forces in the background and as late night ferrymen. We became regulars at parties given at neighbours' homes. Some parties could be rather formal;, and more fun were the informal gatherings, sitting around chatting in someone's kitchen over coffee, or soft drinks in the evening, with gramophone records and laughter and endless planning of trips to the cinema, or to Laughing Waters

In sum we very content, and we were adventurous within our own closed world, but we were not yet looking for life on a grander scale or attempting to mark out future territory. It was a transition stage when my outlook remained essentially home-oriented and my life was yet disambiguated even if I was starting to learn to live as part of a group: to recognise the need for compromise, to learn how to handle suspicion, doubts or negative feelings and more consciously to find things and people I enjoyed, choosing some and rejecting others.

In the school holidays we also both had friends from school to stay at Heron's March, who, as far as I can remember, fitted in to our existing life there easily enough; and we stayed with other families ourselves. I spent a week or two's holiday with my School House friend Des Sykes at his parents' home on the edge of Bolton – another change of perspective for me. His delightful parents were immensely hospitable and I joined in the life of Des and his younger brother, Bill, at the local sports and social clubs. Desmond and I played together in the Easter tournament at the Tennis Club and became involved in a hectic social round of young members. It was the first time I had seen this sort of thing in action, and there were girls in the group who thought we public school boys from Sedbergh were definitely rather smart. That same summer I also spent a week at Myles Moffat's home on the Lune. His father was a farmer and the water bailiff at Killington, and their home life was unfamiliar: a bath tub on the kitchen floor in front of the open range – embarrassing to be left bathing there – a dunny at the bottom of the garden; no squash or water to drink, but tea after meals and of course Yorkshire pudding and gravy for a first course before meat. I grew accustomed, and it was a most enjoyable experience; and we mucked about all day long by the river and on the fells, up the lanes and fields; and at nights were cosily housed under the small garret roof.

At this period Sandy and I also stayed a few times with our grandparents at their cottage at Bemersyde, near Melrose, where the process of learning and lessons continued much as in the past. I played the clarinet, with Dear Man accompanying, playing highland airs and Scottish dance songs; learnt lots about fishing and fly tying, and much enjoyed watching Dear Man painting his watercolours in the nicely lit upstairs attic studio he had designed for himself; and there was a highly intelligent border sheep dog to look after and teach tricks.

We fished the Tweed, mostly on the easier St Boswells town water and occasionally on Doigh Haigh's water at Dryburgh, with its overhung trees, dark pools and pebble banks (dangerous wading). I recall the late evenings with the midges, and one year the rather sinister appearance on the stony shores of many huge, dead, diseased salmon of 30lbs or so. And as it became dark there were bats which seemed to attack one's rod and line, and casts became knotted and you had to try to undo them by moonlight. Dear Man liked fishing right through to dark but after his death Sandy and I never dared go very far from the foot of the bridge. We also enjoyed touristic travel with Dear all around the neighbouring countryside visiting grand houses and ancient memorials. and learning the history and legends of the Borders. And in the summer we sometimes slept in the caravan rather than in the house.

But Surrey was not my father's idea of the English countryside; there was no shooting and fishing, for instance, or serious golf courses. He also soon came to dislike the commute to London by an unreliable train service, especially in winter, as he found increasingly that he had to stay late in town for reasons of work. A change of home was needed and the next step was a move to London.

The Ockley period at home thus equates in several ways with life in the Junior Dayroom at School House, Sedbergh, where, similarly, all aspects of life were similarly contained in a single sphere. It was something of a continuation, in fact, of Dragon School days. New friends were chosen by propinquity rather than by common interests; personal interest was often, and contentedly, submerged into the common interests of the whole tribe. And at every point a new identification with your surroundings, and your new friends, was reinforced by rote, traditions and a strong ceremonial element. At the age of thirteen to fourteen this was happening for me both at home and in school life.

My second year at Ockley also mirrored in many ways the second year at School House, when responsibilities first surfaced – for instance being a junior day room head (there were three), or captaining a very junior team; and then came the move to the Senior Dayroom, which, with boys in both second and third years present, was something of a house crucible. Life changed, and instead of pursuing general goals, ready to try whatever was going on, and play with whoever was around, one started to mark out gently one's own field of interests and preferences.

In the senior dayroom you came to know a wider group of people (including some from the year above you) and you got on with them if required to (for example, if in the same team) or if they were pleasant and engaging; or, inevitably, you might find you preferred to avoid one or two. This was not dissimilar to our way of life and our changing social horizons and personal interests at the end of our time at Ockley in 1955-56.

Chapter 1:   September 1954 to July 1955[3]

J   21 Sept 1954 [Thursday]

Please excuse the pencil for my pen is empty and anyway I am still in bed (7.30)

We had a good journey to Euston and I was there in plenty of time. There was a very nice Welsh engine driver and he told me a lot on the journey.

I didn't meet any Sedbergh new boys until we got on the bus for Sedbergh. I did meet the school 'priest' or whatever you call him. It was thundering when we arrived at School House.

The Head of House[4] showed me my bed in the 10-bedder[5]. Then I went to see Mr Thornely[6]. I met his wife. They were both very well.

Then the new boys had 'tea' (High tea) in the dining room (We all have our own pots of sugar[7]). After that Mr Thornely and Mr Durran[8] told us what books to get.

Important. Please will you send me my Bible and my dental plate - in the bedside drawer – also its key next to the ink well in the top of my desk. It looks like this [sketch of bent pin].[9] Thank you.

---

[3] Jamie's letters only from September1954 to March 1955. Sandy arrived in May 1955.

[4] David R.C. Kelly. I remember confusing, on the day of arrival at School House, masters, prefects and older boys. The house tutor was dressed in games clothes and I took him for a prefect; I thought that the youthful looking Kelly, wearing shorts, was a second termer appointed to look after us new boys and one overweight, older figure wearing a tweed coat and flannels whom I took for a master turned out to be a fifth former. Senior boys seemed very old in those first days, with their faded uniforms, 'colours' in scarves or squares and impressive badges of prefectorial office such as umbrellas.

Boys started in the Junior Dayroom, where there were two large tables and benches used for recreation and prep alike. Each boy had a locker for school books and a few personal possessions, and a tuck box under the main stairs. We competed to sit on the old iron radiators for warmth as the evenings got colder, and got on with each other.

[5] The larger of two open dormitories for junior boys; the beds were in two lines and each boy had a chest of drawers for his clothes, and a basin (filled in the bathroom) and washing things at the foot of the bed. With the windows always open, the water in the bowls sometimes froze solid overnight in winter. Dorms were places for chat, especially in the light of summer evenings, some noise and ragging, but we were generally well exercised and tired. After a year or so in the Bedders, one was promoted to having a cubicle, some of which were shared by two boys but most were single.

[6] G.M.C. (Michael) Thornely became Headmaster of the School and housemaster of School House in September 1954. He was well known to my parents and the Bruce Lockhart family, having been House Tutor at School House under my grandfather for the previous fifteen years. He had married Jennifer, née Scott, older sister of one of the senior boys in the house, the same year.

[7] We were also issued with one small cube of margarine, the unused part of which one stored in one's jam or marmalade jar (or might trade for jam).

[8] John ('Jake') Durran was House Tutor in School House throughout our time there.

[9] A bane of my life, which I regularly (usually intentionally) lost or broke.

We don't have jam at school. Most boys brought some back. If it's not too heavy for posting please could you send some. Thank you.

I will write about the chaps and what we do on Sunday.

J   Sep 26 54 [Sunday]

... I am having a jolly good time here. The beds are very comfy as school beds go. In the mornings we get up at 7 (i.e. the bell is rung then and we have to be down by 7.30 having had a cold bath). Most chaps stay in bed till 7.20. I usually get up at 7.15.[10]

There is a chap called a time caller who yells out the time every minute till 25 past.[11]

At 7.30-8.00 we have morning prep, then we have breakfast. Porridge, bread and Stork[12] and marmalade on Weds and Fridays and a sort of hot course, Scrambled egg, sausages, kippers etc.. After breakfast we have prayers in the chapel or Powell Hall. We work until 12.25 on all days except Thus, Wed and Sat when we work to 1.10.[13]

---

[10] School uniform was blue shorts and long blue stockings – with garters. In winter, vest, blue shirt, short sleeved or long sleeved white pullover (or both in mid-winter) and blazer on top with your house colour (pale blue for School House) shown in the badge (two intertwined Ss). Games clothes were kept in the bootroom on the ground floor for dayroom boys and in the upper bathrooms for senior). The smell of encrusted mud and sweat in old sweaters, woollen socks and games shorts is never forgotten. Equally, newly laundered games clothes were a source of pleasure. The junior bathroom on the ground floor had three baths, grimy with mud and dirt but the water was piping hot. The Boiler room, Mr Peck's Hole, was beneath the Junior Day room, which was wonderfully warm in winter as a result.

[11] The daily round began with the wake-up calls, the time being called, by a fag appointed for a week, every 5 minutes for the first quarter hour and then every minute for the next ten until five minutes before the breakfast bell. That was the call to the cold baths, with usually a prefect supervising the juniors to make sure that you dipped low enough to get your shoulders wet (didn't need to get the hair wet) and to ensure that no one played the fool, spilling out huge amounts of water, or skipped the bath. It was all done at great speed, so you could sprint out again with a towel wrapped around you back to your bedside to rush your clothes on and get downstairs in seconds (especially in the cold winter mornings).

After which there was early morning prep for half an hour, then breakfast - a comforting occasion with warm food, warm room, familiar jam pots, the giant metal urn of hot tea, familiar faces and friendly chatter - a pleasant and undemanding, slow entry into the working day. The morning post was put out on a window ledge in the Common Room, sometimes after breakfast, sometimes not until short break, and letters out were mailed in a box there. Time was set aside for writing letters on Sunday mornings, but as you got older you increasingly chose your own time.

[12] a leading brand of margarine at the time

[13] The school day started with an assembly in Powell Hall, a hymn, short prayers and any general announcements. In mid-morning one had a twenty minute turnaround break between the two main lesson periods in which you rushed back to the house to collect new books for the next two lessons. At lunch time we left school at or shortly before 1.00 p.m., walked back fast for a very short break and then into lunch at 1.20. On full working days (M,W,F) in the winter terms games were played straight after lunch, then we went back into school for a couple of hours; so you changed immediately into games clothes and by 2.30

We have lunch at 1.20. From 12.25 to 1.15 is called the long break. On the last long break, Charlie Ward (I think you know him)[14] taught me fives. It's a jolly exhausting game and rather painful but great fun. I practised in the afternoon. We have half days on Thurs Tues and Sat.

All the chaps here are jolly good blokes, all the new boys and the junior day room boys. There are 8 new boys and 8 other boys.

I have played two games of rugger so far. I played on the parade league (under 15 ½) for the house against Sedgwick[15]. We got beaten 3-0. They had big centres though. I played fly half on a school House private game.[16] When you don't play games you go for a house run[17] instead, up Higher Winder[18] etc.

Thinking about what you could send, Bible, plate, a little grub (hem hem!)[19]

---

you were out on the games pitches or running on the hills.. In the summer term, school started after lunch, and games at around 4.40 pm.

Before tea (high tea) there was rather more spare time, which was usually spent in the dayrooms in the winter terms. In the evening after tea, there was half an hour's break and then one and a half or two hours of prep. This sometimes included a half hour 'reading prep' for juniors when one had to read an (approved) book. The day ended with evening prayers. First came the roll call, which we soon all knew by heart; and then a hymn, lesson and a couple of prayers. We got to know the hymns, which were chosen by the prefect on duty from the Sedbergh School hymn book (a collection put together by JHBL). By the middle years I found it all a restful occasion with its firm traditions and easy repetitions.

[14] Son of the housemaster of Sedgwick House, whom we had met in holidays from the Dragons, was in the year above me.

[15] There were seven houses, each with about sixty boys. Four were purpose built at the same period and in almost identical layout (School, Sedgwick, Hart and Winder). Neighouring Sedgwick House was a special rival for School House.

[16] Games at both house and school levels mattered a lot, rugger being the most important. School games, however, were not very meaningful at first, or until by size or talent a boy became a candidate for School Under 16 teams. Inter-house- games at junior level were good fun; almost everyone under 16 had to muck in to make up team numbers – with the result that all levels of skill were represented and there was a cheerful spirit about it all.

[17] After rugger running came next in importance – with the Ten Mile Wilson Run and the Three Mile race for under 16s. The sport was not only about personal achievement but also house representation. Boys had to be deemed fit by the school doctor and have parental permission to participate in The Ten. The race was followed by the whole school, supported by the town and parents galore (especially those who had run it themselves). Obligatory 'House runs' were generally unpopular because the pace was set by supervising prefects and times of return noted. Furthermore, runs were almost by definition held in dreadful weather when it was impossible to use the playing fields. There were a number of set courses, each of about three miles in length, around which all houses sent their boys in three packs of runners (senior, middle and junior) in rotation.

[18] Sedbergh lies at the south-western foot of the Howgill Fells. Three hills directly above the town were a constant feature of the school landscape: Winder, Higher Winder and Crook.

[19] Food played an enormous part in school life: meals in the house or snacks in between, from one's tuck box, purchased or gifts received from parents and relatives. Among my great favourites were (small size) tins of sweetened condensed milk and mandarin oranges. Then you kept sugar there in a 1lb jar, which I sprinkled together with Cadbury's drinking powder onto bread and margarine.

There is a grubber[20] here where you can buy sugar, sauces etc.

Weather awful...

As for our masters. Mr Forster is very nice and so is our other Maths master. Thornely (nicknamed Prick) takes me for French and a certain Mr Coates takes us for Latin and English. He is very snappy and is packed full of rockets.

The boys who do Greek with me speak in a quite different pronunciation to what we were taught at the Dragons.

J   29th September 54 [Wednesday]

We've just had orchestra practice. I'm in the C section[21] – it's good fun and we're playing nice tunes.

Everyone is very nice and now I'm getting to know my way around.

I'm in the ten bedder and my neighbours are Matthew and Lowe[22]. Matthew[23] is a new boy, fairly quiet and pretty d. He plays rugger well.

Rugger games reports – Colts B[24] etc. ... Those boys who did not play rugger this term yet have now run in house runs 23 miles

Sykes is my pal at the moment. He is very small. He is a very nippy scrum half. I had a 'grub up' with him at the grubber after a very exhausting game of rugger. We walked round the Three on Sunday.

Both services went well on Sunday. Being in the choir is great fun.[25]

I've still got another week of rest. After that I fag. The captain of rugger asked me to be his private fag, which means I clean his corps boots[26], brush his shoes and keep his study etc tidy[27].

---

[20] The 'Grubber' was the school sponsored tuck-shop-cum-café where boys could buy sweets, food and drink to take to their houses or could eat on the spot simple refreshments such as buns and cake. Boys could also make purchases down town.

[21] The school boasted three orchestras. 'C' was a rehearsal and learning forum for new boys and beginners until they ready to join the Second, or First, orchestra according to ability.

[22] Yorkshire farming background; a keen rider and Pony club aficionado, known as 'Foxy'

[23] H.C.G (Colin) Matthew became a close friend. He was Head of House and Head of School in our last year. he became Professor of History at St Hugh's Oxford, distinguished biographer of Gladstone, and Director of the Dictionary of National Biography; sadly he died at the young age of 58 in 1999.

[24] The school's rugger was divided into Bigside (30 top players) and Littleside which together providing the School Teams from the 1st to 4th XV; and at Junior level there were Colts A and Colts B, similarly taking 60-odd of the leading players aged 16 and under.

[25] School House had strong traditions in music. Michael and Jennifer Thornely were both good musicians and excellent pianists – and had two grand pianos in their drawing room. I was propelled (for want of unbroken voices) into the inter-house quartet singing competitions in my first term, singing the alto part in the Ashgrove. I enjoyed the music but did not enjoy the experience very much. I was also put in the choir as an alto u until my voice started breaking - and was not asked to return.

In chapel, as in Morning Prayers in Powell Hall, we sat by houses and by years within each house. I enjoyed singing psalms, antiphonal in particular. Hymns could be stirring too: on the other hand, the Sedbergh school songs (which we had to learn by heart) were not so uplifting. Only 'Winder', the School song, compared.

The dorm prefects are making us have a press-up comp. I have managed 15. One chap did 33. So far we have beaten the Upper Cubes (year above us)[26].

I should say that the food so far is better than the Dragons.

NB I repeat the S.O.S. for my Bible.

The School House library is jolly good. I'm reading the Sign of the Four at the moment. They've got lots of Agatha C...[29]

Mr Thornely takes me for French, He goes very much for loquorial /sic/ French. We are learning idioms all the time.

Mr Reynell who takes the Upper VI classical takes me for Greek. I think he teaches jolly well, I am a bit ahead of the others in the form but I find the chance to revise a jolly good chance.

Mr Coates who takes me for Div, Latin and English is extremely sarcastic and very snappy. Everybody comes into the lesson well in time.

Mr Foster who takes me for maths is very nice.

Lord Bracken[30] has been here since yesterday. He saw me but did not recognize me and asked my name. Realizing who I was he said 'come along

---

[26] The Combined Cadet Force, which boys joined once aged fifteen and a half played an important part (both in terms of psychology and of time devoted to it) in the life of the school. Its existence, in days of National Service, served to embed in the school some of the ideals (of purpose, service and sacrifice) and practices (of discipline, responsibility) of two earlier generations who had fought in world wars.

[27] Fagging was part of life and I don't recall ever objecting to it. There was house fagging and private fagging. The former consisted in public duties such as cleaning the baths, tidying up the bootrooms, brushing out dayrooms, stairs and stairwells, serving and clearing away plates at tables, time calling in the morning, etc. As to personal fagging, you got appointed by a prefect, with Head of House approval I guess. Chief duties were cleaning shoes, including rugger boots (but not any CCF equipment), making tea and toast, and tidying the prefect's study. In exchange one had use of the study now and then.

In addition there were the calls for fags – which could be for private fagging duties, say to replace a fag who was absent or for running errands, such as taking a message to another house. Calls for a fag were bellowed from the top of the steps – and the last to arrive got the duty. In my first term or two but the practice was stopped not long afterwards, fags were sent on icy winter mornings to warm the seats in the B's (outside the main building and not heated) to prepare them for a prefect's use.

[28] The cubicles lay on two floors across the centre of the building. I particularly remember being in south facing cubicles when one could see moonlight and stormy clouds flying past. In winter you put on a tartan rug and dressing gown, and often pullover(s) as well, making a great heavy heap of bedding. The windows were always open, the room lofty and airy and in summer it was never stifling hot and uncomfortable.

[29] In later years we made more use of the House Library. I read through all the war stories and there were many (great favourites were The Wooden Horse and Colditz Story and I recall The Caine Mutiny (abridged version) with horror. I read all of John Buchan and plenty of light entertainment, such as Bulldog Drummond, school stories and adventure novels such as Hammond Innes. I enjoyed factual material (sports books) as well but never got into the 19th or early 20th century classics. Newspapers were available in the library but I do not remember reading them regularly or very seriously.

and have some tea' and pushed me outside and taking me by the arm lead me down to the White Hart.

There were four of them waiting for him: McGee captain of rugger, Mackintosh, son of Loretto's headmaster and some other blokes. We had a smash up tea, cakes and cakes. He held the conversation talking about rugger mainly. When I got back I could hardly eat my School House tea.

Lord Bracken and another Governor had lunch in the dining room (That's why I think we had such a jolly d lunch).[31]

J   Undated Sept/Oct 54   [3rd October]

...Rugger... games...

Yesterday we had a marvellous time. I went round to Cautley spout by the fells. We had a midday half 1.30 to 5, Straight away we started off up Higher Winder. We missed out Winder's cairn and Higher Winder and came up the Calf[32]. It's jolly tiring and there was a howling wind. We ran hard down the gentle slope to the crags and then down to the spout. We clambered down the far side, our party then increased by 2 who we met on Calf, and went along the lower crags to slide down the scree. We walked and lingered till we suddenly looked to our Watch keeper who said there was only 55 mins to get back to work.

We ran down by the Cautley beck and decided we had to cross. We had to jump across onto a stone in the middle (about 1 sq foot). You can guess what happened. I lost my balance and fell in - ohhhh gosh it was cold. I was absolutely sopped mainly because I was face up to the flow and it came pouring down my shirt. Then realizing we had to go 5 ¾ miles in ¾ of an hour, we ran along the side of a fell racing against time in a jolly close race. We came to the road just over Red Bridges it is called – and finding

---

[30] Brendan Bracken, an Old Sedberghian, was Chairman of the Board of Governors. He was a personal friend of Dear Man's and close to my Great Uncle Bertie (Sir Robert Bruce Lockhart) who had been Director of the Political Warfare Executive when Bracken was Churchill's Minister of Information. He was a regular visitor at School House in the holidays when Sandy and I were staying there.

[31] Tables in the dining hall were set up by years. The House Matron sat at end of Table 1 (first and second years) by the windows, Mr Durran, the House tutor, at the head of Table 2 (third and fourth years) under the boards. Table 3 was for senior studies and non-prefects of fourth and fifth years, and Thornely and his wife (at lunch time only, not tea) sat at either end of Table 4 (with the prefects). The urn of tea and vast square loaves of bread, 2 ft. long, were put out at tea time, to eat on the spot (dayroom boys), or to take to studies. I had no difficulties with the food in general, although there were one or two dishes I did not much like (semolina, cabbage and fish).

And with food, of course, must come a note on lavatories. The 'Bs' were outside the main building in a lean-to at the end of the little covered yard. They consisted of urinals one side and on the other a row of some six stalls with a wooden half door. There was only one loo per floor indoors, used by prefects during the day, but principally for use by boys in general at night – with queues at bed time and first thing in the morning.

[32] The central peak of the Howgill Fells was formed by Calf (2,250') and The Calf (2500')#.

that we had to run our fastest to get back to school 3 miles to go and 40 mins, so we ran back and absolutely fagged got to School House with 10 mins to bath and get into prep.

I was absolutely dead tired and sapped but soon got warmed again. Luckily those who had to get to School got there in time. But next time I'm going to start off earlier.

Mrs Thompson[33] wrote to me this morning which was jolly d and also sent me some fudge. Richard is now at Shrewsbury.

J   undated Oct 54 [10 October]

Thanks for letter. I hope the jam comes down quickly from Scotland because I've only got rations enough for about 2 weeks.

...Fortnightly orders... nothing known yet.

Mr Whiteside gave me another clarinet lessons, I think he is a very nice man and I'm sure I'll do well with him.

My impressions now of the other new boys – in School Roll order

Howard (IV Mod). Top scholar, pretty fat and about 4' 11". I should say his parents are pretty rich and he always has stores and stores of grub (which he doesn't and won't part with). In fagging he is very very slack. He does less work than anybody else and would be the slackest[34].

Matthew. Not terribly bright. 5'.6". A chap from Edinburgh Academy. He is very d but he is rather quiet, He is a good rugger player (well at least in the Colts B).

Sykes 4'9" - very nice chap[35]. He is my best friend at the moment and he is going to take me out on Nov 14th. I do a lot of things with him. He is pretty nippy in rugger and yard soccer. Grant. Very Scottish - a fairly quiet chap but pretty d. Mad about fives, about my height. IIA[36]

Laird. Again about my height. He's got the queerest voice imaginable, He is quite nice, Bit of a chump and not terribly good at games.

Moffat. About 5' and very thin. He's a local bloke and very nice. Rather noisy but not rough, just talking a lot, Plays the violin in 3rd orchestra[37] (same as me) and is cracked on classical music[38]

---

[33] I boarded out, with one other boy, in my last term with the Thompson family. She was an Old Dragon, and wife of Chemistry professor Thompson.

[34] Later, scholar to Queen's College, Cambridge; he became a City stockbroker.

[35] Desmond (Des) Sykes was the son of an Old Sedberghian; he was joined at School House by his younger brother W.A (Bill) a couple of years later. He later emigrated to South Africa where he worked as a chartered accountant.

[36] From Inverness, nicknamed 'Granny' Grant; his older brother, Ian, was also in School House at the time.

[37] Being in an orchestra involved giving up arts and crafts entirely, which with hindsight was a pity; and in later years there were quite a number of extra rehearsals which meant giving up free time (for instance after chapel on a Sunday evening), but I accepted it as a given and came to generally enjoy the experience.

[38] Later won an organ scholarship to Keeble College, Oxford

In fact a pretty d lot of boys....

J   Tuesday [17 October 1954]

I am having a lovely time now. It's a jolly good place, but the weather isn't. The last few days have been simply pouring with rain and not at all enjoyable to walk around in.

I had a type of hay fever for the last 3 or 4 days and I had to go off exercise. It was a bit of a swizz but I only missed one day.

I went up Winder with Sykes and on the way we rebuilt the dam we made last Easter hols[39] up in Settlebeck.

We started fagging on Sunday. I am on 'Bootroom; and Scivving. That means in Bootroom I clean out the baths and basins and hang up all the towels. The other chaps on bootroom do the changing room part i.e. tidy up all the games clothes and shoes and boots.

Scivving is clearing up the meals, bringing in the courses and fetching more spuds etc.

Also in private fagging I clean Mageen's shoes and tidy and clean his study and run any errands he wants. He is a jolly nice chap and I have his study on Sunday evenings.

We change round our fagging every week (that is, not private).

Please could you send my Bible and please write soon, I haven't had a letter since Friday week ago (Hem Hem!)

J   Oct 54 [24 October]

...Thankyou very very much indeed for the lovely grub you sent, the jam will only just be in time, I hope, for I've nearly finished the apricot. I prefer that to pineapple jam it is absolutely wizard, but of course any type does.[40]

#...Reports: 3rd in Latin, 5th (same place) in English, 9th (up) in maths, 4th (up) three in Greek.

On Thursday I had a simply marvellous game of rugger. It was a filthy day, pouring with rain and the pitch was an utter bog. I played wing forward for the first time and thoroughly enjoyed myself there.

I have become suddenly mad about fives. I've played lots of times lately. It's a jolly good game but a bit sore on the hands. Please do you think you could send my woollen gloves, that is if I still have any, because they are wonderful for 'inners' in the rather bad house gloves.

---

[39] On holiday from the Dragon School, staying with Dear and Dear Man

[40] We received very welcome parcels of food, tinned fruit, jams, cakes, biscuits, etc., from time to time from home (and sometimes from grandparents or other near relatives). Not only was the food from home of superior quality, but it also freed up our pocket money to be used for general tuck (chocolate and sweets and fizzy drinks) or other purposes.

Last night we had a 'sharp' debate; that is there are 7 or so motions and names are drawn to speak against and for the motion with no time to prepare, My name wasn't drawn (thank goodness) but it was jolly good fun. Far more so than the ordinary debates.

...1ˢᵗ XV match...etc. Peart 6'4" and scrum half 5'3"... walking back from a conversion they look terribly funny.

Everything is going well and I'm having a lovely time.

J   Oct 54 [31 October]

Hope you had a good time with Granny

My fag master has come back from the san[41]. I have to clean his study and his shoes every day. He is jolly nice.

1ˢᵗ XV matches...

Yesterday evening we had a lecture by Mr Spencer Chapman, the author of 'The jungle is neutral'. He gave a wonderful lecture on his travelling in a van through Africa. He is a marvellous photographer and gave us a jolly good show of slides - animals, wild game... He spoke very well, with no hesitation etc.

Last Sunday we had a cine show. We saw the Titfield Thunderbolt; a very funny film in colour and the news.

On Wed we had a cello recital by Maurice Eisenberg. He was absolutely wonderful. It was a real delight listening to him. He used his fingers so quickly. He was jolly good.

J   3ʳᵈ Nov 54 [Wednesday]

Thanks for pineapple jam... Hope Jeb likes London...[42]

Sorry you've got a cold. I'm not in a terribly good way now because this morning (on a fag call) I fell on the stairs and have crocked my ankle. I thought it would wear off but it hasn't, so I'm going to see the matron because it still aches and makes me limp slightly.

It was really very nice of Dowcs[43] to send me that money. Bad luck in the golf, Dad. I did receive a letter [i.e. envelope] with no innard letter (paradox) – but thank you for the last one.

Don't know my place in French but it was probably bottom.

---

[41] The school's medical centre and wards were in the charge of the school doctor and used by all houses. They were manned partly by professional nursing staff with other part time help in cases of epidemics.

[42] My mother was staying in London to take Jeb the wolfhound to Crufts Dog Show; sale of Heron's March and a move of home to London was not yet being considered.

[43] My godfather Peter Dowson, a very old and close friend of my father's from Rugby School where Dowcs had been captain of cricket. He had gone into Shell before the war, served in Burma, where he won an MC, and ended up as a director of the company in London.

First fine day this term, so Prick gave us an extra half. It seems too bad to be sitting up with a crocked ankle on such a day as this but life has its own ways with everyone I suppose and I mustn't grumble.

I played squash with Sykes and fives the day before...

.... re Dragons: are you going to Iolanthe? I expect it will be pretty good with Burleigh and Evers still left over. Have a lovely time in London

PS   Love to Jeb from the Afghan puppy I met in town.

J   Nov 54 [7th November]

...Am going to get Sandy a sheath knife for Christmas.

Jolly good about Jeb's parents doing so well. You really must enter him somewhere again.

Went on an outing with Mrs Sykes... We had a jolly good day although it poured, and wizard meals. We drove round to Kirby Lonsdale. The whole place was in floods like before. Did I tell you that the waves at Millthrop bridge were 6 ft high and the water ran along the path up the side and covered all the pebbles. Lovely waterfalls... We had tea at the Moorcock in the middle of nowhere under Boar Fell's eastern foot.

I think Mr and Mrs Sykes are very nice people. When you come we can take Sykes out.

A few days ago there was a voluntary concert. Two boys played their own composition. One was Senior[44] he played jolly well and has written a very good tune

...Am reading a lot, mainly about sailing – Voyage in a Barquentine, Sailing around the World alone...

Although I was off ex Mageen, asked Miss Pringle[45] if I could play for the paperweights XV v Lime House prep school (6 miles outside Carlisle). She let me out without doc's consent and I went with my foot in a bandage.

The day before the doc had said if I was not careful it would take just as long as a broken bone to mend. However I never felt any pain, so it's none the worse at all (except a little dirtier, the bandage I mean). I played centre, I scored one try and missed two dives by about 1 ft each time I was held up from grounding the ball... We had a smashing tea. Over Shap we got caught in a cloud or fog for about ¼ hour in pitch dark...

J   Nov 54 [Extract of Letter from Keith Sykes, father of Desmond, to my parents...]

... I was greatly struck by James's love of the open air and the fells... delightful and unselfconscious... they were a lively humorous lot and left

---

[44] Ian, son of Mrs Senior who taught the clarinet at the Dragon School in Oxford; she was sister of the French master Bill Gairdner, known to the boys as 'Horsy G'.
[45] School House matron.

14

my wife and me with no questions as to whether they were all enjoying themselves... all is well in the BL world in Sedbergh...

J   Nov 54 [14th November]

...I'm having a jolly good time although nothing interesting has happened.

...Hope you are having a good time in London. must be difficult exercising Jeb there.

Yesterday we had a film The Belles of St Trinians and a cartoon. They were both terribly funny; especially the latter which was absolutely side splitting

1st XV Loretto match...

...Mrs Thornely's brother is our dorm prefect. He's a jolly nice chap too.

J   Letter from the San – Nov 54

I came into here on Tuesday morning after a terrible fevering night. It's a pretty frightful place here except one thing which is that we have a wireless on from 1.30 to 10 pm. We get some jolly good stuff.

Weather frightful... Rawthey rose about 8 ft.

The San is a good chance for reading but the library here is rotten but some of the boys have brought good books.

There are 10 School House boys in a pretty full San.[46]

Will we have a chance to see Dear Man's exhibition[47] in the holidays?

J   undated, late Nov [28 November]

I'm afraid nothing very much out of the ordinary has been happening. Thank you very much for the gloves...

Boar Fell and Wild Boar Fell are covered with snow and even Higher Winder. Today it is bitterly cold.

I have been playing a lot of chess, and drawing too. My clarinet is going well but I think I have gone down a bit in work.

Have you actually sent the jam? Nothing has arrived yet? Tell S if you see him that I would like a camera film for Xmas.

J   Dec 1954 [5 December]

....House matches, Confirmation Sunday...

Oh Yes! Prick (Thornely) gave out if anyone was interested in a naval career they should see him I thought I might find out what it was about.

---

[46] 'Flu epidemic
[47] At the Society of Artists in Bond Street

Between the age of 15.8 and 16 you take (try) a schol[48] which includes Intermed. and general Cert A for Schools and if you pass, the college (RNC Dartmouth) accept you and help (according to your parents' income) your next two years school fees. Then you have to take Higher Cert for Schools at the age of 18. If you pass that you go as a cadet. But if with any luck you get a univ. schol. anywhere; and wish to give up the navy all you have to do is pay back the money they spent to help pay your school fees. There is a long time to wait, and Prick says he will talk to you about it, but I thought I might tell you now as an idea.

... Am now convalescing in the san... Convalescers still listening to the wireless. All very comfy but I don't know when I'm coming back. I've been up for 3 hrs a day now and I feel quite well with no temp.

Plans for train journey home...

It snowed yesterday and things are fairly white

J   Undated Dec 54 [12 December]

Thanks for letter and music

We've had a miserable week with lots of house runs....

List of books for Xmas wish list...

J   Tues Dec 54 [14 December]

Things are now more arranged. I'm coming home on Thurs.

Four others are going so the taxi cost to Oxenholme will be worth taking (3-4/- each approx.). I'll take a tube across London to Victoria or Waterloo and find a convenient through train. I will ring from Ockley station. If anything takes place to the contrary I will ring from Euston or Victoria or Waterloo.

Terrible weather...

Easter Term 1955

J   no date [c. 23 January 1955]

I got here all right but not quite as planned. The train at Banbury arrived several minutes late but the connection was at 10.40. Senior decided to go to Wolverhampton and Crewe so I left him there. I waited about 35 minutes at Woodford and I got into Rugby on the LNER line (central station) at 20 to 12. So I changed stations (10 minutes in a taxi) which I thought was better than walking seeing I didn't know the way. I had

---

[48] Scholarship

some squash and some grub and the hopped on the train. There were lots of Sedbergh blokes on it. I went in a carriage with another School House chap.

At Preston we changed into a special school train for Sedbergh. We ragged in the carriage (5 School House junior dayroom fellows) and I found out later that during that I dropped my wallet (with £2, Health Certificate and other things were in it) and never noticed it's missing until I was walking to the school from the station with Sykes.

At school we have 4 new boys in the house 2 very d ones, 2 boring chaps. I am still in the Junior Dayroom and the 10-bedder, Sykes is now in the 10-bedder too.

I have moved up 1 maths set and to Up 4th classical. We haven't yet really got down to work so I can't tell how I'm doing.

I got some skates (2nd hand) on some boots at Teddy's[49] and tried them yesterday on Lilymere[50]. I haven't paid for them though yet. They are jolly comfortable. The skating there wasn't terribly good but it was great fun. It was rather rough. Some boys are jolly good skaters, but not Mageen.

More later.

PS My wallet has just come from Tebay station – Hooray!!!

J   undated [30 January 1955]

As I just noted in my last letter, my wallet arrived with nothing stolen, pretty lucky. I am not in the choir now for a term or so until my voice has settled as Mr Regan put it – as it's breaking. So I have letter writing prep today.

Time rushing by... sun shining ever since the day (Thurs) we skated on Lilymere. The second hand skates screwed into corps boots I got from Teddy Dinsdale went very well. He has been very decent about the money side too. He said he would put it on the school bill and then I would pay you later – less trouble.

Yesterday and the day before we were clearing the yard of snow - with about 20 boys and a couple of wheelbarrows. A very tedious job but worth the while for we can have yard soccer[51] now.

---

[49] Teddy Dinsdale, owner of Sedbergh's shoe shop, much liked by Dear and the family, was known to Sandy and me from our holidays in Sedbergh in earlier years

[50] Lilymere was a most beautiful lake of some 20 acres surrounded by woodland and open moorland in a bowl in the hills between Sedbergh and Kendal. It belonged to a widow Mrs Williams (who bred dogs), a friend of Dear and Dear Man. She allowed the school to use the lake for skating when the ice was bearing. Sandy and I had skated and fished there for trout a few times on holiday from the Dragons.

[51] An enjoyable game played in the house yard often in short breaks - a form of 'mucking about' in which normally any number could join. Competitions were also held, from time to time with scratch teams within the house, but matches against other houses were very rare. Some boys were very skilled, and clever use of the stone walls of the yard was a key ingredient. A kind of touch rugger was occasionally attempted, but never really worked. I

We have a new English master, Latin and Maths Mr Pentney (Dick P or Bod P) takes me for Latin U4C. I think he is a very good teacher indeed – better than Mr Coates. Rev A.T.I. Boggis (ATI B) takes me for English and he seems good too. He makes it interesting and seems to have good ideas on essay writing.

A chap called Mr Underhill (Unders) takes me for [incomplete]. He really knows nothing at all and makes us do most of the blackboard work. He has quaint ideas of discipline to. He roars with laughter when someone makes a joke then suddenly stops and yells at the miscreator [sic] 'Take 2 maps'[52]. He is a very nice bloke though out of form (not that we see much of him).

Yesterday Kelly came round for names of chaps who might be any good at boxing. (He is Head of House, 2nd Prefect and secretary of Boxing now Highton has left). I have tried yesterday. It's good fun and it's a good thing to know how to do. Last year we won the pot for it, so we're going to try and keep it. However I'm not really going to take it up

Haven't been for any runs yet because of the snow...

J   6 Feb 55 [Sunday]

Not now in the San. It was an absolute fraud but absolute luxury. I went in on Monday morning with 4 other School Housers (including Sykes) and I felt very well all the time. I read 3 Agatha Christies and 'The Red Cockade'. My temperature never went above 99.1 and I only spent one whole day in be[53] . The other two and a half days I spent up., I was in a single ward because I was not so ill as the others so I couldn't catch their 'flu. I had a wireless by my bed and I had a wonderful time, No injections, no more drops or cough mixture.

Sykes came out yesterday (Sat) and the others too. I got out on Wed. I have now finished convalescing and am quite ok.

3rd in Maths. ... don't know other fortnightly orders

---

didn't especially like yard soccer; the ball was too heavy, the yard too crowded, and people came at you from all positions and angles (obviously no off side rules were applied), and skilled older boys could slam the ball very hard.

[52] Maps were a system of punishment for minor misdemeanours such as failing to put books away, late appearances, playing noughts and crosses during reading prep, untidiness etc. They could be given by dayroom heads, as well as by prefects or masters. They had to be drawn on particular paper. Blue paper was drawn from the Head of House – who was thus made aware both of the misdemeanour and of the prefect's action) and red paper had to be collected from the Housemaster. The system was based on numbers, usually 5 or 7 for more serious offences. '5 maps' meant that you had to draw in your map 6 administrative areas (states or counties) each with five towns in and five rivers or other geographical features. The detail was copied or traced from your atlas; and large maps could take up a lot of otherwise free playtime.

[53] Perhaps worries about another epidemic may have led to quarantine for suspected cases.

On Friday we had an operet[t]a here performed by the Intimate Opera Group. We saw the 'Musick Master' and 'Three's Company', both intermezzos so we were told; acted by a soprano, baritone and tenor. They were both jolly good and very amusing. The baritone in particular was very good.

Sunny days... We got up on Sunday 1½ hrs later than usual and when I woke up at about 7.20 there was a wonderful noise of birds singing..

Played a lot of fives, squash... sprinkling of snow on Higher Winder and Boar and Wild Boar fells and Riseall – looks really beautiful, lovely. But down in the valley it is quite warm....

Have bought some orange squash to take in little goes (half or quarter tumbler) when I feel totally fed up and bored, or hot and absolutely done in by exercise. I diluted it in my locker which serves as a good fridge because it is under the stairs..

Today we have a 'Bootroom' – I think I explained last term. It is an exam on the local geography, the school and school songs.

J   Feb 55 [13 February]

The snow is still lasting, in fact it has become deeper. I have done a lot of sledging, mainly on Logie's 'Flexible Flyer', a house sledge. There are some wizard runs and it's jolly good fun. It has been freezing hard for some time now, 12 ½ degrees of frost for 2 nights, last night it was 10 and Lilymere is bearing. I could have gone yesterday but didn't really want to seeing there was 3 ins of snow on the ice. It costs 1/6 to go up there on the buses and back again which can be done for 6d less if you catch a town bus. We tried making a skating rink in the yard but the sun thawed it all through the day.

In the boxing I qualified for the competition but Kelly said it would be more advisable to leave the competitions to next year as I had hardly boxed at all. School House hold the cup and we have a fairly strong team. Since the beginning of term when I weighed 7.8. I have put on 4½ lbs – this is mainly because of the snow and there being no running or rugger lately. My provisional boxing weight is Paperweight (7.10 to 7.5) but no one knows that except Sykes when we weighed ourselves after boxing on Friday.

Wizard snowball fights against Sedgwick – both houses produced about 70 people and we ran all over the place slogging each other with snowballs, retreating, attacking and wheeling – all sorts of tactics in formation.

Film 'Roman Holiday'... It was quite good but not as good as some – there was a wonderful cartoon with it though.

Fortnightly reports – 3rd in English, near the bottom in English and French, 4th in Maths and I think 6th in Greek. However I managed to come 4th in the form order.

Snow falling harder and harder now... the fells absolutely white and the dales too.

It is not too miserably cold. We spend most of our time reading books and warming our backsides on the radiators.

...Sorry that Smith[54] has been ill...

J   Feb 55 [20 February]

We have got Lilymere in full swing now, going up there every half holiday[55] by bus delivered to your front door step. The ice is simply wizard and my skating is getting better and better. I can now do a fig 3 but I mainly play ice hockey though.

A few notes for next year.

I definitely need a pair of warm long trousers, a scarf, my hockey stick. Am freezing up at Lilymere, but it does not matter now.

Another motherly notice: my Sunday trousers when hitched in their normal place round my waist are 3 ½ ins (measured by Sykes) above my 'ankle bone' (the nob on the ankle if you see what I mean). But they can do for now.

I have been skating on Bruce Loch on whole school days (Mon Wed Fri) which is fairly good but a bit bumpy.

Last night we had a 'Mock Trial' which was great fun. VIth form boys (The Forum society) acted it with the help of the masters. It was a kind of satirical play on the masters, imitating their ways of speech and action.

The tobogganing season has produced quite a lot of damage but I have had none at all and it's been great fun[56].

There is a craze in the house in singing hit tunes of South Pacific. Do you remember those records we had of it in Virginia[57]?

I am playing the clarinet in the 3rd orchestra in which we are playing two rather nice pieces, Chanson de Florian and Scipio. I am playing the clarinet as an equal 1st clarinet (there are 3 clarinets playing the same part).

Jolly good Scotland yesterday. The hopes of the Triple Crown are getting nearer and nearer

J   6 March 55 [Sunday]

---

[54] The part time gardener at Heron's March

[55] Half-holidays were Tuesday, Thursday and Saturday afternoons - with no classes, but games and sports in the afternoon and then some free time in the house.

[56] I enjoyed all winter sports. Lilymere was always a magical place but, curiously, I do not remember skating on Bruce Loch. I remember well tobogganing on Frostrow – the nearest decent hill – and the excitement of going at speed so close to the snow. You had to aim through a hole in the stone wall to be able to continue down a second field for a long run; and a really good run got your right down from the fell edge to a chicken hut.

[57] When my parents were in the Embassy in Washington, they lived in Maclean, County Fairfax, Virginia (then in the depths of the countryside, now an exclusive suburb).

You couldn't make out my PS. I said I gained a merit in the Junior French Wakefield Prize.

Extra half on Wed – a really beautiful day. Went round the ten (we have to do it twice a term) in 2.7 [2 hours, 7 minutes] pretty slow but on the other hand we hadn't ever done it before. There was snow in some places about 3-4 ft deep in the ghylls on Boar Fell. I am now doing 3 miles training and have to ask your permission in this letter to run in it. I don't know how you mean to answer but just tell me and I'll tell Kelly – simple.

Started rugger again, snow nearly gone.

Going out with the Sykes... Please can you tell me when you're coming up and when I'm coming out and whether I can take someone out etc..

Just had a letter from John Hordern[58]. He has gone to Hurstpierpoint and seems to be enjoying himself.

The interhouse boxing is going on and so far School House have won all 6 fights which is quite a good start.

We have started playing yard cricket[59] which is a wizard game. We use hard balls but luckily us new chaps aren't bowled at fast. The ball jumps off the concrete and can be jolly nasty. However it's great fun.

J   March 55 [13 March]

We are just about beating all Sedbergh's records – of rain. But now better... I even took my vest off this morning...

Yesterday was a good day. In the afternoon I went round the ten mile in quarter of an hour better than last time[60]. I took 1 hr 43 mins. Kelly thought that was jolly good when I went to tell him. I even beat our 3 miles 'spec' by 12 mins – however I prefer long distances like that to 3-4 mile runs.

In the evening we had a film show – the Cruel Sea and a James Thurber cartoon. The latter was appreciated much more by the senior chaps whose verdict was 'killing' and 'terrific'. The Cruel Sea was terrific particularly the photography of the sea and storms. I really enjoyed it.

On Thursday we had Field Day when the corps go off and have fake battles with blanks, and again they had a lovely day for it. As usual the

---

[58] Dragon School friend, with whose family I spent an Easter holiday near Stamford.

[59] Yard cricket was fun was amongst one's peers but differences of age and ability could complicate participation. Whoever got hold of the ball (usually a battered tennis ball) could bowl and if you got the batsman out, or caught him, you batted. Some natural cricket stars had to retire because no one could get them out. 'Bs door' cricket was played in the covered veranda (about 15 yards long and 3 yards wide) between the house door and the Bs. The door was the wicket. This was more fun. It could be played in any weather, and the smooth concrete floor provided a truer surface for the pitch than did the tarmac of the yard. There was also the enjoyable complication of a wall to the (leg) side.

[60] I ran in my last year and came about halfway down a record field of almost 120. I did the run in around 1 hour 30, but Sandy beat me by a long way coming about 15th in 1 hour 20.

school had a free day as well, I mucked about with Myles Moffatt and Des Sykes on the fell and we had a wizard day.

Last Sunday went out with Des and his parents. We had tea in Kirby Lonsdale and before that a whacking great lunch at the White Hart.

...Maths 1st in form, Greek 3rd.

...Looking forward like anything to the end of term, soon now.

J   March 20th 55 [Sunday]

Have now been dropped from the 3 mile, as not being a fast enough runner, which is quite true as I usually come last in all the training or equal last.

The effect of that is that I play fives or squash every day as the ground is not fit for rugger and anyway there is none now just before the race when everyone is training or slacking.

The house has been robbed of another cup. We shared the boxing cup with Powell House....

Another thing is that every holiday we have house orchestra now.

Another thing at the end of term is that 'Kenny' Anderson is getting worked up about the school orchestra and providing extra practices for that as well

Reports. I came 2nd in form order. I think I came top in Maths. These are provisional last reports but later in the holidays we get the White Book which is our final order[61].

On Tuesday there is the Ten, and concert ....

I am going with a couple of other chappies to St Boswells. That is the best near station so I'm told. I leave Sedbergh at 7.00 and it is due to get there at 11,14. I will send my trunk on PLA to Drum Mhor[62] and how it gets there it will have to find out for itself – perhaps I will at Sedbergh station.

J   26th March [Saturday]
Addressed to MEBL

End of term activities... [results of house competitions in sport and music - School House not doing so well...]. In the Ten we got 3rd and 6th places. Did not do so well in the 3. Winder House dominated.

On Sunday night I had a bilious attack and retired to the sickroom for 2 very peaceful days with books, the wireless and the Chinese Pagoda puzzle which I got quite a way in doing. Dear will remember that I think.

---

[61] The draft of form lists for the following term's Brown Book

[62] My parents were visiting Dear and Dear Man, at Drum Mhor, their cottage at Bemersyde, near Melrose, to which they had retired after leaving Sedbergh in Summer 1954.

I have reminded Daddy about the kilts in the cellar and told him about the sledge. It would be much easier if he took that I think. Daddy and Sandy arrived yesterday at about 5.15 with Mrs Senior. I went along and gossiped with them until tea. I am taking Myles and Desmond out for lunch, we don't know where. In the sports line we have been playing fives and squash but we haven't played rugger for some time now.

Summer Term 1955

J   No date [1 May 1955]

I'm having a grand time and everything is getting under way – except my trunk has not arrived. I am having to borrow ties, collars, games clothes, bats and all kinds of things and that is most annoying.

In our house we have 3 new boys. One is a French fellow who is only coming for one term. HM put him in my charge. However I'm not benefiting much as he speaks English fluently. The other two blokes, a yank and a blond, are both very shy and quiet.

Yesterday we had our first game of cricket. I tried spin bowling and took 2 wickets but for rather a lot of runs.

I have gone up one set in Maths and am now in kappa[63], I am still in the same other sets.

Of course we are playing lots of yard cricket. We have fielding practice too every night.

The timetable for the summer is all changed around. We have ex[64] after school and on Sunday evening we are allowed to go up Winder and rag around up there after chapel till bed time. On Friday we get off the last lesson.

Journey up - everything went quite satisfactorily. I arrived at Euston and got a ticket with half an hour to spare. My ticket was 38/5.

J   8 May 55 [Sunday]

Continuous bad weather... Got a game of cricket on Colts B, Under 15, next year's colts A... I played quite well...

Maths considerably harder in set kappa...

Swum every day and trying for my bronze medallion. It is quite a hard test and I need a lot of practice. The baths are about 75 degrees Fahr. which is nice and warm.

---

[63] Sets named by Greek letters for classes taken outside one's own form.
[64] Shorthand for exercise, meaning organised games and official sports

Invitations to speech day have been sent out. Do you know if you are coming up here then or at all this term?

In the summer we have no runs except with squash and when there is no cricket we just have to be out.

A couple of days ago I went down the river bird watching with Desmond Sykes. We saw a tree creeper and several bullfinches but otherwise nothing interesting or uncommon.

J   mid May 55 [15 May]

Term is simply whizzing by now. I am on Colts B final list. I took one for 11 and hit a six and two singles in my short innings.

Yesterday there were five matches – cricket, shooting, tennis, swimming...

On Friday we had an extra half, the first fine day for some time. I went off with Moffat and Sykes up the back of Winder and those hills. We looked for birds and saw dipper, wagtail, grey and pied, stone chat and moor pipit.

An important matter: Myles Moffat would like me to come and stay for the last week of the holidays. I would take my trunk up then. The 13th was the date implied (September). I would go straight up to school from there with Myles.

Do you know if the watch is getting fairly near ready now?

...The house challenge cup for fives (which Dear Man won three times) has been renewed....

J   late May 55 [22 May]

I got a letter from Ruth[65] with The Old man of the Sea which she had meant to give me before. She asked if I could come out and take a couple of chaps...

Thank you for telling me about the squash racquet. I did actually know before and I won't need it. It is surprising what one does do this term. Cricket continually postponed by bad weather. Colts B. Fives, squash and yard soccer on other days. Not much chance of tennis either...

Practising for the Bronze – to get Bronze privileges. It means I can go with 3 other fellas [Bronze holders] on long breaks and swim without need for a master or a prefect.

On Thursday we had Dennis Brain giving a horn recital. He played three concertos and some odd bits of music. He showed us how his

---

[65] Ruth Rose, my godmother, who lived at her family's farmhouse at Keisley near Appleby, when in England. Her husband, often absent on duty, was (Major) Jimmy Rose, formerly of the Indian Army, whom she had married in Cairo after the war.

instrument, a modern German horn, worked and he played a tune on a hosepipe. He was jolly good.

It snowed yesterday on the higher fells.

I have been reading several books, the whole of King Solomon's Ring and Requiem for a Wren – the latter, I think, is a jolly good story. I enjoyed it.

J   29 May 55 [Sunday]

Thankyou for the watch. It is going fine and has not lost at all or gained.

Sports...

Second fortnight orders. Greek up a place to 3rd, 1st in Latin, 11th in English 9th in History. Not told our maths or French marks.

School 1st XI doing well, as is shooting Eight....

The schools[66] were taken this last week. The top scholar got £300, £120 more than the top scholar last year. He must be an absolute wonder. I think they had to cancel the other major scholarship for him. He comes from the same prep school as Sykes does. No Dragons came up at all.

Do tell me about Jeb at his show soon....

Your idea of going up to Bemersyde is an extremely good one. I'd love to come down by train by night. Provided I have a good book to read, I will be quite ok.

J   Early June 55 [5 June]

The letter arrived on Friday – the strike is holding everything up here. I'm terribly pleased about Jeb. How much money did you win? Are the prizes pinned up above his bed in the kennel[67]? I'm glad you're getting more news about guitars.

Good weather... cricket pitches concrete... ...

On Thursday prospective Panters (under 16 House team) plus Mageen (Capt of House and School cricket) played the prospective House team. I played on the Panters and [missing word: *bowling*] at 13/2/35/1 not very good, but not an easy job against members of the 1st, 2nd and 3rd School XIs.

We had our film of the term yesterday 'Julius Caesar'. I thought it was jolly good but some people did not.

Ruth is taking me out between chapels to Barbon I think, for lunch and tea. ...

---

[66] The scholarship exams for entrance to Sedbergh, which I had sat in Summer 1954.
[67] Jeb, the Irish wolfhound had an immense (c. 4ft square) wooden bed, littered with straw, built at the end of a purpose built garden shed which served as his kennel

J   13 June [Monday]

Jolly d Jeb getting enrolled in the Irish Wolfhounds Club...

Myles' address in case of need is, Grass Rigg, Killington, nr Sedbergh.

They asked if I could come from 13th to 20th and there to school. Des asked if I could come over the previous weekend (his parents asked, that is), that is to say from Friday till Tuesday and travel to Myles then. I think Papa Sykes is writing to you. I hope we will be able to get them to us some time too, but probably not next hols.

I had a wonderful time last Sunday when we went to Windermere – it's a lovely place indeed.

I expect you have heard of the tragedy by now that happened on Tuesday. To take all in order of events this is what happened.

Tues was CCF inspection day (we had a rather jolly looking Brigadier who took the inspection in for lunch) and the assault course was being demonstrated (lots of ropes over the river) and it had been raining hard lately and the river was in very high spate – about 6 ft. Before they started demonstrating Mageen said to Bromley 'I pity the poor chap who goes over today' the latter replied, 'Yeah, first stop Lancaster'.

As the river was up the low wires were nearly in the water so when you hanged you were half in.

Bromley, crossing, got into difficulties and Fell (SH) rushed out to him and told Bromley to grip him. He did so but lost his grip before Fell could start going back and slipped in. The poor fellow could only just swim and managed to keep his head up for about 75 yards but then yelled for he had hit something and went under. The corps rushed off down to chase him and tried to set a net by Birks Mill but the plank bridge had been broken.

I was at the house during all this, playing yard cricket when a chappie turned up and told us to come to the river and hunt for the corpse. We did so up and down the bank along about a mile of water for 2 hours but in the rain and getting very cold wading about in the shallows and prodding. In prep the studies[68] went out to hunt but soon came back because now they had found him, about another ½ mile further down. We had a small memorial service with his favourite hymns later.

In the inquest Fell was commended for his action.

I have played quite a bit of cricket – Panters scores...[69]

I am getting promotion to the first orchestra after OS day (25th of June)

J   mid June 55 [19 June]

We are having a grand time over speech day weekend and a very slack time few days before.

---

[68] i.e senior boys in their last two years who had been promoted to Studies from the Senior Dayroom but were not prefects.

[69] My July letters contained many school and house sports results. These have been omitted.

I don't know if you've been here for speech day before. It's an absolute farce. They spiv up everything, cut all lawns, name the trees and everyone has to have white shirts on and specially clean blazers – and then the weather tops it up with thunderstorms.

Ruth took me out, to Barbon, with Des Sykes. Ruth told me about the wedding at Wittersham and that Dad had been asked to make a speech.

Also went to Windermere with Des and his family...

... Sir Water Monkton to give prizes but could not come. We had Peel[70] instead who stammered which made his speech rather tedious. Prick gave a jolly good speech.

J   25 June 55 [Saturday]

Ruth's father is ill, so she did not take me and Des and Myles out.

...Form orders, 3rd in Greek...

Cricket not going badly – scores... Captained a 3rd league game. Desmond played well for Colts – he was captain of his prep.[71]

Sports training has now begun. Standards for three age groups senior (over 16 ½), middle and junior (below 15).... Points system explained. 1 pt for a junior standard, 2 for a middle or a senior. I ran a quarter in 68, which got me a junior standard. School House got 143 pts....

School House has a good chance in the swimming this year....

J   30 June 55 [Thursday]

Bournemouth[72] - I'm sure we are going to have a jolly good time there.

I would certainly like to go to Scotch House[73]; it would be no trouble at all.

I have gone mad about John Buchan and have read 4 Hannay adventures.

Have played a bit of tennis, but lots of cricket... – Panters.... Swimming heats... Next Saturday it is the Bronze Examination. –We are being hurriedly pumped full of heart information, resuscitation, circulation diagrams etc

Awful weather...

Came 3rd in the Form, 2nd in Latin, 14 in English...

---

[70] To present the prizes on Speech Day?#

[71] Short for Preparatory school.

[72] Staying with Auntie K, my mother's sister, and Uncle Bill, surgeon at the Bournemouth General Hospital, and cousins, Janet, Patrick and Rosemary in their large and comfortable house in Talbot Avenue.

[73] To be measured for a kilt.

J   10th July 55 [Sunday]

Hope we will see Dad play cricket in the holidays... Sorry Granny is ill....

Yesterday I took my Bronze Medallion life –saving and passed. I now can wear a rather posh badge on my trunks and at school I have various privileges: 4 'Bronzes' can go for a bathe by themselves – ie without a master or school prefect.

We have had out end of term weighings. I am now 5' 5" tall according to our PT master and have put on 3lbs. I should be a better size and weight for rugger now.

Sports training... swimming sports... Cricket matches...

Form orders not known except 3rd in Greek...

J   13 July 55

Sorry for writing late for your birthday[74].. ...

Now got form orders, I came 2nd – in my proper position, I hope exams keep me there.

Lovely weather – temperature in the 80s. On Sunday I went out for a river bathe on the Lune – it was simply lovely. The river was not cold at all...

Played cricket in the sweltering sun yesterday and bowled 13 overs. – got tired and bowled inaccurately – got 3 for 47

J   17th July 55 [Sunday]

Athletics already started.... Ran in the hurdles, 0.8 sec off a standard... River bathing as before...

A boy with a harpoon got a 12lb salmon – shsssssh its poaching - don't tell anyone....

Played a bit of tennis but no cricket this week...

J   24 July 55 [Sunday]

Final Sport Day yesterday – SH came 2nd.... Results...

Mr Sykes came up for the sports and took me and Myles out for lunch. At the end of the holidays they can bring my trunk up to school when they take Desmond.

Afraid I only came 4th in exam. That puts my order down to 3rd. I got 72% on Greek, 38% maths, 70 % in French 82% on science, 63% on English, 79% Latin...

Sent my trunk PLA...

---

[74] First part of the letter intended for my mother, whose birthday was on 11th July.

Chapter 2:   September 1955 to July 1956

Note: Jamie's letters continue on from September 1955. Sandy's letters begin in May 1956; he remained an extra two terms at the Dragon School, before arriving at School House, Sedbergh in the last term of the academic year.

J   Undated, late September 55

Since I wrote last[75] the two days I spent with Des I passed mainly playing tennis. Going to Myles I got a bit troubled as the winter time table for the BR had come into action. I found I had to wait 1¼ hrs at Carnforth before going on to Kendal.

I had a jolly d time with Myles Moffat. I didn't do much but stayed in bed till 10 or even later, mucked about the farm with Mr Moffat and ate a terrific amount of food. I never bathed once and it was horribly cold. We had mushrooms a lot too and they were all over the fields.

At School I have got a double Cube with Des Sykes. I have not played any rugger yet but I have fives and squash.

J   late September 55 [25 September, Sunday]

We are now settling down into term arrangements. We have thirteen new boys in School House and it is quite a job seeing that they get to places at the right time etc, and there's all the fagging to be arranged as well. They're quite a nice hoard actually.

I'm in U5A Classical and the master who takes us is Mr Christopherson. He is the second master. I have only had him for two lessons so I could not say what he is like (he waffles a bit).

In Greek I am in the same set as a year ago but the set is now divided into half and 3 others and myself are going on as if we have done our School Cert – reading Hecuba, Thucydides, etc. Our master[76] (who was married last hols) says we would have passed easily last term.

I am in the top French set for the 5th and the second top Maths set, which I think is too high for me really but I'll see.

We haven't seen the sun since Tuesday and in fact it has been drizzling most the time. So much for school.

---

[75] i.e. last wrote home at the end of the holidays. On the way back to school I spent a few days with Desmond Sykes' family at Bolton and another few days with Myles Moffatt's family at Killington, near Sedbergh.
[76] Ronnie Reynell

J   Undated letter [end September 55]

I'm awfully sorry I forgot to tell you about the parcel of clothes. They would not nearly all go in so, since I have that fairly huge suitcase, I left them with Mrs Moffat and I will collect them later and bring them back home.

I am wearing my kilt now. It is definitely too big but I have hoisted it up good and high and it is ok. I got my jacket and it's a jolly nice one.

I was unfortunately told I was too small for Colts A this year after a couple of games in it.

Playing a house league game I tore a ligament or something like that in my thigh as I kicked a penalty. That put me off ex and I have had to have Infra-Red Ray treatment for 3 days.

J   Undated, [2 October 55]...The date of the confirmation service is the third last Sunday of term, the 27th of Nov. I do hope you can come up. I expect the Moffats and Sykes, in fact I know, that they will be up that weekend so I hope you will be able to meet them.

What language does the Swiss girl[77] speak, or don't you now yet? I'm very pleased about the Oxford (Morris). Will we have it for the next holiday or will you even be able to come up in it if you do come?

Thank you very much for the photo of Sarah[78]. I'm afraid my knowledge of the beauty of babies is inadequate and insufficient to remark on her probably very beautiful features.

The house fives cup, won by Dear Man three years running is now being started up again, but it is doubles instead of singles. I was drawn with the captain of house fives which was pretty lucky. We stand quite a fair chance I think but actually I doubt if we will win it.

Yesterday we had a 1st XV match v Waterloo RFC. We beat them 16-0 that was our second win of the season and that looks promising for a good term

I have not played much rugger.... I captained a third league which won and scored a try playing at stand-off where I have played most of the season. My thigh is healed now and I'm quite fit. Being on light ex which I have been for a week I have played lots of fives and squash.

Our first fortnight's up now, actually 2 weeks 4 days, but I don't know any of my places except Greek when I came second by a few marks. I ought to be top of Greek I think, I might make it. Mr Reynell is the brother of Peter Reynell at the Radcliffe[79] and the Rugbeian.

---

[77] Marie Claire, Swiss au pair girl who was not very accustomed to hard work in the house, and had principally taken the job for English language familiarisation.

[78] Our sister was still called Sarah, not yet Sally.

[79] Colleague of my mother's in the Department of Nuclear Medicine at the end of the war

The inspectors are littering up the place this week and the last week. The 'Fodder inspector' came to lunch and we had a really smashing (as S would put it) feast: ice cream and fruit for pudding and delicious fish pie and chips.

J   Undated letter, [9 October] *55*

... The term is now flying on and we have settled back into the old routine. I have played a bit of rugger and was tried for Colts A. I think I am too slow to get anywhere much this year and I did not play a terrific game.

I have spent a lot of time these last few days teaching fives to the new boys. It is rather an arduous job but they are a nice lot and some jolly good games players amongst them (not only fives)

I am not finding my work at the moment too difficult but I cannot foretell anything. I think I have got a better maths master for teaching but not so for other things I think. We are reading (and reading it very thoroughly) Julius Caesar which is the S Cert Play.

Is it alright for me to be confirmed this term? Des and Myles are.

When does Mummy come out of hospital or put it another way what will the next address be and when will it change? I hope Sarah and Mummy are both well and flourishing.

My kilt jacket has not yet arrived but my kilt has. It certainly fulfils Dad's condition[80]. I hope it is not too long. There is a new boy in SH with a Macgregor kilt[81].

The Sedbergh area has been sticking to her old traditions. We have had rain on and off since we came back. It's a good thing actually because the reservoir was so low we were getting rusty water all the time

J   Oct 15 1955 [Saturday]

Sorry letter late – just written to Granny – weather changed from good to bad...

We had fortnight's orders and I came 3rd in the Form, 2nd in Form subjects, Latin, Hist, Eng and Div) and 2nd in Greek. I don't know where I came in French and Maths but I don't think the latter was awfully good.

A couple of days ago I got a merit for Greek prose, getting 37/40 – which was not bad at all. Now will have '2m' after my name in the Brown book[82].

---

[80] Presumably this expensive garment was cut to allow for growth and to last a few years.
[81] This was R. Fawcett.
[82] The official calendar for each term with lists of staff, boys by forms, form-masters in charge, curricula for forms and sets, sports events, matches, musical events, lectures etc, etc.

I have been playing as usual lots of games and on Thursday I played A house juniors XV against the same of another house. That means house second XV.

In the same game Des Sykes broke a greenstick or something like that and has his arm in plaster. I hope he will not have it in for long.

We had the inspectors last week and they came in and listened to most of our lessons. Christo took an immediate dislike to them we thought. And when one fella stood up and spouted something to us old Christo advanced to him, most pugnaciously too, within a foot of him and then they bloated at each other for a couple of seconds and then Christo retired and the other carried on spouting.

Nest Saturday we are having a film, I think it is 'Shane'. It is a pity I've seen it before but I think it's a jolly good film.

Do you know what day of the week you will be able to come up, I hope you will be able to make the weekend.

J   Oct 23 1955 [Sunday]

Arrangements for visit for Confirmation. Glad you're writing to Sykes to stay on way up north, but they may have other visitors coming in for that occasion...

I hope you can come up for the Saturday, for in the evening some company is putting on the Barber of Seville, which might be quite entertaining.

About those photos you were looking for. I seem to remember you keeping them in Daddy's desk but I expect you have looked there otherwise I really don't know where.

Mentioning in your letter Apple Tree cottage[83], do you happen to remember the name of the chappies you sold it to, because a fellow here lived in Appletree Cottage when he was about 3 in that sort of direction .

I have been playing lots of games, lots of rugger and fives. In the house competition we go through to the second round. I have been practising a lot of fives for the junior fives (the inter-house comp). I will be playing on 1st pair although I'm really on second but we're breaking the stand 2nd pairs up. I hope the House get somewhere.

We have our second fortnight orders but I only know one result, that I was first in Greek. I should say I will be about 4th in the form order.

I do hope old Jebikin's leg gets better before the 2nd. It would be jolly nice if he won anything there. I hope he is good and thick and looking really tough not just be fly hunter's expression.

Last night we had 'Shane'. I thought it was very good although I had seen it before, but it was a very controversial opinion. The cartoon that

---

[83] My parents first home, bought in 1941, in a village near Andover. It was rented to an Air Force office for most of the war and sold in 1945 when my mother moved to Oxford.

came with it was an absolute scream, and Donald Duck and there was no doubt at all that was popular.

Our 1ˢᵗ XV still carries on unbeaten a big game is tomorrow v A.F. Dorward's XV[84] – last year he played the ex-captain for Scotland. I don't know who's playing this time.

Considering the situation of my grub I am in a perfectly good and satisfactory state, but no parcel would not be accepted most gratefully and indeed most welcome.

Considering my pen, the trouble about it is that the barrel that covers the sack is half ruined, therefore I have to use it as a dip pen but at school you see we have an inkwell to every desk that Jock Greenwood keeps fairly full and I'm rather fond of it and it has a nice nib – but however and all the rest I'm sure I could look after a nice fountain pen if anyone should happen by chance to give me one at Christmas.

I hope Daddy is better after his stay at Rye and I sincerely hope he played a good few games there and did well in the competition.

Only another 58 days- cheers

J   30ᵗʰ October 1955 [Sunday]

Thanks... I can well imagine how sorry you felt leaving 'Honey'[85] but I'm sure the new one will be just as good. I'm jolly pleased Packman[86] says Jeb is looking well; I'm longing to hear how he does at Olympia; I can imagine some spot you pointed out was cleared up now – I hope so.

About playing rugger on Saturday I won't know for certain till the Saturday but I should say probably yes. I have been playing lots of rugger, I'm afraid I have not played in the scrum yet but everywhere as an outside – including ½ game at wing (that was when house Juniors mixed with House XV for a practice game) and a game as scrum half.

I have been playing lots and lots of fives and even was induced to try shooting with not much success.

You may be pleased to hear that I was 1ˢᵗ in form subjects in form orders last fortnight I fear though I'm going to drop again to about 4ᵗʰ this fortnight unless I really buck up this next week.

I have had rather a passion for Hammond Innes' books and in fact have read 4 since last weekend. It has been freezing overnight and a jolly cold wind so I have spent most of my long breaks reading instead of yard kicking as we usually do. For if I kick vigorously with my right leg ir tweaks

---

[84] Distinguished Old Sedberghian rugger player and Scottish international, who raised a scratch team to play the school early in the term before the fixtures against other schools.
[85] My mother's much loved, powerful Ford V8 Pilot.
[86] I have forgotten who he was: apparently knowledgeable about Irish wolfhounds, possibly from Mrs. Nagle's kennel from which Jeb came.

the ligament which hurts so now I can kick only with my left just as well as my right, sometimes better.

The Sykes did come up last week and I went out to tea with them. They have just got a new car – a Hillman Hard Top (Californian). It looks quite a nice car.

Our 1ˢᵗ XV on Monday played A.F. Dorward's XV and was only just beaten. They were playing 3 Scottish internationals and I English ex-international our XV gave them quite a fight losing 18-13.

I do hope you can come up.

PS I found a book belonging to Daddy in UVI Cl's Form room. An anthology called 'The Albatross book of living verse or summat like that. Mr Reynell said should you want it, do take it.

J   Undated, Nov 55 [6ᵗʰ or 13ᵗʰ November[

About the confirmation. The service is in the town church at 6.30 in the evening of the 27ᵗʰ. There will be the usual morning service at 1.30. I will get chapel tickets but do not come if you don't want to for it won't matter. By the way you won't see me wearing my kilt on the Sunday because I don't think it would be a terrific idea being confirmed into the C of E wearing a kilt because the bishop might think there was some mistake and that I was really going to the C of Scotland, and had come at the wrong time.

Mr Thornely told me last night that Dear Man's operation went very well. I'm certainly pleased to hear it. I do hope he'll be alright and have no further trouble with his nose. I'm very glad about Sarah too.

About adding another Christian name. I have thought about it a lot and since Dad is not keen about it and [I] don't really feel strongly about it myself and it's going to be rather a bore for you to fix up – I don't really think it is worth it[87].

I have been having a jolly d. time playing lots of games. As usual I am spending a lot of time in the fives court practising for junior fives. I have also played a lot of rugger. I'm afraid I still cannot say whether I will be playing on the Sat., but I rather doubt it. However we will see.

We have our 4ᵗʰ fortnightly orders today. I have a feeling I have gone down a bit further. The only order I have so far was Greek in which I was 3ʳᵈ. I will tell you the orders next week,

You may have noticed or not but I have bought a new pen. I had to – my old one was a bit too far gone and I dropped it one day and smashed the nib up. This new one is a very nice one to write with. Talking about

---

[87] I did add a second forename, Robert, when at Cambridge, principally to separate my letters from my father's - both of us being JBLs.

writing I really must apologise for the bad writing. I do hope this is a bit better and more legible[88].

A thing I would really love for Xmas, that would be a pair of fives gloves. The book I mentioned before was the 'Lonely skier' by Hammond Innes. I am still thinking of a little small wooden dog or animal mascot which in vain we sought for last year. Gold balls would doubtless be a good idea. And camera films too.

You know the dressing gown I bought last hols. Well, I wear it every night after all, I had been meaning to tell you before but I had always forgotten. In the cubes we assemble down the passage in the middle and that after we have washed.

When you come up do you possibly think you could bring two books that I happened to see Dad had at Rugby. Also someone's British History Notebook (a blue book) and a small Latin –English English-Latin dictionary (a black book) both in the far left hand hall bookshelves (I think, anyway definitely in the hall book shelves [sketch of shelves and likely position of books)

I'm looking forward very much to seeing you.

J   Monday 21ˢᵗ [November 55]

... a short note to ask you what time does the train arrive. There are two in the morning, one which arrives at 4.48 am, the other at 8.30 am. Please write back because Syd[89] wants to know.

If I am not playing rugger I will get a leave off ex so I can go out on Sat afternoon if that is all right. Could I take Sykes out on the Sat for lunch or tea or both. On Sat I can be out from 1.15 to 7.15 pm. On Sunday for breakfast and between chapels (9. 0 morning chapel. I'm longing to see you.

In the fortnight's order I came 3ʳᵈ in the form order. That is the only result I know. I got 26/30 for a history essay, with the remark 'the best this term from [Form] VA so far'

J   Undated, Nov 55 [27 November]

I'm jolly pleased about Jeb, I think he did jolly well in spite of this Bermondsey bruiser of a dog that beat him in the undergraduate. I do hope he does as well at Crufts, for that is the really big show.

Last weekend we got our half term orders (everything together). I came 1ˢᵗ by about 3 marks. In Latin 3ʳᵈ, History 2ⁿᵈ English 6ᵗʰ. Form subjects altogether 2ⁿᵈ. At half term I managed to discover the maths places for the fortnights so far which I have not previously been able to tell you. I came 5ᵗʰ

---

[88] It was perfectly legible.

[89] Sid and Hilda Morphet, farmers next door to School House, were good friends of Dear's

35

then 8ᵗʰ then 9ᵗʰ for last fortnight Of last fortnight I think I have only told you so far the Greek. I came 3ʳᵈ in the form order and 2ⁿᵈ in form subjects.

I have as usual been playing lots of rugger and fives and even doing some running which I usually manage to escape by playing fives or squash. Unfortunately Johnstone and I got knocked out of the House fives cup in a very close and exciting game in the semi-finals, which is a pity

Desmond's godfather, Mr Sykes told me yesterday, is Desmond Haskett who I think you knew at St Andrews. They will be up for the confirmation. A great friend of the Sykes is a certain Ken (now Dr) Broadbent. He believes you know him too, and his wife, Mr Sykes says, was at Benenden with Mummy, he cannot remember her maiden name but she was called Bunti or Bunte or summat like that.

... [paragraph about getting tickets for confirmation service, chapel service and Barber of Seville if parents want them – with details of times; and travel arrangements – getting Syd[90] to meet them at Oxenholme Station....

I'm very glad to hear Sahra (Sarah - sorry can never remember how to spell her name) is getting better. Talking about the [word illeg.] and warts a new boy who sits next to me in the dayroom has his left hand dotted with warts. They are quite fowl and since every time I look up I can hardly fail to see the beastly things (he sits on my right) I changed him around with another boy. The same fella in one letter writing prep, his other neighbour said, wrote 43 words including the address in 40 minutes. It's a pain to see him work.

As said before the Sykes are down this weekend and I am going out with them today to Windermere – lovely.

About the greedy list: as usual I can never think what I want for Xmas till Boxing Day, but I would very much like a good pen. Gramophone record tokens always come in handy. 'The Lonely Skier' by Hammond Innes, whom as Sandy says, I appear to have 'gone up the pole about'. I have read six of him that we have here and in the cover of all of them it says something about The Lonely Skier. And I have not read it.

Give lots of love to Granny and Grandfather and to Sandy and tell the latter student that I will answer his 'corking' letter very soon.

PS   I will add to the Greedy List next letter, I hope.

J   4 December 1955 [Sunday]

Thank you very much for taking me out last weekend. I had a lovely time and enjoyed myself very much. I hope you had a pleasant journey back home. Thank you very much for the biscuits and the Penguin book.

---

[90] Braithwaite, garage and bus owner and taxi driver, well known to our family

The trials[91] are rather long winded and it takes rather a long time to get to the point.

I am having a jolly good time and the term is simply flying by. We had the first round of House matches last Thursday – School House drew to Winder and lost 3-0 in the replay after a very tough game; all the house watched the game and there was a howling wind, we were all frozen to the marrow. There is junior fives on Thursday next and yesterday we had a practice game against Hart House (we were drawn against Winder for Thursday). We only had time to play 2 games. The first we won 18-16 and lost the second 15-11, unfortunately thus losing by 7 points. The other two pairs lost as well.

There will not be much more rugger for me this term since all the houses are concentrating on house Rugger XV and Junior fives.

We have had our last fortnight order now (except the exams which count as 2 fortnights in our marking system for the term order). I only [know] 2 orders – 1st in Greek and = 3rd in French. (It was the first French order we have been given this term). I will tell you the other orders next week when I write again (also the orders that go on the reports).

This term's confirmandi candidates celebrated their first communion this morning in the parish church. There was a very large attendance of about 80 people or more.

I'm afraid this week has been a rather boring one and there's ought more to say.

I'm looking forward like anything to coming home. The cost of coming home will be about 41/2d to London, 1/- to cross London & 4/9d or so home. The minimum expense is therefore 47/6d (excluding any food). Railway lunch 7/6d. Should I ask the HM to put 55/- on the bill and get the money from him? I have not got much pocket money left.

J   Dec 11th 1955 [Sunday]

...I'm very pleased you enjoyed yourselves here. Thank you very much for investing our money for us[92]. I am going to keep an eye on the Assoc. Elec Ind. Yesterday they were 84/6. I'm glad you'll explain about the shares business because I'm not sure how they work.

Talking of Xmas present I think that I too would like some poker dice. I'm sure they are not allowed at Sedbergh but I can't see any harm in a quiet game with Des Sykes and others in the corner of the Dayroom.

We are now starting to get down to end of term arrangements.

We had our report orders last week. I came 3rd in the form order, having been beaten by one person who started above me and by one

---

[91] Unclear reference, presumably the subject of the Penguin book
[92] A legacy from our Great Aunts Anne and Mary Weaver, later used for travel during Cambridge years

person who started below me. I came top in Greek by quite a fair margin so I doubt I will lose a place in that subject in the exams. I don't know where I came in the others.

In last fortnight's orders I came 3rd; 1st in Greek and = 3rd in French and I was told I had quite a good maths report so my place there could not have been too low. Next week we have exams (and their results) so as Sandy says that might make 'a tiny bit more life'.

Our rugger for the term is coming to an end. On Tuesday I played in the junior fives and we won our round by 30 pts. My pair won by 11 pts (on 3 games to 18). In the second round we played last year's champions (Evans House); the same team except for one person. We lost dismally. My pair lost by 32 points and altogether we lost by 94 points. Paddy Taylor (Len T's son) was on the first pair. He is also on the first pair of senior fives, playing with the English schoolboy champion.

The only rugger this coming week are the House matches Since we lost our 1st round there will be no rugger. There are yard soccer competitions throughout the week. 48 boys, all the house bar a few, are divided in several teams and they all play each other.

On Thursday night Capt. Knight[93] came and gave us a lecture on Kenya with a couple of films. It was very interesting and brilliantly photographed. He did not bring any of his birds which was a pity although we saw them in one of the films.

It has been bitterly cold lately and on Thursday night there was quite a bit of snow. It went however with the rain which was pretty well continuous on Friday. The pitches are completely drenched but with luck they will not hinder the house matches.

Well, life is a bit boring and the term is beginning to drag along; the hols seem so near yet still rather a long way away. Longing like anything to coming home.

Easter Term 1956

J   Jan 22 1956

The term has started off very well – and very quickly, it hardly seems a week that we travelled on Tues.[94] We have started of the work very quickly

---

[93] I do not recall who he was.

[94] In the middle years the Senior Dayroom was our base. It produced a mix of generations because it contained boys from year two and most of year three plus possibly a couple of boys waiting one more term to go into studies (since there would be further leavers at Christmas). A large square room faced south, with wide windows overlooking the Private Side drive and garden. It was sunny and bright. I recall endless ping pong; much sitting and chatting, and not much reading – it was too noisy, but you could use the Common Room

and there will be no slacking since the 1ˢᵗ fortnight orders are next week instead of usually being after three weeks. In history this term we are doing American history which I think is far more fun that English. In Greek we are reading a far easier play, and work on the whole is not going too badly.

So far this term we have only had one game of rugger because on Wed it snowed but Wed overnight it rained and Thurs it continued raining. The Rawthey is fairly full now and the ground is getting very soggy. In the game yesterday, a house game in the pouring rain, a new boy plays at stand off opposite me and it looks as though I'm going to have to keep a very high standard to get a place in the Juniors, House 2ⁿᵈ XV. This fella is about 1' taller than me and is a very fast runner. I think he captained his prep school.

Mostly this week I have been running (I have also played a game of squash and of yard soccer but one has to go for a short run after both of these games). I don't know yet if I'm eligible for the 3 mile because I don't know the date of entry – anyway I very much doubt if I will run it.

One very important Notice. I completely forgot to get Dowcs address before leaving home, please do you think you could send it?

I am attempting to keep a diary up because I did find they were great fun to read through later. I did not get a diary over Xmas but Des Sykes had two (exactly the same) and asked if I wanted one so I have been trying to fill in the holidays but I can't remember what we did on various days. Do you think that in your next letter you could tell me what we did? - what I mean is write down what you had scribbled in your diary like who was there to stay. The dates I can't remember are 1ˢᵗ Jan, 6, 7, 8, 9 10 and 11ᵗʰ morning. Please would you jot own something to help me remember.[95]

I'm in the same sets as last term for maths, French etc. I was given a merit for my French, The book was handed to the last term for a good term's work. I am in only the 1ˢᵗ orchestra now I think but I'm not sure if I'm playing 2ⁿᵈ or 3ʳᵈ clarinet yet. The trunk had arrived on Tues (and no damage)

PS   Terrible = Assoc. Elec. down 1/6 on Fri to 73/6 but + 3d yesterday.

J   28 Jan 1956 [Saturday]

Thanks for letter and the clothes. I hope you had a jolly good time at the Savoy with the Germans. I think it is a jolly good idea going to Norfolk or Suffolk. Will you keep an eye open for yachting places. I suppose you will be going to see Uncle Logie and co at Greshams. What date exactly is Crufts? Are you going to show him or is Mrs Nagle or someone?

---

next door or the Library. There was also a game of table football which could be put up and played, with up to four aside, whirling the figures around on spinning sticks.

[95] These notes were addressed to my mother.

I have played quite a lot of rugger and there was a practice House Juniors XV in which I played against Evans House. We won 17-5. We have drawn against them in the 11st round too! Yesterday I played on Colts B2 and I scored a try and made another and altogether I had quite a good game. I have also played a bit of squash and even yard soccer once.

The work I'm afraid to say has not set of at a promising start I haven't actually been told the fortnight orders except for Greek where I came 3rd, but I believe I have done rather badly in Latin - which includes not handing up a prose which was incredibly stupid of me and I will be pretty near the bottom if not bottom.

The flu epidemic is running around now and many people are down and the san full already. So far touch wood, I have not caught it badly – yesterday I had a slight touch I think but it has gone off pretty well now

I wrote to Dowcs on Friday, I think, any way the day I got your letter.

It's been a pretty boring week on the whole. The weather has been rather like what Dad says yours is. The snow was here at the beginning of the week, It was frozen, then thawing, sleet & hail. Now lots of rain and a couple of day ago fog, mist and drizzle. Come to Sunny Sedbergh – I ask you!

The house orchestra pieces have come now and mine is a very easy bit in a rather nasty key which is a nuisance. The school orchestra pieces are fairly hard – that means a lot of practising for the clarinet.

About the Spectator, I'm afraid I don't think I would read it here at school so I reckon it's not worth sending pretty definitely

J   5th Feb 1956 [Sunday]

Thank you very much for the letter and the gloves. It was very kind to send me them and I have been using them quite a bit already. This week we have had two days really cold, temp never above 31 degrees max all day and we flooded the house yard which on Friday gave us excellent skating. However all Friday night it snowed hard and thawed all Sat and all hope of skating has now gone., and there is nothing but water and slush on the yard; Bruce Loch and Lilymere which had the freeze continued for one day, says Prick [Thornely], would have been bearing is now quite hopeless – Pity. Yesterday however there was some very good sledging on Frostrow which was fun.

Yesterday everything was white but today it has all thawed and there is not even snow on Holme Fell - Barbon (we can't see Winder's top) and H Winder because of cloud.)

On Sat 3.35 am the upper cubes were woken up by the pres[96] from the lower cubes, on whom some pipe leakage had been dripping; no one upstairs had been awoken by the dripping before and Sykes' cube next to

---

[96] Shorthand for prefects

mine was completely flooded all over the floor and it had crossed the passage and gone into Sugden's opposite. With the pres and everyone else helping we bandaged up with leather the big leak and others sprang up into action (4 in Sykes cube, 2 in mine) so the leather had to be unbound. When the bandage was off not just a steady drip appeared but a furious jet spraying up against the wall. Eventually with the help of Prick and Mason having been called from his house the water was turned off up there. Then for about ¾ hour we had to mop. The water had by then gone about half way down the cube passage. It had dripped through not only down to the cubes below but to the kitchen and dining room below them. The lights were finally turned off about 5.15 am.

Yesterday evening we had the inauguration session of our Scottish dancing. It went very well till suddenly the lights went out and the elec cut stayed on leaving the house candle lit for nearly 2 hrs.

All this week Christo has been in bed with flu and also my maths master 'Pid' (Mr. Ward). I don't yet know my first fortnight's order (just as well) nor have any one in the form done hardly any work at all over the week. (9 out of 18 boys in the san anyway).

As you can imagine we have had no rugger this week at all and Juniors had to be postponed. I played squash though and fives also once. I even tried shooting but I don't think I will ever be a first class shot!

About Des coming to stay next hols, if you could kindly suggest a date because they are quite willing as far as I can gather for Des to come 'when it suits you'. They are coming up here on Feb 10th I can talk it over with them if you have any suggestions.

The term is going along at quite a nice pace now, I'm longing to come home

J   12th Feb [Sunday]

Thank you very much for the letter. The date of the beginning of next term is Tues May 1st. The end of term is Tues July 31st. The Sykes came down yesterday and I went out with them. WE first of all had a smash up lunch at the White Hart and then we read comics and papers in the lounge. We then drove to Dent and browsed in the antique shop there. It's a jolly good shop and most interesting things of all kinds are there. We then drove on over the fells round the back of Whernside, in the snow, and down to Ingleton where we had high tea, ham & eggs cakes, fruit salad. Up in the fells the becks were nearly all frozen over and the waterfalls were mainly ice, a lovely sight.

We discussed about the holidays and Desmond coming to stay and the decision was really the first bit was better, the 27th March to the 4th April. However I expect Mrs Sykes will write. Also there was some vague talk of coming up to school a few days early and staying there mainly [outside

Manchester] to see Julius Cesar (by a man called Shakespear I seem to remember) which is the School Certificate play for Eng literature.

There has not been much going on this last week. It has been vaguely trying to snow and just a vaguely trying to freeze but it hasn't done either actually. We managed to get in two games of rugger and thus Junior matches were played. I played stand-off with Sykes at scrum half. It was a very poor game. They had 8 or 9 of their team ill or off-ex (flu still going round). We beat them 18-0. Two of our men were off. Next round we play Sedgwick who have a very strong team. We are due for quite a beating I think.

On Thursday night we had a lecture on horses – the Olympic games of 1952 at Helsinki, by the Brit captain Mr Hindley. It was jolly good and the film which was half colour was very good. He was most interesting, much better than I thought he would be actually.

On Friday the ground was far too hard for rugger. I played field soccer instead. Unfortunately our rather good game was spoilt by the ground which had been slush being horribly bumpy [sketch of wavy line – mwmwmwm] vaguely like that.

About birthday presents I haven't really had much of an idea. I would rather like a book about yachts, preferably with lots of photos of them. The desks I sit in are full of bumf with drawings of yachts all over them). Otherwise I really seem to have no ideas whatever, if any do crop up I will tell you in my next letter.

Last fortnight's orders – I came =4th in the form order, 10th in form subjects (Hist, lat, eng, div). The HM was not particularly pleased as one might expect. I was 3rd in Greek last fortnight but came 2nd this fortnight. We have not been told any other places yet I'm afraid.

Please write and say what happened at Olympia. I'm longing to know.

J   19th Feb 56 [Sunday]

Thank you for the letter. I'm terribly pleased about Jeb. How did the financial side of the affair work out; were you up or down in the end? Have you even seen the cup? Do we get a replica of the cup or something? Rather chic to have one lounging around the house don't you think. What is a mid-limit class?

I hadn't actually been looking at the prices at all until I got our letter and then I saw they were at about 68/- or something. I have attempted to read the AEI's but I only read the bit you marked with a x (it's rather too complicated (many times harder than the shares problems in Elem Maths III for [word illeg] which are bad enough for me.)

In last fortnight's orders I came 4th again in the form but I haven't been told any others. It looks as though I will the same again; it doesn't look as though it's going to be a sparkling fortnight.

The weather this last week has been most odd. Monday there was snow lying around but not enough for 'boganning. On Tuesday there was enough snow (It snowed overnight) and all houses except SH were allowed to bogan and snowball but Prick wouldn't let us so I went round another run; but Thurs we skated in long break on the yard and also played fives on Wed and squash after ex on Thursday.

On Thursday night we had a piano recital by a certain Colin Horsley. It was jolly good – at least he was but the piano had two notes that stuck and a pedal came off half way through. This chappy also had a slick back hair and 2 or 3 strands of it refused to stay back and hung down in front of him close to his nose– like this [sketch] – this is exaggerated.

It was rather a pity because it was the cause of much suppressed laughter,

I'm longing for the hols, its half term on Tuesday and the term seems to be wizzing by

J   26ᵗʰ Feb 56 [Sunday]

Please excuse my change of writing again but I've decided that my new experiment of writing 'more squarely' isn't any good after all and I'm reverting (if that's the right word) to my old method again.

Thankyou for the letters this week. I went to Teddy Dinsdale and asked him about the shoes and he said that they would take some time when made to measure but there had been some delay and he would find out what it was. He said he <u>did</u> answer Dad's letter of about a month ago.

Thankyou very much for the tin of shortbread cake. I have given up sweeties for lent with a real determined effort, and have done so far, and I think the first bit is the worst in a thing like that, so the S. cake came in much welcomed even more than usual. Was the shortbread from Askews[97]? I never noticed but it was your writing on the outside so I imagine it was in fact. Nothing else has come to me yet.

When we had a replenishment of snow at the beginning of this week we got 3 days of snowballing and boganning which was great fun. We have also had skating but not on Lilymere yet (or on Bruce Loch) in the last fortnight that is.

The yard which we flood at night is quite good but what happens is excellent skating till noon and then thaw and reflood and 5-14" at 9 o'clock and good skating the next day till noon etc.

Of course with this snow we have had no rugger for some time. I have done quite a lot of running which I loathe. – I am not in for the 3 mile actually – too old by 19 days!. In the last run I came 5ᵗʰ in the house handicapped – depart 2.30 Trotters pack, 2.33 Little Pack (that's mine),

---

[97] Grocers' shop in the town

2.34 3 mile trainer pack and 2.36. Big Pack (10 milers). On the one before I came 7th and the one before that 6th or 7th I am not sure which.

I've been playing quite a lot of squash and some fives as well. We have fortnight orders again this weekend and as usual I only know the Greek order in which I am 2d again which isn't too bad though I really ought to be top.

What I think has been happening and that is only my own notion – is that I have been doing fairly well to now – particularly in Greek – because I've learnt more than the other boys when I was at the Dragons. Now we're getting on equal ground I'm dropping down a bit.

Last night we had a film 'Dial M for Murder'. It was jolly good – a terrific suspense and thrill and all together most enjoyable. There hasn't been anything else of great interest this last week so I don't think I've anything more to say I'm afraid.

I hope you are all very well and that Jeb is getting fat and that Sally <u>isn't</u> and that Ely^{98} is learning more English.

J   March 4th 56 [Sunday]

...I'm terribly pleased about the prize. £63/8/4d is jolly good. One could go on spending 2/6 on pools for a leap year of Sundays & not win that much. I think it's a jolly good idea keeping it for the summer holidays or something like that. Jolly good about the cup of Jeb's. Where are we going to put it up?

I'm sorry to hear that Dear Man has to go back to Edinburgh. I wrote to him this morning.

There has not been much going on this week. We are now trying had to resume ordinary life after the snow and ice and genuine arctic conditions and the weather has been helping us by giving us a true Sedbergh extra (rain) and there was quite a spate and flood in the middle of last week.

As yet we haven't had any rugger as the ground was too hard and frozen and I have played squash and fives. The ten mile course is now open and as usual everyone has to go round it twice in under 2 hrs. I was going to go yesterday but the arctic wind resumed its knife edged rush across the valley and one would have been blown off Baugh Fell pretty well. (I found a fives court considerably warmer).

Last night we had a staff play 'You never can tell' by a certain fella by name G.B Shaw if I remember rightly. It was really excellent and I enjoyed it thoroughly. The acting was terrific. Jenny Thornely was <u>quite</u> good. I thought she was the weakest member. She took the part of Gloria (if that helps). OMF (Bill Foster - oomph) took the part - I thought the best part of the play of the play, certainly the most fun to do I'm sure – of the waiter William. I think he was the best actor.

---

^{98} The new au pair girl after the departure of Marie Claire, evidently another urbanite

Last week there were the senior fives. SH got beaten in the first round by Winder by about 60 points. There was also the boxing in which we are now standing third with finals and semis yet to be played – this worked on a pts basis/

I haven't heard any results yet about S but I've managed to pick up odd things. A certain set was read an English CEE paper and they said they had to write about traffic signals which from the question meant traffic signals (policeman standing directing traffic). But this fella wrote on red yellow green. They had to write on their favourite fiction hero and this fella wrote on D.O Brace of Oxford rugger varsity team!! He wrote some more trash, something about canoes that brought the house down with laughter when the master who was correcting them read it to his form. I hope this wasn't poor old S. His Latin (source of information from another boy who wasn't doing his prose hard in Latin but watching the master correct CEE pages) wasn't too bad I gather but started off by [sketch showing, top of exam paper, crossing out his name and re-writing it] .However I expect he will get through all right.

Longing for the hols and seeing you and Sarah. I'm glad she's eating well and is generally a good baby (better than others I've heard of, as you say).

J   March 11ᵗʰ 56 [Sunday]

Jolly good about Sandy isn't it; jolly good of him to get into Form Two, I wonder if those papers which were read aloud were his. I didn't know when he had heard but since I gathered that one was told by letter and usually just over a week after the exam I telegrammed to him saying he was in Form II

It's becoming really like spring, even summer here as well,. Friday and Saturday have been real boilers. The day starting with a misty hazy sun becoming really warm for our yard cricket in long break. SH is always the first to start yard cricket and inevitably does so about 3 weeks before anyone else. We are going to have quite a good panters team this year I should reckon. 3 or 4 new boys, at least winter term ones, are excellent cricketers. One of them played for Accy's[99] Under 13 team and had quite phenomenal scores & averages. One game he made 64 not out and took 6 wickets for 4 runs. He bowls fast and hardly anyone in the yard stands up to him firmly. [Cochrane?]

Yesterday was another hot day. I went round the Ten and it was far too hot to be running so fast. I took 1. 52 which is not a terribly good time the only good bits were to Cautley in 34 and back from Danny Bridge to the Grubber in 23½.

---

[99] Edinburgh Academy. This, I think, was Cochrane, a gifted all round games player.

I went round on Tues as well but lost my way by quite a bit and took 1.56 mins. I was going considerably faster than the time before. We had an extra half on Monday but it wasn't a very nice day. I trotted out Lune Viaduct way for about 3 miles, knocked about there and came back again. Not very enterprising.

We had field day on Thursday and since I am not in the corps yet (15 ½ - i.e. winter term for me I had another kind of extra half. We went to Dent over the top of Holme Fell and then had a pretty slap-up meal there and then came back. In fact we had a jolly good day. We had ragging and mucking about up on the fell.[100]

On Tuesday an ambulance came for Jenny who was seriously ill. It can't have been too serious though as she came back yesterday and is up and about

Last Sunday her dog was taken out on the fell by some prefects and they lost him. There was a furious chase and hunt but it was not seen again for 2 days when on Tuesday it paraded up to the front door and was let in.

I'm glad you had a good time at Oxford. I imagine Elly found Oxford more interesting than our country residence. I expect she will like Bournemouth when she goes there.

I'm terribly pleased to hear that Sarah is chirpy and sings in her pram...

On Thursday we had some more entertainment. A certain bod – 'fraid I can't remember his name – gave us an excellent lecture on the '55 Kanchenjunga expedition. It had some good slides and it was altogether most interesting indeed.

This afternoon the Huddersfield Youth Orchestra are coming to give us a performance. I hear they are very good. Our school orchestra is doing one of the pieces, Handel's Occasional Overtures and March. Unfortunately they could hardly have chosen a worse day to come. Again there is a lovely spring sunshine and it's quite warm and the last thing the school want to do on such an afternoon is listen to an orchestra. However, I do hope they are good.

Only 2 weeks and a bit. 3 Cheers...

J   16 March 56

Thank you very very much for the fly case and the stud box. Jolly useful presents[101]. It was very kind of you to give me these as well as what I'm going to get at home – I'm simply longing to know what it is. I've got a

---

[100] Up until the middle years 'mucking about' included some boisterous ragging outdoors, on the fells for instance, as Sandy's letters record, but general ragging of the prep school type was no longer needed– we got enough of it on the rugger field or were generally too exhausted by Sedbergh's hardy outdoor existence for that kind of fun and games.
[101] Birthday presents (14 March)

few old flies at home which I will be able to put in it. I'm afraid I don't know which are which except the butcher and March Brown

I hope you are having a nice holiday. Do you think we might try sailing on the broads for a holiday some time? I think it might be quite good fun.

I had a jolly good birthday. Dear Man sent me 10/- , which was jolly d. I spent that at the grubber with Sykes, Shiffner and Oliver which seemed a fairly suitable way. I got an excellent book from Granny called 'Come and Sail'.[102] I am reading it for the second time. It's full of all kinds of interesting things and jolly well written. Sandy sent me another jolly d book full of beautiful photos. [103]I have nearly finished it already. Granny's cake was simply smashing - & it's nearly gone now. Robin and Auntie K gave me some money that I propose to spend next hols.

Last fortnight I came 3rd again so unless I do badly this fortnight in the final one I ought to hold my place in the form. My English seems to be rather bad, my history not too bad, Greek ditto, Maths very weak, Latin not very strong. I think I was 7th in French but it may have been lower. We have had our report orders which are our term's orders less the final fortnight. These are what come on the report. The whole term comes in the White Book.

...a lot of writing to do of thankyou letters... weather....

This last week has been rather boring and rather usual. We are doing a terrific amount of practising for the house shout (unison – broken voices)[104]. We ought to win I feel after all the amount we have done but quite frankly I doubt it.

There is the ten and three mile race next week and then all the end of term affairs and time should whizz by...

---

[102] A favourite book, which I still have.
[103] *The Beauty of Sail*, Frank William Beken and *Uffa Fox*; Charles Scribner's Sons, 1938 - which I also still have.
[104] 'House shouts' were inter-house singing competitions (for broken voices only). Everyone had to participate, and those who could not sing in tune mouthed the words silently. I learnt a lot about music from Thornely's enthusiastic coaching for these competitions – and in my last term I stood in occasionally as conductor-coach. We also became more conscious of the music for evening hymns since our friends took turns to do the piano accompaniment, and we all helped choose the hymns. The readings were the prefects' own choices too.

Summer Term,1956

The term that Sandy came to School House from the Dragon.

S   Undated [probably 2 May 1956, Wednesday - Sandy's first letter home from Sedbergh[105]]

I hope you had a nice time in Germany. I am having a jolly good time here. On Friday Jamie taught me to play fives with 2 of his friends. It is a jolly good game I think but jolly hard to play, especially hiting /sic/ the ball hard with the left hand which I am rotten at, but it is a supper/sic/ game.

It has been raining all the time and there has been very little cricket just house runs and fives and squash. I have been swimming nearly every day sometimes twice. There are quite a few chaps with flippers and some with masks and breathing tubes.

I do hope you can find what you said a savings book some time.

And will you tell us the very second you know anything even the tinyest bit about where you are going to next – Singapore?[106]

On Tuesday I played yard soccer which is jolly good fun, then went for a run, then for a swim. If I swim under water my head does not go funny but if I stay under for a long time and I don't strain myself[107].

Today is a lovely day and it is a chiz we can't play tennis or any other ball games. So we swim and play draughts and eat![108]

Will you please send my Bible – very important!

I am enjoying myself very much and will write again soon.

J   6ᵗʰ May 56

...now settled back into the proper school routine... and Sedbergh has given us her usual welcome – RAIN. so far we have only had one game of cricket. I captained one side (a junior house game) versus a fella called Cochrane. I was out for a nice round figure and my bowling was 0 for 7 in 2 overs. Poor old S did not get a bat and bowled 1 over in which he was hit for 14 runs..

Otherwise we have played yard soccer. Yesterday being one of the junior ones on the lists S couldn't play and had to go round a 7 mile run. I did jolly well doing it in 68 which is pretty good.

I am in the same everything and not as yet down for Colts A.

---

[105] Sandy's first letter from his new school, eagerly awaited by our parents, was apparently delayed in the post – see Sandy's letter of 6ᵗʰ May below.

[106] More likely to have been a reference to talk of going to the Middle East, then in crisis, not Far East

[107] Sandy had been plagued by ear-ache and our mother worried about his doing any prolonged swimming under water.

[108] Sandy not accustomed yet to the special Sunday regime at School House

Christo has rather gone to seed rather over the hols and now has a hearing aid. We expect that he will retire soon (38th year coming up)

The Bragdons turned up and came in for lunch which delighted the prefects with their talk, particularly by asking if the matron – an elderly woman of 40 odd - was the wife of Jake Mr Durran the House Tutor, We met them after lunch and unfortunately got no tip (chizz!)

... S had been doing fine. Des is probably going to be the Colts 'keeper. Yorks sloshed up Oxford at cricket... I have played the clarinet a lot and had two games of fives after ex and have swum once. I have just written to Rufie and Ma BL as they are called here.

PS   Please thank Ma Skilly[109] for sending the pens. I got my watch from Dorking on Tuesday. It goes beautifully now.

S   6th May 56[110]

Thank you very much for the flippers. They are supper and how cleaver /sic/ of you to get the ones with adjustable feet strapes /sic/. They really are wizard. I got £1 from Uncle Robin which was jolly d of him , and 5/- from Aunt Hat and six tennis balls and 10/- from Granny and Grandfather and 10/- from Aunty K and 10/- from Dear Man – and of course the shortbread was delicious and so kind of you to send me something as well as the flippers. All together I have had the best birthday I have had for a long time. The cake is simply delicious and getting 3 presents from you was just prang-on. If you get a stop watch, get a farley [fairly] good one for I have plenty of money. If you send me my savings book I can put my money in and get [it] out at home to pay you back.

I am having a jolly good time here. I am playing lots of yard cricket which is a supper game. There are some D chaps here, some jolly D. There are 2 D chaps who came this term and 2 jolly D chaps who came last term.

On Wed it was too wet to play games and I put my name down for yard soccer but there were too many chaps playing who were more senior than me. It was too wet for anything but running so I went round a run called Red Bridges which is the longest except the Ten – 7 ½ miles. Good fun but coming back against the wind and rain was harder going. We eat most of our spare time if we aren't playing yard cricket. It is quite true so far about the butter - we have not any yet at all. The eg /sic/ this morning was hardly cooked at all – ½ a minute about. Simply revolting.

I am in the choir as a Treble but it is too high for me I should be an Alto; all the same I want to stay a treble because I think it is the most fun. On Thursday we have a drawing class and we went down to sketch the town

---

[109] Mrs Skilton, a cheerful housekeeper-cook (not live-in) who helped with Sally, and who spoilt Sandy and me with good solid fare of the kind that teenage boys really like.
[110] Sandy's birthday was on 4th May.

church. It was wizard fun and believe it or not but the art master looks just like you see a picture of an Artist in Punch, he is all complete with a beautiful red beard[111].

By the way I jolly well did you write to you on Wednesday. If it does not come I will say this again.

We went up Winder and Higher Winder on Wednesday.

And I past my eights on Tuesday which is just swimming up and down the bath eight times.

I have to write millions of thank you letters. (If you feel like it you can send me some stamps. I miss Letter prep because of the choir.

J   13ᵗʰ May

...glad you had a good journey to Rome..

... spring weather at Herons M and in Sedbergh.

...played cricket twice this last week, both on the interhouse league games. Rain has postponed it most of the week. In one game I was given lbw first ball (not rightly, even the WK[112] agreed) but Bobby Hamer the Canadian had volunteered to umpire and we all agreed by baseball rules I was probably out. In the other one I was cleaned bowled first ball. No excuse this time! However my bowling was not too bad. In the first one I was 5/2/6/4 which was jolly good but I spoilt it rather by coming on at the end and the tail sweep rather hard when I was hit for 8 runs in one over. Luckily the fella the other end got the last fella out before I had to bowl again – so great disappointment my average was 6/3/14/4....

...Amazon Journey – discussion at lunch. Snow was a relation in a way. What relation to Sandy Sally and I exactly?[113]

...We don't have any form fortnightly orders this week but next week. I don't think I have been doing too badly really, my maths hasn't been supersonic, I rather glad I'm giving them up.

S   no date [13ᵗʰ May 56]

Thank you for the letters and the radishes which are lovely. I am have great fun; on Sunday we had the Bootroom test before Chapel, instead of after it so I d d not miss it which was a pity, though I got 106 out of 180 which is quite good.

The names of the New boys are: Andrew Robertson, Lionel Melville, Wilding-Jones, John Whitman. Lionel Melville is a pretty wet chap with curly hair and a jolly silly face and a soppy chap. Andrew Robertson is a

---

[111] Mr Inglis, well described

[112] wicket-keeper (i.e. of the opposing team)

[113] Sebastian Snow, who was one of two explorers who travelled the whole course of the Amazon, was a (second) cousin of my mother's on the Hone side of the family.

good chap, not absolutely wizard but jolly nice, W Jones is quite quiet (very quiet) and J Whitman is a gorp. Really Robertson is a good chap. They are all nice chaps but some rather wet.

Unfortunately I am doing science which is a big chiz – or chemistry. The work is fairly easy except for the algebra which I cannot do at all, but I am doing better at it now; otherwise it is quite easy.

I am very pleased about the boat, especially the outboard motor, I think it is a supper /sic/ idea and hope that we will be able to sail in the Reggata /sic/, When do we go to Dartmouth and when do we come back? Are we staying at the same place as last time? Have you started looking for a flat yet I hope you do get a good one and in a good place.

Yesterday I was Raidiographiesed /sic/ – had a x-ray of my chest, The whole school had it. Two great caravans berring /sic/ mobile hospital affairs came down here, I have never seen anything so clean and ifficent /sic/. It was not like when you (Mummy) and I spent 3 hours in the Radcliffe Oxford waiting and being X rayed, Instead of doing 3 people an hour like the Rad they did 120 an hour.

I am sorry I have left this letter so late but I was very busy.

We have or first fortnight order on Saturday and I will tell you next letter about my work.

There is a film on Saturday, I think it is the Colditz story which if it is as good as the book it will be absolutely wizard. I wrote to Dear Man on Monday; he should have got it yesterday. Don't forget about the stop watch?!

J   20th May 56 [Sunday]

I'm sorry you've got hay fever too. Mine has gone off now, but this last week I have used a quite incredible number of handkerchiefs not only of my own but I have been borrowing them from lots of other boys.

I'm terribly sorry to hear Dear Man is not well at all. I do hope it's not very serious. It must be great for Jeb to have Penny[114] to play about with, or do they not get on well.

I see that it is obvious that we have to sell the house. I hope we get a good price for it! When will we know for certain what Daddy's going to do and where he will be, if he has to go abroad? It does seem a pity we have to leave HM, particularly after all the work you put into it, the terrace, the drainage, etc..

Last Sunday old Brendan was down and S and I went out to tea with him (and a couple of other chaps). I must say he's quite a talker. Anyone who has any name at all (like Lord... and Lady...) seem to be great friends of his. He refers to nice young chaps, the heir to so and so, and fine old birds, the Duke of so and so

---

[114] Dear's border sheepdog

This last week I have played fives twice in boiling heat... I played cricket twice and had nets once. One game of cricket was house Panters – Under 16 v. the House team. We won fairly easily. I bowled for 3 overs taking 3 wickets for 10 runs..

However for some reason I managed to get on the 2nd Colts XI... I didn't bowl but made 21 not out.

Fortnight orders...

We have the Brad Lads coming (Bradford Boys Club) for their annual visit. The seniors entertain them in various ways – swimming, cricket, yard soccer, going up the fells etc. and there is an extra half, usually a cricketing half actually for the rest. Which means just an ordinary half holiday instead of the usual Monday full school day.

S   25 May [115] 56   [Friday]

Thank you very much for your letter. I must say I am really very sad that we are leaving Heron's March but I suppose it is right. If someone makes a good offer and you sell it will be there [still] in the next hols and the Christmas? And will we be looking for a house next hol?

It will be great fun to have a flat in London and a country house or something down in Rye if you don't go abroad.[116]

This week I have played a great deal of squash with various types. I think squash is a supper game and I hope that I will be able to play with you (Daddy) sometime so that you can show me things about it, because I could not play very well just by picking it up[117].

On Thursday I played cricket and bowled for 5 overs and only got 1 wicket though I kept the runs down.

Really nothing has happened this week but there might be an extra half tomorrow if it is a nice day.

I think I am very near the bottom in maths and top in French. I am in the 2nd top maths set in the Lower school which is called sigma. I think that Mr Begley who takes me for English, History and Divinity is a very D chap. He is housemaster of Powell House.

I am not so sure that Mr Flint who teaches me the trumpet is thoroughly good; as far as I can see he only cleans his teeth once a month (like I do) and showers once a week. All the same, he is a good trumpeter and not such a good teacher. I will write again in the middle of the week.

---

[115] There is a note written by my mother on the top of the letter, presumably with ref. to the previous letter -'P.O. Savings Book No 5591 (Walton St Oxford, Nov 1946)'.

[116] Evidently parental plans were still uncertain.

[117] No coaching was ever given by staff for squash, and rarely by seniors, because it was an informal pastime and not an official school game.

J   May 27 56 [Sunday]

...Terrific Dad making such a score for Ockley II. I Hope he does play for the 1ˢᵗ some day, then we would see it in the local paper, JBL 64* and some terrific writing about Ockley's new star performer.. Perhaps it would be more likely that Dad's scores would be like mine last week. This last week in 2 innings I made 6 and 0. My average is about 8.2 now. I bowled once but not terribly successfully 1 for about 15 runs.

I played tennis yesterday, not a terribly energetic exhausting game because it was so warm, but great fun. I have swum and played squash with Sandy one afternoon and slacked for a couple of afternoons and putted on HM's lawn which is very nice and pleasant. The garden here is beautiful...

I do hope the Benenden golf match was fun. I'll bet it was jolly amusing. Did you play well/not so well, or did you win a goblet/ or wooden spoon?

Came 4ᵗʰ in the form this fortnight, same as last term, but don't know my other places.... On the working part of the time I have ben sloshing up lots of revision and likewise for the exam. There is the French one tomorrow morning but no other exams till 6 weeks time,

S   6 June 56 [Wednesday]

I hope the letter arrived I wrote on Thursday or Wednesday. I am so very very glad that you have such a nice house to live in in London.[118] It should really be fun living in London for a bit though Jeb will need exercise.

There was a 1ˢᵗ XI match yesterday v Durham school... We were 234 for 4 declared. They had made 80 for 4 when play stopped. So it was a draw, in our favour

I played squash yesterday with a new boy called Whitman but he isn't very good (in fact rotten) and I beat him, though it was great fun.

Yesterday I played with Wilding Jones (another new boy). He has only played once before but was quite good. And it was good fun. We have to go for a run if we play squash which is a chiz because if you just watch cricket you don't have to do anything but sit and watch cricket.

Do you possibly think or don't you that maybe you could lend me your fishing rod (Mummy's) and perhaps you could very kindly send me it and my cast and flies and the real I used at Drum Mhor. This is only if its not a bother to you. If it's a bother, don't send them. And it would be very nice to have them here and I could go fishing with Robertson who is very keen to fly fish, he lives at Scarborough and has sea-fished a lot but has never fly fished.

This morning the HM called J and me to his study separately to tell us that he was going to say a prayer for Dear Man this morning in Chapel, he

---

[118] This was Vicarage Gate, off Kensington Church Street; a part of a large vicarage with extensive grounds.

thought he had better tell us first and asked whether we thought it a good idea. So he said one and I thought it was a good thing. Tell Dear Man I send him all my love and I do hope is very much better and will be better soon, which I'm sure he will be.

Yesterday evening we saw the Colditz story. It was very very good indeed, easily the best war film I have seen, some parts were very funny, some very serious. It was really very good. Also there was a news; and a very funny cartoon (Tom and Jerry).

I hope that we will be at home[119] for the Ockley and Capel and Oakwood Hill annual shows. Jeb will win some more cups I hope and they are supper fun.

If you really want to know, the radishes were bad but it was lovely receiving them and it was very kind of you to send them.

On the Thursday was the Drill cup (interhouse). School House normally come bottom but Slater[120] trained everybody very hard but Powell house won by one mingy stingy little point with School House one tiny point behind (87 & 86). Chiz.

I do hope Kirsten[121] will be at home when we are there in the hols.

I am glad that Penny and Jeb get on well, but if he barks at everyone it is fine in the country but in the big city will be a great nuisance.

I have just started reading "The Sittaford Mystery." an Agatha Christie. It is very good but not at all well known so it must have a bad ending but so far it is the best detective story I know.

> After lunch

We have just had lunch – Roast beef (or some hot meat I don't know what), roast spuds, cabbage, then Trifle. Sunday lunch here is supper.

I have been for a walk with Robertson along the river – which is great fun.

I am very sorry but I have just found out that the fishing licence costs 12/6 and as we have already had a whole month of term I don't think that it is worth it. So my message on the other sheat [sic] is completely all false.

If Kirsten goes before the summer hols who will we have to come and help? Will you be getting a nanny for Sally. (By the way you have not said anything about her lately in your letters, but I suppose she is alright and in good health.) And when we are in London will we have anyone?.

Now I am going off to bath[e] so I have to stop now.

PS I am prepared to pay almost £4 for a stop watch.

---

[119] i.e. in Herons March, Ockley still.

[120] Jock Slater, Head of House. He went into the Royal Navy, won the Sword of Honour at Dartmouth and rose to become Chief of the Naval Staff and subsequently CDS.

[121] Kirsten, a young Danish au pair girl, was a cheerful companion, of whom we were very fond and a good helper for my mother with Sally; she loved Jeb the wolfhound, whom she spoilt rotten. She arrived with already first class English and became virtually bilingual after a couple of months – most visitors thought she was Scottish.

J   10ᵗʰ June 56
Letter addressed to my mother, after the Memorial service in Sedbergh School Chapel for Dear Man which my father, but not she, had attended]

It was very nice to be able to see you and Uncle Logie and Paddy and the others last week although the occasion was a very sad one, and it was a pity Mummy could not come up too [Dear Man's funeral]..

Thankyou for the box of chocolates. They were excellent and not so much of a chiz as the usual chocolate boxes with only 1 layer and perhaps only 4 chocs.

weather... cricket...

Not much to say, Dad will have the news

On Friday Lyon, HM of Rugby, came up and spoke to the upper school on careers in industry – he was really excellent - the best of that kind of talk I've heard – not that I've heard many.

Time is rather slowing up now as it usually does around half term...

S   June 56   [10ᵗʰ June, as above]

Thank you... for taking us out ...etc...

I am very sad about Dear Man and I hope that Dear is all right. Mr Begley read us (Form II) an artickal /sic/ about Dear Man out of the Sedberghian. It is a jolly good article and says what a 'D' and wonderful person he was. He (Mr Begley) gave me the copy of the Sedberghian; it has many other articles about Dear Man.

This afternoon Robertson and I went to Cautley Crags over Higher Winder and Calf and back by the road. We could not take a pack lunch with us because so many people had asked for them that we lunch early instead, which was a chiz.

It was a supper day really to hot /sic/| though. It was jolly good fun.

On Saturday I played squash twice, v Robertson and Melville. I beat Robertson but Melville who is fairly good (has played 3 year) beat me.

Is there anything special you want me to give you for your birthday.

If Michael Rowlandson's mother asks me to stay (which I don't suppose she will) could you tell her that I've got to do something else or any way say I can't. This is not because I don't particularly like Michael but I think it is a waste of time,

Don't forget to write to Harvey Askew[122].

Mummy what do you think me and J should do about Granny's birthday.

---

[122] Harvey Askew, retired Sedbergh grocer, and lovable character was a great fisherman. He had fished often with Dear Man (and other members of our family) in earlier years. He taught fly-tying at the School and was a willing helper and coach to any interested boy.

55

There is nothing here I can tell you because Daddy knows all the news. I will write much more next week

❋

J   17 June 56 [Sunday]

Sally sitting up ...

Yes, I think it is about time for re-stocking actually, an excellent idea. I think a bit of butter & a couple of pots of jam and some tomato ketchup would carry me out. Do you think I could buy myself a pair of slippers – my others have worn right through the soles to quite an incredible degree! I could do without any more actually.

I have spent a lot of time trying to putt the weight and hurdle and run. I did the half mile for the fourth time in about 2 mins 40 sec. The standard is 2.71/ I can put a weight about 4 gymshoes and 2 inches off the 31 ft standard. Done some hurdling as well

In work now doing the usual lots of revision....don't know positions except 3rd in Greek

Half term on Sunday and speech weekend so we are going to have a good time

By the way is there any time free in August when I might go and stay with the Olivers[123] at Morston near Blakeney Norfolk where they sail in the holidays. It's only a vague offer since I said I thought we were booked up but I would like to know..

J   24th June 56 [Sunday]

Return next term on Thursday 20th. It is the first time we have returned on a Thursday. I think Sandy has answered the Sharp's invitation.[124]

Thankyou for the food parcel from Askews. Just exactly the right kind of thing in it. Sandy's fishing rod arrived here yesterday which was pretty quick considering the usual speed of transport to Sedbergh.

Yesterday was speech day and after the service in the chapel – we were faced with the usual problem of seating all the boys using the side aisle seats, and several people had to sit in the porch and behind the raincoat stands etc – there was the prize giving.

Lord Bracken gave a short speech about Dear Man first and then Prick followed next. He gave an extremely good speech actually talking about public schools.

The visitor who gave away the prizes was the provost of Eton, ex HM of the same, the first incidentally to come to Sedbergh since Roger Lupton our founder, and for that reason we had another verse put on the school song for speech day, Floruit, floreat.

---

[123] Parents of James 'Dog' Oliver, a good friend who later became a Captain RN.
[124] The hospitable Sharp family, with children our age, were neighbours in Ockley.

He had rather bad luck we fancy since Prick said a whole lot of what he had planned to say all about education of the public school being not only a training for one's future job and he had to keep on adding 'and I must underline the headmaster's statement very heartily" and 'as the HM said' etc. When he finished no one expected him to and there was a silence while the poor fella turned rather red, and then he said 'Well, that's all I've got to say, I'll sit down now' and was rather annoyed, and not much cheered up by Brendan's hearty backslapping.

We had the concerts on Fri and Sat nights as usual which was pretty good this year, much brightened up by selections from the Pirates of Penzance. I played a very boring part and only took part altogether in 3 of the 6 orchestra pieces (including the National Anthem).

I think we are going to Windermere with the Sykes which should be great fun.

house matches... dates for next holidays

cricket practice – exams... fortnightly orders came 4th again. 'Consistent' was Christo's remark, hardly surprising seeing I came 4th, 4th, 4th in the first three subjects.

S   June 56 [24th June by internal references]

Thank you ever so much for sending the grub. It was and still is absouloutly [sic] delicious. It was very kind of you to send so much and so clever to know just what I wanted. Dear also sent me some grub which was very kind of her. And thank you very very much for sending the fishing rod and flies and casts and reel, and also for the letters.

Sorry I couldn't write yesterday – there was such a lot to do.

Yesterday Lionel (don't you think it is a pretty pansy name) Melville whom I think is a big dreg and like the chap who sees fairies at the bottom of the garden in 'Down with School' asked me out with his parents. This was a mad thing to do because he knows I don't like him but I thought I could not refuse for I said I was going fishing on Saturday which was a rather feeble excuse and as his parents were standing about 5 yards away I said yes I would like to.

In the end it was not quite so bad as I thought it was going to be. We went by car (Austin) to Kirkby Lonsdale to have lunch with the ex head master of Cressbrook prep School. He (the ex HM) was a very 'd' chap. We had a super [sic] lunch of cold chicken which was very good and potatoes (boiled) the best I have ever tasted. I have always thought that spuds were things to fill up the gaps between the delicacies but these were potatoes which were really good, simply prang-on – and then salad, and then lemon marang [sic] pie!

Then we went off to fish near Cautley which was where I was going if I had not gone out. We had great fun fishing. He (Tich Melville[125]) has just started fishing this term (I think). We did not catch anything – which is not surprising as there were no fish to catch. We took a picnic tea and then came back to the evening service, then to the White Hart where we had pork chops and veg and then a fruit and ice cream dish. Mr Melville is a v. v. nice chap which is not surprising as he went to Sedbergh. Mrs Melville is just all right.

The concert was very good. I am sending the programme. Slater played his flute beautifully but the extracts from the Pirates was very good.

On Speech day in the morning we did not work. At 10 we went to chapel at 11 to the speeches. B. Bracken made a very good speech, a tribute to Dear Man saying what a wonderful man he was. Then the HM made a very very good speech lasting a long time though it as not boring. Then the Provost of Eton made an appauling [sic] speech, really bad It was a terrible anti-climax and a rotten speech all together except for a story he told.

There was a man weling [wheeling] a barrow of manure and he past a luny-bin and a lunatic looked over the wall and said ' what are you going to do with that manure?' and the man said I am going to put it on my straw berries, and the lunatic said 'well I prefer cream on my strawberries.'

Yesterday was a half holiday[126] so I went out river bathing in the Lune. It was beautifully warm and we swum in a long pool about 16' deep and then we swum up through the salmon pools to some rapids where we had supper fun.

Today is the CCF Annual Inspection[127] by Sir Robert Mansergh..., so we have lunch early. It does not affect us guys under 15 ½, so we play cricket (some of us).

---

[125] Common slang for younger brother as well as a nickname for a very small person

[126] Extra half holidays were always a great excitement – a chance to be off on the hills, with the grubber open afterwards, offering not only the relief of getting off school, but also the chance of a break from an otherwise structured, hierarchical existence. Especially in the summer, the time could be used for longer expeditions. In School House many such expeditions were supported by Jake Durran, the House tutor.

And river swimming was another possibility and enjoyed all the more once we were able to go off in groups without supervision after we had passed our Bronze Medallion Life-saving exams. Each house had its own official pool (Lord's Dub on the Lune for School House) and some other favourites. It was a long walk or jog, to get there, carrying swimmers and a towel. Sometimes the water was too cold or, in dry spells, there was not enough of it; nettles, prickly grass and sharp rocks were a nuisance, and clegs and horse flies a menace, but in the right conditions it could be glorious fun, as Sandy's letters make clear. Another liberating activity for many, including Sandy and Alan Macfarlane, was fly-fishing for trout.

[127] The CCF took up one afternoon a week. We started with square bashing in house yards and a lot of cleaning of kit, and then weapon and general training in the gym and on a .22 rifle range, following the formally structured curriculum of Certificate A, Parts I and II, and examined by professional NCOs in keeping with the needs (national service) and spirit of the times by staff with Territorial rank and Sgt Ernie, who maintained the stores. Then there

Now it is lunch time.

J   July 1ˢᵗ 56 [Sunday]

...re possible visit to the Olivers...

Having a jolly good time here. The weather hasn't been too bad and this week I've managed to do a bit of everything.

I have played tennis twice (not too badly I think) and I've done a bit of athletics – I can now get the weight to about 5" off the standard. I did a bit of hurdling, the 100 in about 13.7 and the half quite comfortably in 2.52 in which I should be able to lower that a bit. I have played cricket with no terrific score – went in 9th in Panters

Field Day – always good for those not in the Corps

Went out with Sykes to Windermere.

Prick has just told me that Dick and Kay Weaver[128] are coming on Tuesday and we are planning to go out and have tea with them or something.

School exams start on Monday – doing lots of revising.[129]

S   c. 1 July 56

Thank you for the letter and the photographs. I think the one of Sally is jolly jolly good.

This last week has been very boring and there is next to nothing in the way of news. On Tuesday I played cricket versus Powell House. I bowled four overs and had 3 runs hit off me for 1 wicket. Then I scored 29 of which about 20 were fours, but no sixes.

On Thursday I went fishing by Jackdaw bridge. I did not catch anything but there were many fish around and when I hid half in a bush and casted it so nearly on their noses [but] they still did not take it.

Yesterday I played two games of squash and won them both

On Wednesday evening there was a Junior Dayroom concert in which every single person had to play something in front of the house (not the

---

were field days for practical exercises – an art form of its own, which Sandy and I usually enjoyed, as our letters show. The CCF in the context of potential mobilization was a serious business, and staffing of a good professional army was an important government aim at that period – as is evident form the extraordinarily high level of visitors who came for General inspections of the CCF.

[128] Second cousins of my mother's; he was a doctor in Hamilton, Ontario.

[129] In my second year I took my first exams - sat in the main school hall, which itself was a experience so different from class rooms. The hall was huge and tall; and I can see still now the specks of dust flickering in the morning sunlight coming through the big windows; I remember the shiny exam papers, the lined writing paper, the long rows of desks. As I became more confident, I came to enjoy exams more – except for the horror of hay fever, which I suffered badly at that time of year from about the age of 15 to 25. I had to take Piriton pills, which hardly helped the sneezes and sniffles and only made me sleepy.

building, the boys) and the HM, the Matron etc. The HM and some prefects judged it. There was 5/- for first and 2/6 for second prize. I played 'Passing by', the thing I played at the Dragons. One chap who lives in Surrey played the trombone. He just started this term and never played a tune on it in his life before the afternoon of the concert. He rather cooked his own goose when he went in laughing and you can imagine what it sounded like as he was laughing – so was everyone else. I think it is a very good idea of going to Paris in the Christmas holidays instead of these.

This fortnight I have not done so well in French but better in maths and English.

I'm very sorry there is nothing else to say at all.

Oh yes, I just remembered yesterday I did some training and did 73 secs for the ¼ mile beating my previous record by 6 secs. 72.4 secs is the standard for the ¼. I also did the ½ mile but I'd better not mention how long I took for it – it was not brilliant

PS   Stop watch.

J   **July 8ᵗʰ 56 [Sunday]**

Tuesday was Field Day, which we get free, since I am not in the Corps, from 12 to tea time. Unfortunately we waited for the Weavers the whole time, going down to the White Hart at intervals and playing games and mucking about in between. They turned up at about prep time and came round in reading prep when we went to see them at the private side. We went out for a terrific lunch with them on Wednesday which was very nice. It was jolly nice to see them.

cricket games and scores.

...done a bit of training when I've had free time and can now get about 9" off a wt [weight] standard which gets a house qualifier to go on for the wt. I did a quarter in about 68; I'm not running in one actually and a rather slower half about 2.55 but I was doing it quite comfortably.

revision with practice questions...

I'm glad the house hunting in Rye was useful. I do hope we find a good house there.

It's very nice of Kirstin to knit me a new pullover, and you as well.

I don't suppose Sandy's told you but he might have done that he only has one pair of long trousers which he uses all week for cricket and then on Sunday. He hasn't yet acquired the name of 'bags' Lockhart [sketch of boy with very crumpled trouser legs.] He seems to be having a 'supper' time.

The stop watch[130] is terrific, I used it down at the track once or twice yesterday; it was a very nice present for him...

---

[130] Sandy's stop-watch, received earlier as a present and just recently mailed to him at School.

J   July 11ᵗʰ 56   ]Wednesday]

...sorry about the birthday cards, you see we bought them both at different times without the other knowing[131].

We have now had our first week of exams. Mon & Wed we had only Additional Maths (I and II respectively). Both papers were pretty hard and in the first one I did a bit of bungling in trying to get a graph done in 12 mins instead of the other half question and the trouble was I failed to finish the second graph of the two.. Not everyone did Additional Maths only those in the top two of the five fifth form maths set. It's not a compulsory subject.

On Friday we had American history which wasn't too bad a paper and yesterday we had Eng Lang II Essay. The choice was 'Teddy Boys', 'Monday' 'A touring holiday', 'One side of a debate' something about the H-Bomb, a short story about 'The Lifeboat' or 'the Bend in the Road'. I took ages deciding which on I would write and eventually I wrote on Monday.

Sports training and swimming – speeds and times given, chances of getting a standard.

We are doing all sorts of revision, it seems quite endless. However I manage to get time to read Peter Cheyney and play yard cricket a bit. Hols coming jolly soon – Hooray!

J   22 July 56 [Sunday]

Thankyou for the reminder about the bathing trunks[132].

Sports and School exams. Everything seemed to go well. I did a 100 in 12.3 - 0.1 of a sec under the standard time; a half in 2. 28, 3 secs under the standard; and 110 yards 10 hurdles in 19.9 - 0.1 under the standard...

On the work side of this last week we have had exams ranging from 5 minutes after breakfast to 9 o'clock at night.... Engl Lang I, comprehension, précis – fairly hard. 3 French papers, all pretty easy, I got 2 mistakes in the dictée which could have been worse. Eng Hist quite hard unfortunately and Latin I on Friday was an absolute piece of cake. I took about 1 hr to do the 2 hour paper. Yesterday there was Greek 1. The trans was a gift but the prose Gr-Eng was not at all so. Eng Lit Julius Caesar – not too bad.

Won't know the results till next hols when the HM will send round cards saying what we failed and passed.. Like all public exams it depends on how the whole lot do for a pass mark and perhaps everyone took 1 hour on the Latin paper.

Next week we have Engl Lit II – Chaucer's prologue and Greek II and Latin II – and then we stop work for the term. Lovely!

---

[131] Sandy and I had evidently failed to consult each other and both gone and bought an identical card for my mother's birthday.
[132] A reminder to bring them home with us

S   July 1956 [22 July]

I am sorry I did not say about the trousers before but I just did not understand them for I don't see how I lost them (which I don't think I did) for at the beginning of term when I unpacked my trunk I put all my clothes in my draws *[sic]* then a few days later when I played cricket they were not in my draws. So either Matron lost them in the Linen Room or I lost them.

Yesterday evening a guy called Ward and I played tennis v a House prefect called Lord and a guy called Smith; we won 7-5. That was in the third round so now we are in the semi final; and there are 26 pairs who entered but so far we have been very lucky.

I have just been washing up some prefect's egg pans which is a super waste of time and before that I was swimming.

There have been sports, which are jolly good fun, especially as I have my stop watch and it is great fun timing the race. I have gone in for the Junior High Jump but [expect] no standards for anything. The Quarter (71 secs) I did in 73. The half (1.52) which I did in ?. The half was terrifically exhausting and you had to go jolly fast all the way to keep up with 9 other chaps. All the others were 3-term chaps for I was the only School House newbug to enter.

Also I entered the 100 yards which has a standard for my age of 12.2 sec which is jolly fast; but as the 13-14 years olds have the same standard as the 16 ¼ year old ones (Long Jump 15'9", 100, ½ mile, hurdles) it is hard for a first year guy to get a standard...

This morning there was a Boot Room test which was jolly hard but I think I did alright; there are the papers, Geography, General and Songs.

I am looking forward enormously to the hols and dying to see you all, especially Sally.

Background: The middle years at home, 1956-1957

My parents moved to London in late 1956 and rented half the Kensington vicarage, a fine and large Victorian house off Kensington Church Street. For Sandy and me London was exotic and a novelty, still with some overtones of excitement of previous occasional visits through Dragon years, being met at railway stations, overnight stays in flats, trips to a cartoon theatre or to toy shops or – less welcome – to the dentist. But I doubt now whether I grew up a great deal in London – superficially possibly, but perhaps not much in character or mind set, essentially because it was in a number of ways a rather sheltered existence.

We saw more of my father, being on the spot in London. Even if he did not normally return home till late in the evenings, he was able to organise some weekends and free time at least a bit around us and to be with us. From him, and his friends whom he brought to the house occasionally, we learnt a little about current party politics, domestic policies and foreign affairs. I also began at the period to learn from my mother, and her friends more about English poetry and the creative arts; and from both of them we learned something about music, a wide range of music. London inevitably produced more of an indoor life than Heron's March, so we started listening, as we had not done before, to music in the house: classical music such as Bach's Brandenburg concertos and his Great A Minor Fugue, Beethoven's Piano Concertos, snatches of Mozart operas; and a lot of popular music of one kind or another, Porgy and Bess, Glen Miller, music from early musicals, traditional jazz, Fats Waller and Satchmo Louis Armstrong; and then West Side Story and recent hits. I recall too one memorable outing to hear the Messiah in the Albert Hall. We were taken to the theatre (never to opera or ballet) or cinema – for entertainment rather than for a cultural experience and what we enjoyed was the Crazy Gang, Arthur Askey at the Palladium, Sammy Davis Jnr, Salad Days, West Side Story, and westerns at the cinema in Kensington.

As to learning more generally at home, parental teaching, never easy for any teenagers (who would rather be doing other things) to imbibe, was limited. My father, perhaps because of being short of time, tended to inform and tell rather than explain, while my mother chose to teach and lead by enthusiasm – for instance her enthusiasm for poetry, novels (both 19th century and contemporary); but we did not receive much in the way of direct coaching.

In winter we were mostly indoors, not least on account of the Smog – from which I suffered badly because of tendencies to hay-fever and asthma. And outdoors we were restricted to well beaten paths for safety. First there was the Park, accessible through a back door of the vicarage's large garden which gave onto Kensington Palace Gardens, between two embassies, and then directly through to Kensington Gardens. There we messed about like any Londoner, usually with some sports equipment, but our first duty and pleasure was walking Jeb. Jeb was much admired and always drew attention – and we ran free with him all over Hyde Park to exercise him. He had to be kept on a lead; but in term time he became too much for my mother to look after and exercise and was eventually sent to my uncle Logie at Gresham's School, Holt, with its vast grounds.

Often we were taken out by our parents, and we were rather spoilt. I suppose that was in part the bribe to help us accept departure from Ockley because of my father's preference to be London-based. In town we accompanied my mother on shopping expeditions into the West End, but we did not go out on our own exploring. In a way we had returned to a more primitive, house- and home-dependent life even if it was combined superficially with a new urban existence of a more sophisticated kind.

Life thus became a kind of equivalent of the Senior Dayroom stage of School House life. In London we joined things - or rather my father joined us up. We were made junior members of the RAC, London for swimming and squash (a most enjoyable facility, where in morning hours we had the place essentially to ourselves) and of the RAC Club Epsom, when our parents could take us there for golf and tennis as Junior country members; but actually it was too far away, the course was rather long for teenagers with more enthusiasm than skill and we only went a couple of times. At the RAC Club in Pall Mall an added enjoyment and sophistication was meeting my father for the occasional snack lunch at the poolside tables. All very luxurious.

We were also given junior membership of the London Corinthian Sailing Club at Hammersmith. It was a chance to build on what we had learnt about sailing at Herons March and on holidays but the Thames was very difficult sailing for inexperienced youngsters – with powerful tide and current and all kinds of river traffic menacing a small dinghy. Light airs meant a drift along the river with poor prospects of safe return; and stronger winds gusted in alarming bursts round the edges of buildings, factories and screens of poplars and other trees. But it was lovely by the gardens and quayside and we enjoyed just messing about on the pontoons and making short outings across the river and back.

And once there was a great scare. Sandy and I had spent a couple of days sandpapering and varnishing the boat in hot sunshine and worked the whole day long bending over the upturned hull, shirt off and without a hat. I felt faint, and that evening at Vicarage Gate I stiffened up like a board with cramps –and a doctor was hastily summoned, my parents fearing a diagnosis of polio. The doctor identified sunstroke and ordered rest and a couple of days' peace and quiet indoors– and to wear a sunhat in future.

In Kensington we participated a little in a wider family life which was different from our Ockley experience. (Great) Aunt Freda, who inhabited a wheel chair, was fun. She had been on the stage before becoming disabled; and had become a respected film critic for the Woman's Own and the

Catholic Herald and for some twenty years a standing panel member of the BBC Radio's programme 'The Critics'. She treated us to our first grown-up drinks, small glasses of sherry or vermouth at her house down the road in Holland Street where eccentric London friends and remote relations would appear for entertainment and chat; she took us to one or two (suitable) film previews; and on occasion we would join my mother and her lunching out with other friends and relatives (Uncle Rupert, the opera singing teacher), for instance to Freda's favourite local restaurant, Ciccio's in Church Street Kensington.

We also entered on the edge of a new world of London acquaintances, sons and daughters of colleagues of my father's. The boys were mostly just a little older than us and their friends seemed enormously suave and sophisticated. The difference in outlook between 15 and 16 year-old Sedberghians and sophisticated 17 year-old Etonians or Harrovians in their exquisite homes, was considerable. We joined them at the occasional party but never quite clicked with their circle of friends.

At home, my mother was mostly occupied with Sally and with friends and relatives based in or visiting London. She enjoyed gardening in the Vicarage garden where she took responsibility for the borders (not the vegetable garden); and my father signed her up for a series of rides at a stables on Rotten Row. Thus family holidays were the big excitement for Sandy and me. I well remember a trip to Paris in 1957 for three nights or so in a small hotel for some sightseeing, dinner on the Ile de la Cite and drinking grenadine in small café-bars with zinc counters – a wonderful treat. And dinner with a wartime colleague of my father's, where Sandy and I held back and refused second helpings having been warned to expect a feast of many courses; but to our chagrin there were only two – and all very cuisine mínçeur - and then we were dismissed to the drawing room with a box of marrons glacés to watch television.

Then there was Dartmouth and sailing lessons in a Dart One Design. We spent all day down on the waterfront, relatively free from parental supervision. I remember there was a waterfront fairground too, another new experience for us. My father was there only part of the time, and my mother was busy looking after Sally. And my fascination with things nautical was increased by visiting Great Uncle John Brougham, retired naval captain and Jutland hero, who lived on the river near Dartmouth Naval College. The possibilities of a life in the Royal Navy were enticing; and my interest continued for a year or two until my father and Thornely insisted that university, not naval college, was the right route for me.

Two holidays at Aldeburgh were similar, but without the waterfront town atmosphere. We went sailing and messed about by the river while my father played golf and my mother was once again occupied with Sally. And I once spent a week's holiday at Blakeney with the family of my Sedbergh chum James Oliver in their cottage with a little rose girt garden right beside

65

the marshes. We mucked about on the shore and in a small boat. He came from a naval family and both of us were Swallows and Amazon adepts.

And holidays in Scotland were very much still on the menu. We made a short stay at the Murray Arms in Gatehouse of Fleet – a lovely country hotel offering us a heady combination of excellent food and shooting parties on private moors and marshes, or fishing in the spring for Sandy who went again when I was on language study abroad. And of course there were further excursions to stay with Dear at Bemersyde, after Dear Man's death, and renew the happy experience of fishing the Tweed.

In 1956 Uncle Logie took over as headmaster of Gresham's School, Holt; and our family started a practice of spending Hogmanay there in large family parties of fifteen to twenty in the boarding house where they lived. We youngsters played in the main boys' dining hall, where meals were taken, while the private side drawing room was reserved for grown-ups. Music was being made all the time, and we played endless monopoly and racing demon, and whiled away New Year's Eve with Scottish country dancing.

These holidays were a kind of fusion of school and home. We and our cousins slept in the two dormitories (with cubicles, just like School House), one for the boys, one for the girls. Games and sports of all kinds were played and the whole of the spacious school grounds, squash courts and playing fields, were at our disposal. Indoors there were house games, cricket in the corridor of the cubicles; sardines, charades, murder in the dark, you name it. Logie and Jo were very hospitable, and it was a time full of family fun.

Our life had in some senses reverted to a world of enchantment, a traditional and sheltered family home (with my father more present than before) with organised excursions. But if it was largely parent-sponsored, it had nevertheless changed from a homely scale to something more sophisticated and urban. I guess I learnt a bit more about how to cope with unknowns and continued the process begun in Ockley of learning how to create my own space inside groups. These were important experiences and increased my general confidence – even if still anchored in a family setting.

In 1957 I went on a four week holiday to Italy and Sicily which had an educational purpose too. My Uncle Robin (Head of Classics at Clifton) took a Clifton boy of my age, John Whitley, who was going into the Upper Classic VIth and myself, then in my second year in Lower VI classical, on what was for Robin a recce for a sabbatical to study Greek remains in Sicily. We visited Rome, Pompeii and then made a circuit of Sicily. It was great fun. John and I got on well, and Robin was an enthusiastic and knowledgeable guide – and allowed us a modicum of time off for swimming.

* * *

Home life in Kensington compares interestingly with my middle years at School House where life in the Senior Dayroom and then in the junior studies was a somewhat similar period of experiment; our spheres of life began to divide out, notably in choices of activities, interests and friends. The Senior Dayroom had a mix of generations because it contained boys from year two and most of year three together, plus possibly a couple of boys waiting one more term to go into studies. It was a noisy place, and we spent time getting out of it, either outdoors or by making make more use of the Common Room (for papers and the radio), the music practice Cubes and the Library. This implied new choices and new companions for the different activities, as opposed to all messing in together as in Junior Dayroom days.

Pursuit of particular interests according to preference and abilities altered various aspects of life. Sandy went off on expeditions with Jake Durran, the House Tutor, while I played duets with the Assistant House Tutor, Ronnie Reynell. We were now allowed to use the house grass tennis court, and started playing squash. Whereas the Junior Dayroom boys were generally left to their own devices, in the Senior Dayroom we began to specialize, picking and choosing activities and connections and engaging with youngsters of different ages, and even grown-ups – just as happened in our brief London home life.

Chapter 3:   September 1956 to July 1957

J   30 September 56 [Sunday]

Sorry about the trouble I caused with the shirts. They arrived on Tuesday morning.

Work is completely different, an absolute change from last and previous terms, it is taken from a different angle completely. We are given so much to read through the week, or an essay to write in 4 days, and the preps are hardly organised exactly. For example, we are told on Tues that by next Tues we are to have read Chap IV of British Democracy and written an essay on 'The power of government through the centuries',

Latin and Greek – no more parsing and construing, and no literal translation. That makes it easier. We are starting Latin verse this week which although it is difficult is rather fun.

School Cert results[133]

Latin I		82%
Latin II		74%
Greek I		65%
Greek II		76%
Eng Lang		66%
	Essay	50%
Eng Lit	Shakespear	45%
	Chaucer	68%
Hist		
History	Engl Hist	82%
	American Hist	68%
French		
	Unseen	52%
	Comp and story	64%
	Dict	90%
	Oral	83%
Maths		
	Elem Maths I	79%
	Elem Maths II	64%
	Addit Maths I	52%
	Addit Maths II	40%[134]

---

[133] i.e. at 'O' Level.

I think there must have been one or two narrow squeaks – French [Unseen] wasn't very good and Addit Maths pretty lucky to have passed. Only 8 boys in all got 8 subjects[135]. And now it is 2 years before my next exam.

Joined the Corps this term, being 15 ½ and we had our first parade in battledress. The Under-officer and Platoon Cmdr congratulated me on a very fine turn out! It's a terrific fag having to blanco belts and polish brasses and things.

Rugger... played three times on Colts A; scored a try and made some playing at fly half. B.C. Gadney[136] came and talked to the halves[137] right through the school from Bigside to Colts B.

Please send two books left at home. Virgil crib, translated by Lewis or someone, and Homer Odyssey[138]. If you find any ping pong bats lying around could you send them.

Played squash with S and we had a jolly good game I won in the end but the first two games were very even, 10-8, 9-7.

Went to see Dr Morris[139] about Dr Bott's letter[140] and he said I should not take the pills unless necessary[141] but report after a few days to see whether that was all right.

Reading Hammond Innes, Victor Canning and Damon Runyon. I suggested Runyon last term on the literary [library] suggestions list and they got it. Prick however thought no one would be likely to read it.

At talk of the top table at the HM's end last week was a letter from Sandy to Uncle Logie at Gresham's. 'Mingey breakfast, Went into town. Some boys went to see the pictures (art gallery) but I went to Dixons and had a coke.'[142]

At Jenny's end the talk is apparently always about fridges, washing machines etc and a great strain for the prefects!

S   30 September 56 [Sunday]

... I hope this Swiss person is a sucsess *[sic]* and when is she coming and where will she sleep and eat and read and write (if she can)?

---

[134] As I recall, we did not hear our full GCE O Level results before going back to school, only what exams we had passed or failed.

[135] Presumably I was one of them.

[136] Bernard Gadney, one-time scrum half for England. His son, Reggie, was at the Dragon.

[137] i.e. Scrum halves and fly halves, also known as 'the half backs'.

[138] Books borrowed from my mother: Odyssey selections translated by F. Lucas, King's Cambridge – I still have the copy; and Virgil's Aeneid by C. Day Lewis.

[139] The school doctor

[140] Family GP in London

[141] for hay fever and allergies to dust (and smog), which I was suffering badly in London.

[142] Presumably Logie had told Thornely about this typical prep schoolboy letter.

This week I have played rugger every day but Saturday was an off day, and I am playing on Colts B 3, and I am a wing forward. Yesterday I played squash in the afternoon in long break. Yesterday and the day before I have played and practised

On Thursday after rugger Ward (a guy in the studies who is in charge of fives taught some other guys in the Junior dayroom and me how to play fives, but I think it is not such a good game as squash; and anyhow I think it is better to be better at squash because after you leave public school no one plays fives but squash you can play with anyone.

This week in house master's time Mr Boggis should [showed] us some slides on Switzerland. He is a wonderful photographer and they were all beautiful photos in colour. He went last year with a party of Sedberghians and climbed mountains. Mr Durran and Mr Mills also went.

Yesterday evening an OS gave a small lecture and a 40 minute film on Kenya. It was very good and gave us a very interesting talk on the Mau Mau.

I have been on no runs this term of over 1½ miles.

Did you know that Dear has Uncle Logie's old kilt jacket for me ; it will be a perfect fit when ½ an inch is off the sleeves, so Dear and I think 'why get a kilt or hire one'.

There is not anything else to say for I have said all the news.

PS I went through the solles /sic/ of my slippers suddenly on Thursday. Shall I get a new pair?

J   Oct 7ᵗʰ 56 [Sunday]

Thank you for the books. We are doing Odyssey Book 21, which is 200 lines from where a selection begins in the book you sent. The Virgil is most useful.

I expect to start playing the clarinet with Mr Reynell soon, which will be very nice. The orchestra this term is rather boring, in fact more so than usual. I find it a good time to catch up on Damon Runyon.

Economics and government - we deal with Current Affairs up to date with goings on. We have side tracked into the pending economic crises and government policy.

We had a lecture on the League of Nations, the UN and the Security Council

In the 6ths we don't have fortnightly orders but a half term report.

Played rugger...

Corps learning how to salute – and I would never have expected to find so many goons among 30 boys when ordered to Right Turn.

Trouble with my right leg again. Can't walk. Doc said it was a minor muscle injury and I've had infra-red heat for 3 days. I hope it goes off. Fortunately it won't affect my fives.

Recitals... The Camden Trio came and played. Annie Campbell bassoonist, Leonard Brain, oboe and Welford Pace (?) a pianist. They were only quite good. The piano drowned the bassoon and all one could hear was the oboe, who was very good.

Last night however was far more fun. A pal of Prick's from Trin. Cambs was staying. He is a professional singer, Ian Wallace, and he sung to us in the evening in HMs drawing room – about 20- boys - various selections, and was terribly good. He is going to sing with Robert Morley in Drury Lane on Nov 15th onwards. I hope we can see him.

Turned cold...

S   No date [7th October 56 by references]

This is my last piece of writing paper, so if I can get as far as the far side (there is not much news as usual) ...[143]

One thing that is very important: can you send me my 5/- postal order for it has to be cashed at Sedbergh by 1st November or sometime around there. It is in the top or maybe second top drawer of my Wellington draws /sic/[144]. Then I will buy some stamps and writing paper and I will write some letters to Granny and Dear etc..

One of the Prefects has started a squash ladder. There is a six penny entrance fee and there are about 40 people entering. Everybody starts off in house order and then can challenge anybody to 3 games within 6 places higher than himself and if the challenger wins they swap places. So the idea is to reach the top. So far I have played a guy called Collins who is a 4th termer and I won, and a guy called Hamer and move up another 4 places and then I played another guy in the senior dayroom[145] called Nelson and he was 6 places above the other guy and I beat him 2-0 so I have moved up about 15 places. I hope to stay where I am but probably someone bellow /sic/ me will challenge me and beat me so I will go down again.

On Tuesday there was a super concert by three very famous people. One is Archie Camden who plays the bason [bassoon], the other was Denis Brain['s] brother Leonard Brain who played the oboe ; the other's name I have forgotten but he played the piano. First they played a Mozart thing and the oboe took the main part. It was very good. Then they played an oboe solo and then a bason; then they fidled /sic/ about on their instruments. They showed how long they could hold their breath which was amazing. They played a tune on their reeds only which was super and then the oboist played a tiny tune on the oboe without the reed. It was very very

---

[143]Sentence incomplete; presumably Sandy intended to add 'I will have to stop'.

[144] Sandy had a pretty little Wellington writing desk with drawers and I had a small tall boy. These (gifts from great aunts Ann and Mary Weaver) were where we kept our valuable papers and belongings in our room at home

[145] The Senior Dayroom for second and some third year boys. There were tables and lockers; and the Senior Dayroom also had a ping pong table popular in the winter terms.

good. I have just found out from a guy that the other chap (the pianist) was Wilfred Pary.

Last Sunday evening Mactaggart gave me his study and some tomato soup so I made some soup for myself and had a super time drinking soup reading and listening to his [word illeg., *records*].

This week I played rugger on Mon, Tues Wed and on Thursday I was going to play fives but we couldn't play because the court was being mended.

J   14ᵗʰ Oct 56 [Sunday]

Thankyou for writing to Mr Reynell. I've been up to play with him once already and am going up again on Tues to his house. I think it is very kind of him to play the piano with me. He himself it appears disapproves of Mr Whiteside and says he ought to belong in a military band and that his tone isn't worth two pins etc. etc.

Thankyou for the cuff links. They are a spare pair – actually to which the other (both Woolies) are very broken indeed. I have a nice pair here at school[146].

...Lots of squash and fives played – scores, Played 3 games for 1/- and fortunately won.

A thing I hadn't realised about starting to shave. I did once last term to tidy up and was advised to do it again at the beginning of this term, with the effect that I have had to do it twice more already this term – and I'll have to have a razor soon – as I haven't been doing more than scraping yet – and have to borrow at the moment. It's rather a bore but it has to start sometime I suppose.

There are short sprints this afternoon which rather spoils Sunday!.

S   14ᵗʰ Oct 56 [Sunday]

Thank you very much for the letter and the postal Order, but I have not bought any letters yet because I played squash by myself a [and] practised the shots in the corner like you said (in long break).

On Tuesday in long break I played fives with a guy called Melville. It was good fun; then on Wednesday after noon I played with a guy who came with me a [and] two guys who came this term. We had a very good game.

I haven't moved up at all on the squash ladder this week. I have stayed still.

On Monday there was a 1ˢᵗ XV match v. the OS. It was a very good match and the OS side won 14-8. The referee was a super chap just like a retired colonel he had a beautiful moustache and was very funny.

---

[146] Cuff links, and collar studs, were needed with our formal shirts, for Sundays, etc..

On Friday the HM and Mrs HM played a concert to us (Junior Dayroom). It was very good. They played a thing called 'Handel in the Strand'. It was in their drawing room where they have two grand pianos. They also played a thing called S... M... [2 words illeg.] or something like that; then they played something by Mozart, then to end up played Gilbert and S which was very good. They played everything and it was very enjoyable.

Yesterday evening there were two French films, voluntary, for the Sedgwick Society[147]; it was simply awful; out of all the French films I have seen both spoken in French and English they are simply awful, partly helped by the fact that the people working the camera didn't know what they were doing. The first film they put on upside down and back to front and upside down, and then the second real [sic] snapped off twice and broke the film and the film we were supposed to be seeing which we were all waiting for and which we had gone to see was not shown because they took years mucking about with the stupid film on champagne and because they had left the film on underwater diving by Dumas and Costeau last (for a treat) so we did not see it.

After the French films I played squash for two hours on and off, first with a guy called Whitman and beat him (he came last term), then with a guy called Bowra who came two terms ago, I beat him; then with a guy called Robertson (who came last term) and I beat him. We all had a leave off reading prep

The lunch bell is just going so I better stop now any how there is nothing else to say.

J   21 Oct 56 [Sunday]

Kendal had 20 hours of rain and R Kent overflowed...

Rugger and lots and lots of fives.... Lowis and self the first pair in Junior Fives...

On Thursday we had Field Day which was torture and fun at the same time. Went up on Frostrow and learnt about rifles, camouflage and moving under cover. After our packed lunch No 1 platoon (us) slogged a couple of miles over the fells to above Garsdale. Got to the position we had to defend with quarter of an hour to spare and fought a battle with 15 blanks each, which was rather fun except lying in a marsh waiting for No 2 platoon to come. After that we slogged home along the road.

Last night the Brad Lads, the School club at Bradford came and gave us a variety show, which was great fun; some excellent imitations of crooners and jazz singers – and some good jokes pointed at us. For instance an old man came on and the wit asked him how old he was; when he said 94 the

---

[147] A natural history society, named after Old Sedberghian Adam Sedgwick, the distinguished Cambridge geologist

wit said, 'Ha, I suppose you must have seen School House win a match'. Great applause and laughter. The whole thing was a roaring success except a joke about Mr Madge[148] which apparently made him fume with anger.

Work going ok.

S   Sunday 21ˢᵗ October1956

Thank you very much for the letter and for the packet of Smarties which you sent me about three weeks ago but I didn't open the parcel because I thought it was only a jersey which you had just washed so I put it in my draws /sic/ and did not open it until this morning, anyway thank you very much and it was very nice of you to send me some.

On Thursday it was field day and I and 5 other chaps (the other 4 chaps who came with me last term and one other who came this term) we went to Gawthrop Caves[149]. We all set of about half past 11 with our pack lunches tied up in our white pullovers. We had lunch at about half past one on the bank of the Dee, consisting of

6 spam sandwiches
1 bun and margarine
1 pie (meat)
1 piece of cake (fruit)
1 apple

It was very good – at least there was plenty of it but not wonderful quality. We foled /sic/ about on the bank of the Dee for about an hour then we got to the caves.

They are enormous, for the little tunnels stretch for miles. First we went along a very big tunnel for a very long way (about 300 feet). It opened out into a large cavan [cavern] with a gigantic waterfall coming out of the roof. We had one candel /sic/ and 3 torches. Another guy and I had nothing so we went in a line No 2 and me no 5. Then after a bit me and a guy called Melville went up a very very small tunnel. We both had torches (another chap came half way and then turned back). Anyhow we must have crawled on our tummies for about 100 feet or so then we reached the end, but he could not turn round; I turned (because I am smaller than he is) but he got stuck and I was the far side of him as I went first. Then as he tried to turn (and got stuck) my torch suddenly went out, then his went out so we were stuck in the pitch darkness. We shouted for the others to bring a light but the tunnel was too long and they did not hear. Then he banged his torch by

---

[148] A senior science master and housemaster of Hart House; we knew his children who were of our age from earlier holidays at Sedbergh.

[149] The first of Sandy's many expeditions to the fells and places of interest in the surrounding countryside (some at considerable distance from Sedbergh) which he undertook mostly with the same group of friends.

mistake on the roof and it went on again; so when we had eventually managed to turn round we crawled back to the others.

I have not moved up in the squash ladder but I was challenged but won so I am still where I was last week.

I do hope you had an enjoyable time in Athens and sorry that you (Mummy) could not go.

Last night the Bradford boys gave a play to us. It started at 7.30 and was a sort of variety revue affair, and it really was terrific. They sang songs just like you see six chaps all grouped round a microphone waving their arms trying to sing rock and rool /sic/ or something of that sort on ITV but they did it very well indeed. One boy with a spicy [spikey] hair came on and sang some song like 'I wonder with love' and also he sang 'I walk with god', he had a wonderful voice though. They had many funny acts and some of them came on and pretended to be the Sunbeams of Manchester (little girls); they were very funny.

One man who ran the show came on between acts and cracked jokes; one of them was about a baby. He said he saw a boy weeling /sic/ a pram, so he said 'Hullo, where are you going?' I am taking this back to the hospital' said the boy referring to the baby. Why, the man asked. 'Because it leaks' said the boy. The whole show was extremely good.

Yesterday afternoon I had to do two maps (of 55) for Jamie, which I thought was a chiz.

I have not thought yet what I want for Christmas (it is so early) but if anyone asks I would like a record token; and if my godmother asks, say she has to give me a book I want the Guinness book of records or one book written in the last 10 years (not about Art, and not written in the 19th century).

I have just heard that Dear is coming here tomorrow (from Brendan Bracken).

J   Oct 28th 56 [Sunday]

Thanks for letters and sweet photos of Sally. Hope Daddy had a nice time in Athens.

Extra half – just mucked about on the fells.

Played lots of rugger and fives, not too much squash.

I now have a regular date on Tuesdays to play the clarinet with Mr Reynell. I am playing a new Schumann piece which was unfortunately written for an A clarinet. I have had to spend a lot of time transposing it for a B flat (every note ½ of a tone lower).

In form we have Greek and Latin prose, Fr Unseen, Ancient History essay, Eng. and Div. essay and an Economics Test and Govt Essay – otherwise we read, prepare and learn.

We choose subjects from articles from the Economist, and prepare talks as well as essays. My subject for Dec is American Foreign Policy and her attitude to British FP. Which means I read the American Survey in the Economist and Notes on the World[150] on America.

Film Oliver Twist with Alec Guinness. It was very good.

There have been several matches – A.F. Dorward brought down a very strong XV.

Looking forward immensely to your coming up here.

J   4 Nov 56 [Sunday]

It's a pity you cannot both come up but we can see it's obviously nicer to go to Rye etc.[151]

Last Sunday Jake (Mr Durran, house tutor[152]) took 4 of us out to Uldale Force, by his car to Cautley and on foot from there. The valley was really most lovely, the trees all golden over the river. We went through woods which made me homesick for Herons' March, just like them – lots of bracken and bramble and the same kind of trees. On the way back Jake gave us tea at the X Keys which was very kind of him and although we offered again and again to take the money from our house banks[153], he wouldn't hear of it. Jolly D.[154]

You say Dad thinks we don't seem, to be playing much rugger. What actually happens per week is one rugger once (therefore it's either senior or junior house rugger, which means I may not play). We have 3 sets 3 times a week – i.e Colts A. There used to be 3 fly halves, therefore one day I did not play. On Wed we have Corps and Saturday an off day when we watch a match if there is one and then short ex after that....Colts B scores...

We had a civics 6th Forms lecture by Father Huddleston on Friday. I thought he was terribly good, not exactly inspiring but very good, talking about S Africa of course.

---

[150] A bulletin of the period, presumably

[151] A familiar story; Sedbergh's distance made short visits from the South of England difficult; golf at Rye was certainly easier.

[152] An increasingly central figure in our life as we progressed through the Senior Dayroom was Jake Durran, our tall, gaunt, amiable house tutor. A senior mathematics master, Jake was a mustard keen fell walker and geologist, enthusiast for the CCF and a pleasant man with nice humour. As house tutor, who lived in, and played a kind of in-between role, a benign uncle above the prefects but a less stern disciplinary figure than the housemaster. He and the assistant house tutor complemented each other in some ways: Durran, an outward bound figure was a very different from Reynell, classicist and musician (who was never known to have stepped willingly onto the fells). Neither were games players, but Reynell's successor was very much one, Rogers, a club class cricketer and champion fives player.

[153] The house tutor looked after our pocket money, using account books with a page for each boy and cash box. In principle we could draw what we wanted when we wanted (for purchases down town or at the grubber, food, presents, some items of apparel etc). I think a fixed sum was put on the school account; we could also pay in money received (presents or tips) - but Jake Durran could keep an eye on it all.

[154] Sandy and his group of friends formed over the years a good partnership with 'Jake' Durran.

S   4 November 1956 [Sunday]

I quiet [sic] understand why Dear did not see us otherwise she would have been hear [sic] all day having to call on half Sedbergh.[155]

Are you going to Cyprus or Libya or somewhere because of Suez or will you stay in Vienna or at home [?]

Quite a lot of lessons know [now] are spent by us asking questions about Suez and Hungary and the master says he will tell us the broad outline for ten minutes. Three times 3 masters have said they would talk for ten minutes, one went on for 20 minutes, one for 45 mins and one for 49 minutes. It is all very interesting to hear their different views.

Mr Begley (Powell house Housemaster), who you might of known in the war (he was in the Secret Service), he foretold 5 weeks ago that Israel would attack Egypt at the end of October – and he is quite right and all the prefects and masters say what he does not know about politics is not worth knowing.

If you sent some of the coloured photos (say 3 in 5" letter and 3 in nine, then they would arrive on Thursday and Friday and we could send them back to you on Sunday; for I am longing to see them.

This week I am afraid has been very uneventful. I have played a bit of rugger. I played fly half once and wing forward the rest of the time.

Also I have played a terrific amount of fives. Yesterday I played twice, once in the afternoon with a guy who come this term and 2 other guys in the studies and in the evening I played with Gurney head of House and a House prefect and a guy who also come last term with me. It was teriffic /sic/ fun and I think it is a very good game.

In work I came 11th again and the new boys who are placed at the bottom in brown book order have come top or about top.

Also in the squash ladder I have moved up another 4 places. I beat the chap who Jamie beat for 1/- (a bet) Now I am within six places of Jamie so I could challenge him if I want to.

I hope Mactaggart[156] gives me his study tonight (He has done every Sunday so far) for he might give me some grub (my grub locker is empty)

On Saturday there was a match v Rossall. It was very exciting and we drew by 3 to 3. It was easily the best game this term. I can't think of anything else to say more for I am sure I have told you everything – except what do you want for Christmas. If you can't think of anything special I will.

---

[155] A variation on the theme above, suggesting that time would inevitably be taken up on a visit to Sedbergh by duty calls on old friends from her Sedbergh days.

[156] For whom Sandy was private fag.

J   Nov 11ᵗʰ 56 [Sunday]

re Dances[157], we agree that the one on Jan 8ᵗʰ, the Pony Club Dance, would definitely be the one to go to. It would be a pity we think to have to go to one at the beginning of the hols just before Xmas.

Am glad that Claire Lise[158] seems nice and helpful, I'm sure it will make all the difference

House rugger and Colts. 2 paras... As usual I've played hoards and hoards of fives.....

Today we have a collection for the Hungarian Refugee Fund. We think it is an excellent idea sending the old clothes to them.

S   No date [11th November 56]

Thank you very very much for both your lovely and interesting letters. You must have had a very interesting time on the Hungarian border. Talking of Hungary I am sure that sending our clothes to the refugees was a very good thing to do.

Jamie and I have decided to put both our letters in the same envelope from now on to save stamps. If you['d] rather we didn't, just say so in your next letter.

I think the coloured photos are really wonderful - just like the photos in the American Geographical magazine with blue skies and purple hills in the background etc. You simply must take some more. I hope you have received them for we put them all in one envelope on Friday or Saturday and sent them back (I hope they weren't overwheight /sic/.)

On Monday there was an extra half. I did not go anywhere interesting. I went with a guy who came last term. We were going to go to an Inn and have a good hearty meal but the HM did not allow it as we went to the Cross Keys with Mr Durran last extra half holiday to have tea. So we just went up Calf and down a little gill [ghyll] to the road. It was not very far – in fact it was not 3 miles but it was great fun and it was a hot day so we stopped very often by the stream and just mucked about. Tonight I have got Mactaggart's study and also this afternoon as he is going out today.

Jamie and I have decided we would like to go to the Pony Club dance and <u>not</u> the one on the 22d for if we arrive home on the 20ᵗʰ at about 4 o'clock that means we have the twenty first in London and the twenty third and if the dance ends at about 12.30 (which it did last year) we will have to travel up on the following day when we won't be feeling very bright! So really we only have the 21 and 24 before Xmas which is not long enough to do everything in.

Dear sent me the most wonderful food parcel I have ever seen. It really is wonderful and so kind of her. And I hate to think how much it cost for

---

[157] Arrangements for Christmas holidays at home
[158] The new (French) au pair help for my mother at home, replacing Kirsten

they ['re] not ordinary sweets, they must be about the best in the world; and I hope I don't eat them all to[o] quickly.

In all these services now (especially the evening ones)[159] I get dreadful indigestion or tummy rumbles' at it is embarissing /*sic*/ during the sermon & lessons & prayers. Luckily I didn't have them badly in the '2 minutes silence' this morning.

I think today it might quite likely snow on the hills or even right down here. Last week one night there was the most lovely gale and with all the windows wide open it came flying in; but with the lovely new rug you b ought me I have not been cold yet.

I will tell you what I want for Christmas letter [later].

What day and what time are you coming here and going back home?

J   Nov 18th [Sunday]

House games of rugger... with much detail. Junior fives pairs... games and results...

Hart House play, the Merchant of Venice, a film and the Intimate Opera Company coming up.

S and I have been looking at the ads for plays.[160] Perhaps we can discuss with Dad when he comes up.

I seem to be gaining some wisdom teeth – I now find I can hardly blame Sally for yelling. I hope they come through quick.

S   No date [18 Novembr 56]

... I suppose you must be back in Bemersyde after your shooting. I hope you had a good time and shot lots and that the food was better than it was.

Lovely weather... Today we are going to Barbon. (When I say 'we' I mean the three who came my term who are Lionel and 2 others, and 2 that came the term after us who one of them is the son[161] of Broadbent who won the Harkness scholarship to St Andrews about 1933 or 34). Anyhow we are planning to go there.

On Friday was an extra half so we all 6 went to try to go and have a meal at the Swan which is about 5 miles out on the Kirby Lonsdale road – actually we went over Holme Fell making it shorter, but when we got to the Swan it was closed down for the proprietors were away; isn't this against the law? Anyhow we then went back to the Railway Inn at Middleton. It is the sort of place you never go unless you are desperate for food or a drink but

---

[159] They took place very soon after House Tea.

[160] Presumably for a show to see in London for a Christmas treat

[161] John Broadbent, who became a Director of Marley Tiles and was a neighbour in Kent and a life-long friend of Sandy's. His father was at St Andrew's with my father.

when we got there we knocked at the door and nothing happened so we went round to the back and this great big bloke and said what did we want, and we said ham and eggs or something and he then closed the door till it was nearly shut and growled at us that 'this is a pub not a bloomin café' and slammed the door.

So we set off back and met some of our studies' and slung some mud balls at them; but they ran off ahead without us knowing (about a mile ahead) and they ambushed us along a thin lane and we had a terrific fight (not serious of course); and we fought and then we ran to plank bridge and stopped them crossing so 3 of them waded across and the others waited till we went – it was all great fun.

No concerts this week; only a mock trial; Sir Vivian Fuchs is coming next week to lecture to the school; this should be terrific. The following week Leon Goosens the oboeist is going to give a concert; and there is a film on the Saturday you come – we seem to be doing quite well this term (nearly as good as the Dragons).

The mock trial was last night. Only 25 could go from each house, and as I went last year I thought I had no chance but I got chosen again. Maybe Runyon was wrong and life is not 6-5 against. I expect Jamie will tell you all about it as he was on the jury; the only thing he won't tell you is that the only thing that was wrong was the Jury. For apparently two endings were prepared with great care: one if the jury found the prisoner was 'Guilty' and one if they found he was 'Not guilty', But the Jury found her guilty of Manslaughter and not guilty of Housebreaking. So the judge Mr Gairdner gave her one day's imprisonment.

It is now Monday and there is a match against Dorward's XV who have 6 Scottish international s and 4 who have been on the Scottish trials, so it is a pretty good team.

Yesterday we went to Barbon (6 of us). We got there in 1 ¼ hours which is quite good for a Sunday carrying packed lunches. It is 8 miles away. We bought pop and chocolate to go with our lunch and then went past Barbon a bit and ate it in a field and went slowly on. We got ten miles on before coming back very slowly so we went 20 miles in all. Next Sunday or sometimes we are all trying to get to Kirby Lonsdale without lifts which would be about 26 miles.

I am so sorry that my letter went to Bemersyde. I thought if I posted it on Tuesday it might miss you because I thought you said you were leaving Westwick to go to London on Wednesday; anyhow I hope you got it. I Hope you remember about my jersey. Will you send it?

My pen is running out. See you very soon, will right /sic/ on Monday.

J   Nov 25ᵗʰ 56 [Sunday]

I do hope Dear has a nice trip. She sent a postcard when abroad saying that people called Low (the two boys were at Sedbergh, the younger left a year ago, a very nice chap) were going to New Zealand[162].

You seem to be having quite a job with the leaves there. You need a lesson from Perry (as we call him) Mason.[163] He's an absolute expert in the yard and there are quite some piles of leaves around.

It's terribly disappointing that Dad can't come up to see us this weekend. I do hope he can come up this term. We were looking forward terrifically to his coming yesterday. Has Dad had to go abroad or something?

This week we had the Intimate Opera Company which was quite good but not as good as the Barber of Seville last year.

Rugger... Corps was a double parade – with practice passing out parade, saluting etc. I came 2ⁿᵈ, having lost one mark on turn out.

We had Civics on Friday by a Yank on the Presidential Elections. He was terribly good – most amusing and informative as well.

Junior fives scores...

Reports – we only hear if the reports are bad.

Xmas presents ideas: a schoolboy size weight – 12lbs, record token; books, Stephen Leacock or Damon Runyon, a book about sailing boats would be good...

One large thing which I would like to pay half of myself would be a portable wireless, as I hope to be in the Studies next or summer term. Another thing which will be very useful is a razor, which I will have to get very soon.

J   Dec 1ˢᵗ 56

We're having a terrific weekend. Dad got up overnight with Brendan Bracken and is now staying with Bill Forster – rather de-grading for a SH parent! But I suppose it's all right really. (Winder is fearfully non-U and the spiv house. We look down upon them mainly (through jealousy?) because the dayrooms are allowed to cook, a privilege here only for studies.

Loretto match yesterday and written up in the Sunday Times and quite exciting. Then we went to fix up about Dear Man's grave, had ginger beers and a terrific lunch, watched the Colts match for a but who were very good indeed and then Dad went back for a read and a nap and we mucked about. Supper at the W. Hart and played cards after that...

Friday was the Hart House play, Merchant of Venice, which was great fun and very well acted.

---

[162] The Lows were related to the Bruce Lockharts through the Macgregors (paternal great-grandmother).

[163] School House gardener-handyman

Weather ... pitches too hard for rugger...

S   2 Dec 56 [Sunday, to my mother]

Thank you very very much indeed for the letter and taking us both out. I enjoyed myself enormously and thank you for the sweets and chocolates which you brought us and the lovely biscuits you sent us. It was very nice of you to come up all this way just to see us both.

I think the arrangements for next hol are just wonderful and I do hope that the kilt will be ready by the very beginning of next hols. I have wanted a kilt ever since I was about 6 or 7 and I am now getting one after about 5 years of waiting it makes it all the better.

On Tuesday there were house runs which were not half as bad as everyone makes them to be. In the Trotters (there are three packs. the most junior is Trotters with 18 people in it) I came third. One starts off in a pack and spreads out quite quickly; one prefect goes behind and takes the slow people, one goes in front and takes the fast people. In the trotters there is a difference of about 6 minutes between the first person and the last person. Everyone says you nearly die but they are really as bad as all that[164].

Don't forget about the tickets for the Gilbert and Sullivan. I hope we will be able to get some.

I hope Dad gives you all the news.

Oh yes I have just thought: another thing Granny might give me or you or someone is a portable pocket chess set because I am beginning to like the game a good deal.

J   Sunday 9th Dec 56

E of T[165] arrangements went up yesterday.

End of term yard soccer competitions – six teams all play each other. House matches, we got beaten... Junior fives – we beat Hart House... Our

---

[164] Different houses had some traditionally preferred runs of their own.

[165] Ends of term were of course great occasions. The general feeling of prospective freedom started to work its effects a couple of weeks from the end of term, with variations in celebratory activities, house concerts in winter terms, and so on. As can be seen from our letters, there was a lot of preparation for this end of term carnival – a cheerful authorized opportunity to poke a little bit of fun at prefects, staff and the school.

The final morning was memorable. Special 2-carriage trains were brought in to Sedbergh station (normally used only for goods trains) specifically to take Sedbergh boys off to connections to other lines. The Scots left first for connections to Glasgow and Edinburgh; southerners next, going via Oxenholme for a whole day's travel to reach London. A few headed to south Yorkshire and Lancashire the same way; a few from the North East went to Carlisle for a train across to Newcastle; and probably one third of the school left by car.

junior house seems to be showing itself – we won the recruits Cup [junior shooting].

Practising for the House Concert; taking part in the band which is going quite well; also taking part in a Corps band.

Last night we had a film, Whisky Galore. It wasn't quite up to my expectations but it was jolly good and amusing.

Today we have 2 orchestra practices which as far as I'm concerned is a waste of 2 ½ hours on a Sunday. We are playing the London Symphony – the whole of it. I have 596 bars rest and play about 300. However, accompanying the Creation singing is quite fun.

I seem to be playing lots of clarinet this term. I expect that is because Ronny R (Mr Reynell) is more inspiring than Mr. Whiteside].

S   Sunday 9th December 56

...I do hope you are all well. I must say Sally sounds even nicer than she was last hols and I am longing to see her again.

On Tuesday there were house matches. We played Powell House. Unfortunately one of our best forwards had his face cut open in the 1st 3 minutes of the game and he had to go to the san so we had to play with 14 people and in the end it was 26-3 to them. It was an extremely good game and all our side played wonderfully.

Also on Thursday there was a Junior fives and Jamie played on 1st pair. We played Hart House as you must know from Jamie and I will not tell you all about it as Jamie will and he must know more about it than I do.

And also yesterday there was the Recruits cup shooting (the school one, inter-house) and School House won with 256 and the record is 257. We have now got 3 out of 12 interhouse cups which is a good effort.

When you say it is my mistakes when I don't come back with clean clothes, well on Saturday is was the last laundary /sic/ of term and so I chucked out into the dirty clothes pile 2 dirty towels and 1 dirty Sunday shirt; as Matron had put out on my bed a clean towel and a clean Sunday shirt; but when I came upstairs in the evening I found out that Matron had put the dirty shirt in my drawers and had taken the clean towel to the laundary (which I had hung on the towel rail) and left me with the two dirty ones.

Yesterday evening there was a film. It was 'Whisky galore' and was terribly funny, all about a ship that gets wrecked on a tiny island in the Hebradies /sic/ in the war. It was really terribly funny. Also there was a good news film which was right up to date and a Tom and Jerry cartoon.

What is Dear's address in New Zealand? And is it too late to send a card by sea?[166]

---

[166] Dear had gone for some 3 months to visit Uncle Rab and his family in New Zealand – her first visit to them since they went abroad in 1950 and for a holiday after Dear Man's death.

I hope you will write to Edinburgh about my kilt and tell them to jolly well get a move on as we want it by Christmas.

Today there was a bootroom test so my letter may arrive late.

You know you said something about lunch on the train and a taxi when you are up last week. Well did you mean it?

There is a house yard soccer competition 5 a side (all those who want to play). The teams are captained by the most senior bod playing and called after him; for example J. D. Dorman's team (a house prefect), his father is Governor of Sierrra Leona so his team is called the Colonial Crackpots. The team I am in is called the Bingley Bluebottles. It is an American tournament and great fun.

I am looking forward terrifically to seeing you all

S   No date [possibly 6 December 56, a Sunday]

...It has been stinking weather here raining all day and every day. The squash courts have got holes in the roves and the floors are soaking so none can play. And because there is nothing to do now, because as there has to be 36 weeks of term a year they plonk on a few extra days at the end of this term to make up the 36; and as we finish exams today (Saturday) we have Sunday Monday Tuesday Wednesday with nothing to do all day long; anyway I mustn't grumble because it is better than work anyway – and all I really mean is that I can't get a fives caught [*sic*] because I have already played today.

There was another stinking House run on Wednesday. It was Straight Bridges. I came 1ˢᵗ in our pack which is not really worth it because the next house run I will be in Middle Pack and I will have to go a jolly sight faster – but I suppose it is a good thing.[167]

The soccer competition has now finished and our team, the Bingley Bluebottles, came 2ⁿᵈ in group B. There are two groups, A and B. It was jolly good fun. The London Lizards won beating the Loch Ness ninepins.

We had an hour and a half's choir practise */sic/* without a break this morning and it was jolly long and boring

What do you think I should get J for Christmas. And can you tell me the address of one of my godfather's as [I] have one lovely card, a Sedbergh school card, and I think it would be a good idea to send him one. Also Pat Carlisle (my godmother). Are you having trouble with the Christmas cards or can you find room to put them?

By the way where is Penny? I thought she was coming here but I haven't seen her yet?

---

[167] First reference to Sandy's prowess as a distance and fell runner

They have put the decorations in the dining room and they look very good[168], especially the Holy [sic] which has thousands of berries on up here. And you see people dragging along long branches covered in berries, which would cost about £1 in London.

Everybody is preparing for the House concert and I have just been turned out of the common Room.[169]

I am very pleased that the kilt will be ready by Christmas.

I am looking forward to seeing you tremendously and the house[170] in only 5 days.

Easter Term 1957

J   Jan 20th 1957 [Sunday]

Good journey up... Settled down into our study which although rather large is very comfortable. The only trouble is that our curtains are rather too short so we use them over a grub box which makes a table affair. Please could you look when you are back home if there are any spare ones 6½ ft high and 6 ft wide and if there are please could you send them. That would be very nice.

It's simply wizard having a study[171]. There are three gramophones and three wirelesses downstairs here, which means there is plenty of music to listen to. One doesn't stay in one's study but [we] sit with others and chat and listen to records – in theirs or they come to yours. What with being

---

[168] A seasonal celebration, overseen by Mrs Thornely, much enjoyed by the boys – adding to the spirit of forthcoming Christmas, holidays and home combined.

[169] The Common Room was used by Senior Dayroom boys for listening to the popular comedy and adventure radio shows of the day (Much Binding in the Marsh, Dick Barton and Journey into Space) and the Goon Show which had a cult following but was incomprehensible to me. I don't remember anyone sitting down to listen to classical music; and am not sure if pop music was allowed. I think there were also some magazines, such as The Illustrated London news or Punch. Some may have been sent from home – and newspapers were kept in the library.

[170] First visit to my parents' new home in Rye in East Sussex – a great change from London and a take off point for a whole new and rich late-teenage home life for Sandy and me

[171] Study mates in junior studies were at first appointed and not chosen by ourselves, but even with a rather disparate crowd of boys who might not yet know each other well, the study was a private hideaway and civilized place after public, noisy dayroom life. Private mugs, a few personal belongings and books on a shelf and not in a locker and our own music at last (whether classical, pop or jazz) – these things gave pleasure and allowed a boy to build his own persona. Furthermore there was the privilege and pleasure at last of making one's own tea, egg and beans on toast on the gas rings at the end of the studies corridor – a smell never to be forgotten. Whoever the study partners, all one's old friends were all nearby, with opportunity to increase contact with others with whom one shared interests.

allowed to cook now as well – things like hot chocolate after rugger – life is most fun and luxurious.

By the way, writing with lined paper underneath – hope it's an improvement.

When I was looking for curtains I came across the old fishing ketches which used to be on the stair landings on the private side, it was all bust up, all the stays broken and generally very knocked about indeed[172]. I asked the HM if I could repair and have it. He let me. It's now in my study undergoing operations, propped up between two tins of luncheon meat (of Lowe's) for blocks.

This term I'm getting the Observer for my Sunday paper.

Hope to lose 6lb for boxing to get into a decent weight. I'm far too heavy for my size.

Played squash and fives and rugger and had rather a good game at wing forward.... Junior...

Squash ladder gone up, with positions drawn from a hat. I'm third from bottom – and S is top!

On Friday we had a deadly boring Civics by an obviously brilliant young chap [who left here 4 years ago from here and is now a clerk in the House of Commons].

It looks as though I will have a super term ahead. Thanks again for all the hard work you did to give us such a wizard holidays. I do hope you have a lovely time in Scotland and gets lots of duck and have a good rest[173].

S   25 Jan 57

I hope you have had a good time in Scotland and shot lots of birds, both of you. I expect it snowed up where you are or were... We had snow on Thursday but by Friday it had gone... We are all wanting it to freeze and freeze so it is [becomes] terribly cold. Then we will be able to skate.

Jamie had probably told you but Mrs Thornely's baby arrived about a week ago. Apparently it is a boy.

Yesterday we played fives twice, once in the morning once in the evening There are nine of us in the junior day room who play fives a lot so I reckon to play every half day which is jolly good. Also I play squash about 2 a week and maybe 3 or 4 times.

Is Jeb going down to London soon and when is the day of his show?

I had a talk with Kenny Anderson the music master and he told me that if I felt I was making no progress it would be best to give it up for it would be a waste of money and I agree with him also, it seems stupid to me that

---

[172] Large model Breton fishing boats built by Uncle Paddy when as a boy he was incarcerated in bed in France for a year and more with polio.

[173] The Murray Arms at Gatehouse of Fleet, Dumfriesshire is a comfortable fishing and shooting country hotel.

you will pay for the lesons [*sic*] of this term when I know I want to give it up after the term[174].

On Monday there was a house run. There is no three mile pack yet and I am in trotters. I came first and took 26 minutes and Jamie in his pack took 25½ mins. I expect I will be in Little pack next house run (the middle pack[175].

On Tuesday there was an off day so with two other guys we went to the Clough and it was a soaking day. The river was going very fast so we chucked a big tin in and raced it down; we could go normally a bit faster than it though sometimes we had to climb over walls or wade streams while it just went straight along. In the end it got caught in the wier [*sic*] in a back current.

Some guys are interested in the idea of going to Canada to earn money so could you just tell me the facts of the idea for we are having a conversation about going to Canada and I brought it up.

This term as a form book we have to read Great Expectations. It is really rather good for a type like Dickens and it is twice as good as Wuthering Heights.

I have also read 3 Piggie [= P. G.] Wodehouse's books.

J   Feb 3 [Sunday]

Fives – Juniors competition... – and lots of squash...

The other thing I'm doing a lot is playing the clarinet. I'm playing Mozart's clarinet Quintet in the house orchestra competitions. I play with Ronny (Reynell)[176] every Tuesday and am playing in a Mozart trio with him and a viola as well.

Doing quite a bit of running as well because of this bad weather.

Tried shooting on the miniature range yesterday evening. A 9lb rifle is considerably heavier than a .22, and shooting is a different game. You have 25 bullets; first you go for a group [taking] as long as you like (5 shots) then five 'snap' shots at a small target 2" diameter – up for 5 secs, and down for 3 secs – i.e. 8 secs in which to load, aim and fire. Then you have a minute in which to fire 10 shots, 1 per six seconds at two ordinary size targets. After all that my arm felt absolutely dead with the weight of the rifle.

---

[174] Trumpet lessons, which Sandy had started half way through his time at the Dragon

[175] i.e. promoted out of Trotters to the next level of three (Big Pack, Little, Pack, Trotters).

[176] Ronnie Reynell was an able pianist and enthusiastic accompanist from whom I learnt a great deal about music. He also played the French Horn in the full School Orchestra. He was a brother of a Radcliffe research haematologist with whom my mother had worked.

S   3 Feb 57

I must say your idea of going to Bemersyde and then to the Murray Arms is wonderful. I did fell [feel] that J going to Italy and Sicily and me not going was a chiz[177], but now I am terribly glad I am not going. I am sure that shooting and fishing for grouse and trout and sea trout is more my cup of tea than looking at jolly old Roman pots and pans etc.

Talking of holidays did you say you were going to Rye or the other place, Aldeburgh next hols or are we staying in London. And talking of sailing I just wondered if you had possibly done anything about the boat, but I expect you have been too busy.

On Wednesday I was calling (I get up when the bell goes and shout out the times, every minute for 20 minutes so everyone knows when to get up). But I did not wake up nor did anyone else in the 10 bedder, so no-one woke me; in the end the head of House came in and woke me and told us to jolly well wake up in future; anyhow it was all right as people managed to dress in a hurry and get down in time for breakfast.

Talking of times of things, I just wondered if ever you go to Gammidges [sic] or past it you might take my watch, but don't go out of your way please because I can't expect you to go out of your way because I was to[o] lazy to go there myself and anyhow you are to[o] busy so don't go except if you are going.

There is now a junior dayroom fives club and we play competitions, doubles, singles and the main idea is to play more so we all get good. I am the president I don't know why but I was told I was, for no reason at all and so I organise the competitions and games. It is jolly good fun.

On Monday there was a House run. There is now a three mile pack between Middle Pack and Big Pack; I was in this with 9 other possible three milers. I came in 4th but I don't expect I will be able to come as high again as there were some of last year's three milers as well. On Thursday we all had to go off on a training run; it was a longer run of about 45 mins. We all went in a pack training this time. There were 16 of us. If I go into the Three I might be told to get fell shoes as gym shoes cannot grip and when on Thursday I had to walk in some places it was so slippery, but chaps with fell shoes could run. There was a film on Thursday about Edison who made the light. It was a wonderful film and Spencer Tracey played Edison. He was wonderful. It was a really good film.

There is a Daily Mail competition in which you have to invest an imaginary £1000 in shares. The person who makes the most gets £2000 – entries by Feb 12. If you entered and found out about it I am sure you would win.

---

[177] I was to be taken by Uncle Robin Hone (then Head of classics at Clifton College) on a tour which had an educational angle – together with a bright Clifton scholar, John Whitely, who was doing classics as I was at that time. Robin himself was making a recce for a planned sabbatical to study Roman archaeology.

J   10 Feb [Sunday]

Thanks for the letter and the parcel. The curtains are absolutely superb - exactly the sort of thing and they are greatly envied. They make the room so much more cheerful; it was really terribly clever to choose them so well. Thankyou very much for the sweets as well which we have shared out.

Lots of fives and squash...

There is a debating literary society just made in the house for the studies and senior dayroom – semi-compulsory though voluntary in theory.

There is a general move in the school for a sailing club at Killington, so perhaps soon that'll be coming into action.[178] It is only a start but we have a master and the problem is being tackled.

Am longing to hear about Crufts and the R Corinthian YC for our boat.

I got an impot yesterday for not reading an economics prep properly . It's the first I've had for some time. A pre in our house got one as well.

Junior rugger – lost to Sedgwick 32-0 who had some very strong centres.

Have been playing the clarinet and practising the Quintet. We have also started the House Unison .

Weather getting warmer. There is a noisy Great Tit outside the study window by the garage.

S   10 Feb 57

It was jolly 'd' of you to go to Gammidges for me, especially as you went only for me. I am glad they were 'd' about it and I hope they can mend it properly.

It has been raining and raining. I am reading Runyon on Broadway at the moment. It is terribly funny. I have only read about 100 out of the 200 pages so far but I think it is wonderful. It even makes me burst out laughing in reading prep and everyone stares and I get dirty looks from the Heads. I like Dave the Dude and the Stories about Sam the Gonoph (or just Sam) the best.

On Wednesday it was housemasters time when records are played in the common room while you read. It is jolly good. They played my favourite classical record. It is a march by Tchakosky /sic/ and is played by millions of Russians. It is a wonderful one and easily my favourite; it is all brass and drums and I think maybe strings every so often.

Talking of music I hope you have written to the HM; he suggests a flute or an oboe or something like that for me to learn instead of the trumpet. What do you think about it?

I am going to buy some fell shoes tomorrow. There were house runs on Monday again and I came 4th again in the 3 mile pack. I am going to run in

---

[178] It was quite some years before a school sailing club was instituted there, but I sailed and taught my sons to sail on the Reservoir where there was quite an active little club in the summer holiday period at the end of the 1970s.

the 3 mile. Unfortunately it is a good year for the 3 mile which is a pity; last year was very slow. There is quite a chance that the 3 and the 10 mile records are going to be broken. On Friday the 3 mile pack went round the 3 being timed by a pre and I was furious with myself. Firstly my shoe come off, secondly I had not bothered to get fell shoes in the morning because I thought there would be not 3 mile training, so I could not run up the fells and kept falling over and some had fell shoes. Third I lost my way and had to wait for the guy behind to catch up to tell me where to go. I beat him though in the end. I took twenty two minutes [and] about 50 seconds; the last [runner] last year apparently took 27 mins, so I was rather pleased in the end.

I don't think there will be any skating this year as it is too hot and it is raining again which is a chiz because I bought skates the first day as J said if you don't go the first day they will be sold out of my size. Anyhow I got size 8 ½ so they should last me for at least 1 ½ years. I can just wear them with 2 extra pairs of thick socks.

Again I have been playing tons and tons of fives. I reckon I am the 3rd or 4th best fives player in the Junior Dayroom; only 10 of us play. I am still top of the squash ladder.

There is a heater like the Pioles[179] in Paris now in the library which makes it twice as warm as it is the coldest room in the house.

Has Jeb done Crufts or won anything? I have not been able to get any papers about Crufts.

Sorry my pen has run out. I am in Ward's study eating a scrumy poched *[sic]* egg on buttered toast which is very very good.

Last night there was a film, [illeg – looks like 'fords are red'], a very new one indeed. It was only [out] about a month ago – [about] the new President - which is jolly good, with a Tom and Jerry, then Simon and Laura[180] which is a very funny film. We were told it was going to be a rotten film and that we would do better to play fives, so we all went armed with sweets and ready to go to sleep (I mean not watch the film) but it was funny and never bored anyone.

I had a card from Dear when she was in Panama.

That is all there is to say so I will go and play ping pong.

J   Feb 17th [Sunday]

What a pity about Crufts. I think it does sound a bit of a racket and it sounds as though Jeb ought to have got something.

---

[179] Colonel Paiolle, wartime colleague of my father's, with whom we dined on our trip to Paris, and with whom I subsequently stayed once in the early 1960s when at Cambridge.
[180] A 1955 British film starring Peter Finch and Kay Kendall

91

Tuesday a heavenly day rather marred unfortunately by a 30-0 defeat against Lupton House in the Juniors XV. Our Juniors aren't really that bad – just young and smaller than some other teams.

Snow getting lower on the fells. some houses tobogganing already – and it froze last night for the first time.

Extra half on Friday – we've been waiting for one since Jenny's baby arrived. I went out 3 miles with a couple of other blokes, just generally mucking about not definitely going anywhere.

Yesterday we had a mock trial which was great fun – the trial of a gang of teddy boys who had committed attempted murder while house breaking. It was most enjoyable,

Lots of fives and squash, ladders...

Birthday ideas – books... yachting and Damon Runyon... and portable wireless.

J   Postcard 19 Feb

Most unfortunate news. I have cracked my thumb – which I did a fortnight ago playing rugger but the swelling never really went down. I went to the Doc again yesterday - I went before when it was properly swollen – and he put a plaster strapping on it for two days. And this morning I went to Lancaster and I now have it in plaster, Senior fives in 2 days time, can't play my clarinet and no more Juniors rugger. Rather a bore. Hope it's not on for more than 10 days or so.

J   24ᵗʰ Feb 56 [Sunday]

You certainly seem to be having a nice time with a 'heaven' – or whatever the collective noun for godfathers might be – around, and going to see films and things.

I went to Lancaster today and after waiting around for 1 ½ hours after being x-rayed, I had a plaster slab put on, not a hole plaster, with a bandage to hold it on. The bandage has got so thin already and is coming to pieces, so that I've had to have a new bit over the top as I'm going out today with James Oliver. The doctor said on Thursday that I could play squash, do short runs, skate and snowball, not fives, rugger sledging. Since then have played endless squash and am now 3ʳᵈ on the ladder....

Half holiday, played fives...

I was tried at the beginning of the week for tenor for the House Quartet but I'm not going to do it although I'm singing in the octet, so I will be the reserve.

Friday was a terrific day: the government option class went to Kendal to the Country Council meeting, which meant missing morning school. When the bus came to go back there were already 8 standing, and we were 11, so we went around Kendal, having fish and chips and going into record shops for 1½ hrs.

Then there was civics in the evening, 'Office automation' that was not very interesting and above most chaps' heads, but at least we got off prep for it,

What with Lancaster and Kendal and a new study light (lamp) my financial backing is rapidly lessening...

Speaking of godfathers there is a picture of S's godfather – he's the HM of Repton isn't he? - in the London Illustrated News.

Out with Mrs Oliver last Sunday. We talked about Aldeburgh; she says it's the one place she would like to go back to, absolute heaven.

Next term's dates... Common Entrance next week which means we will soon know how many new boys we'll have next term

First XV... Senior house fives...

As usual I've been spending a lot of time playing squash... We had a house run on Friday. Everyone was pretty indignant with the head of School. I did Frostrow backwards, being on Light-ex[181], which is worse than the normal way round because of the long slope.

This afternoon I went round the ten most of the way with Oliver but one of his shoes split about 2/3 of the way round and I ran on. I took 1 hr 30 mins which isn't bad at all. Last year my best time was 1.54.

On Thursday we had the masters' concert instead of the New England Orchestra or some such thing. It was absolutely terrific. The best thing I thought was the play 'Cox and Box which they finished up with. Ronny played the part of the landlord and was excellent. There were recitations and all kinds of thing s including an orchestra group with the masters all dressed up.

On Friday night we had a civics on aerial photography which wasn't terribly enthralling though there were some interesting slides.

A jazz club is being made in the house. I've been experimenting playing with my thumb in plaster because the prefects want to make a record of it (EP 10") one side only.[182] It's very good fun.

S   No date – [probably 24 February]

We are having very good weather here at the moment. It hasn't rained for about a week.

Jamie asked me to tell you that he's giving a lecture on Louis Armstrong to the School House Literate *[sic]* society so he wanted you to send him

---

[181] One might be on light-ex or off-ex (as opposed to on full-ex) – according to instructions from the school doctor or house matron.. Light-ex was for when building up strength after convalescence, when some light running was allowed but not rugger or other main sports.
[182] We started with a skiffle band, then fashionable; then formed a house jazz band which played swing at first, then attempted traditional jazz. Until recently I had a copy of the EP.

your book and any information about him if possible as quickly as possible please.

On Thursday there was a masters' concert in the evening. It consisted of some stories and songs and a masters skiffle group and some tunes on the violin and piano which were terrific. They were called the Manhattan Town and Four String Joe. Then Mr Reynell, Mr Pentney and Mr Dane gave a half hour play. It was all singing except a tiny bit. It was about two chaps called Cox and Box who had been given the same room in a house so the Landlord could make double money. One man worked all night in a newspaper office and came back in the morning. The other worked all day in a hatter's shop and came back at night; and of course one day one of them had a day off and they met. Then they came to the conclusion that they were engaged to the same girl and neither of them wanted to marry her. It was all good.

The term ends of the 28 and starts on 30 April

Last week I finished Runyon and have started on None but the Brave and over ¾ of The Man Who Never Was. It is fascinating.

On Friday there were House runs and I came 3rd in the 3 Mile pack. There are two guys who will be in the six who are just out of the san so I may not get on the team.

I'm sorry I'll arrive late – I'll tell you why now.

Today was a lovely day. I suggested to Melville, Robertson, Watson (my termers) that we should take a pack lunch and go to Hebblethwaite gill and caves. So we went to order lunch, but orders have to be in by 12, and we were five minutes late so they would not give us any. So we went and asked again and every time the answer was no. So we bought some pork luncheon meat and made some sandwiches, and we got booze, cake and two tins of fruit, large packets of crisps and borrowed a rucksack. But the HM said that as cook had made us our Sunday lunch we had to eat it. But he signed leave to go out from 2 to tea so off we went. We reached Muddy slide[183] and went up the gill and found a dead pigeon with a ring on its leg and took it off and buried the pigeon in perfect condition it must have died of old age. We are going to send the ring in.

We went past the caves and up to the great cliff fault. There were 3 Powell House chaps (18 [year-olds]) who have climbed in Switzerland with a master there doing real rock climbing with ropes and axes. They saw us eating our lunch and shouted from the cliffs on the far side if we had any sandwiches. (There were cliffs on both sides and ours was smaller and we climbed up the back of them). [sketch of gill in profile, showing one side sheer rock, the other half its height and more slanting profile]. So as we had 4 left over we said yes and they came tearing down and across the gill and round to us in a terrific race. Then when they had eaten our home made sandwiches they climbed back up a more difficult bit. So we started

---

[183] A Ten Mile course landmark

climbing up our side and down. It was not dangerous and we did it on our side; if you fell you would only get cuts and bruises but if they fell they would be dead! We went along home. rolling bo[u]lders into the Gill on the way. We had a wonderful time.

On Saturday we went round the 10. Mr Durran [3 words illeg] and it was quite good fun. I did it in 1 hour 58 mins; we have to go round twice this term on any time we like.

I have been entered in the school House fives competition which is on a handicap basis.

I want to give J something for his birthday because he had so few presents on Christmas day and he is probably feeling a bit down about Christmas days and birthdays[184].

Only about 3 weeks to the hols now.

S   no date probably 3 March 57 [Sunday]

It has been much colder here. It snowed yesterday and there has been some snow on the ground all week. I agree with you about the boat, especially the 1st hand graduate[185] but it is a bit over the limate [limit] I think. Where is the Corinthian club? It is a jolly good thing we will be able to keep the boat in the club. Are you going to start buying a boat this term or are you going to wait until next holidays?

There have been no house runs this week, only training. On Tuesday some people went skating on Holme Fell, the ice only bore for a bit and then some of them fell in.

I went up to Frostrow to try and skate on Friday. We took all our skates and our jeans and our jerseys /sic/ from home (and it was all quite colourful) but the ice could not bear a stone – so as there were 11 of us in the junior dayroom and 8 in the senior day room, the J day room went up one hill with a marsh at the bottom and the others on the far side. The S day room types came charging up the hill; it was half snowballing half fighting. We tried to drive them down the hill into the bog at the bottom, sometimes they won, sometimes we won. It was wonderful fun [sketch of profile of slope with marsh at bottom J day room defending the marsh, S Dayroom up the slope].

Yesterday it snowed from 1230 to 3.30 so we all went out sledging. Jamie borrowed someone's really flashy sledge with automatic steering and he decided to play squash so he lent it to me. But another guy said it had been lent to him so I said he was wrong (which he was) but the guy said he was going to take it. J said to the guy to give it to me, so the guy did. It is a super sledge and the sledging place is wonderful.

---

[184] A kindly thought indeed; but I do not recall the circumstances.
[185] 'Graduate' 12 foot centre-board sailing dinghy – a popular class sailed by two persons

On Tuesday there was a lecture by a type called Seligman. It was on Cyprus. We all went thinking how wonderful to have a lecture and slides on the army etc in Cyprus but it was about Cyprus only. For if a guy went not knowing there were terrorists in Cyprus and British Soldiers dealing with them he would not have known at the end either. It was just about the Greeks and the Turks of about 2000 BC and about the peasants in Cyprus. I thought it was very boring indeed, so did the rest of the school.

You know you told me to get a new pair of walking shoes if my old ones went; well I have a nice pair of new ones now as the old ones have holes in the bottom and the snow came in.

I have nearly finished the Runyon omnibus and I think it's terribly funny.

This morning we had a Bootroom and this afternoon there is House Orchestra in Powell Hall. I am now playing some tunes with another guy (Melville) who plays the clarinet. We do it in the music class and it is jolly good fun.

What do you think I should give J for his birthday?

J   10 March [Sunday]

Thankyou for the letter and the biscuits.

Of course squash has taken up most of my time last week, and running. I had an absolutely sweltering game with the chap who is now top and lost 4-3.

Am still singing in the octet but am no longer reserve tenor unfortunately – because a chap has come back who was going to be away.

Plenty to do, jazz club, reading, liar dice...

Tuesday my plaster came off. More squash...

We went out today with Sir John Shea[186] who is terribly nice. We had a whacking tea and enjoyed ourselves immensely.

Could you please send me some money. I'm pretty well right out, and certainly at the end of term with 2/6d PLA and journeying money I don't know how it's all gone but quite a bit on the setting up of the study and Lancaster etc.

Thursday was Field Day but I was off field day because I couldn't hold a rifle for firing in my left hand. I practised squash, the weight and doodled on the piano and tried playing the clarinet and had a most useful afternoon. I cooked that Instant Whip pudding - 4-6 portions and ate most of it myself; and what with cleaning my battle dress for next week's Certificate A Part I exam, and doing a bit of work on the pamphlet, arms drills, field craft, etc..

---

[186] Chairman of the Board of Governors and a frequent visitor to School House lunches, he well known to my family from earlier days.

96

J cont/....   Friday [March 15th]

Thankyou very much for the superb box of biscuits.

It sounds absolutely excellent about the boat. I can see that a Firefly is not obviously a family boat but it's very like the National which the Olivers have, and they are certainly good boats. If possible we should try to get the modernist possible since as far as racing is concerned F32 does not stand much of a chance against F1045 however well sailed. But that doesn't matter, because we'll be able to get jolly good fun out it....

S   No date [probably Sunday, 10 March 1957]

Thank you for your letter and the lovely tin of biscuits. It was very kind of you. They are very 'd' biscuits.

I agree about the Firefly for it is obviously better to have a boat we can race anywhere and the Graduate is probably a rotten little muck-about boat if the chaps at the C club says it is; and if we can't get moving in a Graduate it is no good.

The School House fives competition starts on Monday and I have been picked against Dorman a school and house pre. He is the best in the house and has a minus 6 handicap. I have + 10 handicap (the best in the Junior Day room has + 7. The lowest of all is + 14. I have not played him yet as he has gone to London to see his father knighted; his father is governor of Sierra Leona.

At the moment I am sitting in the Library listening to a lecture on jazz by Lord who is head of house[187]. We all have books or letters to get on with, when he plays some jazz records to illustrate something in his speech. He has some jolly good records.

Yesterday we went out with General Sir John Shea who is a very nice person I think and is wonderfully fit and healthy for his age. We went to the Bull with his godson who is in the studies[188] and with Tommy Bain-Smith the Bursar's son. For tea we had eggs and ham and piles of chips to start with. Then peaches and cream. The General then looked at the empty cups of peaches and said that this was not very big so he ordered 4 more. We then had brown and white bread and jam; then cakes and tea..

It is now after lunch and I have been playing in the house orchestra and cooking scrambled eggs so I have not had much letter writing time.

Yesterday afternoon we played yard soccer v. Hart House, for Evans play Lupton and Hart play Evans so a few weeks ago when Lord was asking for a few ideas about anything (we were in the 10 bedder) I suggested playing other houses at yard soccer at Junior Dayroom level. So Lord

---

[187] Lord was one of a number, including Gourlay, Laycock, Ward, Sugden, Nelson (more junior but the most gifted player) who took traditional jazz seriously, both to listen to and to play. There was a quite a fad for jazz in School House.

[188] Not named, I forget who he was.

arranged it. We played Hart and beat them 11-2, I scored one goal and 2 goals which our side said were goals but Hart house did not, so we did not count them.

I have moved down again on the squash ladder. I was beaten by one guy in the Studies, so I am now 10 from the top.

I think it would be a good idea to go to a cinema with Michael[189].

On Thursday there was Field Day. Robertson W- Jones, Melville, Whitman[190] and I we went up to Crossbeck gill where we had lunch (9 pack lunches between the 5 of us & 2 tins of fruit) and mustard (in my metal stud box) and HP sauce to go on the bad sandwiches. We built a dam across the beck. Then we went up to Baugh Fell still on the beck and had fights - where 2 go across the river and 3 come after them. He had super fun.

The Three is on the 20th Wed. I will be running if a guy called Cochrane doesn't refuse to run (he is our best runner)[191] and if I don't fail the medical (quite a lot of people do).

J   17 March [Sunday]

Thankyou very much for the lovely presents. The picture is the very one I saw, how clever of you to find it and I like it very much[192]. I'm longing like anything to see and use the putter.

I had a jolly d birthday despite the Cert A exam. I got some tennis balls and a Runyon book from Granny and Grandfather, Three Men on a Bummel from Aunt Hat; £1 from Uncle Robin and a record token from Sandy.

The cake you sent is absolutely delicious, the best and lightest cherry cake I've come across. Needless to say most of it has now gone.

On Tuesday I had my thumb out of plaster. At first it was a bit weak but now it is ok. My wrist is still pretty weak for playing fives. On Monday we had an extra half. I went with Oliver onto Baugh Fell and back round the side. We had intended to follow the Rawthey from its source but it was too hot.

Saturday visibility was down to 50 to 70 [yards]. Going round the ten it was even less on Baugh Fell and people were getting lost.

I seem to be having one long term of ailments – this morning with some septic blisters and had an injection and generally my feet are pretty sore.

---

[189] A visitor at home, son of one of my mother's friends
[190] Sandy's main expedition partners for the rest of their time at school, along with Broadbent and Huxley (who came to School House the term after them); W-Jones was Wilding-Jones.
[191] I think Sandy meant: 'if Cochrane refuses to run'.
[192] Cezanne's card players; or a Monet Argentueil scene with a yacht against a mackerel sky

S   No date [after 14 March] 1957

Thank you for your letter. Jamie seems to have had a very 'd' birthday. He is very pleased with the picture of the Chinese horse[193]. I gave him a 10/- record token. I know it is quite a lot of money but I hear the records as well.

I hope you received my note about the 3 mile. It is not absolutely delfinate /sic/ but I think I will be the 6th runner.

Ruth said she is taking us out next Sunday which should be good fun.

On Monday there was an extra half I went to Nor Gill with 2 other guys who came my term. It was great fun.

On Tuesday there was the school house Relay (10 Mile). I Put my name up for it and was put on Team, 2. There were 3 teams each with 9 people who had each to run just over a mile. Then we carried on round the 10 from our starting place; so if you start at 2 miles from the finish you had to run 2 miles and count it as going all round the ten so it was worth going in if you got a good place. I was 4th runner, from Cautley bridge to Little Gill on Baugh Fell. The runner who was coming to me was first by about 200 yards then my runner was about 100 yds in front of the last. We all kept our places, Our team finished second by ¾ of a minute behind and ahead of the last. The time was 1 hour 16 minutes.

Last night there was a film with a cartoon; it was 'Doctor at sea.' We saw it in Dorking with Uncle Robin and Janet. It is a very good film but not so good the second time.

I am very glad that you are trying so hard to find a boat; it will be wonderful if its ready by next hols.

Mr Fox our form master is reading us The Cocktail Party by T S Eliot; he says it is a bit old for us, but it is better to know it a little before one gets to the 6th. It is jolly good but gets a bit boring in some parts. Mr Fox is leaving at the end of this term (he only came for a term anyhow)[194].

It has stopped raining and better weather now...

On Friday I played Dorman (School Pre) at fives in the House competition, he is the best in the house with -6 handicap. He won the first game 15-11 (I only got one point: I am + 10); the second game he won 15-11 and the third he won 15-13.

This afternoon I am going round the 3 for a tour (all the 3-mile pack) being told all about it by a Prefect.

J   no date, [probably 24 March]

There's a yard soccer competition in the house which unfortunately I cannot play in and the squash ladder and fives are being finished off. I was

---

[193] Print of a Chinese watercolour drawing of a single horse
[194] I do not remember him; but see comment in Sandy's letter dated early May 1957 below.

playing the third round yesterday but we had to leave the game at 1-1. I was playing the head of house, playing level on handicaps (-2).

I got on ex. yesterday after having penicillin through the week and on Friday I had my toe opened to let out the puss; the bottom and side of the toe was all raw skin and it became even worse to walk. On Sat however it was far better and I got on ex.

Playing the clarinet a terrific amount, practising the piece we have for orchestra. Our Mozart Quintet isn't going too badly at all and I have been playing in our jazz band as usual.

Am not longer in the Quartet, and it's really quite good (the reason I expect) and we might win the shield. The house unison isn't terribly good and I shouldn't think we'll retain the cup.

Today we're going out with Ruth which will be terrific fun. The HM says that apparently Penny (Dear's dog) isn't well at all; I do hope she gets better soon[195].

I hope I'm in reasonable training because on Wed I hope to go up Ingleborough and maybe Whernside if the weather's ok.

Getting ready for end of term... Last term we had inter-cube rags, raiding each other and sacking the beds and hiding the blankets and things – everything gets cleaned up by 11.30 when we eventually go to bed.

Summer Term 1957

J   1 May 1957 [Wednesday[196]] – Postcard

Arrived well ... I got all my study furniture straight away. I'm still in L VI doing Fr. and German in the Lower Six sets. There aren't any books other than texts that I have to get. Although I'm in LVI C sets I'm working really in a set of my own in German; and I don't know about Fr. yet.

There's Corps today and practice for the General Inspection already...

S   No date [probably Thursday 3 May 1957]

Thank you very much firstly for such lovely hols; and thank you very much for the camera films. It is just what I wanted – but unfortunately I left my camera behind. It is in the 2nd or 3rd Bottom Drawer in my Wellington. The cake is a super one. It will last a good long time as well as the

---

[195] Penny had been left with the Morphets during Dear's prolonged New Zealand trip.
[196] School returned on Tuesday 30th April.

chocolates from Claire-Lize (I will write to her). Aunt Hat sent me a book[197].

We had a good journey except it took 50 minutes in the bus. We shared a carriage with a chap (60) who had been to Canada to see if it was ok for his family to emigrate to. He was something like a factory worker or an engine driver. He said he earned 90 quid a month only engine driving. He said it was a wonderful place. Then he explained what was wrong with England. He was a very good type I think.

We came back in a taxi with a boy (Old Sedberghian) aged about 18 who was staying with the HM[198]

Good weather... I have played cricket twice now. I am the 2nd Head and the 2 of us have to keep order and quietness and control in the dayroom, and we take it in turns to inspect fagging. We can give maps for slack fagging or any one ragging etc.

We have a new form master an ex-prep school headmaster about 40. He is very strict but rather nice.

I am taking my bronze this term (life saving).

There is nothing much to say in only 2 days

J   5th May [Sunday]

Everything seems to be starting up ok. In French and German I'm in the sets that I would be had I always taken the subjects, although in German I'm really in a set of my own.[199]

I've missed in history two terms of the Revolution and this term we're starting the Second Empire. That means I've got a terrific amount of reading to do in that line. I'm longing to get hold of some German O level papers to see what they are like and start practising them. In French with Mr Gairdner we're reading Les Femmes Savants and learning and writing about the Précocité. We are writing our essays in French now, In German I'm battling on writing prose and things and learning grammar and vocab in preps.

Our study is nicely arranged and this term will probably be more peaceful because there is no gramophone in the lower studies. Granny Grant and Lowe are pretty quiet and hard readers (not workers)

---

[197] Presumably gifts relating to Sandy's birthday, on 4 May

[198] Perhaps a relation of Mrs Thornely's, but older than 18

[199] I made a switch, at the request of my father, from Classics to Modern Languages, as being something more generally 'useful'. The switch took place when I had already done two terms of A Level classics. Thus I started German from scratch (apart from a smattering of kitchen German remembered from childhood), and was behind in wider reading for French and European history having done Ancient History etc. As a result I was doing separate books and papers most of the time, but caught up reasonably quickly, despite appallingly low marks and continuing 'howlers', etc..

No cricket yet but had a nets yesterday. Yesterday afternoon we had 'Classifying' on the range[200]. The .303 didn't give such a bad kick as I expected but both Granny and I who were classifying were deaf till this morning with ringing noises in our ears.

We had a double parade on Friday – horrible. We're having FM Alexander for the Inspection and its being held 3 weeks earlier on in the term than usual. We're having 2 parades per week until it's over and lots of hard polishing and cleaning.

I've been throwing the weight very successfully somehow or other[201] and got about 1 foot over the standard.

Thank you for forwarding the parcel of the record.

Thankyou very very much for all you did to give us such a wonderful holidays; we really enjoyed every minute.

S   no date – [probably 5 May 1957]

I hope you are having a good time in Scotland and you have shot some duck, both of you. I am having a jolly good time here. I have already played three games of squash and 3 of fives. Yesterday for ex I played fives with 2 house Pres and a guy who came last term. The other guy and me just played the 2 Prefects. They beat us 7-15. We then swapped around a bit and had terrific fun.

Also we played in the evening. I am a Private Fag again to Ward, son of Mr Ward of Sedgwick House. He is a very 'd' chap. He was one of the Prefects I played fives with yesterday. I also played in the Tennis Comp with him when a Senior chap played with a Junior chap.

We have got a new form master called Mr Fox, the new chap instead of Rev We[d]gewood. He is rather a titchy sort of type and is rather like that chap in Down with School, from 'Masters I have nown' – the guy who says 'The boys look on me as a friend'.

There are no new boys to School House this term.

There is another Squash Ladder this term. But instead of the Head of House being the top of the ladder and the most Junior boy at the bottom etc there is a draw for places and I am at the Top

We had a good journey up and had lunch on the train.

There is nothing else to write about.

Thank you for a lovely hols and for taking us to Paris

---

[200] Tests of ability with a rifle, looking for exceptional sharp shooters both for the CCF and for inter-school competitions
[201] an equivalent to 'by some fluke'

J   May 12ᵗʰ [Sunday]

I didn't realize till the beginning of this week that we don't do any history in foreign texts, or any kind of history with our German, but what we do Latin for I don't know. It's an absolute farce as it is and most of the boys do some other work or read and no one seems to do the prep. I'm doing lots of German in and out of school and I felt much honoured yesterday to participate with the form proper. It's mainly vocab. at the moment at which I'm working. French is coming back to me very quickly and I'll soon be up level I hope. That is to say, in standard, not as far as literature is concerned because of the two terms I've missed.²⁰²

Weather changing, drizzle and then rain, much needed by the river.

Played in nets twice, which is always fun, and two games.... I made 14, a six, a 4 and a 3 in 3 balls, then a 1 and out 3 balls later. Short & sweet.

Squash and fives...

I wonder if the threatened rail strike will mean sending us home early?

Playing some jazz records now to see which records I like – perhaps my writing is bad because I cannot keep in time with Satch's Hot Five²⁰³.

S   Sunday 12ᵗʰ May 57

Thank you for the photos . They are good, but there is not enough wind in the second one.

I am having a very good time. Have you written to Mrs Bell²⁰⁴? Also have you written to Harvey Askew; I don't particularly mind if you don't but I want to know what you said, so I know where and when to go if I go²⁰⁵.

I have been playing lots of cricket. Made 18 on Monday and took four for nine wickets, I took one for nought on Wednesday (2 maidens, 1 wicket maiden). I am bowling fast off breaks. Yesterday played and it was so wet (it was raining) that the ball flew out of my hands when I tried to bowl fast; and as my off break only works when I bowl fast, as I do not flick it but let it twist round my hand as I let go. I got no wickets and millions of runs hit off me. I made 1 run as I went in 4 balls from the end...[scores]

---

²⁰² I much enjoyed being taught classics by Ronnie Reynell at Lower VIth level, moving on from a diet of grammar to history, plays and verse composition. I recall making up for fun my own dictionary of all Greek words to do with ships and the sea. I do not, however, remember what other subjects we took in LCVI: English, French and History probably, some religious studies, current affairs perhaps but no sciences, or maths – and my letters are rather silent on the subject.

²⁰³ I still have the record, a 45 rpm EP – with old favourites indeed.

²⁰⁴ Dear's neighbour and kind helper in Bemersyde who was presumably looking after the house. I guess that this related to the death of Dear's dog Penny while at Sedbergh.

²⁰⁵ Sandy needed to know what to say as he was in regular touch with Harvey Askew over fishing, and in fly-tying classes.

My work is going ok in fact rather well all except my maths I have spent over 1 ½ extra hours of my spare time on the last 2 preps alone but seeing as they were problems and I could not get the answer; it did not help much.

I do hope you can think of something next hols as a hol; personally Bemersyde is a super idea also I think my idea is a super one which is 2 days stop at Keisley on our way up. Those 2 would make a wizard hol[206].

Do you remember you might take us round Scotland yard sometime if you had any time.

Sometime, it does not matter so long as it is before May 24th, if possible might you send a copy of Jane Eyre and Pilgrim's Progress and Brazilian Adventure if you have a copy, for it would save buying a new copy of each. But that also does not matter.

I enclose photos of J and the dance band; he says note it is the dance band because in the jazz thing he does not play from music[207]. It was taken in the House concert.

Our form master is a jolly 'd' chap. he is about your age (40) and was in the Embassy in Budapest at the beginning of the war, then the Germans caught him. He is a prep school master doing a term between a headmastership and another headmastership. He calls himself Bolbey or Bulby or something like that[208].

Is there any news about a house? When are you going to Spain?

The HM gave me and Robertson (3rd Head) a foss[209] on being a head[210].He seems to know everything we felt when we were made new heads and told us how to be a good one etc.

I think I have said everything now.

S   ?19 May 57
PS at top   I hope I enclose the photo
Thank you very much indeed for your letter. My fishing rod arrived yesterday and I am sorry if I troubled you about it, but it has been pouring and since Monday there has been no cricket and excellent fishing with worm. And when this bad weather stops I will not have more than one chance a week of fishing.

Anyhow yesterday with two guys of my term, Robertson and W-Jones, we fished up to Hebblethwaite[211] and up Hebblethwaite and then some of

---

[206]. Bemersyde offered trout fishing on the Tweed; and the house and surrounding farmland of my godmother Ruth's house at Keisley, near Appleby, offered .22 and 12-bore shooting and good country food]

[207] i.e. the group was still at the swing band stage.

[208] Bowlby, and later spelt correctly.

[209] a lecture, not in this particular context but usually an unwanted one and often with sanctimonious overtones. The term could be applied to everything from a boring sermon to a lengthy ticking off.

[210] i.e. Dayroom Head.

the way back. I caught one fish of exactly 8 ins but it had half swallowed the hook and after we had taken the hook out with a pair of pliers it did not look so pretty especially when we lost our temper with it (it was dead because we killed it when we saw we couldn't get the hook out). So we didn't take it back to eat. We had a jolly good time and spent from 2.30 to 6.15. We met Jamie who was also fishing.[212]

I am glad you think it is a good idea to stop at Keisley for a night and I think we should stop for two nights, then we could have one day shooting with Ruth's .22. I agree that it would still be fun at the Murray Arms even if Edie wasn't there. How long would we have at Bemersyde and the Murray Arms?

I have become a Saint book fan. I have read 3 Saint books and 1 Sapper[213] this term.

Yesterday I played Rounders in the evening.

In form I don't know where I am yet; I am low in History, over half in Geog and near the top in French; and Maths is a problem for Mr Bowlby said I am top with scaled marks 50 out of 50 but I am not top of my Maths set I am sure. So he must have made a mistake I think. I think I will be about 13th out of 24 or maybe a bit higher.

Thank you for sending the camera; at the moment it is not the right weather for photography

There is nothing else to say except that I have not been knocked out of the Bronze yet though I might be knocked out this afternoon.

J   26 May [Sunday]

Sorry to hear that Sally has been having a rash again. I must say I hope she won't be a hay-feverish girl.

Terrific news – I got my watch back. It was on the lost property list so I zoomed off to the head of school and asked him about it. He asked me whether it was luminous and I said yes, and he said well this one isn't, Anyway I went down to Powell house to look and it was mine, and it was luminous, so I got it back ok. Apparently it had been in Lupton House lost property for some time. Anyway I have it now and it goes well!

Playing tennis and playing well; singles and doubles... sports training... throwing the weight as usual and seem to have lost the knack. or something

---

[211] Presumably starting from near Dowbiggin on the Rawthey, then turning into Hebblethwaite Beck, and then fishing up Hebblethwaite Beck.

[212] I did a bit of trout fishing up small rivers and ghylls but Sandy was an aficionado. In my last terms I did less in the way of long expeditions on the fells, preferring something like a journey over Holme Fell to the Sun Inn in Dent for high tea, then jogging back along the valley 5 miles or so in an hour for a second one in School House. But I had acquired a tremendously strong feeling of place by the time I reached the studies.

[213] Sandy and I were both great Bulldog Drummond fans, the James Bond of the times.

like that as I haven't had a standard for some time... and some cricket, in 1ˢᵗ league which is lighter hearted and more fun than school cricket.

Extra half on Friday and went with Granny Grant and Oliver up to Hebblethwaite and lounged around in the sun.

Field Marshall Alexander's inspection on Tuesday – I must say I'm getting rather fed up with all the blancoing and pressing and cleaning.

We have 6ᵗʰ form reports this weekend. We don't have any places and unless the reports are bad we don't hear anything. French going along ok and I seem to be regaining my stride. Doing lots of reading for my German vocab. – a long way to go to get to O level standards[214]....

Lupton House play Arms and the Man. It was terribly well done and most amusing...

... trying hurdling at 3'6"; throwing the weight a success by a new method, 1' over the standard and should be able to get up to over 2' over the standard[215].

S   Sunday 26ᵗʰ May 57

Thank you very much for the cutting. It is a pity Jeb cannot perform in the play[216]. It would have been such fun to see him. Did you say what the newspaper said you said?

The rod is a 3-piece. It is very short (8 ft). It is the one we found in the cellars on our way to Keisley when you stayed the night and hunted in the cellars for a kilt. The rod is very light and wonderfully bendy.

Do you remember the billiard table that was here in the hols when Dear Man and Dear were here; we used to play quite a lot. It was one quarter size. Whose is it? Do you think it is still here? And if it is, I think someone in the family should rescue it, don't you.

Lovely weather this week... Went fishing on Monday but caught nothing, and I waded in just above the Dee Watersmeet in the Rawthey but I put my foot down and fell into a deep hole; the water came right above my waist.

On Tuesday Alexander[217] is coming to inspect the Corps.

On Friday anyone who wanted to went to hear records in the HM Drawing room. About half the house went. I went and they played some cello thing and my favourite record again. It is the Tchakovskys Slow March. It was jolly good.

In form last week I was not 12ᵗʰ but 2ⁿᵈ out of 24. I don't think I am doing so well this fortnight.

---

[214] In the end I omitted O level and went straight on to take A level after four terms.

[215] I remember the method, which I learnt from a book and was theoretically pleasing but in practice difficult to execute well.

[216] Not clear what play – or why a wolfhound was required on stage.

[217] Field Marshall Lord Alexander.

I am still in the Bronze; it is a bit of a bore because we cannot go out on expeditions but it will be worth it in the end if I pass because 4 bronzes can go by themselves to a river bathe or to the ordinary [School Swimming] bath by ourselves.

On Friday there was an extra half. I went to Nor Gill with guys called Melville, Robertson, W-Jones, Whitman; we had super fun; we built dams and stalked wild sheep.

Thank you very much for taking my stop-watch to Gamadges; it was very kind of you. I think it would be ok here if you would not mind sending it. I will take great care of it and you can tell the chap[p]y at the shop that I certainly did not drop it and it has not been bashed around.

Are you going down to Chichester or anywhere house looking and have you heard anything about Alde-end[218].

I have played tennis every day this week; also swam a lot.

Can you tell me anything about next hols, David[219], Bemersyde, Murray Arms? Only 4 weeks till you come up.

J   29 May [Wednesday]

[Whole letter in French – pretty accurate and with reasonable vocab. Herewith translation:]

Spent most of the week fishing. Went up to Hebblethwaite but don't think there are any big fish left in the river.

Only played cricket once – bad weather, house seniors v juniors

Went up on the fells once, otherwise little in the way of exercise games.

Delighted you can come on 29 June. Pity we could not buy the sailing boat.

Went to see Dear Man's grave and the new tomb stone.

doing lots of French and hope to catch up the others soon..

Been made Treasurer of the Kingfisher[220]

Had civics on Friday and Canon Wickham spoke about missionary work in Sheffield – he spoke well with a strong Sheffield accent, and very vigorous and we enjoyed it – nous nous sommes bien amusés - Playing clarinet with Mr Reynell at his house on Sunday

---

[218] 'Aldeburgh' misremembered, where we had already holidayed.

[219] David Muir, my mother's cousin, on whose farm Sandy spent a year as a pupil before going to Cirencester Agricultural College.

[220] The School House magazine, of which I was, first, Treasurer and then Editor; the cover was printed in light and dark blue, being the School House colours. I recall the jobs being more duty than pleasure, especially the finance and advertising aspects.

J   3 June

[Opening remarks in German - not too bad in vocabulary and accuracy.]

Glad to hear you have made friends with the vicar[221] but a bit much asking you to do the gardening with Sally being ill and lots of visitors coming in...

[continued in English:]

Final rehearsal and then the Corps inspection by FM Alexander. Sweltering hot on the dress rehearsal - several collapsed and staggered off from standing still in the heat and one boy near me fell like a bomb.

The FM when he came was well pleased with our turn out and drilling and we got an extra half (not awarded yet) for it. I was drilling our section in mutual drill when Alexander came round but he only watched and never said anything.

Played house cricket but not so much tennis... glorious weather.

Work going ok I did quite a d. history essay and Horsy G was fairly pleased with my French essay. In German I'm back on doing exercises and lots of grammar.

PS: J. Laycock wants to know whether you want 1 or 2 copies of the Kingfisher.

S   2 June 57

Thank you for your letter. I will not go wading across rivers when the spate is coming down for I know it is very dangerous.

Jolly good you doing all that gardening when you know there is no point at all. I do think it is a pity having a friendly relationship because you get no pleasure out of being friendly with him or his wife[222].

On Tuesday was the General Inspection by Field Marshall Alexander. He came to lunch in School House. I was at the very senior end of the junior table so I was about 3 ft away and I could see all of his medals and things. He has nine rows of medals. He is rather a small sort of chap and all his chest is covered with ribbons and things. It was a terribly hot day and the Corps had to stand on the cricket pitch for 35 minutes without even moving an inch. About 15 chaps fainted from the heat, and one fell flat on his face and two were sick. Apart from that everything was super, especially the band. Alexander inspected every man, walking up and down each rank. He said the turn out was wonderful and better than some army turn outs.

I am still in the bronze and can now bathe without a prefect or master if there are 6 of us. So we bathe in our long break nearly every day. They have also changed the time from Sunday afternoon to Tuesday or

---

[221] The Vicar of St Mary Abbotts', Kensington, and our landlord at 1 Vicarage Gate.
[222] The Vicar

Thursday which means we can go out with a pack lunch on a Sunday which 4 of us are doing today.

I am playing cricket like anything but I got off yesterday to play tennis and another bloke played instead of me.

On Monday we played and were bowling to a much stronger side than us. They slammed 4 off every ball even off our Panters bowlers. There was one more over and 3 runs to get. I was bowling. My first ball I pitched as far to the off as possible so the batsman couldn't hit it; he snicked it and it was dropped by slip; the second he got a run, the third he just hit and was dropped again, the 4th he missed and the 5th I did a straight one and bowled him; the sixth I did a super fast one; it flew over the batsman's head, the wicket keeper missed it and 3rd man missed it and they ran 3 runs, so we lost by one run.

Sorry this is late, it is now Sunday evening. We went out onto the fells. It turned out to be a lovely day so we went to Cautley spout then to Beckside Gill.[223] We took pack lunches and started at 12 o'clock. We reached Calf at exactly two minutes to One. We had lunch by Cautley Spout; my cake fell down a little rock into the pool; it didn't really matter as it was not a lovely cake. We then climbed about by the spout. We then went to Beckside Gill and back by the road stopping at some café place to have a drink (only water – we had no money with us). We mucked about in the Rawthey and then arrived back here at 5.15. It was great fun.

This week I don't know where I am in work but I don't think it was as high as second.

I am playing tennis with Jamie in the House doubles which should be fun.

I am going to stop now and write to Hugo[224].

J   9 June 57

... How annoying about the rudder. I do hope we find it soon. Has Dad got the right mast?

Thanks for the copy of Yachts and Yachting – interesting supplement. In our study we get the National Geographic, New Statesman, Sunday Times, Observer and Sunday Express – so we have a pretty hefty pile.

Do you want us to do any booking of rooms for when you come up?

Speech Day next weekend and there's continual rehearsals for the Musical Society, orchestra, speaking for speeches and chapel. The 29th June is OS day with all kinds of matches and things going on.

I seem to have wrenched my thigh muscles at the beginning of the week and seem to re-pull it every time when I go on to bowl, so I've been off-ex

---

[223] The ghyll immediately to the East (and North) of Cautley Beck and the Cross Keys
[224] Hugo Rowbotham, good friend of Sandy's at the Dragon School.

these last two days. I made top scores in the league games this week – 14 and 23 not out (not such terribly good scores actually)

I've been doing quite a bit of practising for the wind competition. I'm playing a Brahms Sonata and Ronny is accompanying me. I have enormous fun playing with him on Sundays, I was asked to join the jazz band but it is bang in the middle of the afternoon and although the HM knows it exists, it is illegal or something. Ward in our house was asked as well to play the piano[225] – and he didn't join up. I was asked to be 2nd clarinet. I think I will next term if there's a place but not this.[226] I have too much on my hands.

I did a free prose [in German] with the rest of the class. French seems to be going ok. I think I will soon be up with them..

Not much going on. Haven't done much reading this term – except one Sapper! Up to now I've had a pretty good average, of 32 books per term, but I just haven't had time.

Haven't done nearly so much gramophone record listening this term – which is probably a good thing because it grows on one and becomes a kind of fever.

S   9th June 57

Thank you for the photos. They are very good, especially the ones of Sally and Penny [Dear's dog]. And also the Yachts and yachting it was very 'd' of you to send it.

This week has been very usual, nothing unusual at all except an extra half on Monday. This was because of Lord FM Alexander, also because of him we have an extra day on the hols, so we go back on the 20th of September instead of the 19th which is jolly 'd'. Next week is Speech Day week. The school are doing Joan of Arc for a play.

This morning I was terribly keen and so for the first time in a year 7 of us, 5 of our term and 2 others, persuaded a Prefect to take an early morning swim 7.15-7.45. It is jolly good fun once you have actually got up for no one else gets up till 1 ½ hours afterwards. The water was very warm indeed but I swallowed too much I think, by being ducked. We all have great fun ducking everyone else. It is super fun for you see a chap say 10 yards away in the water you dive in and come up about a foot away from him and opposite his waist, then you duck him take a deep breath and swim away under water and hope by the time he comes up you are miles

---

[225] Charlie Ward was a good player of swing and jazz on the piano.

[226] Music was taking an increasing part of my time. In the house there were three music practice cubicles with a piano in each which were quite well used. In earlier years I felt a bit embarrassed about practising the clarinet by itself in an empty room, but in the middle years I began to play duets (clarinet and piano) or learn piano pieces, with others. I remember working at Bach's Toccata and Fugue in D, Jesu Joy of Man's Desiring, Sheep May Safely Graze and a few other classical pieces with friends who played at advanced levels.

away. But quite often he sees you coming and when you come up he ducks you.

A chap in our form in Evans house has been sent away, and he is mad; he was caught in pyjamas and corps boots about to inspect the corps. Br Bishop says he is about to have a nervous breakdown and has gone home.

On Tuesday I played cricket for 3rd leagues (there are 4 leagues); 1st is for the normal older ones; 2nd for the bad older ones; and 3rd is for the normal younger ones, 4th for the bad younger ones – though most people play on both (1st and 2nd or 3rd and 4th). Anyhow I took 6 wickets for 15 runs and I bowled at one end every over of the game.

Yesterday I played fives with Jamie and one of his pals and one of mine.

I have read 6 saint books so far this term

What should I do about Granny's birthday, letter, card or present?

On Tuesday we had a bronze practice; this time we learnt about respiration

Has David written yet? What sort of shooting will we get at Murray Arms, might we be able to take Ruth's 22 as well. I would be perfectly prepared to pay for all the bullets for it. Will we be able to go up into this hut affair for 2 or 3 days?

S   ?16 June 57

Thank you very much for the letter and the stop watch which arrived yesterday.

I am so glad your party went well; the food sounds delicious. I hope we have one when we are at home. Here is it baking, absolutely scorching hot for the last few days.. Yesterday and the day before the swimming baths were closed so we couldn't swim, so I have been drinking booze bottle after booze bottle I have gone rather mad about potato crisps with lots of salt; so the only thing I spend money on at the grubber is booze and crisps, never chocolate

I am so glad we can go down to David's when J is away.

This fortnight I am 16th out of 24, I am 4th in French, 2nds in Geog, 9th in History, 9th in Latin and 9th in my form in Maths, but 21st in English (the top chap gets in all subjects about 180, 50 of these are English and I only got 1 in English. I think I should have got more, so I am -49.

I don't see why I am only 16th, my essays have few spelling mistakes (I look in a dictionary) but we had a terrible dictation from Dickens with millions of words I had never heard of before.

Then I wrote a poem (that was told to be stupid and nonsense in aa, bb, aa, bb of 12 lines). It is a change from Wordsworth's My heart leaps up when I behold a rainbow in the sky. Mine starts

> My heart leaps up when I behold
> An omlet on a plate;
> So it was when my life began

Apart from Eggs and boiled ham
It always was my favourite course
Especially with some HP Sauce.

I thought this jolly good but I don't think he did.

When you come up could you bring a bottle (like one of Sally's orange ones [sketch], not the thing she drinks out of, the one you buy it in - because it would be handy for an extra half or a river bathe or something.

This week I have worked every reading prep, but I have finished our Form book which we have to read by half term; it was 'Brazilian Adventure'. It is quite good but it is a pretty cranky idea writing a book about a party that goes out to find Fawcett and only shoots alligators when it is me[a]nt to be adventure and exploration. The next half of term we have to read 'Jayne Eyre' *[sic]*. If it is anything as boring as Withering Heights *[sic]* it is the worst book in the world.

On Monday the Brad Lads came so we had a cricketing half. I played in the nets which is great fun. How did you get on at Ockley?[227] Was it good fun? Tell me all about it.

Yesterday we got up at 8.30, then chapel, then speeches. The HM made a very good one. The Principal of Studies of the Academy (Sir Albert someone) came as the guest. He asked for a holiday for the school Then Bracken asked HM to say something about a holiday but we have already had one this term because of Alexander.

The concert was really good. They did Joan of Arc and it was excellent.

We won the Panters first house match. I am not on this year, but am still young enough next year. I should get on quite easily

You have rooms in the Bull for 28th, 29th and 30th. Will Daddy and me travel to Scotland by car and Mummy by rail with Sally?

I am still in the Bronze. On Sunday we went from 1.30 to 4.45. It was boiling hot, the river was lovely. It has never been warmer.

J   1957, Jun 18th [Tuesday]

I was talking to Mr Gairdner about what I should do to catch up my French in the way of reading etc, and he said pretty well straight away that going to France on my own would be the thing really.

He went on about what about next hols, and I told him about Uncle Robin and Sicily. We discussed possibilities... He said he might be able to help find somewhere. So I'm writing to see what you think. I think

a)   a swop of house and home is pretty well ruled out
b)   is a paying guest any better?
c)   not next hols. I want to be home some time

---

[227] My father returned for an annual cricket fixture (which he had originally set up) between a FO scratch side and the Ockley village team - who normally fixed the opposition by inviting them to generous pints of Kentish scrumpy before the match started.

d)   it's an opportunity

e)   I'd much rather you decided and you can see him when you are up here.

I shouldn't think S would find much fun in having a froggie at home for the hols.

J   23 June [Sunday]

What an intellectual time you're having [no explanation]

Nice to have gone down to Ockley again and see all the people there.

I think it by far the most sensible idea not to do anything about going to France these holidays

The term is now off on its second run. With no speech day preparations we've done some much nicer pieces in orchestra, and I'm working pretty hard at the Brahms for the woodwind competition.

Three weeks before sports – which means training in the afternoons, less cricket and tennis and more quiet reading and working in the afternoons – a usual mixture this week. We had an extra half on Weds and I went river bathing and river-bathed last Sunday and Monday too. It has been absolutely glorious and the water warm, and my throat and nose has been peeling.

I've been promoted in Op German sets, at the end of last week and I now get 'Bish' Bishop three more times per week than before.

On Friday we had the first film of the term. It was a new projector and screen but the reels still crackled although the sound was much better. It was Dam Busters. I thought it was terribly good and the news and cartoon were better than usual.

I do envy you going to the test match. Not much else going on. I've tried to read Simenon in French, and I've putted a bit on the School House lawn - pretty fast by the end of the week.

S   June 23rd 57

It must have been lovely at the Test Match on Friday. I Hope it is ok on Monday because there will be a big 'do' for the Queen.

It has been wonderfully hot until Saturday; on Sunday I went for a river bathe about twenty of us went. It was boiling hot, both the river and the temperature. I took my stop watch and nearly everyone had goes to try and stay under water the longest. Mr Durran can stay under for 49 seconds; a boy stayed under for 49 seconds as well. That was the record most people do about 23 seconds, J and I can only do about 18 (me about 15) though I don't think there is much point in trying too hard, because I know what happened when I tried too hard in America (I got funny old headaches). I Hope we will be able to swim in the hols a lot & can we swim in the Tweed and the river at Murray Arms? Will we be able to stay at Keisley for a day or so. What river do we fish in at the Murray Arms. Is it the Dee?[228]

If you have five minutes to spare could you go into our room and get my blue goggles (for under water) from the wooden box; they will be at the bottom of that. (If by chance they aren't don't bother to look anywhere else). Could you bring them in the back of the car?

The HM has just called all of us in individually from the thirds. He wants to know (if we get into the 4ths) whether we will take Latin or Geography (Group A) and German or Greek with History (Group B). We have to take one of each group so when you come up on Friday we must decide.

On Wednesday there was the 3rd and last Extra half. We might get one more because the last one was in honour of Sir Albert.

A great pity the game against Ockley is on the 2nd. Could it be in September?

Yesterday afternoon I played in a net with 3 other types. It was an off day, so it was voluntary. It is great fun playing in the nets.

On the extra half I went for a river bathe at Lune's Viaduct. It is a wonderful place and there are many fish in some of the pools; you can dive right down and swim nearly up to them. It is not very good if you have no goggles as you can not see clearly, though if you have goggles you can see as clear as in underwater films, the rocks towering up on your side and fish hiding in cracks. It is really wonderful fun.

On Tuesday I went for a bathe also but had to come tearing back because I had 'four sides' to do for leaving bathing things in the gym. I had to write them on birds. It has to be four sides exactly, every line, no margin, no paragraphs. It took me only 70 mins and I copied nearly all out of a bird book. I was given it by a School Prefect in Powell House and according to a guy in the Junior Dayroom in the 5th he said he could see the School Prefect reading it and pulling the most terrible faces and frowning awfully; he has said nothing to me about it.

Last Sunday evening we went up Winder and were caught ragging, which is very much forbidden on Winder on Sunday evenings; again we were caught by a School Prefect who is head of School House as well, and again nothing has happened.

At the moment I am listening to the Arrival of the Queen of Sheba by Handel on family favourites, which is terribly unusual for the programme.

On Friday there was a film show, the first of this term. They have bought a new cine projector and a new screen and a new sound box affair. They now play gramophone records before and after and between reels. It is jolly good. The film was the Dambusters which is very good but very sad really with all the bad tests and his dog being killed and then he is sad and cross with himself for inventing the bomb and getting all that many men

---

[228] The Fleet was the river at Gatehouse; but the hotel had fishing rights on other rivers too.

killed. There is no rejoicing just Gibson writing letters to the mothers of the killed and the mess with over half the planes empty, The Rooms and beds and clocks still ticking away etc,. The cartoon was very funny indeed though the news was not very interesting.

Next Saturday is probably an off day so we will not be playing cricket. Only 5 days till you come which is jolly 'd'.

J   4 July 57 [Thursday]
[kept with S's letter of the same date (below) in the one and the same envelope by MEBL]

Thank you very very very much for such a wonderful weekend and for all you did to make it such an enjoyable holiday. I've never had so much fun going out in the middle of the term. Thank you very much indeed for the tins and the sweets and 5/-, all of which come in more than useful particularly at this stage of term.

We have been swizzed of 10/- for the balloons, but seeing that it is a church fund etc we'd better leave it at that – but S thinks it is a v. bad thing that a church cause should chiz us and intends to write I think.

There were the second round house matches yesterday. I made one top score or 20 which was a big surprise. I had quite a good day altogether for although I didn't bowl I caught 3 catches, two rather natty ones at short square leg.

Not much else has happened since you left. Ronny Reynell and Mr Whiteside both want me to pay different pieces in the wind competition. I haven't had much practising time lately but I'm going to play the Brahms Sonata in F, or maybe it's in Eb, I dunno, which Ronny wants me to play.

Only 4 weeks now.

S   4 July 57
Thank you very very much indeed for the really lovely weekend, and for the goggles which work jolly well and the grub.

Today is Field Day and we asked the HM for permission to go on bikes to Windermere to go to the Lake. But the HM said no but he would take us himself to anywhere we wanted by car and we could come back ourselves. If it stops raining we will go to the Moorcock [Inn] 5 miles E of Baugh Fell and then on foot to Baugh Fell and Uldale Force and Cautley. It is very 'd' of the HM to take us 12 miles by car.

Yesterday I took 6 wickets for 12 runs, 5 of the 12 were from overthrows (for 4 overs we had no wicket keeping gloves). I did not bat.

I will write a long letter on Sunday

115

Only 3 ½ weeks till we come home and we will probably come on the early train, but we are not allowed to leave the house before 7 so it might be difficult.

Thank you very much again for such an enjoyable weekend.

PS The Balloon people wrote back and said we only get 10/- if our balloon got further.[229]

J   July 7ᵗʰ 57 [Sunday]

Bournemouth sounds most fun for Sally and for you as well after London. I hope there isn't too much of a holiday crowd there.

Quite a successful week at sport this last week. In the House match on Thursday; I got top score and 3 catches. On Friday a hit a 3ʳᵈ XI bowler for a 6 and took 5 wickets for 7 runs. I also won the final heat of the House breaststroke – and did the fastest Middle 220 (under 16 ½) in 26.5 beating a second who did 27.3

A bit of training and clarinet... Terribly close weather and stuffy.

Field Day. After having gone in a cattle truck which only just got up Scots Jeans we went miles out over the Kendal moor. As usual training before and then a battle. The Lithuanian People's Army (us) v. the Sedbergh Sharpshooters. The kick off was an hour and a half late – boiling sun, and clegs everywhere and everyone fed up.

As soon as we saw the enemy advancing Jake, an umpire (school house tutor) leapt over a wall and flung thunder flashes at us and informed us that we were wiped out by mortar. The battle raged for another hour and a bit and we joined in again after 50 minutes of death, watching over a wall. Eventually we got back to school after 8½ hours.

Only 3 weeks to go now and end of term things come into action.

S   'Sunday 6 July ' [either Saturday 6ᵗʰ or Sunday 7th] 1957

I hope you are well and enjoying Bournemouth. When are you going to America and for how long? It will be lovely, especially the voyage out there by sea.

On Thursday it was Field Day. It poured till 8 o'clock, after that it was a lovely day. We (Robertson, Wilding Jones) went to the Moorcock. First Mr Thornely drove us there by car. It is an inn about 12 miles out on the Hawes Road; it is 4 ½ miles from Baugh Fell. We then climbed right up on to Baugh Fell and across the top to the Trig Point Top (2216') and had lunch by a tarn (jam and marge bun – I had two we took 4 pack lunches and shared them between us, one piece of Christmas cake with icing I pork pie, 6 spam sandwiches and an apple. We saw great amounts of baby

---

[229] A charity event, see below.

grouse on the top of Baugh Fell, 5 of them got up about a yard from us. There were millions of curlew and one seagull with its nest in a tarn.

We then went to Uldale Force, a water fall on the back of Baugh Fell. On our way down we were passing a cliff edge near a gill when about 20 yards away a buzzard flew out of the cliff. We went down to see if it had a nest and about 6 feet below us was a big nest with 2 eggs in it. The bird was absolutely whacking. I remember buzzards in Germany but they did not seem half as big as this, we all thought it was an eagle. We saw it coming back to the nest and as we were about 6 ft away from the nest we ran off quickly because we thought it would attack. One of the house pres (Laycock) was once attacked by a buzzard. We saw it miles high in the sky circling above its nest. We thought it must be an eagle, also when it flew off the nest it looked like an eagle; but everyone says there are no eagles around here so it must have been a buzzard.

We then went to Uldale Force and then to the Cross Keys then back by the road. We drank gallons of booze at the Cross keys and staggered back to Sedbergh and arrived back at School House a 6.20 .We went 12 miles by car and 15 up and down on foot; it was the best Field Day yet.

You probably wonder why the HM took us. Well we went along to ask for permission to go by bike to Windermere; he said 'No', but he would take us by car and he said what do you want to do there so we said go in a boat and have tea. So he said No! Then he said he would take us anywhere else by car, so he took us to the Moor Cock. Jolly 'd' of him.

I hope to go fishing with Harvey on Tuesday.

The Bronze exam is next Saturday. I can do all the water stuff easily but it is hard to learn about the heart and the names of all the pipes and valves and things. The Doctor gave us a talk about it on Friday.

Last night it thundered. It has been beautifully hot for the last few days..

Do you think you could write to the Balloon people and demand 10/-. It is a church society but they started swindling and then saying they would give you 10/- if you entered the balloon. They don't say they might give you 10/- , they say they would. So I think I will demand 10/-.

Has Ruth replied yet whether she can have us for 2 days or so?

I hope you like your present from me and J. I hope it arrives all right.

S   10 July 57 [Wednesday]

Many happy returns of the day and best wishes for the year. I hope the present is all right.

Yesterday I went fishing with Harvey. He taught me; then we went to a pool. He told me how to approach it and how to fish it. Then he stood on the bank and I went out to the pool. Then I caught a 1 and a ½ lb trout (1 ½ lbs). It was a lovely fish. It pulled the reel out with a wirrrrrr! I had it for tea and it was lovely.

J   14ᵗʰ July

Glad you liked the snails. I do hope they were good[230]. What a wonderful present from Dad. We'll be able to push Sally along and watch you ride down the Row[231].

Much rain. Buskholme all muddy and track awful, No one's going to get any standards if this keeps on. Cricket is over and I've been playing squash and training [for the sports]. Might get a standard for the half (2.26), but the quarter (62) is too fast I fear.

Squash scores... Swimming... took part in the senior short race. Got 3ʳᵈ, a decent place ,in the senior breaststroke heat but the winner was doing 41 (school record 39.7). I did 42.6 which made it seem not too bad.

Working fiendishly at the beginning of the week for French and German - and recreating my mind with a break from literature with Bulldog Drummond.

Music practice...

S   Sunday 14ᵗʰ July 57

I am glad the snails arrived ok. I am glad they tasted ok

I have just got leave for an early morning swim. It is jolly warm once you get in, though not so nice getting up early.

Yesterday I passed my Bronze exam. In the morning (long Break) we each had to swim round the bath in turn, twice round breast stroke, then without stopping twice round on your back with your arms folded. That is very easy. I was, for no special reason, first on the list, so I did everything first. Then we had to do a duck dive, with feet like this [sketch showing lower leg protruding vertically from the water]; and pick up a brick – which I found the hardest of all. I can go down but not keep my feet together or straight. Anyhow I just passed. Then he picked six chaps to do resuscitation. I was one of the six. It was fairly easy. Then in the afternoon we had to rescue a chap and pull him the length of the pool four different ways. My partner was Melville – who is 6 ins taller than me. When I rescued him he thought he was rescuing me so we both splashed around trying to rescue each other, then he realized. How the examiner did not see I don't know (4 pairs do it at the same time). Everyone passed except 3 chaps. One was Johnny Gairdner (son of Mr Gairdner)

The sports are next week. I am a Middle, i.e. over 15 by the end of term. Middle cannot go in for the quarter mile, high jump and they have the same 100 yd standard as the seniors and the half mile standard is 4 seconds slower (2.32 instead of 2.28). The weight and discus are the same

---

[230] Ordered by mail as I recall.
[231] The present was a set of riding sessions at a Rotten Row stables.

as the senior. So my only chance of a standard[232] is in the half mile, which is unlikely.

The opera you went to sounds terrific. It is a pity that Jeb wasn't there. It certainly was a nice present you, Dad, gave Mum. It will be wonderful fun riding in the park on London's best horses; you must ride in the hols so we can take photos of you charging down Rotten Row with all the dust and sand flying out behind. You could even ride to the round Pond and round to our garden – I can just imagine the vicar.[233] You will probably meet some horsey people and probably some nice ones, which would be good.

The term's work has finished only Exams left which count as 2 fortnights. I think I have done rather well this last fortnight; I got 40 more marks than the one before in English, Latin, Geog and History combined.

I had a wonderful fun with Harvey on Tuesday. It was jolly 'd' of him. Apparently he told the fly tying class about it on Wednesday. He was very pleased and he kept on saying to me 'Well you'll have something to tell your dad about.' And he told me about fishing with other members of the family. And the person who takes woodwork was enquiring about Logie, Paddy, Rab and Dear.

I think I better stop and write to Dear.

J   16th July [Tuesday]

We have booked the rooms for 3 nights and that is all ok. I expect the HM will want to see you but he'll probably be pretty busy over the OS weekend. I'm jolly glad you didn't come up for speech day weekend – the place was crowded out and anyway with house matches there's no time to go out on Saturday – and the concert in the evening.

Actually the concert and the play (the trial scene from St Joan of Arc) were pretty good this year and so were the speeches. Sir Albert Richardson spoke most amusingly and Brendan B and the HM both pretty well.

House matches – all the details... Glorious weather.... I got through a round of the singles tournament but S and I not having played by the required time have to trust to the fall of a coin.

I showed a couple of blokes around the school on Thursday one of the 2,000 per annum prospective parents.

Sir Albert R gave us an extra half and we had our third this term. Otherwise, Speech day, with all the practising etc, took up all the time this week, which I find rather boring.

---

[232] Standards were set by age groups for all track and field events, allowing interhouse competition in athletics on a basis of general representation, not just according to winners of the finals.

[233] The Kensington Vicarage had its own back gate giving onto Millionaires' Row with direct access through to Kensington Park.

J   21 July [Sunday]

Terrific storms and bad weather. The Achilles match[234] had to stop in the middle of the afternoon because of pelting rain, Even so we saw a bloke cover the hurdles in a second under the school record and saw the discus being thrown 140 ft odd. They walked away from us in the 100 despite a handicap and it was in general a really rather wizard exhibition[235].

Had a rather nasty boil on the left arm and the underneath of the arm was all red and swollen. Had plaster poltus [poultice] which was helpful – the doc suggested I should have proper hot poultice with antibiotics. I think it must have been too hot because the next morning not only had it drawn a lot of pus but there were whacking blisters about ½" high. However the swelling is going down now although my arm aches quite a bit still.

It didn't seem to worry my sports... I failed a standard in hurdles, got one in the weight. Came first in the ½ mile heat quite easily but missed a standard. Went first in the 220 relay, and beat the others to the handover. We came 2ⁿᵈ, but in the final Sedgwick broke the record.

In the quarter I got boxed out, but then managed to overtake 5 chaps to come 2ⁿᵈ in 59.3 the standard being 62 secs. That means I get through a round.

Wind competition after chapel. No one was expecting it to be held at this weekend and it's rather a bore, I can only tootle and do my best.

S   Sunday 21 July 57

When you say I will not be seeing Dear next hols, I presume we will see her at Bemersyde, or is she going to the Logies?

On Tuesday there was a sports match, Sedbergh v. Achilles Club; I enclose a programme. Only two things really impressed me; one was the discus, the other the hurdles. The way the chap just glided over the hurdles was fantastic – something like this [sketch of stick man figure hurdling low]. The chap who bunged the weight was pathetic. It only went about 40 ft - though it was a 16lb one..

And in the half mile the two Achilles chaps just paced our chaps round and did it in 2 mins 7 seconds. I was very disappointed for I expected to see them going round as fast as they could but the men just looked as though they were trotting. They did not run the mile or a quarter because of a thunderstorm. On Tuesday was the start of our sports. I did my half mile in 2. 37. The standard is 2.32. I was angry with myself for not going just that little bit harder. Jamie did very well and came 1ˢᵗ in his heat. The rest of the sports are on Thursday and Saturday.

---

[234] A joint universities scratch team for field and track events who visited various schools to compete, demonstrate and encourage.
[235] Sandy, in his letter, was more critical.

I think with Uncle Robin's £1 and Aunty Kay's 10/- I might buy a spinning reel or do you think those are very bad? Then I could try a bit of spinning on the Tweed and at the Murray arms, then if there were no fish taking fly I could try spinning; or do you think the whole idea is very un-Bruce Lockhart to spin for trout etc.

Today we are going fishing straight after lunch – up the Gills, Thrush Gill, Ashbeck Gill[236].

Next Monday evening there is a film. It is supposed to be either 'High Society' or 'The King and I', the court Jester, which I have already seen twice. Still I would enjoy seeing it again as it is a wonderful film

What does Ruth say? Can we stay there for two days or so or is she away

Has anything happened about a house yet?

I am in the third round of the Tennis singles but I have now to play the best chap in the house.

On Friday we played water polo. There were 8 of us (Bronzes) It was great fun. We got all the water polo goals out and a water polo ball. It is great fun.

I took 3 wickets for about 10 runs on Wednesday.

J Postcard at end of term
End July 1957

End of term exams in full swing. Came bottom in English I regret to say. Came 6th in form overall. French 'very creditable'. Don't know other results yet. Mr Bishop was pleased with my German...

Wind competition. Not placed 1st or 2nd; don't know more than that.

In the sports I'm afraid I got no further.

Nothing tomorrow but a film; and then the concert. Compulsory for the school though the Programme still claims 'voluntary'.

Be seeing you on Tuesday.

S Sunday 28th July 57

Very bad weather... Every day of the sports it has bucketed down; and every day the rain has stopped the sports and we cannot go back to the house till exercise finishes. On Friday which was a sports day and I was not in for anything, I played fives and swam. The people doing or watching sports on Buskholme stood in a cloudburst – they could see it approaching across the rugger fields about 100 yards away and it was not even drizzling where they stood. It rained the hardest I have ever seen.

Last Sunday two other boys of my term and myself went fishing up Nor Gill. We went to try and catch them in our hands. You see them in the

---

[236] Ashbeck is East of Winder, coming down between Crook and Sickers.

pools then walk in and notice under which rock they went, then put your hands under and pull them out. It was ok till I put my hands under but when I felt the fish it gave me such a shock that the fish swam away between my legs; it really gives you the most awful shock as you feel it.

Exams were this week and final orders came out yesterday. Last term I was 15th; this term I am 10th (out of 23). So I have moved up 5 places. The only question now is which 4th form I get into – 4a, 4b, 4c, 4d. (4a is for scholars; all the other 4th forms are supposed to be equal but they aren't.) I want to get into 4c because they have the best masters for Physics and Chemistry easily, but I might get into 4b or 4d. I am beating 3 others of my term and lower than one other.

Here are the final places

French	15/23	in 2nd top set
Maths	10/23	bottom of set, but it is the top set
Geography	9 /23	
History	9 /23	
Latin		10 /23
English	13 /23	

I will bring back all the exam question places and all my own answer papers.

Ruth wrote to me (a postcard) to say she will be able to have Dad and me to stay. It came from somewhere in Germany.

I have been playing lots of fives this week, also swimming, our bronze badges have arrived and they look swish

I have read this month 'Diving to Adventure' 'Pompey's private army'; 'Trout fishing on beck and stream', 'Leashed guns', 'Of their own choice' and various short stories.

The film tomorrow is The Court Jester, with Danny Kaye. I have seen it twice already but it will still be fun. And there is a concert this evening. It is a less serious one, and should be good.

Next term I should be in the senior Dayroom unless I am still a head.[237] But all my pals are going up probably, so I hope I will not be a head.

Packing this afternoon. I have had all the clothes washed so I will have a record good trunk I hope.

---

[237] One head, usually 3rd Head, used to stay on in the Junior Dayroom to the next term, as 1st head, in order to take charge of the new academic year's intake in their first term.

Chapter 4:   September 1957 to July 1958

J   22 September 57 [Sunday]

The main news is that I'm not going to take O level German this term – or ever. The HM is putting me straight on so I don't miss a term pottering away on O level.

We've got the study fixed nicely and it is really very gay. It's a much nicer study than the lower treble. It has far more light and has been completely decorated since we have lots of odd bits of material and quite a few pictures.

I caught terrible hay fever at the beginning of term from dust - cushions carpets etc but it is going off now. Dank and drizzle weather has not helped.

Work started with an A level French prose – a bit of a stinker but I've managed to get most of it done. ... I am doing a Fantastic amount of work, using every spare minute, long breaks, after breakfast, after ex etc to get done all the reading, proses, unseens, essays. Mr Bishop is keeping me at it with the O level standard work. No results yet...

I'm afraid I'm on Littleside II – all the 2nd Colts XV there – which is something and I'm trying fiendishly to get up a game. We've only had one game so far but lots of practising and short sprint, because of the flu..

I seem to be climbing up the house now. I am in short break PT[238] (7 or 8 only from each house) and 3rd best fives player in the house and having to coach new boys.

Am on top table now which is pretty superior[239] but unfortunately I have to start the skivving which is a v, complicated affair, as there's only one chap.

Thanks for wonderful hols...

---

[238] It seems that candidates to play in senior school teams took additional PT during the 25 minute mid-morning break, presumably to get fit again after the summer holidays.

[239] A special feature of life in the last terms was lunch at the top table with Michael and Jennifer Thornely. Senior prefects sat next to them and were expected to converse, entertain and answer questions. They were grown up affairs, and conversation could be on any subject from light politics, civics to house affairs, personal interests etc.. Mrs Thornely had been rather withdrawn in her first years – with a brother in the house, perhaps not surprising - but by now she had grown accustomed to her role and the house, with which she had only little to do, and had a warm personality. We were also expected to entertain Thornely's guests, governors, grandees, visiting clerics, lecturers, musicians. That was fun and Thornely was at his best on these occasions. He was witty, and a showman – and he would almost wink at us behind their backs having tipped us off as to what they would be like – and afterwards have an amusing round up on what they had had to say or how they performed.

S   22 Sept 57

Thank you very much indeed for giving us such a lovely holidays; I really enjoyed it enormously.

We had a very good journey up here and arrived about five. I am in the Senior Dayroom and I am in the cubes but they have knocked down about 10 cubes and put 13 people into the space making it a dormitory. There are five people below me in this dorm so I would easily have got a cube and I think it is jolly bad luck that they have been knocked down.

Yesterday I played fives twice and swam once. We went fives training in the afternoon with a prefect; there is only one place left on Junior Fives because all last year's team except one are still young enough. The swimming pool was very warm, 75 degrees, that is 5 degrees higher than the RAC highest[240] and 5 degrees warmer than its average.

Do you think it would be ok if I swopped to German instead of History. Reasons:

- I would prefer to learn German
- If you take history you do 3 lessons of history a week and 3 of Art; if you do German you do 6 German lessons a week
- I would never get an O level history but I could take an O level German as an Option 2 in 2 years' time having dropped it for one year in the Fifth.
- I am much better at French than history (I am in the second top French set out of 5).

If you disapprove of this idea, can you let me know immediately because I think I will go and see the HM about it today.

Also I don't know what you think about this idea: I know it is a long way ahead but Melville and I thought of hiking somewhere probably in Scotland for about a week in the Easter of Summer hols. We have been planning it for about 2 terms now. We thought the best was to go when J was at camp next summer or in Germany at Easter.

Thank you for sending my tie, and garters. My sponge bag is here (in the bottom of my case.

Don't forget to tell us your new job.[241]

J   Sep 1957 [Sunday 29th perhaps]

There is a terrific epidemic on throughout the school at the moment. I hear that in fact we are not suffering too badly compared with Rossall and some other schools. The san was filled very quickly and up to this moment Powell House only have about 20 chaps left; we have lost 23 and Lupton

---

[240] Indoor heated swimming pool at the RAC Club, Pall Mall, where we had been made junior members for the holidays.
[241] With responsibilities, and extensive travel, in Africa as well as the Middle East

about the same. Rugger has had to be cancelled, lower cubes evacuated etc. Singing in the chapel will be very weak I can see[242].

I won't bore you with the detail because I expect S will tell you, but the usual symptoms are burning hot feet, convulsions of the stomach, quivering hands, blood red eyes with a streaming cold and stiff neck. Sometimes the muscles get paralyzed and in fact one chap was whizzed into hospital.

I suppose you believed all that Hee! hee!

I'm feeling extraordinarily fit, playing lots of games – squash, fives. Our new assistant house tutor is the ex runner-up national fives champion of GB. We played with him and were absolutely licked. He makes the game seem terribly easy. Played more squash for 1/- a game – and won, phew!

One rugger game – the detail...

Two of us Sugden and I were bunged upstairs into the empty cubicles as everyone was being moved around– I had a small bed and short mattress, and woke up absolutely freezing.

Talked to the HM about university. He had just been down at Cambs talking to tutors. He said don't worry about College. They are basically only taking scholars – you'll be lucky to get in. I asked about Worcester – and Masterman. He thought that was the thing – particularly with one subject specialisation and doing French with backing of German for the schol.. It would be a terrific bore if I failed my A level this year but not an inextricable problem. Failing all else, St Andrew's of course.

He said he would write to Masterman. He said to keep him up to the £20 odd fund for travel abroad. There's a challenge.

Working hard at the German and hope I don't get bogged down by flu for a week.

S   no date 57 [probably 29 September, Sunday]

I feel strongly about German so I have started it. It is great fun and I'm sure I will come higher in the set than in History, I forget if I told you that if I take German I get 20 more marks a fortnight more than History and so if

---

[242] This was a factual statement, but underpinned I think by further thoughts. My enjoyment in later years of school chapel (and house evening services, but not school morning assembly) worked at several dimensions. One was a feeling for place: the chapel was right beside School House and we walked through its grounds several times every day. Then music, religion and tribe were all subsumed in the experiences of divine services, and especially the singing, in chapel. Confirmation (in my second year) and attendance at early morning communion strengthened the religious element. There was a family dimension too: Dear Man's memorial service was held in the School chapel and he was buried in the cemetery beside Buskholme playing fields. Daily proximity to the cloisters just below the School buildings, a memorial to those who fell in the two Great Wars (with a separate memorial for four Old Sedberghian VC holders) reinforced a patriotic dimension. There were no official services held there, but it is a peaceful place (with a stunning view) through which we walked often enough.

I do well in German I will gain an extra few places in form order; then I am more likely to get into the 5th next year.

Physics and Chemistry are terrific fun. I am 3rd in the chemistry marks so far and we have not had any physics back. We have Mr Taylor for physics and Mr Mawby for chemistry. Both are very good teachers.

On Tuesday there was a shooting trial for chaps in the corps in School House with .22s. We had 5 shots grouping, 5 shots at the bull and 5 at targets that bobbed up. I got 80 out of 80 which is absolute A top and there was nothing phoney about it because it was pretty serious with RSM in charge.

I have played rugger four times this week, three times on house games and once on Colts A3. I played wing forward and three quarter. I scored one try playing on Colts A3.

I have been playing fives every half day this week. I think it is a great game and there are five of us, one from the term before us and the others all in my term who enjoy fives greatly, and I can always get a game when I want.

On Friday I played with 2 of last year's Junior fives and Mr Rogers who was the English Singles Fives champion 3 years ago and the English runner-up in the doubles. He is pretty good and can hit the ball very hard and he kept on hitting me with the ball because I did not get down quick enough, so Ward the prefect in charge of fives has forbidden me to play for three days in case I get a thing about being hit (Ward was watching the whole game). But two others I was going to play with managed to persuade him to let me play. We had a terrific argument and we won. But I cannot play for two days now.

Also I have been playing squash a lot and have done some practising by myself. I played Jamie last night and beat him.

Asian flu has caught the school. We have about 30 in School House in bed; chaps are popping off to bed everywhere. Powell have 40 away and Lupton about 38, and 25 in Evans and 20 n the rest. In fact about ½ the school. All the lower cubes are full up here[243] and the house is in chaos.

You certainly seem to be doing everything you can to get a house, but I am not so sure that it will be a good idea to go to Aldeburgh if you just tear around the whole of Suffolk and Essex looking for a house instead of having a holiday..

I am in the fly tying class. It is super fun really terrific. We do it once a week on Wednesdays from 7.10 to 8.20 (we do Prep in the afternoon. Harvey Askew takes it and is fantastically clever with his fingers.

What a nuisance about your job, Dad, not knowing what it's going to be.

What are the best ways of how not to catch 'flu?

---

[243] presumably being used as a Sick Bay

J   no date [probably Tuesday 1 October] 57

I've been struck – just as I guessed after that bad Saturday night – Sunday cough and a bit of a headache, Monday cold and snivelling, now under the blankets.

A record has been set up for the school in the number of chaps down – over half the school now. Apparently at Rossall, the maids, the house matron and housemaster's wife all had flu so the masters and the tutors all stopped teaching to run the house. It isn't quite as bad as that with us now.

Otherwise life is reasonably gay. Cass Matthew, my study companion, is in the next cube, Fox Lowe has his portable wireless up the other end of the cubes and there are various other characters – Moffat, Oliver and so on – and we yell to each other, doing crosswords. The biggest blow is that afterwards we have a fortnight off exercise.

J   6 Oct 57 [Sunday]

Up again, back to school on Monday. In the sickroom which has been converted – all because the HM's secretary now has the old matron's surgery. It's absolutely wizard here, we have a wireless and gramophone and lots of records. Mrs T lent us My Fair Lady, the 16" long player of the musical everyone is crazy about in the USA. Got up for the first time on Friday evening, feeling well but rather wonky on the legs. I should be recovered enough to go out with Ruth today who is coming Hooray!

When going to the HM to get leave (to go out) he said I hope there won't be any trouble this time about getting back to school on time – and then quickly 'that was a superfluous remark wasn't it.'

It has just been announced that those in the house who have been sick are going to give a concert for the rest for 40 mins – Rather short notice. We're all thinking fiendishly and rather hopelessly.. I have hoards of work on my hands too – Molière, and Hebbel ....

Thankyou for the letter. How awful about the boat. It was very careless of us not to have fastened it securely. Lucky the steward was quick.

Hope Sally hasn't been raided by the flu germ yet – or any of you. Perhaps London is healthier.

S   6ᵗʰ October 57

I hope some of the places you are going to see today are all right and maybe you will see some nice houses. Has anything happened to answer your advertisement in the Times?

I have still not caught flu yet and think it is already dying away slowly. On Thursday there were 250 boys away with flu and there were still some that had to go and some that had come back.. The house was awfully funny[244] but now most people are back; and in my classes, which are normally big compared with the rest, only about 6 or 7 people. It is super fun with so few people and in Physics and chemistry we have practicals every lesson instead of one every 2 in 3 weeks, and in all subjects we get 3 times as much attention from the masters. And as I am doing 3 new subjects it is a great help for everyone to be away. There is no fortnightly order this week either, as you probably imagined.

The people who have had flu are going to give a concert to those who have not had flu; it will be great fun for us.

Ruth is coming to take us out today - J came out of the sick room on Friday - which is jolly d of her.

You can tell Granny that I would love a watch for Christmas. Also if it happens to interest any one I would like some fly tying feathers and I have to have a vice for fly typing and I will pay you out of my Post Office savings for it as it is going on the bill. And would you please send my fly box which is at the bottom of the Wellington and the key for the wellington is hanging on the hook that hangs up in the Mirror in our Room; as I will need it to put in the beautiful flies which I try and make. For Christmas I would also like some binoculars very much indeed. And if any nice kind person asks what I want you can hint that money is very boaring [sic] because an envelope with some money inside is not half as exciting as a parcel; this is not meant to be rude, as money is very very nice but just a little hint and they always like to know what is most appreciated, like a medium nibbed pen, a compass, a record token etc.

Here we are back again. It is now the evening and we have been out with Ruth. She arrived here on time and we drove off to the New Inn and had lunch there. She has not got her Jag yet as she does not yet know when they are going abroad and they cannot have the car more than 6 months before they go.. Ruth has a dog like Penny but smaller. It is just one year's old. It is very nice but it had been chained down all day and kicked about by farm-women so it was very nervous, but it is apparently getting much better and Ruth says that it learns things very very quickly. We then went to Keisley and shot, me and J shot around on the fell then at candles to try to shoot the flame out. Ruth shot the wick and flame right out first shot, just grazing the candle - super shot.[245]

We had a super tea and then came back here. She gave us two cakes and 2 boxes of chocs between us, jolly 'd'.

Next week there is a film as we are apparently getting fed up with the term. I must catch the post that goes in 5 mins. Hope you have a good journey and good time in Cyprus.

---

[244] for being half empty

[245] Ruth was a sportswoman; she loved to drive fast cars fast, was a good shot (but not a fisherwoman), and during the war had been a motor-bike despatch rider, an ambulance driver, and finally a pilot flying small aircraft on delivery runs.

J   13 Oct [Sunday]

What a wonderful cocktail party you gave - must have been pretty swish with a Reform Club waiter waiting around. A pity about the ad, but I do think Dover should be nice as long as there's golf near enough.

My kilt jacket hasn't come yet which gets more and more of a bore every week. The chap needs blowing up.

We had the terrible house concert affair on Wednesday. Although Cass Matthew[246] and I only made up and rehearsed our thing in prep an hour before it went off terribly well. The matron said it was better than the proper one we had at the end of the winter term. There were some very good acts and skits finishing up with a song about pres and masters.

Am still off-ex. Go to light ex on Tuesday and Rugger on Thursday. The latest wheeze is to make us go round walks, getting longer and longer each day, to make us fitter for when we eventually come on ex. It takes about an hour walking fast and is rather a nuisance..

Work – essays as usual... orchestra going ok...

We had a wonderful weekend with Ruth. Had a jolly d lunch in the pub there and then went back to Keisley to shoot with the .22. Ruth has a little dog – a Penny dog (border sheepdog) called Zippy. It isn't terribly obedient – but is very nice looking, not as foxy as Penny, She was badly treated as a puppy and hence is terribly nervous.

J   19 Oct 1957 [Saturday]

We thought the enthralling serial from Cyprus was absolutely wizard... Wouldn't the sleuth perhaps slide his duke round the equalizer?[247]

Will you soon know what Dad is going to do?. I'm absolutely dying to know if we're going abroad. The house down by Rye sounds terrific – almost too good to be true.

I hope it will be big enough because with one bathroom it sound as though there is hoards of space everywhere. It would be absolutely super if it was nice though.

I dreamt last night of reading in the papers, the Times I think, a list of those going riding in the Row – all v. horsey - Maj. so and so, MBL riding a grey I think it was but I'm absolutely furious that I can't remember the name. Hope you'll be riding there in the holidays and we can come and watch - and stare and admire as you canter by.

My kilt jacket came all right...

I'm back on full-ex now. Yesterday we had a Littleside game, very mixed up with a lot of chaps just back on–ex like myself. It was very good

---

[246] The nickname Cass for Colin Matthew came from this skit, loosely referring to a scene in Julius Caesar, in which I played Brutus (for Bruce) and he was Cassius.

[247] Language taken from Runyon as so often, and the exciting story, I recall, had to do with a door to door hunt for an EOKA terrorist.

fun though, very fast and rather tough. I felt as though I had just come from the sickroom that morning

School squash competition...; fives playing and coaching junior house fives...

Nose to the grindstone at work. I'm getting the hang of Mr Hammer's German[248]. It flows at about 304 mph - probably kph - but I can follow him most of the time. I have an essay on Mme Sévigné to be done before evening chapel. If I do go abroad with the aid of the HMs offer, will it be to France or to Germany? I think France would be best as French is my real aim with Oxford in mind. I think the HM agrees but we only talked vaguely about it.

With Ronny I'm playing Schubert 'Shepherd on the rock' with another boy from the house singing. It's a lovely piece I think. Mr Hind the Director of School Music is in a terrific peeve with me at the moment because a) the school clarinet needs re-padding & I have to use it for orchestra pieces being an A clarinet (mine is B flat) and I can hardly get any noise out of it, and, b) because I mentioned to Mr Whiteside that could I change my time because I cannot waste an hour's prep going through orchestra music that I can play anyway – at least I didn't put it in those words. So I'm keeping out of the way of the music staff at the moment.

Have thought of one or two ideas for Xmas. Hope to be getting a single study soon, so one or two pictures would be nice... A book called 'The Beauty of Sail', a propelling pencil, a watch strap, mine is broken... a desk lamp, one with a green shade.

S   20th October 57

Thank you very much for your letter and the airmail letter from Athens which was super, and for the ping pong bat and the fly case. I am doing some fly tying in the house now and have made some quite nice ones, but it is very tricky. At the moment in fly tying we are only making flies with body hackle and sometimes a tail, but the hackle is very hard to do properly. They look something like this [good drawing of a dressed hook]. It is very good fun and it sends the time flying away (very good pun) when it is wet and I have nothing else to do. I am 10th in Maths in fortnightly orders, but I should be higher when we stop Algebra which is the only thing I don't like.

---

[248] I went from scratch to A Level German in four terms thanks to the teaching of punctilious and enthusiastic Ken Bishop first and then the wonderful Jack Hammer. In my first German essay for him I scored 134 howlers - a world record. I made quite quick progress and enjoyed German lessons with Hammer. He was kindly and humorous and very inspiring, and his special succinct manner was in no way stern. One day it started to snow and of course we all looked out of the window; 'Alright, you haf two minutes precisely to vatch the snow, zen ve vill go back to our vork!'

In Physics I think I am somewhere near the top but I don't know, and for other things I will only know tomorrow.

It sounds most exciting about the house on Point Hill. I remember it well. It will be a lovely place to have a house overlooking the sea and harbour and the town, even if it isn't an awfully nice house you can always have it done up. I am sure there will never be another house going on Point Hill so you must get it. If it is so cheap it does not matter if it is only a shack because you can plonk a new bedroom and bathroom and don't waist [*sic*] time buying it otherwise some chap will come along and offer £8,000 for it.

If this turns out ok where are you going for a holiday in three weeks time? I don't suppose you will still be going to Aldeburgh but to Rye instead.

I have decided to be confirmed this term and we have the first address by the HM (who has incidentally been in bed for a week) on Wednesday evening.

Last night there was a film we were supposed to have had last Saturday, 'The Baby in the Battleship' about 2 chaps who went onshore leave and got stranded with a baby and had to smuggle it aboard and keep it secret and fed till next shore leave. It was rather poor. It was supposed to be funny but failed miserably. The cartoon however was one of the best I have ever seen.

There is going to be a house squash ladder again which is a good show. I played some more fives this week; it is a jolly jolly good game..

It is pouring with rain and has been since Thursday.

On Friday there was a Sharps practice. The motions were 'that the Queen's visit to the USA will not improve Anglo-American relations'. It will I say. 'Photography is a great art' I say no. Then chaps had to air their views on how the Russian satellite affects the middle East. And 'Prince Charles should not go to Cheam' I say he should not go.

I did not have to speak.

Are we going to Holt next hols? For Christmas or New Year?.

Thank you for the photo of Sally; it is a very 'd' one.

J   27 Oct

A house looking over Rye to the sea sounds spiffing....

I got my watch strap – 7/6 it was, a nice leather strap

Work isn't going badly in fact French is pretty hot. Came top in the last prose and the last essay. German is tootling on, rather inaccurately is the big fault at the moment. My Latin has been good too.

House game went ok and I ended up winding the opposing fly half (I was W-Fwd). Lost my match on the school squash competition – completely outplayed apart from the first game – but I beat the house champion by 5-0.

Proper parade for the first time after all the rain, going for Cert A Part
II now...

House runs yesterday and last Wed which wasn't very nice. No extra
half given yet this term.

Nothing much happening – sorry for boring letter.

S   **Sunday 27 Oct 57**

Thank you very much for your letter and the thing about the house and
the photos, they are really quite good except how I got a photo of a camel
in that film I just don't know.

It is most exciting about the house and you must tell us as quick as
possible if you buy it. It sounds jolly 'd' especially having a bedroom for us
overlooking the sea. If you buy it before anyone else will you draw a rough
plan of the ground floor, first floor and then attic floor so we can see what it
looks like...

In work this week I don't know where I am but I have found out that
each fortnight marks are out of 310. There are 50 marks for French Latin,
English, Maths, German but only 30 for Physics and Chemistry. This
means that if you come top in English and Latin you get 100 marks a
fortnight to help you on your way to the 5ths, but if you are top in Physics
and chemistry you only get 60 marks which I think is a chiz.

Oh yes while I remember, I'm terribly sorry about the 2½ stamp but I
was in a terrible hurry to get to the post.

On Wednesday we had House runs. It had been pouring all week.
There are 4 packs, now I am in the 2nd top one which has 18 chaps in it, all
the 3-milers except one and some older ones. I came 3rd in the pack; but it
is probably because the others had had flu and were not very fit.

The squash ladder has started and this time I was picked about $2/3^{rd}$ of
the way down but I have gone up 16 places this week. This week I played
squash twice and fives twice and was very fagged out at the end (and about 8
games of ping pong).

There was a General Knowledge Prize on Wednesday. We had to write
on What makes a Power a Great Power and is Britain a Great Power.
Then on Alterations in the Army; then a letter to a newspaper about road
safety; and short accounts of Sir Malcolm Sargent, Tommy Steele, Lloyd
someone and Christine Truman, Alice Markova, J Foster Dulles and
various other types..

Do you know your new job or whether you will find out soon now?

Are we going to Greshams in the new year, and when are you going in
November.

Fly tying is great fun and also a jolly good hobby in the house.[249] Next week I will send a sample of my flies.

PS Wednesday
The thing about the house is most exciting.
Confirmation Sunday is on Dec the 1st.
I was 8th in Physics and 2nd in Chemistry out of 20

J   3 November 57 [Sunday]

Exciting about the house in Rye...

Sorry Granny has been ill....

Played 3 games of rugger, all on Littleside II, and scored some satisfactory tries. In one game I bruised badly the thumb I cracked last year – which hasn't done it any good – painful and stiff.

Played fives and squash on the ladder...

Corps field day postponed because of the continuing wet.

Top in unseen in French, essay on interplanetary contact was rather hard. In a fortnight's time Madame Tartufffe is being acted in Lancaster and 6th formers can go.

Listening to music a lot in the study all day - from Sibelius, Verdi and Wagner to pipe bands Dutch Swing College Tommy Steel and Satchmo and Eartha Kit.

Playing some swing as well as my Schumann and Brahms on the clarinet.

S   3 Nov 57

Thank you for your letter and the Yachting magazine. I think it's absolutely terrific about the house, it really is super and Rye will be such fun to live in. How soon are the other people moving out? and when are we moving in? and when is the plumbing and decorating starting? How much time will we spend there next holidays? Can you tell us everything about it

There was another House run on Monday. It was Slacks, the worst of the whole lot, but I came second in the pack. That is about the only thing

---

[249] There was not much in the way of hobby life in School House. I do not remember boys making model aeroplanes, or playing conkers, for instance. We played some kind of games in the junior, dayroom and maybe in the senior dayroom too, such as dot cricket, battleships and similar paper games, along with some chess and draughts, and Dover Patrol in the Library. We practised music indoors of course, but visits to the arts and crafts centre in spare time were limited. Essentially we lived in an outdoor world and, unless resting and reading, the most usual thing was to go off to practice sports as soon as breaks allowed.

of interest to happen this week. Fortnightly orders come out on Monday and I don't know how I've done..

Yesterday there was German singing in Powell Hall. Mr Hammer takes it; it is killingly funny. He dances around the stage wirling *[sic]* his hands and singing solos or with us. He has a very good voice; and if he tries to get lovely strong German accents and flies all over the stage, he is really very good but just like a comedian acting a German.

I have been playing much rugger this week as a wing forward.

I played an appalling game of fives with the prefect in charge watching, but I don't think it will not matter because the others played even worse so I might get on Junior fives.

I do hope Granny is better. I will write to her today.

Are you coming up for confirmation? because if we don't book rooms very soon they will be gone, if they haven't gone years ago. Do you know your new job yet?

There is absolutely nothing else to write about – except Jamie and I played squash last night and some village boys came along and started turning off all the lights.

J   10 Nov 1957

Longing to hear more about the house. I think it is a good idea to go down there for a week next holidays

It's jolly nice that Mum can come up for S's confirmation, that'll be very d.

I think the HM wrote to Dad some time back, anyway maybe you've written back when I last spoke to him he was - shall I put it – rather anxious for an answer.

We had quite a good field day. Indeed I'm sure I learnt in that day far more than 4 or 5 parades. Absolutely pouring. Did some instruction indoors, then some did a small battle on the near fells, and we did all kinds of things and some nice 'fi e and movement' exercises which are fun, crawling around Akay wood.

Extra half – gorgeous November day, clear sky, frost in the morning, everything white and the leaves on the ground and bracken red. Shiffner, Oliver, Grant and I went to Riseall, not terribly strenuous but very nice. Trouble with winter and easter term extra halves is that it gets dark at 5.15, and there's no sun for most of the afternoon in fact and it's cold.

Rugger – two games, league[250] and Littleside... Fives and squash, Second on squash ladder at the moment.

At the moment preparing for Church Parade in the town – 3 from each house goes to the Remembrance Sunday service – preparation is blancoing

---

[250] Inter-house matches at different levels, probably

and good turn out. School has 2 mins silence in the cloisters which is a thing I don't think has been done for a long time if ever[251].

Work going ok. Mr Bishop is allowing me time to go through the book I missed last year for A level which is very useful.

S   Sunday 10th November 57

I hope you are all well and you are all right without Claire Lise. When is the other person coming and what sort of person is she?

 I am glad Granny is better

I am glad we are spending a week in Rye next hols, camping in the house. I've not got any brilliant ideas about name. I think Hill Lodge is pretty good. I can give you a lot of things it shouldn't be, like Sea View and Chez moi. Incidentally how far is the river from the house? Can one fish in it? How far are the nearest marshes or flat lands where one can bow and arrow safely? Also how far to the nearest tennis court if we don't get one in the garden?[252]

This week there was another House run. I did very badly and came 8th. Also I was beaten on that morning for scabbing a cold bath[253].

On Tuesday it was field Day. In case you don't know I am in the Corps now. Unfortunately it rained very hard and we weren't allowed out of the school grounds; but we are going out on the fells one half day to have a good battle and make up for it. We did things like camouflage, compasses, judging distances, map reading, section attack, gun loading and firing but we didn't fire anything, not even a blank. Pretty stingy I think. The only good thing was lunch which was jolly 'd', six sandwiches, one jam bun about the size of your hand, a pork pie a hunk of fruit cake and an apple and a water bottle of fizzy booze (my fizzy booze[254]).

On Wednesday there was a talk on confirmation and at the end we had to give the name of our vicar and our Parish church; I put Rev Eile at St Mary's Kensington. Is this correct

In form this term I move down 3 places; [because] there are 2 new chaps in our form from 4a. This week I am doing better, and I made some superb crystals in Chemistry.

On Wednesday there was an extra half (the first of this term). I went with 2 others to some gill past Calf where we made a super dam with whacking boulders and moss and turf. It was great fun.

My fives has started getting much better. Yesterday I had 2 good games..

---

[251] Evidently I approved – perhaps from Dragon memories of it being a right and proper thing to do.

[252] The garden was quite small, with a lawn just about big enough for a small croquet pitch, and then to the side a terraced slope with borders and rockery, a couple of fruit trees and a patch of vegetable garden. The tennis courts were half a mile away.

[253] 'scabbing' meant to avoid by cheating; here, trying to get away with not taking a cold bath.

[254] Meaning 'my favourite' fizzy drink

The weather has been much better the last two days.

PS

Good idea about the dancing classes if you can find a good place. But are we going to any dances?

I am going tomorrow to the Bull or the White Hart to see if I can get you a room

J   17 Nov

Thank you for the plans of the house, It sounds absolutely wizard; the more we hear, the nicer it sounds. Wonderful news about the field.[255] I hope other people in the road are not bidding.

Church parade was rather fun, except for an appalling sermon. St John Ambulance and Salvation Army were all there.[256]

Rugger matches in leagues – scores etc.... Fives...

There's no doubt now I feel that essays are the big snag in my work, and I don't really see how they can come better except through practice I suppose.. My proses haven't been bad at all. My German has been miles better lately.

My first prose was 15/ 50 now reaching 27; essays up from 15 to 31. Current essays are: describe a haunted house – in French - and are Hebbel's Herodes and Marianne psychologically convincing.

Had tea with Horsy G which was very nice. He thought the chance of getting into Oxford as a commoner was little, so I'm to work for scholarship level and if I fail St Andrew's is the thing. Horsy G says I must read more contemporary French which is what I'm now trying to do. We talked of this and that, and music and eventually got to my essay which was the purpose of coming.

The Governors have been lurking around. B Bracken was to be in for lunch but I haven't seen him or Sir John[257] this time

S   17 Nov 57

Thank you for the letter and the drawings and plans of the house.. It is really terrific about the field – absolutely super. I hope there will not be too many cows in it, so we can hit a golf ball and hurl a cricket ball and boot a rugger ball. The position of the house sounds perfect. I am absolutely dying to get moved in there. Will it be decorated and plumbed by the Easter

---

[255] A chance to purchase a 6-acre field at the back of our and other houses on Point Hill; my parents sold it some years later for a ridiculously small sum (on poor advice) to someone who promptly sold it on to a developer for a great deal of money.

[256] The pomp and traditions of such a church parade appealed to me – but apparently did not dull my critical faculties with respect to the sermon.

[257] Sir John Shea

hols? Will the present owners be out when we go down to Rye next hols? How far actually is the sea from the house?

I have done much better in form, gone up 6 places in Latin and have gone up 7 places an dam now 7th in maths. In other subjects I have gone up I should think except English which was not so good.

I have booked you a room in the Bull (single for Sat and Sunday night). Shall I order a taxi to fetch you from Oxenholme?

This week has been full of rumours, most of which were true (unlike at the Dragons, where most were not true); there was going to be a film on Friday – yes, Moby Dick; and Sedgwick Society was going to have 'The living Desert'. It did not; but next Thursday there is the Liverpool Phil Orchestra.

Talking about the Dragon I was thinking that it would be a good idea if maybe J and I went to stay with Granny and Grandfather and went to the old Dragonian Supper, but I don't know if there is one these hols.

There was German singing again on Saturday and Mr Hammer was as funny as anything.

Thank you for accepting the dance. Do you know anything about dancing lessons yet?

J is going to see a French play today.[258]

Thank you very very much for the lovely biscuits. It was jolly 'd' of you and they were terrific ones.

24 Nov [Sunday]

How lovely that Dad has got the African job and Middle East.

The more I hear about Rye the nicer it sounds. We don't want a big house there's no doubt about that and this sounds absolutely the thing. With the golf, the sailing, the harbour and country it sounds quite gorgeous.

Thank you for the box of biscuits – a lovely surprise.

Various things to ask.

> -On separate piece of paper please, could I have Sandy's greedy list
>
> -for a form talk I have to give in German – do you still have any photos of Niagara
>
> -Horsy G would love to see you when you are up. Mrs Senior will also be up.
>
> -Jazz concert – for a performance by the Wolverines – one night only – could I borrow, and could you bring up, Dad's blue trousers, and Mum's yellow socks and one of my brightest

---

[258] Sandy was envious because such outings involved having some free time in Lancaster after a matinee – for fish and chips and fizzy pop, etc..

checked cowboy shirts. Will add to that a Derby hat and gymshoes.

-Friend who is leaving this term, Mike Sutherland, the school's no 1 crack shot will be doing a job in Holland Park. He wants to know if there might be a rifle club in Kensington or anywhere fairly near, and also squash courts (I've told him about the RAC squash courts). Does Dad know, could he find out and let me know so I can tell Mike

Work going well. Had the equal top mark on an Unseen and an essay on Mme de Sevigne.

30 of us L and UVI ML to Lancaster to see a performance of Tartuffe – it was terribly good. The acting was superb and it was most amusing and it wasn't too difficult to understand. We had fish and chips from a newspaper afterwards and a gay journey singing out way back to Sedbergh

S   Nov 24 1957 -

I am so glad you got the job you wanted. It is jolly good that you think Anne or whatever she is called is a good thing; I hope everything will be all right when you come up here. I am ordering a taxi tomorrow morning.

We had House runs on Thursday when it was drizzling; the Corps had a double parade and the recruits had a battle with blanks; it was jolly good especially as it was raining. We had four little battles and in each we had to storm some little stronghold. Everyone got terrifically wet crawling around in the mud and things; The only thing wrong with it was the cleaning of rifles and boots afterwards.

Talking of shooting could we have a day shooting hares and woodpigeons next holidays.

Yesterday there was a First XV match against Uppingham; we won 14-3. But afterwards, School House is the only house which has to go round a run after the game, which is a rotten chiz.

On Thursday evening there was the Royal Liverpool Orchestra. It was terrific. The conductor was John Pritchard who was absolutely splendid. He was about 45 big but not fat, black hair going straight back and a little bald patch. He was so dignified; and the way he wirled /sic/ his hands and arms he had no chin at all. The programme was jolly good especially the Fireworks overture which we played in the House orchestra; also the last one the Meistersinger overture. But they were all very good; and it lasted roughly 2 ½ hours. Everyone had to change into Sunday clothes, and all the masters wore evening dress, and it was a very big do and enjoyed I think by everybody. Also in Friday evening there was a film, the Ladykillers. I must say it was really very funny and superbly acted by Alec Guinness was terrific and the old lady is superb. The cartoon was a Tom and Jerry which was average. The news was very good.

I have played hooker a bit this week. It is not a bad place but where I want to play is scrum half, and I'm going to ask next week.

Yesterday I had a terrific game of fives and I also played squash against a guy in another house and beat him 3 games to 2 in about the most exhausting match I have ever played.

I might have told you there is a House concert at the end of term on the 17th of December. I am in a small skit play affair about 3 Teddy boys and 2 Etonians in a Soho café. It is pretty weak stuff but we feel it is better doing something that is weak than doing nothing at all. I am a Teddy boy, so could you bring with you when you come up two of the flashiest American shirts you can find of mine; and an old tie that nobody ever wants to wear that can get slashed to pieces and also one of my pairs of jeans - if possible too small for me - and a pair of my boldest yellow socks as bright as possible.

Melville thought that if we could go for a week hiking in Scotland in the Easter holidays it would be jolly good fun. But we thought we could get together in the hols.

J   early December [probably 1 December]

Corps exam - which I passed - done in parts, weapon training, map reading, field craft and drill. drilling and teaching people was not too bad; on field craft the questions were as expected - although my map reading was messed up by having a pencil that broke and I had to miss out 2 questions. Weapon training I must have been very lucky, because I had completely forgotten how to load a bren magazine and got all fuzzed up doing the IA - 'Immediate Action' when gun stops: cock gun, pull trigger, cock gun, change mag, etc etc. The sergeant from the Kings Own must have been pretty lenient.

Exams start on Thursday have been reading desperately though Moliere, Tieck and Brentano and Mme de Sevigne every spare second.

For House concert practising the clarinet in Wolverines going not badly. I have a Swannee River solo - swing first, then a boogie, finishing in a minor drag blues. Got a part in a skit which is fun, doing a radio play behind the scenes, being a props man opening windows etc and other noises, horses hooves. All that needs some rehearsing too I'll say.

I must say it is a terrible bore about Penny and the vicar's cat - if we shot up the cat with a bow and arrow that would save all our problems?.

I Hope Janet gets through the exams. Will she get a place at Oxford if she gets them?

This morning it has been snowing for a couple of hours - rather exciting, but jolly cold. In fact it has been roaring like a blizzard down the valley. If it goes on we may go home early or something interesting, but I doubt it.

S   57 [Probably Sunday 1 Dec]

Thank you very much indeed for your wonderful letters, Jamie's and mine[259], I think it is simply wonderful of you buying or hiring me a kilt; yesterday I got matron to measure me so I would make no mistakes. My waist is 26" my hips are 34" and my waist to ground when knelling [kneeling] is 22 ½ ".

Also I think the arrangements for next holidays are absolutely terrific and the dances beautifully arranged, also Paris which will be wonderful, also Holt. I think me and J are going to have the best Christmas holidays we have ever had and I am looking forward to going to Holt – they are so nice there and it is such a lovely place.

Last Sunday we had a film in School House by the preacher, it was about the Flying Angel, the society for mission to seamen. But he showed us another film on oil tankers. Then there was the other film about Mission to Seamen which was also interesting.

This term I have read quite a lot of books, the Code of the Woosters, Summer Lightning, the inimitable Jeeves, Something Fresh – all by P G Wodehouse. Then Operation Cicero by I don't know who, the Big Pick Up by E Trevor, Two eggs on my plate by some Norwegian guy, then Hounds of Death by Agatha Christy [sic], The Grand Babylon Hotel by Arnold Bennett, the Secret Adversary by Agatha Christy, the Black Gang by Sapper, and at the moment I am reading Withering Heights by someone Bronte.

This week I have moved up one place in form and am now 10th.

And now I am playing either fly half or three quarter (centre) which is great fun.

Me and J thought we would like to go to the Crazy Gang or 'Ten Minute Alibi' but really I don't know anything about it.

Yesterday I played fives for about 2 hours, It was terrific fun.

Yesterday we had a balloon debate – 8 people were in it and I was one. I chose Humphrey Lyttleton but a boy who chose Leonardo da Vinci won.

I know what I would like for Christmas, at least I don't want you to buy, for the kilt will cost an awful lot, I just want maybe some money towards it from Granny etc.. It is an air rifle for I have wanted one for 4 years now and I am sure I have enough sense to use it properly and nearly everyone here has one and nearly everyone at the <u>Dragons</u> had one and it is their most valued possession of their very own; and if all the 10-13 year olds at the Dragon school have them then I don't see why I shouldn't be safe with one. Anyhow I will buy nearly all of it if I get some help from people like you and Granny.

Last Sunday there was the big[g]est collection of all times during a service at this school (Speech day and all); it was over £40 and for the

---

[259] i.e. separate letters to us, not from each of us.

Hungarian Fund; now there is a big one in all the houses and an awful lot has been collected.

Are you coming up by train and where are you staying? I am looking forward to seeing you very much indeed.

S   2ⁿᵈ December 57 [Monday]

Dear Daddy,

Thank you indeed for the wallet and the letter which Mummy gave me on Saturday. I shall value the wallet very much and always keep the letter in it.

Mummy arrived here on Saturday but there was no taxi for her; note that this was not my fault as I had been down there twice to get everything ok.

Grandfather has sent a small every day Prayer Book and Granny The Book of Verse for Christians which she says is too old for me but will be very nice later on. It is very kind of them [260]

Sorry this is so short but I must get it to the post before you go abroad.

J   4 December [Wednesday]

Thank you very much for such a lovely weekend. You know we love going out [261] and last weekend we really had enormous fun. It was a pity we didn't have the car but we could hardly have had a nicer Saturday and Sunday. Thankyou for bringing up the huge pile of clothes and for the mintcake.

Been having a good week although off ex.. House matches were played but the ground is very hard.

---

[260] Confirmation presents.

[261] Outings from school, which could vary hugely in type, were significant events (safety valves, or energisers perhaps) right through our Sedbergh days. One normally went out, with one's own or another's parents or relatives on Sundays between morning and evening chapel. We were occasionally allowed to go out on a Saturday after lunch too, provided one was not required (e.g. for a school team) and that you returned in time for roll call at prayers, that evening, because there was no prep and few obligatory activities (such as lectures etc.) on Saturday evenings. In later terms, one might be introduced more often than before to the parents of others, and even to parents of boys in other houses, in a more grown-up fashion; sometimes with an invitation to drop in for tea or join a group of friends at the Bull or White Hart.

My father (who was travelling abroad a lot in those years) only visited two or three times that I can remember; and my mother three or four times more. It was a long way to come from the south of England to Sedbergh, but visits could be combined with seeing Dear at Bermersyde. The lack of frequent visits was not a tragedy; boys who did not go out became a clique, mucked about together at weekends, enjoyed the freedom and tended to feel rather superior. Weekend outings could sometimes involve a lot of car driving and eating with some resultant exhaustion, however enjoyable a large lunch in a distant grand hotel, such as The Langdale Chase Hotel outside Ambleside, might be.

I saw the doc this morning and it looks as though I'll be able to have the splint off in about a week from today[262]. After that I won't be well straight away, probably another three weeks without exercise. Ghastly thought. Anyway my leg is enabling me to do quite a bit more work and things such as reading for which there is usually only little time. Practising the clarinet madly for the house concert, orchestra and my music for Ronnny.

S   Sunday 8 December 57

Thank you very much for taking us out last weekend; it was terrific fun, and thank you for bringing up the clothes. This morning I went to communion. It is a very nice service I think.

It is terrible weather here now, raining all the time, but on Thursday there were House matches. We played Evans House and lost 14-0. This was a pretty poor show because everyone thought it would be a good game and that we would just win. Everyone gets pretty worked up, standing on the touchline and yelling and in our case clenching our fists, pulling our hair etc.. It's a good job that I'm not on the house team because everyone blames it on them

There are junior fives on Saturday and unfortunately I am not even a reserve. We beat Evans house easily.

I think the 2nd wave of Asian flu is maybe just about starting so I hope it comes quickly then we can go back home early which would be jolly 'd' but as there are only about 10 days left I rather doubt it.

I have been rehearsing for the House Concert every Half day and nearly all days this week. I think it is really quite good now though unfortunately there is another lot of chaps higher up than us doing the same sort of thing, so maybe one of us will have to give in to the others.

Can you Daddy think of anything you would like for Xmas.

We have now (quarter past five) had a first dress rehearsal and Laycock who is in charge of the concert came and watched; and the first time he watches he either says all right or tactfully it won't do. Anyhow he said ours was very good especially the clothes and dress, so we can now do it for certain.

I have to have my shoes I bought last hols mended, and heels and toes done in leather so we won't have to buy some shoes to dance in.

Thank you for the 10/- It is really awfully kind of you.

Exams start Thursday this week and stop on Saturday; then we have 5 days to go doing nothing but wasting time.

---

[262] My right knee had been badly damaged in a tackle (by my friend Chris Heber Percy) in a an inter-house rugger game against Winder. I was taken to Lancaster to have the leg in plaster, then splint and bandages and was off-ex for almost eight weeks.

J   15 Dec [Sunday] 57

End of term Decorations are very gay in the dining room, balloons and
holly with berries – which I picked in a blizzard - streamers and bells and a
beautifully decorated little Christmas tree.

Exams are over. We had some pretty fiendish papers – at least that is
what I thought. They were:

English essay.	Responsibility - World Opinion*[263]
French essay	exportation - a railway accident*
	or describe a XX century novel you have read
German	a shop window - recipe for a happy life - the car
	has changed man's way of life*

The German was hopeless and for the French I couldn't think of
anything to say let along bung it into French. I don't think my English one
was too bad though.

S   No date [probably 15th December] 57

Snowed hard... but the ground was so wet that none settled down here
only on top of the hills... all gone except on Baugh Fell.

This week there has been the Yard Soccer Competition on Wednesday,
Thursday and Saturday. I am on Ian Grant's team. I am also on another
team because someone is off ex and I am substituting. Both teams played
against each other, but I played on Grant's team. Jamie was refereeing and
I scored a goal which was an obvious goal, to both sides, and Jamie said it
was not a goal which was a jolly bad show; we won anyhow and I scored
one goal that he had to allow. So on Monday I am playing in the final.

In the school matches this term we have scored 31 points and lost 32!

The House concert is tomorrow evening with a dress rehearsal this
evening. Yesterday and today we are spending all our time rehearsing. The
HM told us that after the concert there would be what he called 'some
festivities' given by Mrs Thornely and himself, which sounds as though it
will be great fun. We're searching everywhere for slashers' bike chains and
coshes etc.; so far we have one sand bag, 2 bike chains and 1 slasher. It is
absolutely terrific fun having our own dress rehearsal.

There are now decorations and balloons and holly and a Christmas tree
which is an absolute beauty and beautifully done up in the dining room.
Last Sunday we stirred the Christmas pudding. I hope we are having it
today. Talking of Christmas puddings I hope you get a bigger one than last
year.

This week was junior fives. We played Sedgwick House; they won by 3
points. This was a very bad show as everyone thought we were bound to
win. It was on Friday 13th; it was very bad because the people who did not
get on the team like Melville and I played and practised twice as much

---

[263] The asterisks mark which option I chose.

143

those who did get on the team - partly because those who were on last year were sure of getting on this year so they did not practice.

The second round of the house matches were both drawn and so they both played again, and again they were both draws; [so] they both played again yesterday and Powell and Hart won.

We have finished exams but had no results yet. We had physics and chemistry in one 2 hour paper.

Shall we bring the top hat and bowler back with the kilts and jackets in our trunk?

Next week there is nothing to do, only 2 rugger matches and one concert in 3 days and as our trunks go we cannot play games. See you in 4 days, at about 5.30 as I guess the train will be late.

Background: Later years at home, 1958-60

Just before my last years at Sedbergh, our parents decided that London was not the right base for the family – chiefly because I (in particular), my mother and Sally all suffered asthma from the smog, and constant pollution. So the family beat a retreat. My father expected to travel a lot in his work and wanted to have the family based comfortably in the country near the coast. Woodbridge and Aldeburgh were options but Rye was eventually a natural choice. My father had been a member since the 1940s of the Rye Golf Club, a favourite getaway of his and the spiritual home of the Old Rugbeians Golfing Society. In the autumn of 1957 they bought a house on the edge of the town, and there Sandy and I entered a most enjoyable late teen-age life with a handful of good friends - a step in my upbringing which was a close counterpart to the happy senior studies and prefectorial years at Sedbergh.

We were comfortably ensconced. A small loft conversion added a washroom lavatory for Sandy and me on the top floor, where we had a v iew to Romney Marsh and the sea, and we had been involved with readying the house right from the start, helping my mother choose carpets and wallpaper. The garden was small with a lawn barely large enough for croquet but behind the house my parents had bought a 10-acre field where Sally would be able to keep a pony. And for Sandy (now 15½) and me (16½) Rye offered all the facilities and company we needed. First of all there was the sea, which still held something magical for us (having been distant from it at Sedbergh, in Surrey or London). We either bicycled down a path across the Romney Marsh or we persuaded our mother (or other peoples' relatives) to drive us to the Golf Course, to Camber sands for miles of wide open beach or to Rye Harbour for sailing.

At first it was difficult to find a suitable person to help my mother with Sally and with housekeeping and housework – my mother was unwell through the following six or seven years, and frequently undergoing hospital treatment – and the house, and a tiny attic room, was too small for live-in help. Eventually a fisherman's daughter from Rye Harbour was recruited who was a wonderful help and remained a family friend for years.

Sandy and I were soon part of a happy clan of late teenagers, the children of my father's old friends and golfing companions or my mother's new acquaintances through riding and other Rye social links. In dry weather, all year round, we played tennis, at neighbours' houses or, for competitions, at the town Tennis Club just below Point Hill. And in August, nobody missed the great social event for Kentish youth, the Benenden Tennis Tournament. And golf was an almost everyday activity, whatever the weather, for Sandy and me and one or two like-minded friends. And in winter afternoons we played indoors every kind of house and table game over coffee or soft drinks.

Sandy and I became very self-contained with our gang of friends. We rarely had friends from Sedbergh to stay, as we had done in earlier years (Rye was a long way from the North country), and there were not many other visitors on account of my father's absences and my mother's ill health. At home we messed about in the field, hit practice (aerated) golf balls off a door mat on the lawn; and in the winter sat in the 'Herrenzimmer' (the study) with its gas fire, comfortable armchairs, familiar book collections (old bound volumes of Punch), gramophone – and finally a television. All year round, we took Tappy the Jack Russell terrier for walks; and there were dog shows and gymkhanas, which were mostly of interest when members of the gang came along too.

As we got older, in our close knit circle we considered ourselves rather superior. It was a kind of home version of sixth form behaviour where we ignored younger siblings, scorned most outsiders – whom we reckoned to beat at any sport or game – but were occasionally willing to coach or help younger friends. No doubt we cultivated a style and image, but nothing too harmfully vain. Work of any intellectual kind or serious cultural pursuits in the later years were generally reserved for our 'own time'.

This period also saw my foreign travel for language purposes, to Freiburg for German and Tours for French familiarisation. The German working holiday took me into a German version of my English home and school environment. Both the parents were university teachers, and the son and daughter of my age led the sort of social life with a small set of friends which Sandy and I were embarking on in Rye, combining long walks in the surrounding hills by day (in lieu of tennis or golf etc) and coffee parties all evening with friends.

Tours, however, was quite different. There I was on my own in an ancient small chateau, the only guest of a widowed countess, who was very strict with lessons, then reading prep all morning and conversation over meals. In between I had freedom to wander and a bicycle, and spent most of my time at the local tennis club with usually slightly older teenagers.

* * *

By our second year at Rye, life was all about socialising and entertainment in our private clan, making girlfriends and boyfriends, and taking first steps towards adulthood. We were increasingly free of parental oversight, and heading for driving licences, to be able to get out and about without being ferried. We continued to play golf and tennis regularly with the same gang of friends and their friends. We went shooting, with a variety of arms (shooting balloons on Camber sands in a high wind was a favourite sport). For a couple of winters we skated and played ice hockey on nearby flooded meadows, attended by friendly parents who brought warm soup picnics. And we started sailing.

146

I was given a boat a 12-foot Firefly sailing dinghy on my 18th birthday – but sailing in narrow Rye harbour was difficult because of the strong tide. Sandy and I cruised up and down the river but in racing got seriously left behind a small fleet of expert sailors. One summer there was an incident when I nearly drowned my girlfriend Rosie. We were out at sea off Rye Harbour in the Firefly when the wind got up and a whirlpool of high waves denied return through the harbour entrance. So I headed for Camber beach, but we got swamped in a breaker and capsized. We were not actually near to drowning but the ignominy was having to telephone upset and irritated parents to come and collect us; and take us back to sail the boat back into Rye Harbour the following day.

The pace of parties and evenings of games at homes increased, with trips into Rye or Hastings for the cinema or to taste a beer - but more often to an Espresso Bar for a cappuccino, in those the early days of frothy coffee. We thought it was all rather sophisticated. Then the dances! From the start Sandy and I were personae gratae because we knew how to dance, and had no worries about asking girls to dance. Thus we were generally counted on by mothers and by the local band leader, Waggie Wagstaff, who played at the larger events, to get things going[264]. And girlfriend relationships became more serious and I have happy memories of the first thrills of awkward affection – attended by a glow worm on the bank beside the path on the way back from Rye cinema one summer's night.

And then we started taking holiday jobs to earn pocket money. Sandy worked at Bryant's garage; we both did some fruit picking. I worked in the hop yards in the summer and in the other holidays worked in 'Waggie's delicatessen in Hastings – in charge of the chicken barbecue machine.

Of family holidays the most memorable was a three week trip to S. Jean de Luz, San Sebastian and the Pyrenees – an introduction to southern Europe with its exotic food, unfamiliar landscapes and excitements such as a bullfight or watching pelotte played in a village square. There were further holidays in the north too, with my Godmother Ruth Rose at Keisley near Appleby and with Dear at Bemersyde, but very special was a family holiday in Glenbeigh in County Kerry on the South-west coast of Ireland. There Sandy and I fished the mouth of the river for sea trout, played golf on the little 9-hole course at Dooks, tried riding ponies, but did not much like that, sampled a few Guinesses; and, in true Sedberghian fashion, climbed the Macgillycuddy Reeks, Ireland's highest mountain group, with a narrow ridge with immense drops between the peaks.

* * *

---

[264] At university age I played in his band (paid too), from dance music scores, in local halls or upstair rooms of pubs at various functions, public or private, in small towns around Rye in the Christmas holiday season.

147

As to extra education at home, it was mostly in the form of encouragement to pursue interests identified at school. My father helped me occasionally with both French and German studies, and both my father and my mother were enthusiastic about German literature. On art and painting it was my father who had a keen interest, and on music each had a certain input in different ways. But most of my key cultural influences were developed at school, guided by excellent Upper and Lower VI form masters and encouraged through parallel exploration of the subjects with my peer group. In fact, with respect to wider and future interests, I recall one curious incident of a negative influence. I told one visitor at home who noticed my ability to draw and my interest in maps and plans that I was thinking of architecture as a career. 'Oh no', said he, 'don't become an architect or you will spend the rest of your life designing town drains.' No doubt it was meant to be witty, but if so I missed the point and waved goodbye to architecture.

Thus in all, life at Rye was in its essentials rather similar to life in my last two years at School House with the experience of having a single study and then prefect status. It was a period of rather positive encounter with new spheres of life, focusing more sharply on my own interests and moving towards forming my own identity. I was concentrating on what abilities I had and followed more energetically pastimes which pleased me, from art and music to particular sports – fives and putting the shot at school or tennis and sailing at home. I had by then also learnt how to learn, how to work in a more concentrated fashion, and how to practice; and I was happy taking the lead when opportunity arose – at home as well as at school. In every sense, home and school life were well integrated by my last few terms.

The fact is that we were becoming young adults, with a new place and role at home - with our own circle of friends (not just family or parent's friends), looking after my mother who was unwell, driving a car, pursuing interests (or work) which may have had no home connection. Life had started to bridge the spheres. In my last Sedbergh terms, there was a new degree of cross-over between home and school, for instance in favourite reading, in collecting pictures or gramophone records, in more thoughtful choice of presents for relatives, in planning of holiday jobs or trips independently from parents, exchanges of letters with girl-friends, etc.. The two lives were becoming one. School had done its work.

Easter Term 1958

J   19th Jan 1958 [Sunday]

Thank you for everything you did to give us such a wonderful hols - immense fun – as nice an Xmas holiday as we have ever had. Thrilled about the house[265]...

Rain, snow and bitterly cold... Fun being back though, and getting down to reading, talk and playing cards. Now in my own single study[266]. Study all rigged up – one of the nicest. The pres, even with their nice newly painted studies, are jealous. Admittedly it's a double study and I have hoards of space for pictures, cuttings etc.; I have two nice lamps, two tables, a couch and a grub locker. I have the curtains since there is a big rail, which is a nice way of filling up the wall at the end. I wish you could see it, because I'll never have such a nice study – the actual room that is – I shouldn't think.

I went to see Dr Morris and I'm off rugger and fell running next week – I've played squash and fives and my knee has only hindered me in getting up and bending quickly[267]. Work started. Reading in class with Horsy G setting us down to Racine: Britannicus. Last evening the HM called me along when filling in the form to go to Clare college, which he will be sending to you pretty soon.

J   25 January 1958 [Saturday]

How terribly exciting about Uncle Robin[268]. I'm terribly pleased. It will seem funny to have another aunt. I have seen and spoken to Penny[269] twice, but she doesn't recognize me. She certainly seems terribly well and I think she's going to love being up at Sid's.

We have had a wizard start to the term and have done so much it seems we have been back for years.

5 or 6 inches of snow... Wasn't allowed tobogganing; played lots of fives. left hand getting more proficient – can flick my left wrist and have got far more contact than I used to have. I feel my knee when crouching and getting up, and there's still a trace of fluid on it.

---

[265] our new home in Rye

[266] Having a single study helped me create my own space. I collected my own pictures, photos, books (on sailing and art) and belongings, a Macgregor tartan rug for the couch, a pewter pint mug for cold water etc., my lares and penates. I did not have a record player but listened keenly to all kinds of music in other studies, and sometimes one could not avoid hearing it – I recall Sugden playing endless Elvis down the corridor.

[267] I continued to suffer problems with my right knee for years.

[268] My mother's brother Robin Hone was to marry Helen Caddell in Linlithgow.

[269] Dear's dog was still boarded at Sid Morphet's farm during her absence.

Been skating in the yard. Have attained a reasonable sense of balance, but nothing flashy and there are not any really good skates. One of S's pals Whitman is probably the best. S skating lots...

German prose, says Mr Bishop, was the best I've done. We're reading Goethe's Egmont which is nice. I've been longing to do something of his and apparently last year they went right through A level without doing any Goethe. In French it is Racine and we have finished a novel called 'La Neige en Deuil', which I think is a terrific story[270].

Music has begun and is hitting the school like a steel driver. Orchestra started with a terrific foss about practising. We are doing Orpheus aux Entrees - with a horribly difficult clarinet cadenza – and the whole of the Unfinished Symphony. I like the Second movement very much. For the House Unison we are doing 'Say goodbye to your pastime and play, lad' from Figaro and a song by Gounod or however you spell it. We might win the pot there.

In the Quartet I was tried as Tenor but could not hold the top note firmly enough. I popped down 2 octaves to try bass but could not 'sit on' the F with a proper booming, so I'm chucked. In House Orchestra we're playing a Stanley trumpet tune. We have the best trumpet player the school's had for a long time.[271] Also a Trio for strings and a sextet for clarinet and strings, the Entracte of Rosamund. We start practising that today.

Ten training has started - necessary if one is going to get anywhere in it.

Yesterday we had some South Africans staying for the night. After The Bridge was the best film I've seen for a long time - perhaps I'm always saying that - better than Great Expectations – star studded cast[272]. Good cartoon with it... The S. Africans stayed for tea and breakfast. They were terribly nice. They came from the school where Spencer Chapman OS is Headmaster[273] and each family paid £300 for a tour to Rome, Vienna Innsbruck, Paris and all over Britain visiting various schools, seeing shows, rugger matches etc. .

Nice to see the slush gone now.

S   26 Jan, Sunday, 1958

Thank you for the butter and the gloves. The gloves arrived at just the right time; also for sending the trousers.

---

[270] About an aeroplane crash in the mountains
[271] Nelson had joined the National Youth Orchestra in his fourth year – an exceptionally gifted trumpet player and musician.
[272] Unclear text, because the film shown was Great Expectations. The reference to 'After the Bridge' may refer to 'The Bridge on the River Kwai' which came out in 1957.
[273] St Andrew's College, Grahamstown

I hope you are having a good time in Rye and that Dear likes Rye and the house. Are they going to wall paper our room with the squares[274].

It snowed on Monday but not enough to sledge. I did house juniors training in the snow; and it snowed hard over night, great big heavy flakes, and on Tuesday there were drifts in the yard – and everything looked very beautiful when it was untouched.

Tuesday afternoon I went tobogganing. There were two sledges between the four of us. We did not go on the school run on Frostrow but made many runs on the golf course. It was terrific fun and we went on till about a quarter past five. Then on Tuesday night it froze 26 ° of frost e.g. = 6° F. It was very cold in bed. But all this frost was wasted because we started [making] the house yard [rink], making banks and rolling on Tuesday afternoon; and on Tuesday night the prefects got a hose and turned it on to the snow – it was a fire hose. The snow just shot up in bumps and the whole thing was wrecked. Luckily after about two minutes of hosing the hose broke down. But on Wednesday night we all threw fire buckets on to it to from the top. This worked well but was not thick enough (23° of Frost). We skated for the first time on Friday and there is now very good floodlighting and a loud speaker which plays dance music. This morning it is unskateable but we all had yesterday skating.

On Thursday we decided to go skating on Holme Fell tarn. The snow was very thick but there was also a thick mist. Me and three others set off very quickly and were the first out. Unfortunately we knew it was on Holme Fell but we did not know where. Anyhow we met another guy, a senior in Hart House, and followed him, but he took the wrong route and went up the steep face of Holme fell and we had to climb about 200 yds on our hands and knees. Eventually we asked this Hart House chap if he knew where he was going – and he said No! Holme Fell tarn is about 2/3 of the way up on the Sedbergh side and we realised we were now going down the far side, so we climbed back up and found the cairn. We then went back down and saw the tarn. We realised that on the way up we passed the tarn by not more than 100 yds but the mist was so thick we could not see it. By the time we arrived the ice was pretty thin and very crowded. Most people left fairly soon and it got better but 2 people went through and it was not terrific.

We went skating on Wednesday on Frost Row. We were the first there and it was very good until half the school came.

On our Sunday walk we took Penny who was very well and likes Mrs Sid very much. I hope Dad might remember to get some Eastern rug affairs in the Aden market, which would be jolly 'd'.

---

[274] I remember well Sandy and I choosing that wall paper for our room - a chequered, somewhat psychedelic patter in red, black and grey - in Sandersons.

This term I take Cert A Part I and so I am having C.M.I. in long breaks. I don't know what it stands for but it is to learn about weapons, Bren guns etc.

On Friday night some South African Schoolboys came over; we skated on the rink, then there was a film, jolly 'd', it was Great Expectations. It was done very very well and was a 1ˢᵗ class film, nearly up to River Kwai standard, but not quite.

J   9 Feb 1958

Please don't worry about the dentist next hols. I've been on Tuesday and had 3 fillings and have to have 2 more in a couple of weeks time. About the passport, I'm afraid I have little idea about where it is. I'm pretty certain I never kept it and if I have it, it can only be in the top of my desk or in the envelope and pen holder affair at the very top. On the journey I kept it in the ruck-sack along with Robertson on Goethe and writing stuff and I definitely had it at Dover. What a bore! I do hope it appears quickly.

I quite understand about the Firefly and bringing it up, it would be jolly nice if we could but again we won't count on it.

A second attempt at snow....

Playing fives... Although it's still got fluid on it, I think my knee is ok....

Here is the form for County grants which please will you fill in and send to the Education Officer, see form. I have also done one for Sussex. Middlesex conditions state 'ordinarily resident on the 30ᵗʰ June?

Went to Kendal for my teeth. The whole place and equipment seemed a grade or two below Harley Street, I have to admit to being a dentist snob. It was a filthy day and I tramped around from shop to shop for an hour, in a heavy mac dripping on to the floor and getting embarrassed after 5 mins then walking on to the next. Spent quite a bit of time learning my English prep for the HM in a café with a coffee.

Here is a photo of the jazz band – you can just see the bowler hat but not the stomach [pillow tied in].[275] Pity it wasn't in colour. The bull fiddler's vest was pink etc..

For German I've now had four a minus running from Mr Bishop. I had an equal top French prose and a mediocre German one. French essay this week and I haven't had my German one back, on the Kriminalroman[276].

S   9ᵗʰ Feb 58 [Sunday]

Thank you for your lovely letters, especially the air mail from Tel Aviv. I Hope you are enjoying your trip abroad. Incidentally do you know a chap

---

[275] See Visual Essay
[276] Detective story

in the Embassy called Cowley, for he is cousin of Robertson (chap who came my term).

On Monday there was an extra half and Melville and I organised a paper chase. We did this with chalk marks at 30 yd intervals. The hares set off at 2.15; there were two of them. Then the hounds, e.g. me, Melville and the others, numbering 7 in all set off at 2.30. At about 3.15 we saw one of the Hares and had a super chase right over Frost Row and down into the Dent valley. We caught the hare in a wood. Then we went back up on to Frostrow and saw the other hare; he then ran off and we ran after him but he got out of sight and hid in a bog lying flat in the water (only ½ inch deep but mud and rushes and we could not find him. It was great fun and we will have another one soon.[277]

By the way can you send the address of the cousins in NZ because I have forgotten it and I have written a complete airmail..

On Wednesday evening we had a Sharp practice; in case you have forgotten this is a debate when a motion is read out, then the name of 2 chaps who have to propose and oppose the motion[278].

The motions were 'Whether the fuss made about the dog in Sputnik was typical of the modern age'. This lost (I said no). The second was whether boxing is a game of skill. (this lost - I said yes). Whether Valentine cards should be abolished. This lost (I said no). Whether rock and roll has vanished off the face of the earth, and is this a good thing?' This also lost. I said no. I only spoke on one of these, which was boxing which I said was brute force; but I don't think it is.

On Friday there were House Runs. It was the Three Mile for us (not the actual 3 mile, it is about 4 miles). I am still on Big Pack and came 8th. This does not mean I am the best in the house, because the prefects do not run and quite a few chaps were sick (Jamie did not run). I did it in 26 mins.

Yesterday it was snowing so they cancelled the fell run and put on a road run instead; this I did not see so I went round 3-mile gate up Frostrow; it was not actually snowing but there were many big snow drifts, one well above my knees which was terribly hard going. Incidentally you may be wondering why I was going round by myself. Well this is because I don't like going round runs with other people because they are either too fast or too slow; and if you want to walk up a hill they want to run and if you want to run down, they want to walk it. It is far simpler going round by oneself.

Today Mr Durran took 6 of us to Baugh Fell. It was snowing all the time. He drove us there and back. When we got to Rawthey bridge it had turned into a raging blizzard, and you could not face the wind because of the blizzard There were snow drifts all the way. We went on to Baugh Fell but could only get about half way because of the blizzard in our faces and

---

[277] I had forgotten this rather original project.
[278] i.e. an impromptu debate

the snow drifts which you had to crawl or roll through. We reached Uldale force at about 4.15 and there were millions of icicles about 4 ft long, some about 10 ft. We pulled these off and climbed around the Fall and snowballed. Then we set off back, which was much easier going,, skidding all over the place – and arrived back late for tea.

J   Feb 16ᵗʰ 1958 [Sunday]

Hope Dad is spending lots of time admiring the possessions of Sheikhs and Amirs, because I've been hearing all kinds of stories from a guy called McGlashan[279] whose father was Shell's top man in Persia a year or two ago . He was infested with presents because he thought it was good manners to admire the carpets, watches and jewellery. The boy's brother got a gold fountain pen, when goggling in wonder at it, the Sheikh said, 'take it please'...

I will investigate transport by train. You never know it might be possible to send it PLA.

Sorry, that was from [replying to] Dad's letter: it's called a Firefly.

I've been reading a book with pictures, small size, one from a series, on Picasso. I think one or two of his pictures are terrific, and his drawings in charcoal and ink are awfully good. I would have liked to have seen the film.

About Aug 4ᵗʰ I think it very d. of Uncle Robin and Aunt Helen to ask us to be ushers. I haven't asked the C.O. yet but I will next week. I'm not sure that I'll be able to, but probably – it remains to be seen[280].

Ruth came on Thursday and is taking us out to shoot. She was along at the Private Side, with flying boots, jeans and a vast jersey with a zipper - clearly thought but little of by Figaro[281]. She had just fetched the new Jaguar from Windermere and it looked absolutely gorgeous. The HM fetched me along in the middle of prep and was very efficient, although he had to try three times, in getting me back to my French Prose. Ruth had hoards to say but the HM was very firm and after about 10 mins I managed to get away. The shooting will be a wizard day.

I dreamt about shooting last night which was very vivid and have photograph like pictures of it in my mind – Sandy taking a pheasant right above him, a rabbit running about at Sandy's feet and I simply couldn't fire at it, shot bounding off a tough woodpigeon and all kinds of things.

Ruth comes after chapel. Hoping for a big bag.

Later. It wasn't anything much like that. After lunch in a pub we went out with the .22 and a 12-bore. Long shots at some woodpigeon but could

---

[279] Graham McGlashan was a good friend in MLVI and later at Cambridge where we both read modern languages. He was at Clare, on a BP scholarship. He died in an air crash in the Gulf a few years later.

[280] I was due to be at CCF Camp on the date I question.

[281] The Thornelys' small (cocker?) spaniel

not get any. Came across 5 or 6 hares but never got anything. We put up 2 brace of partridge - the last of the season we learnt afterwards. It was great fun to be charging around in jeans. We came back and did some target shooting and after gobbling down a high tea got back 1 minute before chapel.

At chapel the organ had bust up and we were singing from a single tuning pipe without accompaniment. It was quite good actually..

During the week played lots of fives, sometimes as first, sometimes on second pair...

We had a piano recital on Friday and a talk on mountaineering earlier in the week. In fact a rather gay week. Denis Matthews the pianist was terribly good but it wasn't a terribly thrilling selection. I liked very much the 7 bagatelles by Beethoven. 4 bagatelles by a modern composer which I didn't think was terribly inspired; the Appassionata (Beethoven Sonata) which I liked very much and 3 Chopin pieces

Half term soon. And first plans for end of term travel...

Sing ho for the wind and the rain.

S   no date, [16 Feb] 1958 (per J letter)

I hope you are well. I do hope you manage to go out riding in the Park sometime again.

Ruth was here on Friday night. She came while I was doing prep but Jamie saw her. She came in her new Jag at about 10 o'clock after lights, there was a sudden 'come on Zip' from the front garden, then quiet talking, then Ruth's laugh. Then she got into her new car but could not get it to start; in the end it started and they went off.

Today we are going out with her. She is coming to collect us straight after morning chapel; then we will do some shooting in the afternoon, jolly 'd'. I have kept my diaries up since Jan 1 now, a record though not quite as good as Dear's 50 year.

On Tuesday there was a lecture by [space left blank but never filled] on mountaineering. The slides were the best I have ever seen, mainly on Scotland. Unfortunately the term before I came there was a lecture on K2 and the Abominable Snowman. This chap did not talk about them. He only gave us one shot of a Snowman's foot print in the snow, which was fascinating. The rest were slides of mountains in the Lakes, Wales, Scotland and some in the Himmalers. He was not a good speaker and had a strong accent in some words, like 'Immalers' and he forgot the second part of sentences, for instance, 'Here we have the Temple of Shine where once ... then he forgot what happened; and he kept on repeating 'the mountains give one good friends, companionship and much laughter' – and he wound up with a sentence with millions of long words which was so obviously not made up by him and it sounded very funny. But his slides were wonderful.

On Wednesday there were House runs again and it was a very nice day. I came 8ᵗʰ on Big Pack again and we did Straight Bridges. I did it in 20 ½

Yesterday it rained very hard; the rivers were very high and looked wonderful.

Dennis Matthews the piano player came here and gave a Recital on Friday evening; and he brought a grand piano all the way from Liverpool. He was a very good player and I will try to enclose the programme; I am sorry it is scribbled on but the last half hour was very boring and I had nothing to do but meditate on how hard Powell Hall chairs are after 2 hours of listening.

We went out with Ruth in her lovely new car and had lunch at the New Inn

Shandy, soup, steak kidney pud, carrots peas and spuds, (Orange), Fruit ice cream Sunday. All very good.

Then off to Keisley. Jamie and I changed into our skating clothes and went off shooting; Jamie with the .22 and I with the 12 bore. We had great fun but shot nothing. Twice we saw something and waited, then it got up very suddenly. Once it was a brown hare looking like a brown brick and the other was 2 partridge. We then had tea and arrived back just as chapel started. Jamie dropped in at the back but as I had to go to my place like this [sketch of route from door to seat], and the service had just begun, I had to leave it so I did not go. Actually I doubt if I would have gone anyway because I was very car sick (feeling, not actually, sick) coming back on the stragelly roads. In chapel I sit next to Mr Rogers our Assistant House Tutor but he was also absent so no one yet knows.

Melville wonders if it would not be best if I went to him next hols as we are nearby. What do you think? I am 50-50.

Is Jamie going away in the summer hols?

J   23 Feb 1958 [Sunday]

Sounds as if there is a lot of work going on at Westwick[282]. Looking forward to it so much, and the 'Vorfreude' of a slow two-day journey down to get there via London.

Maddening. Am not able to run in the 10. Doc says with water still on my knee 6 weeks ahead, I can't expect to be able to train for it. Playing fives and squash instead...

House orchestra going quite well. There's a chance of winning the cup.... Have been playing clarinet a lot and piano too.

Question on my note pad. Are my braces still at Vicarage Gate, probably on the back of the cupboard door in our room If so could you please send them, I need them for Corps. The other note is 'Dew Line'. It

---

[282] Our house in Rye was named after the house outside Guildford of Great Aunts Anne and Mary Weaver, whose generous legacies helped finance the purchase.

took me a while to unravel that. It is a camp in Northern Canada where one lumbers, traps, digs and drives for $400 a month. One does all sorts of things from running stores to driving bulldozers, shooting and fishing. It sounds a rather good idea for when I go to Canada, if I do.

I keep forgetting to tell you. I am now Editor of the Kingfisher. My problem at the moment is how to get rid of 39 copies of October's one – i.e. last year. Because there's that pile looking at me from the shelves, each worth 2/- to the good when sold. It's going to be a very worth while experience dealing with the printers, advertisements and receipts and book-keeping etc. I'm wanting lots of ideas from Dad on the next edition too.

Doing lots of French reading in particular, determined to be right on top of French prose and Unseen and I'm doing hoards of contemporary writers as fast and thoroughly as I can. My German Unseens are considerably better than my Proses – which suffer more from inaccuracy and small vocab than lack of feel for the language.

Got a rather annoying cough at the moment, but it is going, otherwise everything is fine

S   Sunday 23 Feb 58

Yesterday it snowed again and this morning there is a good covering of snow again..

The builders and people seem to be doing things very fast. I am longing to see the house again, especially the alterations. Has the gardener sowed the grass yet on the new house? I think the corner cupboard for the Herren Zimmer[283] is a very good idea indeed. The more that I think of Rye and the new house, the more I look forward to seeing it and being there.

If you write to the Logies sometime could you ask if J and I could borrow their discus next hols. Dear says that it is actually yours, so maybe they could send it to you. And while I remember do you think it is possible to have the furniture van take down our bikes, as that is how we will go to the town, tennis, golf and sailing etc and it would be awful if you forgot.

I think it is a jolly jolly good idea giving up smoking in Lent even if you have 2 a day if necessary.

Yesterday there was a Firsts match against Wakefield Grammar School who have played 19 matches and won 19. It was a really good game and we won by a drop goal and a try. Also there was a running match against Ampleforth and we lost! I think that is very poor as we are supposed to be good runners if not the best running school; but of course the race was only about 5 miles and lasted 28 minutes. Also we did not have our best team,

---

[283] Our family name for the study-cum-library. It was normally my father's den, but in the holidays Sandy and I took it over for ourselves by general agreement, rather than having to use the drawing room where everything had to be kept tidy. The gramophone was moved in there and in Rye, for the first time, there was a television set there.

because Scott who won the Ten last year, Thompson who came 5th and Taylor who came 7th did not race – for Scott was on the First XV, Thompson was off-ex and Taylor did not want to. On Ampleforth's side, a Pole came first and a Spaniard 2nd. The HM does not know about my not being in chapel – which is a good thing. I have just written to Ruth.

When is Dear coming up here to fetch Penny? I don't think Sid knows.

I think it will probably be best if Melville comes to us as there are more things to do at Rye. There were House runs on Friday; this time it was Western Foot, which I did in 22 ½ mins and came 7th in Big Pack,.

We may be coming back by the early train but there is an awful muddle about it, and no one knows who is going for there are too many people for 1 taxi and we cannot get 2.

Can you tell me what Jamie wants for his birthday?

J   2 March 1958

Thankyou for the biscuits. They are a most wonderful selection of mixed biscuits and it's terribly kind of you to send us such a delicious box each. Thankyou also for sending the braces – I'm not a pessimist but they are indispensable[284] I'm very glad they were at home actually because I could not remember whether I had taken them back or not.

Daddy must be back now. I hope you got the rug back through the customs and any more interesting things you've acquired from more wops and such. I hope it was a nice journey back. How lovely that Dear's coming up here on her way[285].

Had a lovely week – but nothing in particular. House fives we got through another round, beating Powell by 2 points. I was playing on third pair, which is supposed to be our point scoring pair. We won by 15 pts and 1st pair won by 13. Our group is weaker than the other, so we needed do very well in the next to have a chance of glory. And we beat Winder by 51 pts and are now in the final. Rather wizard but I don't think we'll win..

Got work piled up all round me and am determined to get through it well. I had been hoping to read 3 Bulldog Drummond at the weekend and play the piano a lot. Tant pis!

Which reminds me, quoting from my French prose, 'If I chose the country it would certainly be somewhere near the sea...' Not that I am an enthusiast for boating but I like the idea of a boat and even an occasional ten minutes' row. I think I could be happy there if it were far away enough from London and at the same time near enough to London... That is the

---

[284] Battledress trousers were normally worn with braces – which helped ensure their correct and smart hanging when pressed.

[285] On her way back home to Bemersyde, presumably in order to pick up Penny as well as to visit friends in Sedbergh after her absence.

chief problem of the man wanting to live in the country- to be far enough from London and yet to be near enough at the same time...

...Other usual topics mentioned in very brief references: ... fives, work, piano, reading, clarinet... – very happy.

PS What's this I hear about cousins Karen, Kim and Malcolm coming here and Rab and Pip going to Fettes. Has he been offered the HM there?[286]

S   2 March 58 [Sunday]

Thank you for the letter and the biscuits. They are (or were) absolutely terrific biscuits, millions of cream and chocolate ones and even marshmallows. It was very kind of you to send them.

I expect you Daddy will be back in England by now. I do hope you had a good time.. It must have been jolly interesting meeting all the Sheikhs and Khans and important people.

The snow up here hasn't been too bad at all – in fact rather pathetic, only 3 ins on the flat but plenty of big drifts. The only day it snowed was on Monday and there was an awful wind. And then there were House runs, which was jolly stupid as we were running along the top of Frostrow right into the blizzard which really stung as it was very cold and I had only 1 games shirt on. I came 11th in big Pack which isn't so good and took 22 mins. I hope that is the last run of term in fact until next November.

I don't want to argue or be a nuisance but I do not know how Uncle Logie cannot send Dear's discus for that is very simple, as if it is like the school ones it will weigh 4 lb and is only 9 ins in diameter so he could send it by post. The reason why I would like it is because it would be great fun and also I am sure I could get a discus standard next term if I could practice; and the discus as opposed to other things is 2 points not 1, also the standard is only 66 ft.

On Tuesday I went up Winder in the afternoon snowballing. It was great fun especially when we ambushed 6 other chaps in Settlebeck and had a terrific fight.

There has been a stupid new rule saying we have no sauces on our food for tea or breakfast (we never do anyhow for lunch). Why I don't know but this is the Head of House's idea when they [the prefects] came up into dormitories the other evening. We argued with one who went out to fetch the Head of House. We asked him and he could say nothing except that it showed good manners;. We won the argument and the Pres got very cross and walked out in a huff.

On Thursday I played field soccer, the first time since the Dragons. It is taken very light heartedly and is great fun. We won 6-4..

---

[286] It was Loretto School, Musselburgh, near Edinburgh.

Yesterday the 10 Mile course opened but I did not go round. In the senior Dayroom we have to go round twice in under two hours.

On Wednesday there was a Voluntary service. Nearly all the school went. They are held on Wednesdays through Lent..

Next week there is a piano and violin recital on Friday and I think a film on Thursday. There was going to be a film last Friday but the film had not arrived.

The day Dear comes up I am taking Cert A Part I; I should be finished by 3.30 but I am not sure. At the latest at 4.15

I have just heard from Morris that Uncle Rab has been offered the HMship of Fettes; jolly jolly 'd'. That means they will be coming back soon, I hope. Will you tell us all about it?

J   9th March 1958 [Sunday]

Had a vivid dream about Heron's March– passing the bit of Friday Street (in the picture in the Field, which I have in my study - of the pink snow scene), but the telegraph wires were on the wrong side. It was very vivid; and then we managed to have Jeb with us somehow and went in through the back door to the new glory kitchen and I remember feeling very alarmed by Jeb's footprints on their linoleum floor.

Longing to be at Westwick next hols; it all sounds a bit different, the lawn, the dining room, our bedroom[287].

Fraid I can't get down by the early train. The school rule is not before 7.00 except to go north on a fixed train.

Fives matches and scores...

German Essay on Egmont which is going to mean a lot of sorting of my notes.... French...

Hoards of orchestra practice (House orchestra) going for the cup.

Field Day yesterday was the best yet. It snowed the night before and there was a covering everywhere. Although it was cold in the shade the sky became perfectly clear and it was fairly warm; not too much running, fired off lots of blanks, had an hour for lunch in a gully and marched 2 ½ miles back.

We had the film 'Kind hearts and Coronets' which was absolutely wizard and a good cartoon with it to end off a very satisfactory day.

On Friday we had a recital by Howard Ferguson (piano) and Yrak Neaman (violin)[288]. Apparently the HM was very pleased with the choice of programme, none of which I particularly liked except some Ernest Bloch, some rather oriental atmosphere music. There was a Cesar Franck Sonata which bored me, a Mozart sonata which was all right and a sonata

---

[287] Our parents had had several minor works done and added a small wash room/lavatory on the top floor to be shared by Sandy and me and any live-in help.

[288] Yfrah Neaman

composed by Howard Ferguson himself which they had played on 4 continents or something – which I thought was a waste of time rather, but perhaps it wasn't as bad as all that.

S   9 March 58

I cannot understand how you do not know about Uncle Rab. Maybe it isn't true but Mrs Morris came up here last weekend and had a letter from Rab telling her. If you do not get to know soon I expect it is some funny sort of rumour, but I can't imagine how one would start about Uncle Rab.

It is a terrific coincidence about Mr Spens[289], especially you just finding him and finding out we are friends here.

I am dying to hear all the stories of your trip abroad, and I hope it is a nice day in Rye for your golf today.

Thursday was Field Day. It was a day without a cloud in the sky but the wind was awful. Our platoon of about 30 chaps went up on to Frostrow, having got rifles. Before lunch we divided up into sections and did weapons training etc. A Brigadier came round to inspect the Corps. He came round to us and made us give a demonstration of field signals (5 of us). Then we had lunch and sat in a barn for about 1 ½ hours. After which we had a battle; our platoon defended a position; we were only allowed 5 blanks each; we had six because our section commander was feeling decent. Our platoon was in the front line of defence and after a bit we had to retreat. We retreated to some wonderful trenches in a marsh and held out there for quite a long time; and after a bit they got to within 30 yards we stopped the battle. It was jolly good fun..

On Tuesday I went round the ten mile, with a chap of my term and we had a race with Mr Durran and the four chaps he was going round with. We raced all the way to Cautley and we got ahead; then they caught up and went ahead. In the end we won. I did it in 1 hr 40 mins exactly. I was going in for the House relay yesterday but it snowed so hard that we could not have it, but I expect we will have it sometime next week.

I am taking Cert A Part I on Tuesday this week not Thursday so I will be able to go out with Dear after all.. I am looking forward to is very much indeed, It takes years to clean one's kit; I am using Jamie's belt and gaiters which are very very good ones.

On Thursday evening there was a film called 'Kind hearts and Coronets.' Alec Guinness plays 8 parts of which all were murdered. It was very good but not terrific. And again on Friday there was a Recital in Powell Hall, by Ifrah Neaman and Howard Ferguson. It was quite good, much better than the piano one earlier on. Ifrah Neaman (violin) was very good indeed though the programme was a bit stodgy.

---

[289] Presumably a Sedbergh parent whom my father met on his travels somewhere

Sorry this is late but I have had not a minute spare with pressing, ironing, polishing, scrubbing and brushing my kit for Part I – which I took yesterday and passed.

J mid March 1958 [separate letter to JMBL]

Dear Dad,

Many thanks for the wizard box of Turkish Delight and for the lessons to come from Willy Anderson. The Turkish Delight from Istanbul is superb and I'm eating it as slowly as I possibly can to make it last. Very hard!

Dear was here on Thursday, and after running in the 10 mile relay (S and I both did the first bit[290] (which was 1 ½ miles, I came 1st and S came 2nd out of 4) we went out with her for a terrific 'binge' at the X Keys. It was very nice there and we had a vast meal and lots of talk.

Had an extra half on my birthday which was terribly nice. A bit chilly despite the sun. We walked about 4 or 5 miles, snowballed and ran a bit but nothing terribly strenuous.

Saturday just the normal one, but this term Saturdays are rather marred by constant orchestra practice. I still can't play the cadenza for the Thursday concert and am getting very 'pumped' about it. The house orchestra bits aren't so hard.

I doodle at various pieces on the piano – but no hard enough. The first movement of the Moonlight is just about coming under control...

Art is my craze at the moment. Am plodding conscientiously through 'Outline of Art' from the start on. Have got to Michelangelo now. Also managed to do a lot of contemporary French reading. Am never sure whether it is better to look up and write down everything unknown or to read on and get the sense of it and only look up when really stuck. I prefer the latter, otherwise I get bored with the book.

I quite agree about not reading modern languages at univ[291] but what I'm not sure. I'm certainly keeping the architecture business in mind, and would like to know what the training entails for one thing.

Hols soon here

PS please can you tell me what the Freiburg professor want me to bring along[292].

---

[290] First section of the relay run

[291] I was evidently reviewing options with my parents but this is a puzzling reference given my father's previous keenness on my doing modern languages, My interest in architecture lasted for some time, but an Exhibition to St John's to read modern languages settled the matter.

[292] A reference to a planned 3-week Easter holiday visit as paying guest to a professor and his family (2 children of my age) in Freiburg im Breisgau for German language immersion. Both husband and wife taught at the university.

J 16 March 1958 [Sunday – to both parents]

Thankyou very, very, very much for the beautiful book and the print. I can hardly stop looking into the Queen's Beasts[293]. It stands next to my Design of Yachts [Also still in my collection]. Lovely frame for the print too – simple and nice proportions....

Granny and Grandfather gave me a very nice Kent hairbrush and 4 golf balls as well. S gave me two little books on painters from my favourite series, one on Cezanne, one on Klee ([still have them both and some others]. I have one on Vlaminck which I bought with money Aunt Hat sent me and Uncle Robin sent me a £1 which was terribly d of him. I'm hanging on to that for the moment..

Sunny and cold but Monday was a heavenly day and everyone was rather peeved at NOT being given an extra half and there was a general sulk strike in afternoon school.

I had a good afternoon however. Bendle and myself, specs[294] to lose as 1st pair, beat the specs to win in two games.

On Wednesday went to Kendal for my second and last dental appointment and had two fillings. It started snowing a quarter of an hour later and going back over the fells it was very heavy snow and looked wonderful because it was the sticky kind that sticks to every branch and twig.

S   Sunday [16 March] 58

Thank you very much for your letter which was a lovely long one. I have not heard from yet from my godmother. I think it was very nice of her; also I think it would be lovely to go round the National Gallery and choose a picture to get printed. Talking of pictures I gave Jamie two small books containing 30 colour pictures each, one by Cezanne and the other by Klee[295]. He is starting a collection, as they are in a series of some 30 books. He was very very pleased with your picture you gave him.

Dear arrived on time on Thursday and took us out to tea at the Cross Keys where I had as good a tea as I have ever eaten, specially ordered, ham and eggs, apple pie, hot scones cakes, biscuits then fruit salad and cream. It was absolutely delicious. Dear was very well and told us all the news. What a pity about golfing at Rye when you went with some chaps and it snowed; it must have been very disappointing.

It has been lovely weather for the last few days but on Wednesday it suddenly snowed. On Friday there was an extra half. I went with some

---

[293] A book on heraldry, which I still have

[294] A 'spec' is someone seen as the hope (say, of a House) or someone widely expected to win at something; for example, 'he is the spec for the Ten'. Thus here, Bendle and I (School House's first pair) were not expected to beat our opponents, the favourites to win the fives match in question – but we actually did.

[295] I still have them too, along with a number of others from my collection from those years.

chaps over Crook, Scissors then down a frozen scree. Halfway down we got stuck and it was very slippery. We took hours going back up it. We took every caution, as if we had started to roll down there was 200-300 ft of snowed over rocks. Apart from this it was great fun. We stalked sheep and tried tickling fish. I can still get a junior fishing licence for next term which is very nice as it is 17/6 not 45/-.

There was the 10 mile relay on Thursday and both Jamie and I were running in the 1st leg which was from the start to the first farm in 10 mile lane (about 1 ½ miles. There were 4 runners in each leg. Jamie won ours and I came 2nd, quite a long way behind him. It was very good fun. Unfortunately our team lost, in the end, and Jamie's came second.

I think it would be great fun trying some decorating ourselves, though we would have to get some tools. I expect you really know quite a lot about it for I thought you did some of the Herons March spare room.

Cert A was on Thursday. In the morning I got up in uniform, then after one lesson we came back and had a drill test and an inspection. The examiner calls each chap out in turn, who marches up to him – Halt, Salute, Stand at Ease, then answer any questions, then attention, salute, about turn and back to his place. Luckily I did ok although two chaps forgot to salute. Then we did map reading tests and message writing. After lunch we did field craft, crawls, field signals, use of flags, and how to move without being seen. Then weapon training. We did not finish till 4.30. About 30 people did it; 2 failed. It was quite fun doing it.

There is a house fives competition – double in an American competition but in senior, middle and junior groups. I am playing with a chap who has only played 3 times. in his life, so I doubt we will win, but it will be good fun.

Yesterday I went round the 10 again. I did it by myself and did it in 1 hr 36. Near Green hill I was attacked by 2 geese who came charging at me with necks stretched straight out and hissing away. I ran as fast as I could up the hill and they stopped chasing.

It is a lovely day today and I am going on the fells after lunch.

J   23 March 1958 [Sunday]

How infuriating about the Huns but 'so ist es im Leben ...' we might say.[296]

We've had our last English lesson – with the HM who does them very well – and I finished Latin on a triumphant note with the best piece of work to date – cheers cheers. In German more on Britannicus and Eduard Mörike whom I like as a poet definitely.

---

[296] Reference not clear; something to do with the planned Freiburg trip perhaps

I got a merit for my French essay Tempête en mer and an A- for that two – but might have got a Distinction if it had not been marred by 11 elementary mistakes (gender etc.)

School orchestra has finished so that's that. The cadenza went off with only one squeak – and that in a place I've never done it before. Rather lucky. I thought I was going to bish the whole thing up[297].

The 10 Mile concert was a terrific success this year. The house played the Toys in the Toy symphony and the Masters quartet was awfully good – and of course Orpheus was very popular too

There was the Ten on Thursday which no doubt S will tell you all about [he did very well]. The run was just a gallop of dark horses, and it was definitely a good day. A beautiful windless sunny morning. Heavy driving snow in the afternoon. Le voila Sedbergh. However it didn't deter the runners and 2 records were set up - 12 chaps under 1 hr 20, and 64 chaps under 1.30. Pretty fast.

On Tuesday we pairs of fives played 2 pairs of Cambridge fives, (both OSs). It was terrific to watch although their standard was not phenomenal except for the 2 Smith brothers who hardly ever made mistakes or put up easy shots.

Been playing fives and running and now it's yard soccer competitions. S's team are winning at the moment – under the title of B-Lzebubs Ha! Ha! There are some quite good names this year and quite a lot of spirit about the whole thing.

House orchestra and singing cups this week – and needles s to say more feverish practising on all of those. Hope we'll do well, but not become too much of a musically minded house...

After a term off full exercise, the Doc thinks it's nearly all gone now and I'm allowed on the fells, yard soccer etc. and I reckon that is that, if I'm not absolutely stupid – c'en est fait de lui.

Packing on Tuesday – only 4 days. Orchestra rehearsals

J Letter from Cambridge following an interview at Clare College[298]. Late March 1958

Thank you first of all very much for a most enjoyable 24 hours or thereabouts. It was awfully nice to be back home in Rye, for I really do feel it's home now, no doubt at all, even for such a short while - a very pleasant and peaceful break. There's nothing like a long train journey and an

---

[297] Common slang: to make a total mess of it

[298] This early visit to Clare College, Cambridge, was a preliminary excursion arranged by Thornely presumably to find out where I might stand with the college for a possible place based on summer term exam results rather than on scholarship entrance. I was not at that point a firm scholarship candidate.

evening at home with time to sit, think, read and have peace particularly from this kind of peak period of the term. The outcome of the break as far as peak period is concerned is 8 repeat 8 essays by coming Saturday

I got to Cambridge ok at the expected time. There I got chizzed by the taximan having been previously that it was a long walk to Clare and I didn't know where Clare was at that, who took me an extra long way round apparently. I found my room eventually in the new buildings of Clare, the other side of the backs and had plenty of time to change and wash. Then the interview. It was with one man, this doctor Northam himself only.

In short the outcome of the interview was hard work wanted. Not much that I expected came up at all, Most of the time he spent on explaining that it wasn't fair (horrible expression) to the student or the tutor to take in a guy who had just scraped his exams for it meant he probably wouldn't get through his university ones. More than a pass is needed and as far as I can see; what he next wanted are my marks at 'S' levels in August. Whether he'll be saying anything before he's seen those I don't' know – but I'll tell you if I hear anything from him. Politics never came up, we discussed work and languages reading, why I changed sides, nix about who wanted to come to univ; he refused to follow up any of my 'interests' except the standard of my clarinet playing and a bit about art.

The total result was therefore rather negative except that they aren't being difficult by saying you mustn't go anywhere else other than here; he said rather that he thought it was a good thing to try a second college.

I had a very enjoyable time there. Went to the hall of culture cinema to see 'The Captain's tale' with another guy from Sedbergh[299] and a pal of his. The next morning we looked round a few colleges and generally around the place. I got back lateish, all well and without much spent. Nice to be back again except for the prospect of the Ten on Tuesday

We have hoards of hard work taking exams this term and practices for everything going on wildly. Then there's Easter at the end of the week. We're having some form of amusement and dinner next Sunday which should be rather gay

Thankyou for a lovely stay at home & looking forward to the holidays like anything

Summer Term 1958

S   no date [c. Monday 5 May 1958, just after his birthday on 4 May]

I have played some tennis and some cricket. In the first match of term I took 4 wickets and in batting I hit a four then was run out.

---

[299] possibly Graham MacGlashan, see p. #, fn. 263, above

Dear came Friday morning and I saw her for a few mins; she gave me a Selkirk Bannock which was terrific. It is just what I wanted as we have a new cook who has not yet got the hang of things; actually we think she has not yet found the fridge as we had sour milk on Friday and Saturday and it was very sour today.

Jamie was back this morning[300] and brought his lovely knife with him with a deer handle, also your lovely peppermint creams which was jolly d of you to give me, and Granny and Grandfather's record. I seem to have had a jolly 'd' birthday.

Today the weather is not so good...

Thank you very much for the cake which was delicious...

J   Sunday 11 May 1958

Dear Mummy

Thank you very very much indeed for the lovely but so short holidays and everything which you did for us. I'm sure Rye's the place for us and we're going to have a gorgeous time there. I only wish I could have been longer there these last holidays as well as my stay in Germany which I enjoyed v much.

Thank you very much for the kilt, slippers, Goethe's poems, Rock and handkerchief. Sandy hasn't received his slippers yet but he will soon because I only opened it this morning to get my kilt out.

I'm sorry I didn't write to you before at Vicarage Gate. I should have done but somehow I just didn't get to it. The kilt is absolutely fine with braces and certainly more comfortable as well. This morning I got up in a frantic rush. I had forgotten about my kilt, I couldn't find my studs. Then to crown it all I couldn't tie my tie and Cass Matthew had to do it for me, I just couldn't - I had no idea. Incipient madness I should think.

I had a very nice journey up here indeed. The steward on the sleeper, which was superbly comfortable and luxurious, was Uncle Rab's old batman as I expect Dad told you? Small world, what? My companion was a very nice chap who was going up to Barrow and who had come down with his three pals for the Cup on Saturday. I was woken up with tea and biscuits, all terribly luxurious but rather early and then I walked up the train to the Windermere half, at least portion.

At about 6 o'clock I scrambled out onto Oxenholme station. No buses running till the afternoon, so I read on the platform till a man coming for the Sunday paper turned up and he gave me a lift right to the door at the House which was very d. There I had to do some more sitting and reading till chaps went to Communion, because I was locked out but it was a very nice crisp morning.

---

[300] from Freiburg

Life as a prefect is absolutely super.[301] I can hardly see how we lived before with all those petty things like roll calls, out of the house on time and so on.

One bit of news for anxious mamas: I have a bath every night. Most odd. Feel unnaturally clean and so forth. Shoes bright clean every morning, My fag is a guy by name Dorward, son of an O.S. and nephew of <u>the</u> A.F. Dorward, Scottish rugger player, etc. He isn't a terrific games player but is very brainy and definitely very nice & a pretty efficient fag too.

Of course there are all kinds of things to do as a prefect. Sitting at the Junior Dayroom table is rather an effort; working out a haircutting list took me an hour. And then things like seeing that the ten-bedder don't talk after lights, that they strip and make their beds - and generally tidy up after them like a nanny. In the evening we don't have to go to bed till half an hour after the others, which gives you an extra ¾ of an hour to work, read or play records in or something, which is very pleasant and makes all the difference too.

I haven't missed much work and what I missed in French I made up in tutorial with Horsy G in the week and I've only got to copy out what little grammar I missed. We haven't had any work back yet so I 'm still in suspense for results. I'm still thinking a terrific amount in German and a French essay meant for this last Friday which I still haven't done is absolutely hopeless. I seem to have forgotten all French and try putting German words in. I have no problems now in understanding what Jack H is saying and I have far more confidence in talking myself and answering questions and things. We have a German essay on the Free Trade Zone for this weekend, which I just must do well.

Weather frightful – hardly any cricket. I've only played twice. Once on Littleside and I bowled quite well but I doubt if I'll stay on because 18 chaps have been weeded off the gigantic Bigside, which now stand purely at 22, the two elevens. I played in a first league game which SH just lost. I got a hat-trick and took 4 wickets for 22 runs, which wasn't too bad. I had a short but sweet innings, scoring one very long six which was a real wizzer 200-yd golf drive. I was bowled a bit later trying to do roughly the same in a different direction to a straight ball.

Talking of golf I bashed round the Riggs yesterday in drenching rain. I think I found nine tees and nine greens. I only lost one ball, not too bad at all and it was very good fun but rather cold and wet. So I ran back afterwards to get warm again.

---

[301] My last two years at School House were most enjoyable. Seniority often really began in the Spring term (i.e. Jan 1958 for me) when the scholarship takers and top prefects of the previous Winter term had left, and there was another move up the house. Responsibilities of a junior prefect were light – such as junior dayroom supervision at preps, or organising a squash ladder – but one made new friendships among the older, more senior, prefects as well as among one's peers; and in addition one got to know better boys a year or so below through involving them in the organisation of teams or other aspects of house life.

I have been swimming again and find the pool terribly shallow for diving but I expect I'll get used to that soon. I'm the pre in charge of swimming and also of fives. Swimming isn't taken too seriously so I have nothing to do there really except practise and try to get into the final of the diving or something myself as an example. Fives is definitely more important and in these wet days I have played quite a bit, getting the juniors playing a bit. They have to start properly this term if they're to be any good for the junior fives comp. next term – and they've got to be!

About the wedding[302] at the beginning of the holidays, another boy, who came the same term that I did, in Sedgwick House, who I've seen quite a lot of in various things, is a cousin and also going. He says that they can take me out by car to Linlithgow which is a very nice offer. How long am I going to be away from camp? This guy, Jock Stein, is staying the whole of the next day as well – on the pretext of clearing up I gather. I could I suppose also have permission to stay away that day. Please could you tell me soon as I have to work it out with Mr Macdougall, the Corps Major, and there are all the problems like taking up kilts etc.

We've had a civics and a recital this last week, both of which were terribly good. Civics by Mr Alrego the Dead Sea Scrolls expert, with slides. It was first class, absolutely super photographs and most fascinating. Last night we had the Linden Singers. I thought they were pretty good but when they tried some lighter stuff it didn't quite come off. Their madrigals, folk songs and negro spirituals were terribly well done and their conductor spoke quite amusingly. A very pleasant evening is what I would say. There's orchestra this evening which is a terrific bore with all the work I've got in hand, but we're playing some quite nice stuff, 2 Gilbert and Sullivan overtures, 'Iolanthe 'and 'Yeomen of the Guard'. We're also going to play the whole of the Unfinished Symphony which I like very much and it's certainly a great piece of music but I should think the School are going to find the Powell Hall chairs rather hard on the Speech Day Concert.

Am eating a piece of the Edinburgh Rock at the moment and it's wizard. Thankyou very much for it. Sorry again I haven't written earlier and thank you for the parcel again

lots of love to you and to Granny and Grandfather from Jamie

S   11 May 58

I hope you Daddy had a good Birthday and are having a good trip abroad. I have been sent 1 parcel from Uncle Robin and 10/- from my godmother and 10/- from Aunt Hat which is jolly 'd'. It has rained without stopping and the School Fete was postponed till next Thursday which was rather a pity. I went fishing instead and went right down the Rawthey practically to the Lune. After about 5 mins the chap I went with wanted to

---

[302] Of Uncle Robin Hone to Helen Caddell

try a cast or two with the spinning rod and reel and he got it in such a tangle that he could not undo it as our hands were so cold. Unfortunately Harvey Askew is rather badly ill and has been in bed for the last week or so. The river is in spate and it should be wonderful with worm this afternoon.

On Thursday when I played cricket there was a lamb which went on the next door pitch and the sheep dog went after it. They chased round and round the stumps for literally 4 minutes. It was very funny especially when some boys tried to catch it but eventually the farmer caught it by tripping it up with his crook. I took 3 wickets that match and as we won by 7 wkts I did not bat.

I hope you agree about hiking down south after camp? We have everything planned out it is all very simple. Do I get 1 ticket to Melrose on the end of term day and will Dear meet me or anything? The north train leaves here at 7 pm [a.m.] which means changing at Carlisle and going on the train to Edinburgh

I have told the HM I am leaving in Easter 1960 although I don't think it will make any difference about being a prefect as I will not get a study until say next summer even Winter (1959) this is because so few chaps are leaving though Jamie will know when chaps are leaving. Jamie was a Prefect on his 12th term. If I am a pre on my 12th term it will be Easter 60. But as I will not be a prefect on my 12th term I will not be a prefect, all because I came at the wrong time, chiz!

Do you know if there is a 3 year commission and all about it as I would rather like to know.[303]

On Wednesday there was a Corps and I am now in B Company (having passed Cert Part I). We do drill all the time now and it is much more fun. Three of us who have only just started arms drill do it in the House in the evenings with the Prefects for the Drill cup which is sometime at the beginning of next month.

Last night there was a recital in Powell Hall by the Linden Singers who are a group of 4 women and 4 men. They were very good and sing on the Radio and TV and big concerts. All of them had lovely voices especially the Sopranos and Tenors It was a very good programme consisting of Part songs 16th century madrigals folk songs two parts Negro spirituals. They were very good. There were 6 encores done especially and they sang a pop tune as a Finale at the end.

The school library opened on Monday and we had an English lesson there. It is being photographed by Country Life this weekend, so you must buy one when the photos come out. Thank you very much for your Edinburgh rock which is delicious.

J 18th May 1958

---

[303] Sandy was starting to think seriously about what next after school

I haven't as yet actually dealt with the wedding problems, but they'll be ok. As for the trunks, it doesn't matter what ticket is going when it's done through the house on mass and no one even bothers to investigate whether your ticket tallies with where your trunk is being sent and all the rest.

Yes, we're suffering from cold weather... and rain. Only managed to get one game of cricket so far. I didn't bowl terribly well but I managed to get 1 wicket for 21 runs. But for a change I managed to stay in and make some runs. I got 26, which was top score. I succeeded in keeping up my record of getting a six every game in the term – but I rather feel my supply of runs may have exhausted itself now and I'm going to be in for a whole series of noughts.

Fives... coaching juniors ... and I also had one game last night with more senior blokes, Lionel Melville was playing and he plays very well indeed now with a left hand like a gun shot. Not much going on. I've put the weight a bit, played golf with my niblick and swam a bit.

So I've had plenty of time to work which has been a good thing. The German Oral exam is tomorrow which is very early in the term – but for me rather a good thing, while I still have German on my mind – although it seems very long ago now. I'm spending this weekend trying to germanicize myself for it. I've gone past my previous best marks for German raising it to 58%, which is not enough yet but there is a bit I could cut out from that. In my German prose I only had 5 mistakes in the whole thing which with Mr Hammer would give me 82% It was rather wizard to get back work with hardly any pencil marks at all on it. I find reading in German infinitely more easy now – not the reading but the understanding I mean.

I got my first French essay which wasn't too bad. It was horribly full of anglicisms and germanisms but I reckon I'll put those away with concentrated reading – hoffentlich, The exams don't begin till July 7th so there's quite a bit of time still.

I seem to have been back for absolutely ages but it's only a fortnight really. The postponing of the fete which we had, seemed to draw things rather on and in general a rather monotonous week. We had the fete for the Parish church who were asking £100 for the heating. The school succeeded in getting £130 in the end which was a very pleasing effort. There were all kinds of fascinating things there and quite a crowd of people, Unfortunately – and my throat is suffering for it now – I spent the whole of the afternoon yelling outside our show and didn't manage to see anything. We were giving Sputnik rides into space and it was a roaring success. A system where a chap goes in blindfolded and mounts on the rocket, a duck board, with noise effects from earphones plugged in to a gramophone and is boosted up into the air about 4 inches – with the impression, because his hands are on the manipulators' heads, who crouch slowly down, that he is 4 or 5 feet up in the air. Then he gets yelled at to jump and is scared and usually has to be tipped off and gets a gorgeous shock when he hits the ground about a second before he expects to.

171

Apart from that nothing terribly enthralling but jolly good fun as usual of course

France is in a super mess up[304]. I hope Dad will straighten it out for them.

S 18 May 58

It has been raining except on Thursday when we had the School fete and it was lovely.. The fete started at 4 and went on to 6.30, and the side shows were rather original especially Jamie's which was a ride in a sputnik. Jamie stood outside dressed as a sort of door man or what have you in a flowing coat and top hat. For part of the time I was helping raf[f]ling a cake with Lionel. Actually it was not a rafle /sic/ but a guess the weight. Unfortunately the person who guessed it right was one of our friends who also came our term which looked rather fishy especially as only 5% of the entrants were boys; so we had to swap that [ticket] and gave it to the next nearest who we looked up to find was another of our friends (this was Broadbent son of Mr Broadbent who won the Harkness Scholarship at St Andrews the year before Dad); so this was also swapped and we gave it to a person living in the town. There were many good side shows such as kicking a soccer ball through tyres and knocking a 6 inch nail into a piece of wood in x gos and many good rafles and the band was very good. Also there was a donkey ride for the small town's children and a skiffle group in the fives courts[305]. Altogether it was a great success and made £!27 and our rafle made £3

Harvey Askew is much better now and ought to be out of bed in about a week according to Ed...[illeg.] his son.

Today is quite a nice day and am going out with some other chaps. I don't know where yet. There is not a cook in the House, so Sunday lunch is not worth staying in for. I'm back and it's now 8 o'clock.

3 of us went to Barbon where we had pack lunches ices and pop; then we walked up the car track place and up and down the ghylls and it was gorgeous and sunny. We got a lift from a person who turned out to be a Sedbergh mother. She asked what house we were from and was surprised that anyone in School House ever took a lift. This is extremely true; but on the way back it was very funny as we took a lift with a chap and his daughter about 65 and 30; and he asked 'what time does the headmaster have his tea as we are going there to stay? This was rather a shock to us especially when he said he would drive us right into the house. So we hopped out just outside Sedbergh hoping he would not mention that he took 3 boys back

---

[304] Algiers coup attempt of May 1958 and political crisis which led to the return of De Gaulle. Algeria was in my father's Middle East and Africa area of interest in the FO.
[305] Alan Macfarlane's skiffle group.

from Barbon as the HM knows we went to Barbon. The chap was the preaching tonight, and is the Very Rev Provost of Wakefield!

Do you know about the Theatre after the wedding or whether it is a theatre or not? I have a 10/- cheque from my godmother which is signed to Margaret Bruce Lockhart which is not very helpful as I cannot get it cashed; or can I? Or shall I send it to you?

J   25 May 1958 [Sunday]

...Westwick seems to be coming along superbly. I can hardly wait to see all those lovely things that are being put in – cupboards, curtains, wallpapers, etc, and of course all the stuff from Vicarage Gate too.

About working in the holidays, I'm investigating. From what I gather as far as making money is concerned working on a farm, although possibly nicer, is hardly worth it. It may be, I'm not sure. Do you think you could possibly ask in Rye somewhere about such possibilities. One thing could be to try in London at the Jo Lyon Corner House or one of their places. Apparently working overtime one guy managed to earn about £10 in a week, pretending to be over 18, which is another thing these days. If under 18 it cuts the week's wage by $1/3^{rd}$ if not more.. If it is for a matter of a fortnight it would clearly be worth getting down to it properly. Any ideas and opinions?

Not much cricket because of rain. Managed to stay on Littleside. Bowled quite efficiently. Haven't taken many wickets but I've succeeded in keeping the spinners to a reasonable length and have not been clouted about too much. I have a batting average of about 13 which is better than the usual 4.. I had one 19, a top score on a 1st league game.

Have been putting the weight and should be able to get a standard pretty easily now. That's 31 feet for the 12lb weight; the first qualifier is 35' and the second is 38' I don't expect to get to those yet. My record so far is just short of 33'... practising discus, long jump - I don't think I am a serious long-jumper but the 16' standard is not terribly far. Played some fives and golf on the Riggs and around the Lupton House field which is free for golfers in the summer – and sheep, which are quite sensible sheep and keep out of the way.

Have been working pretty hard – nearly ceaselessly. Essays all over the place. It was 3 and an Unseen for last weekend and its 2 and an Unseen this; but they aren't so stinking this time. .... I got an AB for my Antigone Anouilh essay which was top mark. There are three Moliere Misanthrope essays in the coming week. Am trying to read as much French as possible and have also bought a Penguin European Architecture book with 72 plates (for 6/-) which I haven't had time to delve into yet.

Have been down to the Art School and watched Charlie Ward paint in oil and tried manipulating it a bit, also tempera. It looks terrific fun and I'd love to have a go at it seriously. The trouble is of course the cost. A tube of white costs 3/6 and small tubes range from 1/4d upwards which don't go very far although one can dilute with turps and so on. It's something I'd like to investigate further in the hols....

Have played quite a bit of piano in my spare time and tried pen drawings a la Paul Klee – becoming very cultured.

The ok word here for chaps who don't do anything is 'They've got character'.

S   25 May 1958

Happy Whitsun greetings etc...Have you got anybody in to cook and help or are you waiting for the hols? The food here is getting much much worse. For one meal (pudding) all they gave us was chocolate sauce. And we often get for lunch soup with bits in and then a 'teeny tiny' bit of pud. This would not matter so much but unlike last term we can not have as much bread and marge as we want. For we get so little marg and jam that it all goes years before the end of the meal.

Last week in fortnight orders I came 16th in Chemistry but 4th in Maths and 2nd in Physics.

It has been a very boring week. I have played lots of fives but it has been too wet for much cricket yet. I am on [one of] the 13 people of whom 11 will make the House Panters, which are to be played on Friday 13th of June. If I get on, it will be as a bowler (off breaks) though I can not decide whether to bowl them medium fast or medium slow.

We are contemplating going to a motorcycle scramble today. It is motor like racing along mud tracks and through water splashes etc. It is near Kendal, but it is not a very nice day and we may not go.

I don't suppose you have thought or have anything about going to France in a sailing boat?! as I think, and I am sure J does, it is a wonderful idea.

Back from chapel now, raining hard so we can not go out to the Bike Race

It is a lovely day (Monday) Sorry this is late but I went up Winder last night and had great fun fighting other houses.

Everybody is getting rather fed up because School House is to[o] cultured and if we do anything wrong everybody flares up especially the HM. For instance when I got beaten for scab[b]ing a cold bath, he called me down and told me the Prefects trust us to have them and therefore I was untrustworthy, but it is so obvious they do not trust us as they try to catch us. Also in School House you get a Housemaster's beating for scabing a lift but in other houses you only get a Pre's. Also the HM sends up Dayroom heads and Pres on Winder on Sundays to see we don't rag; but other school pres don't mind at all if their house rags. So what with this and the rotten food there is rather an anti-people who run the house' feeling.[306]

The Bradford boys are supposed to be coming today but they have not turned up yet but there I still an extra cricketing half

We have super new fire alarms installed that make the most terrible noise. We had a practice on Friday[307] and from being in bed to getting downstairs in slippers & dressing gown (it was not actually in the night) and all the windows and doors to be closed and the cubes searched by prefects it took 70 seconds. Though the HM says we are going to have a proper practice in the middle of the night sometime.

There is a film on Saturday (Rear Window) should be great fun seeing.

I have been having a very good time here.

J   1 June 58 [Sunday]

Thanks for the parcel, slippers and magazine. Yes indeed, I did get the kilt stockings from Dear; sorry I should have told you before. They are very nice.

It is possible that I may not have to go back to camp after the wedding at all. Jock Stein isn't going to. I hadn't realised that Wednesday is the last day... Anyway the decision is not mine. Major Macdougall will tell me whether he thinks it's worth my coming back for just a day and a half.... But will need an extra ticket. The army does not pay the rail fare for something like that – only the ticket to your home. Where do I need to get that ticket to?

Busy weekend and lots going on. Freihandelszone essay I was quite pleased with. Got 58%. Came second in a prose which was a bit of R. L. Stevenson (Treasure Island I think). 3 essays in hand on Le Misanthrope and a German general essay and one on Gerhard Hauptmann. I had quite a good French prose.

There's been time for other things too though – a lot of knocking about on the golf course with a 7 iron only. Went round in 51 playing except for one hole pretty well immaculately. If I can hit my other clubs as well as the 7 iron I'll be doing quite well.

Cricket one league game and one Littleside game – but don't suppose I'll get on to the 3rds. We, the 4ths, beat them in a practice game anyway, which was rather A1. Had one good game of fives with next year's seniors – which promises well.

Last Sunday Mr Lyon and Mrs Same were here from Rugby (former headmaster). He does career interviews. I had one. We discussed

---

[306] First signs that Sandy and his friends, who had been boxed out from responsibilities by unlucky timing of arrival behind a large intake, were beginning to feel rebellious

[307] Fire drills normally involved orderly, daytime, exit from the house and head counts; but chutes and ladders were installed at some later point and tested by a handful of volunteers.

architecture without coming to any particular ideas. If anything it made me rather negative. The whole thing was rather negative. They send their love to you.

We had an A+++ film last night, Rear Window – absolutely super, thrilling, gripping and amusing and thoroughly satisfying. No cartoon but the film made up for that.

½ of the term has gone – hooray!

S   3rd June 58 [Tuesday]

... hope you had a good Whitsun...

This week has been much better weather and I have played cricket most days, twice captain for 3rd Leaguers (this is a house team under 16 friendly games v other houses). Yesterday was one when I was captain and we got them out for 23 and then one [won] by 10 wickets; Morris[308] is a very good bat and always makes about 25 going in No 1; he is also a very good wicket keeper, and on Thursday he caught and stumped a chap in one ball.

On Thursday the Bradford boys came and there was an extra half and I went with some chaps up Hebblethwaite Gill. We tried to stun some fish by throwing a big rock on top of a medium size one and thus stun the fish underneath it; this worked once on a fish 2" long, and it became unstunned in about 5 seconds. Also we had good fun in Hebblethwaite Hall grounds which are lovely, old with miniature lakes and one good size one, all terribly posh although people only live there for about 2 months in the year.

Nest Thursday is Drill cup so we have to clean all our Corps stuff extra well. I really rather enjoy the corps now we do arms drill and have finished learning stupid things for Cert Part 1

We have just been out five of us. We passed Dent and up Crag Hill which is 2,200 ft; we got to the top at 2.15 and had our lunch but it started to rain hard so we ate it in a cow place, rather fun. We came down and bought lemonade and chocolate in a shop and just as we came out there was Ward our school prefect, but we were rather lucky as he had been caught himself the day before drinking beer while away on a match, so as he was going to the HM in the evening he could not very well report us for drinking lemonade!

On Sat there was a film It was 'Rear Window' with Grace Kelly and James Stewart, it was a murder story about a man who had a bust leg and sat by a window looking over a block of flats and in the night he saw a man carrying something to and fro across the road in a case; then he saw a man with butcher saws and knife and the man's wife had vanished in the night.

---

[308] John Morris, son of my Aunt Pip Bruce Lockhart's sister, was at one time my fag. A gifted games player, he later returned to the School as a master, becoming housemaster of Hart House, master in charge of cricket and Second Master of the School.

A dog found his wife's finger in the garden and it turned out he had chopped her up and laid her in parts all over town. It was a very good film.

This fortnight Order I went down in General but up in Maths and Chemistry and 6ᵗʰ in Physics.

What do you suggest we give Granny for her birthday – on the 16ᵗʰ isn't it; I think a small present would be nice but what I have no idea; maybe you have some.

House matches next week. I don't know yet if I will be on Panters. I will either be only just on or not on at all, and I will not know till the 12ᵗʰ.

I quite agree about Jeb and also I think it would be quite nice to have a small dog[309]. You say in your letter about the cook, but do you have one? I presume you mean in Rye; but is she a Ryean? Will she just cook or be like a cooking Annie?

J 8 June 58 [Sunday]

Thankyou for the wedding plans – I still don't know the verdict about camp. Jolly d. about the Derby win. The chap next to me in Form won the Evans House sweep. I don't think he even shared it. There must have been a lot of sixpences for him

Sorry I didn't tell you about the German oral. (French oral at 9.20 tomorrow morning.) First it was a matter of reading a short passage, from Buddenbrooks I think – preparing it for a couple of minutes and then reading it aloud.. No easy questions such as in O level orals – like which fellow has a beard, but I was asked to talk about it and when I had babbled on as long as I could about this character who had a stutter who became a schoolmaster although he wanted to be a priest; he just said 'Danke'. Then he asked me what my hobbies and interests were and what I wanted to be – ich war immer noch ganz unsicher, I hazarded architecture and found myself in the soup. I turned that away as soon as I could. I should have mugged that up but we were mugging up all our lit books of which I was asked nix thank goodness – and then Brussels and hence the fact that I had been in Germany, which was safe ground. A few minutes on the Freiburger Dom and that was that and he turned into English.

Another week has flown by. At the beginning we had the drill cup. SH came = 3ʳᵈ which with our vast contingent, the biggest by far, was a pretty good effort. Apparently it was over eagerness and exaggeration that lost us the extra points. We came top equal in the actual drill. Have played a bit of cricket on yet another victorious 4ᵗʰ XI against the rest of Littleside and 2ⁿᵈ XI. I got a duck.

It's been heavenly weather this week and cricket was most enjoyable. I managed to scrape into the bottom of the House XI. We have on paper quite a nice side with 1 1st, 4 2ⁿᵈ and 3 3ʳᵈ elevens, a tennis VIIIer and a

---

[309] A reference to the inevitable difficulties of looking after a dog of Jeb's size

Shooting VIIIer both of whom could be pretty hot stuff. The first round is next Saturday, I don't see why I shouldn't keep my place too.

Most of the house went up Higher Winder yesterday in a pack which was pretty killing exercise. 6 weeks till the sports. I beat the breast stroke standard by 3 secs which means at least that I can get the one standard to uphold my position as swimming secretary.

Exams 4 weeks tomorrow. First A level exams – horrible thought! The final push... looking forward to a nice peaceful Speech Day weekend to get quite a lot done in. Orchestra having rehearsals madly all the time and Ronny Reynell has got rather fed up with it all – but unlike the others can show it. He walked off in the middle of a rehearsal last night and was in an A1 peeve about these damned Americans[310] and so on. It looks as though we might be one horn short. I went round and played the clarinet with him on Tuesday which was fun as usual.

Any further news about what I might do in Rye or Kent?

Fight the good fight... lots of love

S   Sunday 8ᵗʰ June 58

...Played a lot of cricket. On Friday I played for 'Panters' v 'House Team' but I do not think I will get on the team on Friday when the first match is, but I may.

Yesterday it poured with rain and the whole school went up Higher Winder, except the junior dayroom, and we went training for the sports. We walked all the way up and ran all the way down. There was a lovely mist and at the top it was pretty dense.

A chap came from Clifton (a master) and he looked round our Arts and Crafts and came into our fly tying class. He found out which one I was and introduced himself; he was rather a nice bloke and I think he is trying to start arts and crafts at Clifton,

I feel I would like to know more about what I want to do when I leave school. It may be rather early but no harm can come from finding things out. If I leave when I am 17.11 or 18.2 I will go to David's[311] till I can get a 3-year commission is the idea. If you have time do you think you could find out if there is a 3 yr commission and about it.

But what I really want to know about is the following: for there are 3 boys of about my term who also want to become farmers and they have different ideas; the idea has been for me to go to a college and then get or manage a farm. But the chaps here say (they are probably talking rot I don't know) that one cannot just get a farm without about £2,500 capital but if one passes one's degree in agriculture one can get a £2,000 grant from the government to start a farm. It is also very hard to become a manager of a

---

[310] Possibly with reference to the crisis in the Fourth French Republic
[311] i.e. to go as a Pupil on David Mure's farm in Kent

farm because there is an awful lot of competition. Do you think this is all true, for although it may be nearly 10 years ahead I like to have the facts clear because I think it is stupid to go with a definite idea without knowing anything about it.

I think the idea of letters on Monday and Thursday would be easily the best days especially as I can have mine on Monday to greet me on Monday morning.

It was the Drill cup on Tuesday and we were hoping to do rather well but only came =3ʳᵈ. The chap who inspected us was rather a good type and he said that our only mistake was that we were trying too hard. I can't see why this is a mistake but I suppose he means we over-exaggerated our movements.

I went for an early morning swim on Sunday, very keen. We got up at 7 and went down there but could not find the key to the swimming pool; but some chaps from Winder house came and they knew where it was. It was jolly good fun.

I bought my new blazer yesterday like you told me to and got the best quality. So I should have one pair of shorts to buy when these get drab. Is it best to get the more or less expensive ones?

On Sunday we went up Winder and Crook in a heavy mist. It was terrific fun; we chased sheep and wild ponies on the top; it was wonderful up there all alone.

Lionel and I think it would take about 4 days to come down south with a tent and a stove to cook on. Do you think when you come you could bring it?

J   15ᵗʰ June [Sunday]

I agree with what Dad says about de Gaulle but am not finding it so easy to express in French – which is my present headache.

I think a half time garage job would be a really good idea and I would probably learn something about cars which would be very useful.

No I'm not a secret drinker – Sandy was exaggerating and had no idea about this[312]. I bought a little bottle of whisky on the boat (cheaper of course) for our pres' booze up at the end of term. But then got into a funk about taking it to school, so left it behind without thinking much about it. I had a swig on the boat, and can't say I terribly liked it. Any way the event may not take place after what happened to Charlie Ward after an away match. And the pres keep company with those who are leaving and there is only one school leaver from the house this term. But please do not mention it to our dear Housemaster who might become obsessed by the same idea[313].

---

[312] My parents had found a quarter-bottle whisky in my desk at home.
[313] i.e. secret drinking

The French oral wasn't too bad. We know that the good lady was terribly pleased with our A level candidates but whether that had any exceptions I don't know. I found it rather hard but was more prepared than in the German one. Fortunately a) she asked no questions about the reading passage, which was about the Romantic movement and I didn't understand it fully and b) talked a terrific lot herself.

Speech day weekend... and hoards going on. No prep and little form work since Friday, so have been busy revising.... Kingfisher things to do,...

Many concert rehearsals. Managed to stay on the House XI which was nice although it meant having to clean my boots which were like an old pair of gardening boots. House match – descriptions.... We lost but I got 3 wickets.

On Saturday another full day. I did 1 ½ hours car parking duty; then had to stand in the porch for the speeches. The HM laid it on superbly and one could fairly see the parents lapping it up. Lord Chandos spoke terribly well indeed and most amusingly and the whole thing, with Sir John Sloan in the chair, whom one could hear, was a great success. Then back to the car park duties and lovely sunshine but not a very good lunch – with the rice hardly cooked.

The concert was a success although the Schumann was nearly boshed up by me. I made up for it however by playing the clarinet solo bit well in the Schubert. When we first went on stage I found the top of my reed had caught on my sleeve and was broken and I could get no noise out of it; and then I found that either I or the second clarinet Jacko Jackson was out of tune. 20 bars before the solo passage I realised that I had the wrong clarinet (A not B flat).

Nudged Jacko, swopped clarinets leaving him holding a virtually useless clarinet. No noise. Can't play on Jacko's reed. Ten bars to go. Try swopping the mouthpiece end of the clarinets, eventual success. Recognize place by ear and start up the passage – 2 bars too early! Kenny Anderson saved the situation by taking up the passage on the violin. Still flustered I could hardly play the second solo piece properly with the new hard reed. Haven't seen Mr Hind[314] yet, not looking forward to it either.

Met Mr Sugden who sends his regards. Had dinner with Cass Matthew and Charlie Ward with Mr and Mrs Laycock which was very nice, and met Mr and Mrs Morris[315] who send regards, and Mr and Mrs Grieve, something to do with the Radcliffe or St Andrews?, or was it Greycoats? – also send regards

Times flies, here is a quote for Dad, from [Goethe's] Egmont – a bit like Dear Man's 'Don't worry about what you can't help'. Soll ich den

---

[314] School Director of Music and conductor of the orchestra
[315] John Morris' parents - see above p. 200, fn. 292#

gegenwaertign Augenblick nicht geniessen damit ich den folgenden sicher sei?[316]

S   Sunday 14ᵗʰ [actually 15ᵗʰ] June 58

Thank you for letters...

Yesterday was Speech Day and we had a great time. In the morning we had the speeches. Lord Chandos was the guest of honour (Chairman of the AEI).

The HM made a very good speech, much the best I have heard him make. Then Sir John Shea made a little speech, partly about Viscount Bracken who could not come as he is ill in London. Then Lord Chandos made a good speech. The start was very very good but it [he] did not quite keep it up which was a pity. In the afternoon were the House matches. I was 12ᵗʰ man for Panters. As this is not the final team, I might still get on, but I cannot say. Next game is on the 23ʳᵈ and the final team plays on the 3ʳᵈ of July. So yesterday I scored; actually it was quite fun scoring. [Details of match scores listed.]

If we do get into the final we play Sedgwick (who we beat in a friendly Panters game last week). It is very queer as we often have the best team on paper but they never come off. This is not because people don't try hard enough, because we are told we try too hard. I think that if we won one thing only it would change everything; but at the moment we always flop. I expect Dear knows this situation well as it is bound to happen every so often.

Thank you for your letter Daddy. I think I would like to go into the Guards for a short commission and be a farmer very much; but I am not sure if farming in England has much future, but as you say first things first.

The Concert was on Friday and Saturday evening, the best things were a violin solo, a piano concerto and Schubert the Unfinished piece, I cannot remember if it is a concerto a Prelude or an overture or what, at least I know it is not one of these. This was very good.

I had 10 of my flies in the Speech day exhibition. One [word illeg.] and the best 2. Also while I remember I will send my Godmother's cheque to you. I will not be able to send the flies this week as they are with the Art School.

Yesterday four of us went out with a packed lunch. One chap's mother had to go back home after chapel so she picked us up outside Sedbergh and dumped us just past the Cross Keys. From there we went up the Rawthey to Uldale force, which is a lovely 60 ft waterfall with a terrific pool below the fall. We had our lunch, then bathed and climbed around behind the fall. We got right behind it where it was quite dry. Like Niagara, what!.

---

[316] 'Am I to not enjoy the present moment in order to be certain of the following one?' Goethe's Egmont; it should read 'gewiss' not 'sicher'.

It was very hot and great fun. We then ran down to Cautley without shirts or shoes and it was terrific fun. Then we got to the Cross Keys and bought lots of lemonade and sat by the river boozing it. Then we walked back along the road.

Today is lovely as well. I hope it is as nice in Rye when you arrive tomorrow.

By the way when do you all go up to Scotland?

J   Sunday 22 June 1958

How wonderful you will now be in Rye, our proper full home. I'm longing to get down there. Hope it hasn't been too hectic getting the things moved..

My pen keeps flooding and drying up and wont write properly....Little happening. We had an extra half on Wednesday...

A Brig came down to inspect CCF and fossed at us on initiative and leadership.

Three of the prefects – the non-leavers, because the leavers are allowed to have bikes at school and went off together – took a herd of 25 round Black Force. It was rather fun. A nice day and no smalls[317] dropping out or twisting ankles and things. The Force itself is fun to climb down and being a rocky steep ghyll with shale etc; the cascades must have looked like Blackpool Tower on a Bank holiday – and only a few scrambling down slowly.

Trying for a discus standard. Managed to throw the weight 4 feet over the standard which was unexpectedly hefty. More hard concentrated practice needed.[318]

Of course the whole time now is dominated by exams. German Unseen for practice on Tuesday. The trouble is the pass mark in German is on average 170 out of 220 whereas in French one can pass on 140 – ie they reckon it [German] easier, or the general standard is higher or something like that.

No orchestra this week which is gorgeous but I have been playing with Ronny Reynell and practising.

[Sketch of figure at a desk with lamp and quill pen and upholstered chair, hemmed in by narrow walls, with motto
'Unleidlich war
Mir's schon auf meinem Polsterstuhle'[319]

---

[317] i.e. younger boys

[318] In athletics in my last year I practised hard at putting the shot. I built a pit at back of the house gardens, and trained others' and came second in the Final. I could not throw the discus so well, but got my standards in the other events, doing best again in the 200 yards.

[319] 'I already found it intolerable to be on my upholstered chair', Goethe's Faust

S   June 22ⁿᵈ [1958] - dated by **MEBL** on the letter

How is the house, what wall papers etc are there by now? Do you think the decorating will be finished by when we come next hols. I hope all the things we measured for in the kitchen are all right and you can get the cupboards in.

It has been raining nearly since Thursday and the mist was thick right down to Fell gate and I and another chap tried to get up Winder, Higher Winder and Crook. We got to Winder ok , then to Higher Winder as all you have to do is keep climbing; but then we went down the wrong side of Higher Winder and got lost. We wandered around and after half an hour found ourselves on Winder again; we found Crook in another half hour. It was a drizzly mist and as I only had one jersey on I have a superb cold.

We started throwing discus on Wednesday and I was 5 ft short of a standard; with practice I might get it. Also the House tennis court and putting lawn has been opened. I was thinking that Dear must know exactly where the tin of grub is she planted in 1941 or whenever it was, because it would be terrific fun to go and try to dig it up sometime when everyone is out or it is dark or something. Also, do you know what is in it !??

The general inspection was on Tuesday. Did I tell you about it or did I tell Granny. Oh yes, we have sent them a small Wensleydale cheese for her birthday. I am not sure if it is only Grandfather who likes them but I hope not.

The Inspection was by a Brigadier (a rather unimportant chap after Field Marshall Alexander last year) T Hart Dyke DSO. He spent years and years over the inspection; it was about 50 mins, he spoke to quite a few people but not to me.

There was an extra half on Wednesday and 3 chaps and myself tried to get a leave to take a pack lunch and run to Windermere and bus back, but the HM would not sign it. So after lunch we changed quickly and split up into 2s.

I went with Lionel; we went first and ran to the 3 mile post and caught a lift to Kendal, then we ran through Kendal and caught another lift to a place called Crook. This was with a chap in a biscuit van; and then we ran another mile and caught a chap in a sports car who took us right into Bowness (a town near Windermere). We bathed there and drank orange and ate ices. This was at 3.40 (we had left at 2.10). We had arranged to meet the others on Bowness pier at 4.00 but they were not there so we wandered around and left Bowness at 4.20 and caught a lift into Kendal and then walked along the road for 3 miles. There had not been a car for half an hour and it was 5.30 and it would have been very difficult to run 7 miles along that road in an hour and change for tea. But one car came and took us along, and we picked up the other two a mile further on and got off by the Lune. We arrived back at 6.20 having gone nearly 40 miles. Unfortunately the story has a rather sad ending because Mr Ward saw Lionel and I a mile past Kendal at about 10 to 3; so the HM asked us where we had been and how. The four of us got beaten[320] which was hard luck on the other 2 that only got to Kendal and did not get caught.

A lovely day today and we are going bathing in the Lune.

About the hiking I will just go and ask Lionel so as to get everything right. Here is my list if you could kindly bring these in the car when you come up

1 tent (I will have to buy pegs in Melrose)

1 ground sheet

1 rucksack (the biggest one without the iron backpiece)

2 shirts

1 big green pullover

1 wind jacket

1 pair shorts (will have socks and 1 pair long trousers here)

Lionel has a primus

We think it will take 4 days starting on Wednesday

Today it rained and we did not bathe in the Lune but just fooled about there and tried to catch fish but as always they were too quick. Have not been fishing this week as I have been playing in house matches, and I am on Panters this time. We are playing Lupton House.

Hope this arrives on Wednesday; got to catch the 8.35 post.

J   29 June 1958

June is nearing its horrible end, a week and a day to go now. This next week I'm going to have to devote to learning of quotes for the literature papers and re-reading the books...

All exams and preparation and nothing much else happening.

Weather has held off cricket. Third round of house matches are being held however. We play Lupton but it is clear that neither of us can get into the final since Powell has already won 2 matches. Training for swimming and athletics – putting the weight as usual – and a bit of piano and drawing...

Yesterday was OS day. Some left only a year or two ago. I played squash with one – a tremendous game which ended 8-8 then back to 5-5 (the accepted thing) and was finally won by yours truly. Then today a morning service with OSs reading the lesson and giving the sermon. Clarinet and

---

[320] This was a housemaster's beating. More common were beatings by prefects - for offences deserving more serious punishment than 'maps'. They were performed with a 'bim stick', a CCF officer's short cane or swagger stick. Three or four strokes were usual; six was serious. In the case of the housemaster, the beating was taken over a chair. Prefects' beatings were taken bending over the end of the bath, sometimes with trousers down (ie underpants only) or in pyjamas. When the victim had dark blue trousers on, the cane could be chalked, and the chalk mark of the first strike would enable the prefect to target the next strokes on the same spot. That could hurt a lot more. Talk of putting blotting paper or an exercise book down the trousers was nonsense: it would be found out.

orchestra continues.... Hay fever attacks now and again but otherwise am in great form. My knee gives no trouble.

Regards from a certain Mr Wilson, whose son was at the school in 1943-45?

S   Sunday 29ᵗʰ   June 58?

The cook person sounds wonderful; it must have been very funny trooping into supper when the gong went. It would be terrific if she stayed on till September....

Yesterday, Saturday, we were going to go round the 3 Peaks but the HM would not let us go. Actually I think he was quite right as it is a lot further than we thought. But Mr Durran offered to take us to Pen y Ghent the furthest of the three. We took pack lunches and went in Mr Durran's car. We stopped on the way at the place on the Dee where we stopped when going to Ingleborough last summer. It was a cave over which the river was flowing and it was covered in fossils. I am not very attached to them but they were fantastic. I found one fossil on a rock as big as my hand. I brought it back in the car; and there were many small ones almost perfect shells. I hope I enclose the last of those I found. Went on to Ribblehead from where people start the 3 peaks and three cars were there, Mr Mills and the Sedgwick House prefects and Mr [name illeg.] and the Evans House prefects, all going round the 3 peaks. They would come back to their cars at 7.30 in the evening as it is 7 miles from the last Peak. Mr Durran left a note on top of Pen-y-Ghent in a bottle on the cairn saying 'strain and struggle might and main, scorn defeat and laugh at pain – then in brackets 'Only 7 miles to the car'. Then on the cars we left For Sale Notices and one Police one.

We had great fun rolling boulders down Pen–y Gent and rock climbing; and Mr Durran took 4 or 5 photos I will get some if they are good. We had a look at some pot holes on the way down and went back in the car and had some orange booze in the Sportsman Inn. It was very good fun indeed.

On Monday there were house matches and I was playing for Panters. I did not bat but bowled 3 overs and took no wickets and had no runs hit off me. They only made 86 and we made 88 for 5. Today we are playing Powell and I am playing again.

Last week it rained and it was mostly sports training. I went round Winder. Higher Winder, Scissors and Knot on Thursday. On Wednesday I suddenly got the [k]nack of the discus and got a standard 6 throws running. But this morning I had completely lost the nack again. I hope it will come back.

Only 4 weeks left today. Field Day is on Thursday. It is raining hard now and I doubt there'll be Panters this afternoon.

Have got your letter from Paris and thank you very much for the 10/- , very 'd', but how was it written on British Embassy Paris paper saying sent from Rye in England?

J   Sunday 6ᵗʰ July 1958

Here we are - the worst or at least the most interesting weekend of the year. Desks have been moved into Powell Hall. We've had our Exam instructions; things like no boy shall occupy more than one desk, only one boy to a desk and other such frightfully important information. We have two weeks of exams. The second half is slightly fuller than the first.

We have French lit on Tuesday, French Prose and Dictation on Thursday, German Unseen on Friday and German Translation on Saturday. French Lit is pretty well under control now – just need to learn a few quotes. My German ones seem more complicated. Last week we've been handed out summaries. Jack Hammer is the world's hottest summary man. He summarizes all books he reads, novels and things, articles from the newspapers and of course all the work books he has to deal with. The questions and whether we are prepared for them is fate. but I'm going to do my very very hardest and hope things aren't too bad..

Other things are coming into action too. The main one is the Kingfisher. I hope I will have the text of the thing ready by the end of term but much depends on how quickly advertising blocks get sent and so forth. Do you have any possible contacts for advertising because it helps immensely to have a few well paying ads. Tennis competitions, wind competitions and the sports of course.... I have bust up a muscle on the back of my hand by the knuckle which means I have pulled something – which I did throwing the weight – which keeps me from training at the same or the discus.

I'd like to ask for some extra money to take to camp. At Rhyll last year, where the camp was fairly near the holiday resort people took £4 or 5 but camp living was pretty expensive there. Crieff should be a pretty dead end I think, and about £2-10 should about cover things[321]. I may not use all of it and can bring back what is left. We have to pay for all camp amenities and camp cooking isn't famous for its exquisiteness. And oh yes I don't need to go to camp for the last 2 days, so I am free from Monday 4ᵗʰ August which is nice. Where are you staying for the night of the 4ᵗʰ/5ᵗʰ? Should I come there, or go down to Bemersyde, or stay with the Steens?

Mr Begley, who takes us for Current Affairs once a week, has come up with a rather thrilling idea - of a trip for twenty top boys from a good public school who are interested, at a price of £40 per head, to go to guess where –Germany? No. Norway? no; Malta or Greece, no! – To Russia and Peking, repeat Russia and Peking. It's something he's got on to through

---

[321] The camp was not far from Lochearnhead with access to both the hills and the lake itself.

education authorities in those countries. Boat to North Russia, air to Moscow and China. We may need brainwashing afterwards; but if there were to be anything in it, it would be a gorgeous idea. To take place next summer holidays. I don't lay any weight on it yet, but it's not joking.

To return to earthly things we had another house match this week and got beaten – pity. All our big men flopped. I went in 8th but never faced a ball. We were all out for 83, Lupton got 84 for 3, and one of them, a member of the 1st XV got a 56. They made their runs very quickly and this one batsmen dealt beautifully with everything that came his way. At cricket Desmond S has been playing quite well on the 1st and may get his colours soon.

Longing for the hols – can hardly wait to come to the house with all the new things in it

S   No date [6 July 58]

Thank you very much for your letter. I hope you had a good journey to the Middle East. It must have been terribly hot. The weather here has been better in the last few days but it poured all the first half of the week.

It was field Day on Thursday. It rained in the morning but was boiling hot by mid-day and we marched with kitbags and rifles to Danny Bridge. We had lunch there and then we practiced Section in attack, each taking it in turns to lead the section; this is for Part II next term. Then it started to pour with rain and we were going to attack No 1, 2, 3, 4, 5 Platoons who were all searching for 6 chaps in the fells. It was great fun as we were only 1 platoon of little squits compared with their 5 senior platoons. It was very good as we came up the fells behind them without their knowing and suddenly attacked not even the masters knew we were coming to attack and we had a terrific battle; one section commander led his section in a heroic charge and about 10 yards from the enemy they fell slap into a bog right up to their knees and had to be fished out. But all through the first half of the battle I was having a battle with our Platoon Sergeant, a School Prefect, 1st XV, head of Sedgwick House. He had no rifle as he was a Pltn Commander and came up to me just before we attacked and said 'Let me look at your rifle', so I thought maybe there was something wrong with it, anyhow I gave it to him to look at and he quickly grabbed it and charged off and fired off all my ammunition inside the gun which was all I had (swiz chiz). In the end he gave it back and gave me 4 blanks and went off to get somebody else's and fire off their ammunition; there was nothing anybody could do about it. We bashed up the enemy completely. They say they bashed us up as well. A chap's rifle in my section split in half, this is not surprising as most of them are 1915 ones.

Went for an early morning swim. It was fairly cold but it is ok as one can go to sleep for ¾ of an hour in a chair in the common room afterwards, for nobody else comes downstairs till 2 mins to 9

Today I went for a river bathe in the Lune with 7 other bronzes. It was very hot and we put on many sweaters and ran out there and got very hot and had a lovely bathe. I took my gog[g]les and we could see many fish. We found an old canoe and had great fun. It sank about 3 times and it was great fun all diving from it. It was very very hot indeed.

There was Panters on Wednesday and we batted and I went in No 11 and made 3 not out. The whole team made 128.

In last week's orders I came 3 in Physics and Maths but 15 again in Chemistry, in which I don't seem to get much higher.

Here is another list of camping things, a revised one
1 rucksack (biggest without metal base)
1 tin plate & knife fork and spoon
1 mug
2 pairs shorts
2 big pullovers
1 sleeping bag
1 windsheater *[sic]* (my green one)
No Primus as Lionel has it
I think that is all as I have the rest here which I can take to Melrose.

J   Sunday 13 July 1958

Cannot reply to your letter because I cannot find it. There's nothing on my desk or in my pockets except Kingfisher letters. I hope there wasn't anything terribly important. I'll add a PS if there is. And yes, Grandfather's letter with the texts was a Godsend – I found them terribly useful.

The pressure has relaxed at last which is absolutely gorgeous. The worst exams are over. We started with French – three hours writing as fast as possible. The questions weren't too bad and I knew my quotes ok for that. I kicked myself for one stupidity and not following Dad's advice to ask myself what is behind the question. I was muddled by one of these triple choices: 'either a) do a translation... or b) write an essay and do a (smaller) translation. I only did part of the alternative and since each question is 20 marks I may well have missed out on 10 or 15 marks. Then French prose and dictation which were quite hard. Friday and German was better... Thought I did all right.... Next week we bang off with French again but now my major revising jobs have come to an end. Will spend more time on the kingfisher – still chasing ads....

Sports start next Saturday. So far only swimming. Swam in the breaststroke and came 2nd behind the school champion in the second heats and in quite a fast time, even though he was half a pool ahead.. Our relay which I thought would be by miles last, won our heat.

Only a fortnight to go – superb! – Of course there's always camp but that's only 5 days.

S   13th July 58

Thank you for your letter and Daddy's nice long one from Geneva. The chap with his artillery sticking out of his shirt sounds a terrific chap.

Westwick sounds lovely now. How is the new lawn? and do you think there will be any apples on the apple trees? I hope Mrs Virgo will stay on; she sounds terrific especially as I presume she does all the cooking and washing.

The food here is getting slightly better, probably as [because] if the food is bad or not enough the Head of House goes round to each table and asks about it then stamps out to see the HM or Mrs HM. Very good of him. Marg and bread gets put out every afternoon now and if we want more we have to go to see Mrs HM instead of just asking a sciv; so obviously not half as much is eaten anyway, we are getting strawberries for lunch today.

Today is the last fortnight order. They come out tomorrow but the Final order is after Exams; this is the order that gets me into the 5th or not, so I have to do well in my Physics, Chemistry and Maths exams. As I said last week my Physics and Maths are good but my Chemistry's bad, so I hope it will not hold me back. If I do not get into the 5th I will not take 'O' level till 1960 and that would be perfectly g[h]astly; but if I get into the 5th next term I will take O level in Summer 1959 and then if I fail my chemistry I can take it the term after (Christmas 59). And then if I stay till the summer I can always take anything if I suddenly wanted it. My Chemistry will be about average for the whole of the 4ths.

Mr Strahan my form master has been finding out from my set masters whether they think I can pass 'O' level next year. This is what gets you into the fifths – whether they think you can pass in a year's time, 'yes' and 'probably yes'. Anyhow they all said more 'yes' than 'no', which is very good but all the same you will have to keep your fingers crossed in case I don't get up.

What does Uncle Robin say about the Wedding and after it. Sal will be getting a present here, and also I shall buy some white gym shoes as I will need some probably and mine are black and 2 terms old (in rags); and I'm also to get some tidy walking shoes I think you said.

A new cricket and rugger pitch is being built on Akay. It is now flat mud and we have just started picking up the stones. We do it in parties of 10 for about an hour, each house has one party all the time. It is an added bore especially when it has been raining. On all the other days I have been training. I am in for the Half, 100 yds, hurdles, long jump and discus

I have written to Dear say[ing] I arrive at Melrose at 1626 starting at 7 o'clock, breakfast at 6 o'clock, up at 5 o'clock. I hope you will remember all the things for our camping? What day do you drive South?

189

S   no date – 20 July 58 [Sunday]

Thank you for your letters. My Fair Lady sounds terrific. I would love to see it at a matinee next hols, Are Granny and Grandfather coming to stay at Westwick?

Nothing much has been happening except revision for exams and sports training. The Exams start on Tuesday with Maths (I am 4th in Report Order in Maths). Exams go on till Thursday. Sports started yesterday and go on till Saturday. There's a Sedgwick House play on Saturday, it is Pygmalion; then a concert on Saturday, a film on Monday and up to Bemersyde on Tuesday. Quite a busy time considering

There was a Sharp Practice on Friday. The motions were all rather stupid. 'It is better to score 50 at cricket faultlessly than 100 with a few mistakes.' This was supposed to be about life, not cricket. The second was 'Is it better to win the Ten than get a University Scholarship?'. This is also stupid as it depends on what you want to do after you leave. The third was 'Should the second serve in tennis be abolished'. Fourth was 'Will the Middle East crisis grow into a World War?' Fifthly, 'Is jazz just the sign of the baser animal instincts of man? All these motions lost.

There was weighing and measuring. I am now 5' 6 ½" and 8 st 5 lb.

I hear Uncle Logie is coming to preach next term. It is raining again

O yes the other motion in the debate was 'whether Spanish should be taught in this school?' 'The younger Shiffner, the one we played golf with, had to propose this motion. He gave a lovely speech: 'Spanish is spoken in Spain; wine grows in Spain; therefore Spanish is written on wine bottles. As wine is very nice to drink you must learn Spanish to read the bottles.' He just got up and quickly said that and sat down again. It was very funny.

We're getting Uncle Robin and Aunt(ie?) Helen's [wedding] present here from the Dent Antiques shop or Jacksons.

How super getting asked to the palace[322]. Do you go for Dinner, and will there be millions of other people? It sounds rather fun.

Have the other people moved into Vicarage Gate? If so when you go up to London will you be getting a small flat with somebody else near the office where we could sleep on the sofa when we go to London in the hols? For I was thinking how do we come back to school next hols. If we start from Rye it would take 3 hours to get to Euston and we would have to start by 6 in the morning?

I have been sports training hard. Discus was not as good as it was last week. I have lost the knack. I hope it comes back in time for the Standards. On Saturday I ran in the 100 and hurdles not getting a standard in either, but in the half mile I got a Standard and won my heat (5 chaps) so I am in the semi-final on Tuesday which is just before the discus. And I hope it will stop raining otherwise it will all be cancelled as it was yesterday

---

[322] As part of a Foreign Office team accompanying the Shah of Iran.

S   27 July 58

Thank you very much for the 3 letters and the money. I Hope you are well and that Daddy does not have to go off to Beirut this weekend.

All the camping stuff we need we have now got as Lionel is bringing the cooking stuff. Thank goodness you have sent some clothes to Bemersyde otherwise it would have been awful.

We have had exams and sports. I ran in the middle half semi final and threw the discus, but I did not get a standard which was a bit of a chiz because I had practised a lot, in fact more than I have ever practised. I came 4th in my heat in the Half but that did not get me into the final as only the first two went.

I was 10th in my Maths exam which was down a bit but gives me a final place of 6th in chemistry I was 8th in my form, in Physics I was 2nd and I don't know where in the form. In all the other exams I was about 10th except French which we have not had back -so altogether it was not too bad

I have played lots of tennis these last few days when it has not been raining – only 3 days in July so far when it has not been raining. On Friday was an extra half and we went bathing near Killington. 5 of us found a terrific place, much better than the house pool where everybody else is, so we are going there again today.

J   Mail received at home in summer holidays

i)   Self addressed Postcard   and completed by Thornely in early August [with two remarks]:

A Levels

French	Pass
German	Pass
General Paper	Fail
	This doesn't really matter

V. good effort. GMCT

ii)   Telegram from Granny and Grandfather, Oxford
'Well done Splendid.'

Chapter 5:   September 1958 to July 1959

Winter term 1958

J   19 Sep 1958 [Friday]

The main thing, before I forget same: corps boots and gas cape; the latter is in the [word illeg.] somewhereabouts and the former in the [word illeg] hanging cupboard [massive ink spill in the crease of the paper]... but could you please send   the boots for Wednesday parade[323], i.e. quam celerrime, I'm terribly sorry about that – and the other things, in advance, which I don't know about yet but probably left behind and am going to cause more trouble by asking to have them sent on.

I'll be able to get along somehow for the rest of the things, but if possibly please by Wednesday for the boots.

Thankyou for all the things you did... - such a lovely home... There's no place like home, they say and I'm sure we could have had no better holiday anywhere or anyhow in the world than last hols.[324]

Everything coming along fine here... [illeg ink spill again]... German good result, although my French Λ was a pretty close thing, I passed equal top of the whole form including scholarship people. I got 243 marks, pass being about 160 and in French 181 (gone up from 150 odd. Odd)

Some squash and fives, but mostly settling in. My study is nearly fixed now and quite nice....

[At bottom of page a cartoon sketch of 'Charlie Dragon au coin du feu' – a dragon seated in arm chair with pipe and a glass of 'petrol' – for Sally.]

J   21 Sep 1958   [Sunday]

Thank you very much for sending the cape and shoe cleaning equip. The parcel and letters will have crossed in the post.

All is under control here and the term is settling in with the usual dust and hay fever. Lots of nice things all over my study and the general effect is very gay. Lovely that you're coming up – and you'll be able to change your ideas about my termly environment after the last study you saw.

---

[323] From Corps camp boys went directly home for the holidays, hence Corps equipment might carelessly get left at home.
[324] Rye .with its golf course, beaches, sailing and tennis and the young friends we made, provided a wonderful environment for Sandy and me, better by far than London.

I'm officially allowed my wireless – we're supposed to have an electricity economy campaign. But if the wireless was on all day and night all term it would only cost 2/6 .The head of house worrieth not.

Having music lessons with a new chap who is decidedly odd. He was the band master of the Duke of Edinburgh's Regt but although he claims to play all wind instruments, the fiddle and the piano I've only heard the clarinet and piano and he could hardly play either. I can't see how he'll be able to teach somebody who is new at a clarinet, but I think he knows a thing or two about the general mustering of an orchestra or band. In orchestra we are playing The Water Music and Egmont, both of which I like[325].

Lots of training done for rugger and played one game on Littleside. Played at lock which I didn't want to. The game was very fast for this stage of term but I wasn't in too bad training.

Coached fives but not played yet...[326] Corps this afternoon, I 'm a corporal now and in charge of a section of new recruits, to make them spick and span. I got a pair of boots left behind by a guy who left last term. If you can't send mine, perhaps you could bring them up when you come.

Otherwise all going well.

S   no date [20 September 58 - Saturday]

Thank you for the letter and black tie. I will send a postcard on Sunday (tomorrow) to Sally. We had a lovely hols. It is so nice to have a permanent home now, especially with all the things around to do.

On the first day of term school train started at 1030 not 1040, so what with the Rye train being 15 minutes late we might have missed it. I think quite a few people missed it because of it going 10 minutes early.

When I came back the people who came 1 term before me said I had a cube which was perfectly true but they had not got one, so HM was consulted and we changed the beds back so I am still in a dorm. I am now the 2nd chap to get out of it and I am the 8th to get a study.

I have Mr Taylor for Physics, Mr Mawby for Chemistry, Mr Moore who was new last year for Maths, Mr Gairdner for French and a new master for

---

[325] Music took an increasing part in my life in my last year. As in other spheres, I responded best to personal enthusiasm, from Reynell and Thornely and even from some boys in the house – and learnt more from them than in formal lessons and practice. As the letters show, there was plenty of informal music, classical, jazz and swing, to ring the changes.

[326] In my last two years I spent a great deal of spare time playing and coaching fives. I had been well taught and by practice had got over a weak left hand. In my last year I was in charge of house fives. We did well in competitions, with players such as Lewis and Lowis, but were ranked second rather than top. In winter the walls and floor of the fives courts could become wet and slippery, which could prevent play. I also played a lot of squash, but there were no formal squash competitions. Most of the squash court roofs similarly dripped rain, making dangerous wet spots on the old wooden floors.

Latin and Mr Alban for English; so I will take 7 'O' levels next year Chemistry, Physics, Maths, English language and English literature, French and Latin. So far work has not started.

Our trunks were here when we came which was a pretty good show.

Lionel did not get his £5 back; he got back to Fordingbridge that afternoon. There is a new matron this term who seems very nice and efficient.

Nothing has happened yet, except I played rugger once at wing forward and swam twice and squash twice. Also I have unpacked and find that I have no slippers and no squash raquet /sic/ but this does not matter, so you can bring these up in October.

Yesterday it was house runs. It was awful having them on the first day of term; we had 'Slacks' the worst one; I was in Big pack and came 10th. It was about the worst house run ever.

I had a letter from Kim[327] this morning in reply to one of mine.

I hope you are making arrangements to buy a dog, a Jack Russell terrier. It would be lovely to have one next hols..

Sorry this is so short I will try to write a longer on Sunday.

S   no date: Postcard   with date stamp 22 Sep 58 [Monday]

Addressed to Sally (sister aged 3.0 – i.e. written for parents, etc.)

Hope you are well and your finger is better. The picture on the front is our school, our house is the one over the chapel. We have just had a house run and despite all our exercise in the holidays I was in lousey training. Tell Mummy that I will send her a letter on Tuesday when there is something more to say.

love from S

PS tell Mrs Virgo[328] it is [was] lovely fudge.

S   27th September 58 [Saturday]

I hope you are well and that Daddy's cold is better; also I hope that you played a good game of golf with all the important people. It rained all week except Wednesday when it stopped for the Corps. I am now in the 4th platoon which is when you take Cert A Part II but this is being changed this term to an exam called the Army Proficiency Test – which is arms drill, taking a section, map reading and inspection.

---

[327] Cousin, son of Rab and Pip, who had returned to UK ahead of his parents; he was due to come to School House in 1960 and came home early to visit relatives, familiarize himself with life in UK after being brought up in Canada and New Zealand, and to do some language training in France and Germany.

[328] The cook/housekeeper who also helped with Sally

195

I am making ginger beer with a chap with whom I share a grub locker; our first lot will be ready on Thursday; we can order ginger and sugar at the grubber now.

When you come up on which weekend is it 30th October? Will you be staying in the Bull or where? For it will be fairly near half term and we will have to book rooms for you soon.

I have played more rugger this week and am on Senior Game 2. The games for 16-upwards are Bigside, Littleside, Senior 1, 2, 3, 4. Jamie is on Littleside; I have played wing forward all the time.

Yesterday the Corps shot 15 rounds for the Empire Test. I got only 58/80. This was pretty poor as I got 80 last year so I should have got 68. I got all the shots in a 2" group but the group was not beside the bull.

Rain, and more house runs likely...

Have you got any tickets for My Fair Lady? Personally I would have thought that they would be nearly all gone by now..

About the pullover, I think dark green or lightish blue would be very nice. My tweed jacket is here so now I have three but I will have to travel back in my kilt because of the dances at the beginning of the hols and my kilt is pretty [word illeg.] and creased in the wrong places, so I think I will have to get it cleaned here if I can.

I cannot understand about my squash ra[c]quet. It is not here and I remember packing it...

Where are you going in Scotland at the end of the month?

J   28 Sep 1958 [Sunday]

Many thanks for everything – watch in beautiful sponge packing, corps boots, slippers, collars, jersey, etc. All going well except for a rather nasty boil at the back of my neck; using poultices but it's being rather stubborn.

Played stand off on Littleside and had a most enjoyable game. First house game, although we have no Bigside there is a little talent lurking around and a lot of spirit from some guys.

Good day on Saturday – played squash with Sykes, and it's good for my game to play for a change with someone who beats me. Played fives with the juniors, and then shot in the Empire Test and out of 80 I got 69 ad 67. I threw the weight to keep up the practice, and then more fives.

In orchestra we played Egmont last night – not too difficult for my clarinet part thank heavens.

Gorgeous weather.

Uncle Logie comes next weekend which will be fun and it will be interesting to hear him preach.

J   October 1958 [Sunday 5th]

Thanks for letter and glad you enjoyed your stay at Joanne's[329]. Good about Jack Russell terriers – they sound just the thing

Sorry I forgot to tell you about the Kingfisher. The HM and Laycock both thought it was awfully good, just the stuff, which is very nice. The HM thinks the whole thing is pretty good and is generally pleased. The trouble however is the advertisements. I haven't got 2 of the 5 yet although both are ordered. The proofs have been dealt with and returned and that is all that we're waiting for.

I've played a lot of rugger, always on Littleside but Littleside is unfortunately a bad game to be on because it is so fluid. There are 9 wings and 7 wing forwards and only 1 official second row man. It's all most peculiar. Sykes is official captain of the 3rd XV which is good. However all the games are with people I know and are very good fun. The 1st XV is pretty hot stuff. The pack is tremendous, and pack is the word, but the centres aren't too good.

Squash still unbeaten record except for that game with Sykes...

Newboys started fagging on Thurs and I have a new private fag who is a very d chap I think and pretty talented too at rugger and running, one of Edinburgh Acys' crack shots, and most important, efficiency personified[330].

In French I liked Atala and René very much and found Balzac's Le colonel Chabert most amusing. Phedre, Ruy Blas and Le Notaire du Havre are keeping me going at present.

The new music teacher is a bit of a problem at the moment; he can't play the flute, or more than an octave and a half on oboe, or clarinet properly, he isn't bad on brass and can play the fiddle. He accompanies on the piano with only one hand, and makes too many jokes through the lessons, e.g. 'syncopation is wandering from bar to bar on uneven feet – a thing you'll do some day too.' The flutes are stopping their lessons and I'm going to consult the HM because I don't find I gain anything from the 4 or 5 guineas a term. I hope you will understand.

All is well otherwise and time is flying on. Logie drives up today and arrives only just before evening chapel.

S   8th October 58 [Wednesday]

Hope you are all well and Sally is better. What a pity that Mrs Virgo has gone if she said that she wanted to stay; still maybe she will come back some other hols. If you remember, she told us she would.

So glad you have arranged for us to have a dog. It will be jolly 'd'. We will have to think seriously what we call him.

---

[329] Hedley Saunders, a close friend of my mother's from Germany days
[330] This was Fawcett, a distant connection/cousin who also wore a Macgregor kilt.

Pouring with rain – don't know why we didn't have house runs on Friday possibly because of a Firsts rugger match which was a match against Waterloo schools a team of men who play against schools. They won 0-6. We have a good pack this year – very heavy. King's school Canterbury are coming up here at the beginning of November which should be rather fun. This week I have been playing as hooker; I have never played there before but I think it is quite a good place for me, at least that I like it.

First fortnight orders out tomorrow...

Have been playing lots of fives and squash and have not been defeated at either yet. Maybe there will be a squash ladder as it is Jamie's job to start one as he is prefect for fives and squash.

I've been going through the Nevil Shutes in the library; they are all very good I think. I am on my 6th now.

We have just had the Old Sedberghians in. It was a very exciting game – 3 all at half time and then at the end 13 all. Uncle Logie came up just after lunch having started at Greshams at 8, which is pretty good going. He preached a good sermon and we then sat in Jamie's study together and talked. He sends his love. Mrs Thornely had her baby on Sunday night. It is a boy, Charles. Fig[g]lers their dog was killed by a lorry while the nurse was out with it and the pram on Monday which is very sad.

In fortnight orders I have some marks and places now: Latin 12/30, Maths 31/50, Chemistry 33/50; French 2/ 30, English 12/30, Physics 44/50

Every week on Tuesday I have CMI which is learning about mutual drill and such things for Cat A Part II now Army Proficiency Test. Just played rugger as hooker, we drew 8-8; and fives, won 2-0; both very good fun.

J   11 October 1958 [Saturday]

It was nice seeing Uncle Logie last weekend. The Logies must have driven up here at break neck speed. He left at 8.15 and said he could have been here for lunch but preferred to have lunch in Settle. thinking that better. He preached a good sermon and was most listenable to, with his pleasant voice. He was here the night the Thornely's baby arrived, so generally with the governors meeting, and the OS match next day life was pretty hectic that evening.

An old stamp block[331] was unearthed in the cellar and put in the common room for general use – I haven't paid hoards of money to have it done!

Only played one game of rugger on Littleside, there was a 1st XV match. Played fives twice and Des Sykes and I have some pretty close battles at squash. Training, short sprints, throwing the weight....

Good week at work. No essays which makes life far more enjoyable. Done lots of reading and tutorials in French and German. Doing now

---

[331] Plate imprint: School House, Sedbergh, Yorkshire

scholarship paper proses and Unseens in both languages which is quite a business; a great deal harder than A level standard... We do French language work with Mr Mills this term and I think he's better than Horsy G at that, though not so good at literature. In German we are doing Goethe's poems virtually from the beginning to end. There are more from the earlier years that I like very much. I enjoy La Fontaine and Victor H's Hernani for that matter.[332]

I had another music lesson on Tuesday and it went better. I took a very firm line and told him what I wanted him to do, and I don't think the lessons will be wasted, so I'm keeping on with him for new pieces and I think his musical understanding makes up for his lack of technical knowledge.

Last night one of England's top tympanists gave a concert. He was quite superb. He had about 30 instruments up on the stage and demonstrated his virtuosity on all of them. He spoke amusingly and the whole evening was most enjoyable. He's the chap who made the noise for J Arthur Rank's gong, and rolled the drums when the Queen was crowned. He played the interval noise at the BBC at the end of the war and all kinds of things. He imitated jazzplayers and Edmundo Ross terribly well. He did train noises for the wireless and did a guards band playing bass drums, cymbals and side drums all at once.

S   11 October 1958   [Saturday]

Hope you like the stamp which is in the common room. Hope you are all well and that Daddy had a good time with his Imperial Highness the Center /sic/ of the Universe.

We have had a more interesting time here this week. We had a concert by Mr James Blades who is a precussionist /sic/; he apparently is the chap who sent out tom tom messages on the BBC in the war; he also played the solo drum during the coronation in Westminster Abbey; and although he is a little fat man of 55 he is also the chap who hits the gong at the beginning of J Arthur Rank films – at least that is the audience of the film see this

---

[339] Bertie Mills, brilliant but rather vague, was loved by all. Bill Gairdner, who spluttered as he bubbled with excitement over his favourite authors, was such an enthusiast one could not fail to learn from him – but one also took care not to sit in the front row. By the time of S levels we were pared down to four students and increasingly worked by ourselves in a new study, built like a railway carriage, of white wood, with individual desks.

One pleasing feature of sixth form life was that it produced for the first time close friends in other houses. Our group of four scholarship candidates was Graham McGlashan, Tom Boyd, Chris Marks and myself – die Vier, im Schweisse unser Angesichts (the four, by the sweat of our brow), as Tom inscribed under a desk lid. The MLVI became a kind of home from (House) home.

Herculean chap hitting a cardboard gong and Mr Blades is behind the seens [sic] with a gong making the noise.

He brought along 30 instruments with him all precussion ones. He played them wonderfully, he explained them and played them all in turn he was especially good on the drums he had, side drums, brass ones, 2 kettle drums, a Chinese one and 2 African ones. He was I think a little soft up top or else he was used to giving concerts to 8-year olds; he was very funny, sometimes meaning to be, sometimes not, but he acted very queerly indeed as well as getting three boys in turn up on the stage to play the drums, and the thing you shake and hit with your fist that goes click. This was generally disapproved of by all; it is a bit much to ask three new boys (they were all new boys sitting on the front row) to try to play things they can't do properly in front of all the boys, staff and parents. Actually he picked them very luckily and they were all quite good. After that he played wonderfully on the xylophone the zither and some others that you hit like a piano; he played all his instruments very well.

Today is so far a lovely day and we will be going somewhere probably Barbon or Whernside.

Incidentally on Saturday the 1st November, the day that you are here there is a 1st XV match v St Bees and a film which is rather a waste considering you will be here.

We get an extra long Xmas hols. Last year it was from 20 December to 17th Jan. This year it is from 18th December to 20th January, but Easter term ends of [on] Thurs 2nd April; which gives us Easter at school for the first time since our first or second year at the Dragons. All this fascinating information came out with the Brown Book which we got yesterday.

We went 6 of us to Dent and past it up the valley on Sunday. It was a beautiful day and quite hot. We bought pop and chocolate their [there] and had a lovely lunch up past Dent beside the river. Then walked up a gill beside Whernside and back through Dent and up Tweedledee and Tweedledum and back to Sedbergh.

House runs again on Friday, I was 10th in Big Pack again.

Sorry about the ghastly biro as I forgot my pen in Rye (I do not know where it is in Rye but I expect I will buy a cheap pen some time when the biro runs out...

I have played fives twice today. They were both good games. There is a squash ladder starting this week (when Jamie has written up the names on pieces of cardboard)

Jolly 'd' going in for competitions – maybe we'll get the Aston Martin even if it is a 1 to 100,000 chance– wouldn't it be wonderful – going along the straight stretch into Rye at 100 mph.

J 19th Oct 1958 [Sunday]

Jolly good idea doing these competitions[333], I hope your ideas of humour are the same as the honourable judges'.

Played 3 games of rugger. Played for the Assassins against 2nd XV. The Assassins are a collection of masters, Old Boys and connections with the school who happen to be around and two or three boys to fill the gaps. The game was very good fun and I had a good game, scoring the only try for the Assassins from a line out near the line. The final score was 3-3.

I enjoy the back row but have been playing all over the place – which qualifies me well to go as 16th man for the 3rd XV. We went to QEGS Kirby Lonsdale yesterday but were beaten pretty thoroughly – 26-3. It was good fun and they weren't a bad lot. Good food.

Played squash pretty madly and held off all comers – forging my way up the ladder, where I started at the bottom.

More boils. This time I'm having them properly cleaned up and have two days with a giraffe bandage and hoards of penicillin – 4 days' worth in 2 days – a constant series of pricks and punctures.

We're painting up, plastering and decorating the rooms in the cellar. I expect S has told you about that because he and Lionel M are the accepted expert polyfillers!

I've tried my hand at that and the other forms of exercise devised down there – whitewashing ceilings and distempering walls.

Plenty of work – three essays this weekend to be done by Tuesday. Usual reading. Musset armchair plays I find good fun.

My study is in an awful mess this morning because last night we had a Mock Trial. I was one of the 12 good men and true – who were the most honourable collection, 9 of them from the Mod Lang 6. I doshed up[334] as a local farmer looking smart in gaudy tweeds, bright red waistcoat etc – corduroys turned into breeches, bow tie etc. Everyone enjoyed it; and our verdict too surprised one and all especially Judge Horsy Gairdner – but he managed to concoct a pretty good sentence.[335]

Looking forward to your visit on 1st.

---

[333] My mother enjoyed competitions in the newspapers such as writing advertising jingles, and occasionally won some good prize money.

[334] I do not recall the term 'doshed up' for 'got up as...' or 'dressed up as...'.

[335] Alan Macfarlane (his letter home of 19 October) took part as a 'communist demonstrator', which was good fun, as we just had to do a bit of shouting, distribute some pamphlets, and then got seats in the front row! I dressed up as an extremely dirty looking communist - more like a tramp, with a bristly moustache and a black chin. And I wore an old rain coat and a highly disreputable hat!'

J   26 October 1958 [Tuesday]

How nice that Dad found out why he isn't shooting straight[336].

Had a good week. The big excitement was a lecture by Sir Vivian Fuchs[337] whose boy is at the school, a school pre in Powell House. It was tremendous. He gave us the whole works 2 ½ hrs of superb slides – it was terribly interesting and we now know all about it.

Thinking of entertainment there is a classic film on the Saturday evening next week, Twelve angry Men. All are supposed to go – so it's a pity that it's the weekend you are coming – but it may be possible to miss it. It will be terribly nice to go off in the car somewhere, seeing you've got it this time. On se debrouillera.

Work ok. Essay for Bertie Mills on 'Le problem des races de couleur', and one on 'All knowledge is useless'. And usual reading – and enjoying doing it all.

House rugger games and more Littleside games swapping round positions generally. I played in the front row. Not too bad but not very interesting and I have no intention of remaining there, and the games weren't too bad with forwards playing as backs etc.

Fives and squash... S's fives has taken a big step up. Had an enjoyable fast game with him and others.

S   No date – [26 October] 1958

Thank you for the letters and the lovely picture of you with Sally. It certainly is a very good one.

I am very glad about your shares and I hope they will go on going up, then you can sell them and then when Daddy goes to Athens of Spain or somewhere you (Mummy) can go as well. (Sally can go to Aunty Jo).

Dear came here on Monday (I think) because a boy called Ventners saw her car outside Mrs Lason's house.

Rain but no house runs... Friday was an Extra Half. Mr Durran took me and 3 other chaps who came last term and one who came the term before us to Cautley to the Cross Keys. We started off late as Mr Durran had to give out money to those going to Inns (incidentally he told us that £10 had been drawn in 2 days). We got to Higher Winder and took a long time looking at the Lake District Hills, so when we reached Calf it was 4 o'clock. Then we climbed down the crags by the spout and from there to the Cross Keys it was 4.30.   There were some people already there and the Proprietor did not know that it was an extra half as the telephone had broken down and no one had rung up to tell her. Consequently she did not

---

[336] With his 12-bore shot gun. Being a right handed shot, his dominant left eye vision had had to be offset by use of a patch on the barrel.

[337] The Antarctic explorer. Peter, his son, has run for many years a trust encouraging young people to engage in the world of exploration and outward bound activities.

have anything ready and it was 5.15 when she brought us our tea which we scoffed as quickly as possible (eggs, homemade bread, butter, jam, cakes, buns, tarts etc). But it was twenty five to six when we finished and we had to get back by 6.15 (just short of 5 miles by road to run in 40 minutes which would give us time to change and go in to tea at 6.15. But when we started we certainly regretted having eaten so much tea. We got back at 6.20 but tea was late – not that we wanted any but we had to be there. It was very good fun and I enjoyed it very much.

On Wednesday we had the Shea General Knowledge which the whole school did. The Junior one was (as far as I can remember).

> a) either write about the Suez dispute and say whether you think the general attitude [incomplete], or what is a ram jet , a turbo prop?
>
> b) write brief notes on 9 of the following Nixon, Gaitskill, Macmillan, Nehru, Stanley Matthews, Donald Campbell, Laker, Krushev, Menzies, Humphrey Littleton, Mozart, Douglas Bader, Benjamin Britain, FM Montgomery
>
> [c] Review a book you have read in the last 6 months
>
> [d] What are the Olympic Games? Where are they going to be held?
>
> [e] Do you consider that international sport contests do more harm than good? Give at least 2 good reasons for your opinion.

I did the Suez thing and the nine names I have underlined# – and the rest.

Yesterday morning we had a debate. The motion was This house is glad it does not exist in Scotland. The debate lasted two periods (one and a half hours). I backed up Scotland but we lost 5-9. It was very good and some boys got very cross because of the rot the other side said about England or Scotland.

I have been playing a lot of fives and squash in my spare time.

Yesterday evening there was a film show. First was the news (only about 2 months ago); then a cartoon which was fairly good, then Oliver Twist. It was an 'A' film with about 3 murders and was rather spooky but it was an extremely good film and the acting was really wonderful. Alec Guinness was Fagin and was really wonderful.

Looking forward to seeing the house.

If you are coming up when are you coming?

J   no date [Saturday 1ˢᵗ November 1958 – addressed to JMBL]
Please excuse the pencil but I'm not allowed to use ink in bed.

I haven't actually done any serious damage to my knee. I did it on Tuesday playing rugger, intercepting a pass from the scrum half and being run down by half the pack I was thoroughly tackled just short of the post.

The next morning it was much swollen and I was taken to the san and had a splint of plaster put on and went to bed. The swelling is still up but my knee doesn't ache[338].

Then next day I was taken on a journey to Lancaster, facing backwards in a joggy ambulance on the twisty road; kept waiting sweating away on a sheet for an X-ray and then back to the san.

Haven't done much in the san, just reading, French and English, adding a couple more Aggie Christies to the vast number I've already read of them.

Mum arrives this morning and I'm getting up somewhere around lunchtime. Am terribly sorry you couldn't come up this weekend but I see that you have a lot on hand[339]. I expect we'll have a lovely weekend. Jolly lucky I didn't have to stay in bed for 2 more days.

I won't be able to play on house teams – maddening. I had played second row on Monday just for a change. Quite a different job – it was great fun.

No news from here in the san. The trees outside in the doc's garden are rather beautiful – nicer without leaves than with the leaves on. Out of the side window I have a view of the back of Loftus Hill houses and of television masts – not very inspiring, particularly as it doesn't get light till 11 o'clock and lights are on again at 3.45. My 4 days rest come to an end now – a good thing to have it I suppose

Breakfast ahoy. It isn't beer and chips but it looks pretty d.

J   9 Nov 1958

Thank you for a superb weekend...

Played on the 3rds away at Rossall. We had a splendid day. Left at 10; coffee an d biscuits the other side of Lancaster and arrived there (it's about 3 miles north of Blackpool) in time for lunch. Lunch in a communal hall was not very good; then we looked around library and houses – very like Sedbergh. It was a very good game which we won 6-3 in the last two minutes. It was a penalty all at half time.

I had quite a good game; I caught the ball from a penalty against us and was haring down the line with 25 yards to go but unfortunately got caught. Got offside twice in keenness to get the opposing fly half – but otherwise nothing horrible. Don't know whether I'll stay on the thirds.

On the way back visited a gramophone record shop and had fish and chips.

Thursday was Field Day. Being a NCO in the bottom platoon we didn't do anything very thrilling but had quite a good battle on Frostrow and lots of lecturing.

---

[338] Water on the right knee yet again
[339] A familiar situation

On Saturday evening we had a concert by Leon Goosens the oboist. It was tremendous stuff. One or two of the pieces he chose were a bit obscure but on the whole they were enjoyable and it was certainly good. It was livened up a bit by some local Teds putting an atom banger (on what the North calls mischief night – 4th November) in the passage beside Powell Hall.

My work is going ok except that I'm behind hand as quite often happens. I had a rather bad German Essay on 'der Kampf um Weltherrshcaft'. I got 19 out of 50 but in fact the German was bad and I had 57 mistakes, I've come top in French proses out of three but my French Unseens aren't quite so hot.

The address of the kilt shop is 37 Chambers St, Edinburgh. I have had some ideas for a Greedy List. I hope they are helpful. Possibly some to be shared: a full sized rugger ball; the New Statesman for a year I would like to get very much (perhaps there is a cheap rate for schoolboys?) An art book, large, called 'The Moderns' to be found at Smiths etc. A record token is always more than welcome; fencing foil, maybe 2 pictures for the study – can't think of any particular ones I want; cartridge paper or whatever it is called for watercolours. We've got paints and brushes. Golf balls of course more than welcome – afraid my list is running dry..

Time marches on. French plays at Lancaster this week. Thanks again for the lovely weekend.

S   No date – [9 November] 1958

Thankyou very much for your letter and for the lovely weekend you gave us. It was great fun; the shortbreads were jolly nice too. I hope you had a good journey down and Granny and Grandfather are well.

There have been two more 1st XV matches [...narrow wins against Uppingham and Rossall; scores given...] This means 7 unconverted tries; if we had needed the points it would have been a great pity not to have a kicker.

Wednesday was Field Day and I am in 5 pln. I was in the main exercise which was called 'Operation Hitumhard'. We went up to Killington in luxury coaches. Ours was so full that it could not get up Scotch Jeans so we all had to get out and run beside it. We got to our destination which was a marsh surrounded by little hills at about one; then we did section in attacks with blanks; then we had lunch of spam sandwiches which was like that [drawing of fat rectangle] – that thick each piece of bread – also they had been made the day before at lunch time which I saw. It looked so silly because most of the other houses have lettuce and tomato and egg sandwiches which are properly made and they are about [sketch of thin rectangle] that thick. After lunch we marched to meet another platoon and then we did the big march to hunt out the terrorists. They were hidden in some hills on one side and we had a lovely battle but when we had used all

205

our cunning moves and had got right up to the enemy and were about to charge them the battle stopped and cease fire went. The buses came back in the end and we went back singing all the way which was great fun.

Then in the evening there was a concert by Leon Goosens the oboeist. He played the oboe wonderfully. The piece I liked best was the oboe one that we have; it is Cantata or OP 47. He played it with part of the orchestra accompanying him. It went on or about 2 hours (and 2 encores); and in our row in Powell Hall we played that game where the 1st chap thinks of something and tells the 2nd who draws it, the 3rd says what he thinks the drawing is and then fold the drawing over, the 4th draws what the 3rd chap says it is etc. There were 11 in our row and we had two rather funny answers, 'one was a ham sandwich chained to a house in a gale'; the other was a boy wanting his hair changed to Julius Caesar before a battle. It is rather a good game to play for quarter of an hour or so because one only plays it for about a minute at a time then you pass it on.

The things I would like to put on my greedy list are probably the same as Jamie's; we thought of for both of us a rugger ball, fencing things and of course record tokens. Even better are records themselves as it is always nice to get presents on Christmas day; a skiendu or however you spell it[340] and anything else that you can think of; surprise presents are always nicer I think.

Jamie and I think we would like to go to the dance with Ann Garde or whatever her name is, if it is not too much trouble. Also I wrote to Valerie Sharpe and refused the dance in London; I could not think of why not, as I had said before we were having a dance; anyhow I said how very much I would have liked to. which is true, and said maybe another time; and she replied saying then come to the Pony Club one in Ockley – but I am only 50-50 for that one, maybe 60-40 against so what should I do? It is on Jan 8th. Her letter came on Saturday so I will have to reply fairly soon.

There are only 5 weeks till the hols now. If we keep the cat please don't call it Mitzi – maybe Mit or even Mits but not Mitzi.

PS   We have nothing against cats that are not called Mitzi or Sugarkins.

J   16 November 1958 [Sunday[
Glad you had a good journey down.

Had a good letter from Granny, saying what a good little girl Sally was – on the whole. Can this person who is with us now cook? She'll be all right if she's got the right ideas and is happy about hard work.

Would it be OK for Sug [Sugden] to come in the afternoon of the 22nd so he wouldn't have to help prepare and stay till late afternoon the next day, so that we can do something with him? A tremendous muddle it must

---

[340] correctly, skein dhu

have been chez Bayley when it actually wasn't Rosie's half term, but I think everything is straight now[341].

Good week of games. I managed to keep on the 3rd XV. We played a Balshaw's GS[342] XV –They were huge and rather rough. Unfortunately we lost 5-0 but it was pretty even. The pitch could not have been muddier and we were all half dead by half time with the effort of wading. I didn't have a bad game and was awarded a match tea – captain and man of the match chosen by him.

Real November day – fog, rain and mists. Rugger practices....

The French play at Lancaster was good fun. It was Le Barbier de Seville. It was most enjoyable and Figaro was awfully good. We had a good ¾ hour afterwards in which to hog fish and chips.

Had quite a lot of work. Been reading Le Monde with Horsy G daily...

At piano am practising some straight forward pieces.

Before I forget, a form herewith to be sent to the Medical Officer at the Sanatorium all filled out, not back to me please.

About the dance we have been asked to[343], S and I don't agree about it. That is to say in my view is a) a long way away and a nuisance to have to go whatever it was for, b) driving back at 2.30 in the morning seems senseless, although we could leave early which would be one solution. c) stay the night, although nice in some ways, on the 23-4 [December] would be rather a bore, d) we won't know anybody and are unlikely to keep in touch with anyone we were to meet there. However, there would be some nice people probably and it would be gay and I wouldn't mind going if S is keen to.

My first reaction is that I have not yet reached a stage of 'ennui' in the holidays where I would consider this necessary to make the holidays gayer; the hols could not be better if we stayed right at home meeting hardly anyone the whole time. There's so much to do and I have all kinds of ideas as one always does in term time. The need to go to this dance seems an insult to Rye, Westwick and our own capacity for doing worthwhile things without having to tramp off 45 miles to people we scarcely know[344]. So much for that outburst.

Today Charles William Alexander Thornely was christened and the house are giving a rather fine mug. Tonight we having the evening service in the Parish church, once per year, which will be a nice change

4 weeks on Thursday...

---

[341] Rosie Bayley was a neighbour and soon my first girl-friend.
[342] At Leyland, near Preston, Lancs
[343] At Horsham, by old friends from Ockley days
[344] The invitation had come from one of Sandy's friends, and my initial negative reaction may have been prompted by my interest in Rosie Bayley in Rye.

S   November 1958 [16 November]

Thank you for your letter and telegram. I have written refusing, I hope you are all well and the cat is ok; sad about the small one. Are you trying to get the dog soon as I think Mr Taptoe would be a very nice name.

It has rained a lot this week and the pitches are practically unplayable now. I played wing forward on the house games and hooker on the school ones. If I get on Juniors which I think I will it will be as wing forward but that will not be till next term. I will also be old enough for the ten mile which I think I shall go into. Then I will also be playing fives if there are one or two illnesses for there must be at least ten fives players to make up a team of six; so, I shall be pretty busy but that is not quite far a time yet.

This Sunday we hope to go somewhere with a packed lunch, possibly to Kirkby Lonsdale. Sunday is really rather boring if you always stay in the house as there are no games to be played at all. The idea of staying in for a Sunday lunch has gone now as you get no more than on any other day, and that is very little.

Here – I hope I will remember – is the polio form. The HM says will you fill it in and return it to the doctor to the School Sanitorium.

Yesterday the XV beat Ampleforth, 17-3; so out of 4 matches we have 9 points against us and 78 for. This is pretty good. Last year was 41-42 for the whole season.

Today we went out. We went about 20 miles and my feet are very sore. We went about a mile short of Kirby Lonsdale, and we ate such a big lunch that we could hardly bear the thought of going there and having eleven miles to go back; for lunch we had egg and tomato sandwiches, apples and chocolate marshmallows and fruit tarts an chocolate buns and Cydrax (we were only given the apple and sandwiches). We found a banger and let it off which was fun; also we met some Casterton girls and had a long talk with them; they had gone to Barbon.

Monday

I have got your letter which bore a 'Settle, Yorkshire' stamp mark. I refused the Sharpe's invitation as you said. I don't think it would be a dance worth going 90 miles for, especially as there would be know *[sic]* one I knew there. Good news about the flat. Where exactly is it? as I can see in my London map which I have in my diary.

Jamie has got his 3rd XV colours, which is jolly good. We have a bye in the first round of house matches; then we play the winners of Powell and Sedgwick which are the two best teams; each has 6 people on the 1st XV. Part II exam is next week. I hope I pass. I should unless I flap over something as the written questions are just a question of time.

Did you order 1, 2 or <u>No</u> subscription concert tickets? This is v. important as they are just coming out.

Jamie says he said [sent you] a long talk about not going to the dance; but he said it was bosh and you must take no notice.

Sorry this is short. I will try to write a longer one next week.

S   no date – 1958 [Tuesday 18th November]

Thank you very much for your letter and the invitation. We are making our final decision about it today. I entirely disagree about your views (in Jamie's letter). It seems stupid to say we can entertain ourselves at home, of course we can, we would be very happy putting shot and discus and being around the house all day but we like to play golf and tennis and sail as well, this is even better. It is the same thing with things like shows in London and films etc; obviously one could survive without these things but as they give great pleasure why not go to them as well and have the pleasure. This seems a much better line of argument than saying to look for entertainment away from home shows lack of power to entertain oneself, so to prove my point it seems obvious we can entertain ourselves at home but for the whole year's entertainment we like about 3 shows, 15 films and 5 dances out of 365 days, this makes it seem better; so it is bosh saying we cannot entertain ourselves.

Anyhow, we will make a decision about the Wallace dance and reply to it.

There is going to be a house concert a t the end of term probably on the Tuesday (we come back on the Thursday). I think 4 of us are going to do a short scit *[sic]* on the ITV advertisements, things like those you can see before films, such as Make the Day, Make the Day, Cadbury's Milk Tray and The Great Little cigarette Woodbines and OMO and Persil etc. We will I think a short skit on 3 or 4 adverts of this kind. This is what we are going to practice and if, by next Sunday, it is not very funny we will scrap it and either do something very small or nothing at all. It should be fun anyhow.

How nice about this Jill person; she sounds very nice[345]. Up to what extent is she a member of the family person. I presume she eats with us; does she sit in the drawing room or her own room? - but if she is nice it is all that matters. We seem to be having luck with her and Mrs Virgo being so good.

The 1st XV won again; this time it was against Uppingham, the score was I think 14-5, I am not sure. Anyhow you can see it in the Times, Sedbergh v Uppingham. Talking of things in papers it said something about Sir Rob BL in the Punch Almanack this year. It was no more than 2 or 3 lines and can't remember what it said.

We have been practising our house concert thing. It is terrific fun to practice; we have only 3 weeks now to do it in, so if I need any clothes will you send them.

Jamie and I have decided we would like to go to the dance at Ockley as it will also be fun to walk round there again the next day. So we will reply to the invitation.

---

[345] She came from Rye Harbour, and married a Rye fisherman. She was an excellent helper in every way and became a good family friend.

Jolly 'd' about the kilt shoes. I hope J said it would be better for you to keep them; if he didn't that's what we think.

Today is Tuesday and I've not even had time to do anything these last few days, the whole time has been polishing and swatting for the Part II exam. I don't know any marks but we all passed except 2 chaps in other houses. So that is a great relief

Are you getting the dog soon? Good about finding a good home.

J   23 Nov 1958

Thankyou for the letter and the invitation. S and I will discuss after letter prep. I agree that Ann Garde's dance is a bit different from the one at Ockley and that we might meet people who we'll continue to know around Tunbridge W. I think it would be good fun to go.

About the dancing shoes,[346] I think it'll be fine to have them sent to you. they would be very flexible being soft and as you say you could stuff them with tissue paper. 91/2 to 81/2 is right. Talking of shoes please may I buy a pair of black walking shoes –the request is fairly urgent as Teddy [Dinsdale] says they - my non-brogue shoes - are not worth mending. The leather is so wrinkled like paper it has broken at the side of the instep. I use the brogues for tough wear and for the kilt for evening wear. So may I buy a tidy ordinary black pair suitable for Sunday best, ok?

I'm glad to be able to proclaim my 3rd XV colours. I was lucky to get them after 2 matches, most people have waited for five – and there are only 4 colours now. I wear a gold badge on my jersey but it looks rather non-u new. We had another match yesterday against Lancaster GS and won 21-3.... I scored one of the tries from a loose scrum after a line out, barging through with thousands hanging on, cheers cheers.

Thinking of rugger in the holidays I feel that going to play in London Scottish B team would probably be rather a business for this year, a long way, admin difficulties etc. Could Dad possibly try Sussex or Hastings of something Juniors as an alternative suggestion?

House matches, rugger and fives, training etc.... 3rds have one more match v Rishworth away at Halifax, The red carpet is coming out for this occasion, all their governors etc are turning up. Should be fun except for the journey.

S and I have discussed the dance at Horsham and we would like to go. It t's rather fun to see old friends, there would be quite a few people we know, even if we don't see them again, and it would be fun to muck about round the woods, and snoop round Heron's March.[347]

---

[346] Soft, black, pumps with calf length laces to go with highland dress
[347] Evidently I changed my mind - or Sandy changed it for me.

S   No date – [After 23 November] 1958

We have just got your letter Daddy.

[re Ockley dance plan] There was an offer to put us up. It was on the back of the invitation but maybe you did not see it. We have accepted the invitation which is a pity as I thought you said it was up to us to decide and you did not want to stop all invitations; actually you did say this but maybe not seriously.

I quite agree with you, Daddy, about the dance at Westerham and My Fair Lady and our dance, but we will have to go to this one now. It will be very good fun there and at Ockley the day after, so we will hike or bike there which should be better fun that the whole lot. As you say Enough of that, but I don't see what being at Ockley again and scouting around Heron's March etc and dancing thru the night before gives you a pain in the neck, but as it does it is very 'd' of you to let us go.

I am 2nd in the squash ladder at the moment but don't suppose I shall stay there long as I have been challenged by the chap who won last year (you have to play within 4 days or the challenger gets a walkover).

House matches today – we have a bye. Jamie says we are coming South in time for the match v Marlborough whatever happens. Will you Daddy, be able to see it too as it is in London?

There was quite a lot of ice here today and it is very cold; maybe they won't play house matches today.

I have just refused having my hair cut this time so I will not look completely like a scarecrow when I come back. It was cut 3 months ago anyhow.

J   30 November 1958

Thank you very much indeed for the 2 letters and for the 10/- which I assure you it was spent in traditional style.

Re Dad's question for next holidays after some match experience I think it would be better if I stayed in the back row.

How fascinating that they are going to dam up Rye harbour, would make for good sailing.

About the dance at Ockley? I imagine you didn't see the note on the back saying Mrs Johnson [348] was offering to put us up. We answered saying yes please. It was for Jan 9th.

I have bought a super pair of most comfortable, new shoes, and not too expensive I think.

House rugger. Just lost to Hart House who are about the same standard as us. The other matches will be harder with 7 or 8 Bigside as position....

---

[348] Another Ockley parent, whose children we knew well

On Friday had the film Modern Times with Charlie Chaplin. It was absolutely first class. We were laughing so that it hurt - even though I'd seen it before, There were some superb scenes.

The weekend was also the Loretto match and the memorial service for Brendan Bracken. This was only quite good I thought and didn't quite carry atmosphere. The HM read the lesson badly which I know a lot of people commented on. Dear came for it and watched the start of the Loretto match. Neither S nor I saw her as it was only a fleeting visit, but she left some provisions for us with the HM, sweets, cake, bannock etc.

Wizard day yesterday - 3rd XV match away against Rishworth. Mummy knows the place outside Halifax. 3 hours drive in thick fog... stopped in Keighley for coffee, meat pies and fruit. Excellent lunch at the school. Only just arrived in time because of the pea souper all around Halifax. Fog as heavy as ever, it was almost twilight. Pitches are up 800 feet above sea level and it is a bog - like playing on Frostrow or Holme Fell, black and smelly. There were times when goal posts the other end could not be seen. After the match they produced beer or shandy - a new institution by their HM, in the pavilion. No objections. Baths, then sausage and chips and back to the bus - Capuccino coffee in Skipton, fish and chips in Settle on the way back. That was the last match of the term and a thoroughly successful trip.

Had an extra half and had an amusing time going out to Cautley and back doing nothing in particular but walking and talking.

The house concert is drawing near and ideas coming in from all sides....

Fives, squash and recreation, meaning rest, very necessary - and the Kingfisher comes along next week

S   Sunday 29th November   [actually 30th November] 58

Hope you had a good time in Switzerland with the Centre of the Universe[349]. About the Ockley dance Mrs Johnson had written on the back of the invitation to offer to put us up. What a pity about the Aston Martin; I see some garage chap has won it, I think it matters a lot on who you are who wins it.

Yesterday there was a thanksgiving service for the life of Brendan Bracken in chapel. General Sir John Shea addressed the congregation, I thought he spoke very well indeed. He outlined Brendan's life, his character, his love for the school and the things he had done for it and the great example he has given us. The governors are meeting this weekend to elect a chairman

Also yesterday was the match against Loretto - it was 42-3 for us, 7 tries but again none of them converted; it is an awful pity but the points are now 116-17 in 6 matches and everyone is pretty confident that we will beat Clifton and Marlborough.

---

[349] The Shah of Persia

Apparently Dear came here yesterday. We did not see her. I expect she probably did not want to stay long; anyhow she left an enormous food parcel, bananas, shrimp paste, Selkirk bannock and butter and a vast tin of chocolates and a chocolate cake – all very 'd'. We don't know where Dear is to write and thank her so we shall wait till she goes to Rye.

Monday was an extra half... We went to Dent over the top of Holme Fell. We had egg and chips in the George and Dragon and at 5.15 we came out feeling hungry so we went and bought some chocolate and ate this while we ran. After about 3 miles we were all nearly sick, and we had to walk the rest of the way arriving about 5 mins before tea. It was pitch dark going over Frostrow on the way back and as we felt ok we sang all the carols we knew. It was great fun.

It was a [word illeg. ?CCF] day yesterday and we got up a game of seven asides. We play 20 mins each way, so it is not as energetic as the 7 mins game. I played scrum half. On Friday I played for a Senior 2 side v Senior 3; we won 46-0 which was a decisive defeat; or victory.

J   7 Dec 1958

Thank you for the lovely card – I now have nearly 30 of these reproduction art cards. I like the Pissarro you sent very much indeed. Can't say exactly about the train times – we might be down in time to catch the 3.8 form Charing X arriving at Rye at 5.15 – it depends where the match is played and whether trains are on time.

Pleased to announce my house colours for rugger[350]. We played Powell House, a much stronger team but gave them a good fight.... Shiffner had his knee wrenched... – a most enjoyable game.

Could I buy a house tie and square? Most people have them knitted and if you have time, a nice plain one would be lovely. Ten feet long is the rough length – to be wound 4 times round the neck with games clothes. The sensible Dragon blue would be just right, only longer but not very wide – it requires 26 somethings? Would it be ounces, balls, scathes? I could of course buy a school one but this would be cheaper and MUCH nicer, if you have time.

In the exercise line time has been taken up by practices, short sprints and junior fives.... We've had frost, fog, sun, drizzle the lot and it looked as though games would never be playable.

Lessons are devoted to one or two seniors who are trying for scholarships – and I've been mostly revising from the beginning of this

---

[350] In later years inter-house competitions, especially in games, were ever more serious affairs. It was all part of becoming a full member of the School House tribe and winning house colours was the ultimate trophy, a plain blue silk square (worn inside the shirt collar (see House photographs in the Visual Essay) and plain blue woollen scarf to wear outdoors.

week. I've been trying to read English as much as possible, essays and poems, such as G.K. Chesterton.

The house concert is the next thing of importance. We're going to have a dance band and all kinds of gay things. Unfortunately a bug has struck the school but I don't think I'll succumb. 8 of Winder House are down, 4 Luptonians and about the same from all other houses.

11 enjoyable days to go, and Dear will be here tomorrow which will be nice.

PS   Will ring up from London. S and I have just parleyed and we might do some shopping there.

S   no date [c. 7 December] 58

Dear is coming here tomorrow which is very nice. I Hope she will be able to see Harvey Askew as last week he heard that she was watching the match and he walked all the way to Buskholme to see her but she had gone.

All this week there have been practices for house matches against Powell. I presume you heard that Jamie got his house colours which is jolly 'd'.[351] As Powell House have five on 1st XV and we have no one on 1st or 2nd XV. We did jolly well I think especially in the first half when it was 3-0 to them at half time.

Did you send in the subscription to the subscription concerts? I can't remember if you said you would get us some [tickets] or not. If you did, mine haven't come; not that I really mind.

I've been practising for the House concert most of the time. We are doing it as from behind shows and we are doing 4 short advertisements; the best at the moment are Woodbine, the great little cigarette, and the other is on Alkaseltzer – nearly the same as the Lucozade one. I think it is quite funny but one just can't tell as when you have done a joke for the hundredth time one can't tell if it is funny or very weak. And if one gets a chap in to see it you can't expect him to say the whole thing is lousy and not worth doing. But we are getting gin the Head of House to come and tell us about it, sometime today probably.

Have got your letter and just written a postcard to Sally. Not a very thrilling picture You can tell her it is a picture of Windsor

We have had our house concert seen by Laycock and he has ok'd it.

Mrs Thornely has dressed the Black Man as a highlander of the 18th century with a kilt, loose shirt, jacket and sporran, buckled shoes and everything he should have including a shield and claymore. It is very beautifully done.

---

[351] My house scarf was knitted at home, an especially long and warm, double-skinned one.

On Sunday it snowed for about 5 mins and it is pretty cold all the time. I Hope it snows before Christmas it gives an atmosphere to the whole thing, but I hope it does not snow on the day we travel.. Which reminds me that the game against Marlborough is at Teddington which is somewhere near Twickenham which is further than we thought, but it doesn't really matter; it is easy to get there by train..

Dear came here yesterday. We saw her after tea. She is driving down today and will get to about Cambridge and then to you the day after.

Only 8 days till we see you; hope you Daddy will be there Thursday night.

...[yet more requests for clothes from home for the house concert: checked shirts, jeans etc.]

J   December 14 1958

The flat sounds quite superb[352] with all the room and service laid on and the car for Dad. It must be good fun giving a party or a dinner there. I'm looking forward to seeing the seascape too

Glad Dad had a good visit to the centre of the universe.

We saw a little mention in the Daily Mail of what we thought must be a similiar meeting of the Shah going for highly secret talks in Geneva

I had no idea about the expense of wool but the scarf goes round three times which is absolutely as good.

Comparatively little exercise. Junior fives lost by three points in a very close game.... Done a little squash and the usual end of term yard soccer competitions. My team is not very good, the star performer being a new boy who is a very gifted rugger player. We are called the Rye and Dry – not of my choosing.

House concert has taken over, hectic... learning songs, rehearsing, helping people with things. The Rigoletto opera skit which I'm conducting is coming along nicely.

We had exams at the end of the week which went along very nicely but I haven't heard how they came out. A rather mixed selection I suspect. I know that some weren't very good but others will be better I hope.

cont/ Thursday

We had the Liverpool Philharmonic – absolutely superb, a wonderful evening of beautifully played music – Brahms academic overture was the nicest and some Elgar strings I forget what t was called. I didn't think the school's cheering was terribly hot which was a pity because it was rumoured that the March Slav was going to be their second encore. We did get to it eventually which was nice.

Film was the Ladykillers. Alec Guinness was magnificent so were the others – superb fun.

---

[352] A reference to rooms taken in Hyde Park Gate

3 games of rugger last week....

S   no date, End of Term December 58

Please tell Dad we are being driven to anywhere we like in London by a Canadian Aluminium car[353] so all is OK I think.

Thank you very much for the letter and the shirt & socks. They are fine. Everything is very gay here now with decorations all over the house.

I have only had two results so far, Physics 10th and French 12th. Our exams have been pretty hard this term, for maths we did a complete O level paper in the proper time and conditions, so I will know tomorrow whether I would have passed it.

Yesterday we had Junior Fives final. We have been in every fives final senior and junior for 2 ½ years but have not won one yet. Winder beat us this time.

The house concert rehearsal is tonight so we have been dashing and collecting things and making things. Yesterday we finished making and painting our camera which I think is really quite good. It looks something like this [sketch of large TV camera]. We have thousands of things to get, including ear phones and about 100 yds of wire from the corps and all the small things to use in the advertisements, which we have decided to be 'Woodbines', Alkaseltzer and Bobby [name illeg.] advertising White Label Scotch whisky. We are going to make them all as silly as possible with lots of big advertisement smiles, if you know what I mean.

We have seven people, 3 actors, 2 technicians, one powder girl and the producer, which is me, and are finishing it off with one actor tripping over a wire and most of the place and all the lights blowing up. It seems as suitable an ending as any.

The exam results are all over now and I was 12th in Exams and 16th in Final Order.

We pack this afternoon and I will be super specially efficient.

Easter Term 1959

J   25th January 59 [Sunday]

Thanks for the copy of the Draconian, with Granny's cutting. Fine journey up. The train was stifling and sleep making...Breakfast at Euston on a cup of coffee peaceful and enjoyable journey – greeted by the usual rain...

---

[353] Presumably laid on by the father of Bobby Hamer, the Canadian boy at School House

Back to the deserted, calm, peaceful harmony of school routine - wonderful.

They were splendid holidays and Rye is a superb place, but we really owe it to you Mum for everything you do to give us such a glorious holidays – for all the time you give up and the trouble you take – thank you very much. Golf, skating, tennis, parties, everything,: three cheers for the holidays..

Rusty wheels as term gets going. Wireless seems to be working better than last term. A powdering of snow and packed ice in the yard. There's some skating going on on the fell tarns but I haven't been up. Squash competitions at this time – some of the saps are off training...

It's a superb day sun and snow, dazzling white and beautifully fresh. Sandy and his pals have very sensibly gone off on the fells or somewhere.

Lots of work. Mauriac in French; and Jack Hammer not content with Iphigenia has pushed us on to Goetz von B.

First subscription concert[354], by Alan Loveday, a celebrated voilinist. I've never heard such wonderful tone – real swinging strings, He played among other things Bach's sonata for unaccompanied violin.

My new office (school prefect) is rather fun - with crest on the blazer and brown tie with gold rosettes.... Have been promoted to Sgt and platoon commander which is also rather fun.

S   Jan 25th

Thank you for your letter and for making last hols so enjoyable, they really were wonderful fun...

Am feeling virtuous, having written to Kim a complete airmail letter.

Today is Sunday and me, Lionel and another boy are going skating on Holme Fell Tarn. Conditions are perfect... perfect snow, blue skies, really is lovely; only people going skating from School House.

Uneventful journey; played poker dice; on special train to Sedbergh and Casterton; the door between us was locked, but after 10 minutes it was broken down.

Joined the RE Sappers for this and probably next term. We are going to learn to make bridges, and work out how much load bridges will carry, and how to blow up bridges or anything.

On Holme Fell there was nobody else there when we arrived and then lots of people came, and when we 3 were off, the ice cracked up and 4 people went in up to their waists.

---

[354] A new scheme introduced by Thornely whereby boys, with parental agreement, could subscribe to a series of concerts at a fixed price (put on the school bill), which school staff and nearby parents (and others connected with the school too) could similarly sign up for.

Today we went skating on Lilymere; there was about 1 inch of snow but very very powdery. It was terrific fun; we made an ice hockey pitch for tomorrow.

The subscription concert was on Saturday. It was Alan Loveday, violinist. He was very good but it is not my favourite instrument. The 'Opera Players' are coming sometime soon.

J   26 Jan 59 [Monday]

Can you please, you plural meaning Daddy really I suppose, fill in this Sussex form tithing and then, which I think is best, could you possibly return here so that they can all be sent off together in one batch.

Skating on Lilymere has begun. It's good but there's snow on the ice which slows up the skating and makes it harder work.

Not much else has come to pass in the last 29 hours. Thank you in anticipation for the paperwork. I had meant to enclose this all yesterday but forgot.

J   1 February 1959 [Sunday]

What a terrible thing it must have been to see Mr Taptoe[355] fall in –it's nice to know he can swim though - and maybe this fondness for water will allow us to bath him now and then without half murdering him. I hope Dad wins the rest of his matches it would be rather fun to get the salmon and the money[356].

The address of E Sussex Education Council is...

It was Johnny Gairdner who wrote that awful thing in the Draconian - and it is an understatement[357].

Everything going along fine, but slowly as yet. The advantage of having 7 prefects (which hasn't many advantages) is that the senior two are only prefects of the week once. My choices – reading roll calls, ringing bells, locking up - are over the term on Tuesdays.

Skating at Lilymere at the beginning of the week. The trouble was there was one or two inches of snow over it, which slowed the skating a lot. The surface was quite good but not as good as it was at [place name illeg.]. Bruce Loch was quite good too and I went down one afternoon when there were only 4 or 5 people on it on a gorgeous sunny day and it was great fun.

Rugger has been out of the question. Fives – the house should have the second best house team I think....

---

[355] The name of the family's newly acquired Jack Russell terrier, usually shortened to 'Tappy'
[356] Presumably prizes in some golf competition
[357] He had contributed (anonymously) a note to the Draconian magazine about ODs and their doings at Sedbergh.

My study has been littered with paper all week – fiendish. It's a matter of fighting it just to keep one's head above water – prose, unseens, essay on de Vigny.

The HM gave a sermon on the road to hell being paved with good intentions. Afterwards I went over it with S and we worked out what he really can get pat[358] for the exams, knowing the set books and the set formulae and what he should do to help on some other things.

Could you possibly send some records to me. There's Des Sykes's one which John Laycock brought with him, Rhapsody in Blue, which I forgot to bring back. Could you also send the Dvorjak symphony. I feel that if I heard it more I might like it more; also the Dichterliede. Would be very grateful. Sorry I forgot to take them.

S   No date –[possibly 1st Feb 59]

I have actually been doing some work and have hardly had any spare time except for exercise and skating. Most f the time I have been reading St Joan in and out. I think it is a very good play – until the trial scene starts then it becomes very stodgy. Everyone is spending 1 ½ to 2 hours trying to get good prep marks. The problem is where to work so that it is easy. The library is full of people reading the Daily Mail, playing chess or writing letters, 2 or 3 talking. The common Room is worse with the wireless and everyone talking. And the dayroom is worse still; which is probably a good thing because it makes the thought of work more pleasant, because really hard work is impossible.

Skating on Lilymere was wonderful. On Tuesday we went from 3 to 4.30 and played ice hockey, which was wonderful fun, especially after our practice in the holidays.

On Thursday there was a mist down over Lilymere and the thaw had turned the snow into a thin layer of water all over the ice. We tried to flood the yard and the prefects sprayed it on Tuesday but there was not enough to skate on, and then the thaw came and the water we put on did not freeze and it all turned to water.

The big news is that I have got a cube this term. With nobody leaving, 2 of them will not get them for a term or two, so I am not so badly off as some people are.

There were House runs on Friday, the first exercise proper of the term, and because of all the skating and the wonderful things we did in Rye, skating, tennis and golf, I seem to be very fit; and I came 2nd in Big Pack , probably the highest I will ever come for a long time..

At the moment there is a big flu epidemic going on, mounting and mounting. I expect it will peak about Tuesday. Some houses are down to

---

[358] Slang for to know perfectly or 'inside- out', or in some cases 'by heart'

about 1/3rd left, but it has only just started here, so we are going out again today to get away from the flu.

We are also going to get Polio jabbed quite soon which I suppose is a good thing.

I hope your training with Mr Taptoe is going right – it will be wonderful to have a dog that comes when one calls (sometimes)

We did not go far today, only to Inglemire Hall[359], where we first of all sat on a hill looking at the place and watched while eating our lunch; then we went around the house and peered in to the chapel and it was all deserted and nobody around. So we went round to a door which had a large handle and creaked and groaned, when we heard a door slam and footsteps coming towards us. We ran away and watched, and looked through the chapel windows and we heard footsteps again and a scream. So this time we ran 200 yards away and watched and saw a lady coming out carrying a baby. I can't imagine what she was doing in that deserted old place but at least it wasn't Dracula or some such thing. It is a very spooky place but it was very funny indeed – afterwards. After that we found a wood of enormous rhododendrons which one could only get through by a route in certain places; we had great fun in there..

Will you be coming up for the 10? It is on the 24th of March; and next term begins on 30th April and ends on Tuesday 28th July.

With a little bit of luck there might be a skating extra half this afternoon.

S   8 Feb [Sunday] 59

Nice that Taptoe and Penny are good friends now. He sounds an intelligent dog; I hope so but of course we can't tell yet.

Yesterday Lilymere was lovely – it was the first day since Tuesday and the surface was very good for ice hockey for it was not too fast, six of us in the senior day room played some senior Powell House chaps. Jamie and the Head of House came along for quarter of an hour and all together we played for about an hour. It was a very good game but we lost 10-8 after having led 8-3. Then on Tuesday the ice was even better so that even a little flick of a hockey stick sent the puck about 100 yards or when we shot a goal or passed hard it went straight into the bank and after having fished it out of the rhododendrons for the fiftieth time we gave it up. All the snow had melted on the top and it had rained as well, and then frozen over again which gave it this lovely surface.

Just about half the school is down with flu and about half are back now though they have to spend their days up in the house, but not at school lessons etc. Jamie and I have been very lucky; actually only one of our prefects has flu. Two of our masters have had it and are in bed. One is our

---

[359] Ingmire Hall, a part-derelict 16th century house attached to a mediaeval pele tower on the outskirts of Sedbergh.

Latin master so school prefects take us for these subjects. And on Tuesday Jamie took our form for Latin, in which we wrote out prepared prep and then did scanning with Jamie showing us how. It was rather funny (peculiar and ha ha!) to have Jamie taking me.

Tomorrow there is a concert; in fact it is a conjuror. It is a good idea, I hope he is a good one.

Also tomorrow is pancake day which is jolly good. Talking of food it is really quite good this term, and we get a lot more than last term, but on Sunday we get starved. It is very good quality but it is far less than any other day

Last night it froze very hard and should be another good skating day; but there are too many people off for there to be an extra half. So there may be House runs like last Friday; although there were many people away. I came 5th which was not very good..

I hope you will have a good time in London. Maybe you will see Gigi; it sounds wonderful.

J   15th February 1959 [Sunday]

What a terrible, terrible thing about Jeb. It is lucky he was not shot there and then by the Polizei – something like that was bound to happen – in fact it is pretty remarkable it did not happen before.

Skating – getting better at my edges, pretty competent at 8s and 3s. Games opening up madly. Only 5 weeks to the Ten. School squash competitions, inter-house fives...

I'm on Bigside for rugger now, and the first pitches are coming back to being playable. There aren't many 2nd XV matches. There's also junior house rugger to help with.[360]

Mad rush this term with music – with house and school orchestra... House unison and I might have another go at the quartet, as a bass.

Work all around me... Preparing hard for the Wakefield French prize. Thinking of French do you know when exactly and where and to whom I'm going next holidays?[361] Lectures (on coal) and recitals thrown in, and I'm reading the lesson in chapel and Powell Hall next week – rather frightening. In Corps, being a platoon commander requires more time for preparations. Gramophone and piano for relaxation - and spent a whole afternoon talking to Sid and Hilda

Flu seems gone and passed for this term, except for the HM who, as last year, got struck down last of all, yesterday evening.

---

[360] In my last years at rugger I found a niche as a wing forward (not being fast enough for backs, not heavy enough for the main pack). In my last term I played on the First XV a couple of times but ended up as captain of second XV and stood sixteenth man on some First XV away matches. Coaching house rugger teams was an important prefects' job.
[361] Plans for a language familiarisation visit to France were in hand.

S   15 Feb 59 [Sunday]

How awful about Jeb. It must be awful for the Logies especially Rhu; but I expect Jeb will be happy in his new home, although it is a bit late in his life to change hands again[362].

There has been a complete thaw here and we had the first game of rugger for the term, in pouring rain. It was only 9 aside juniors practice as there are only 30 people on ex in the house at the moment and only about 15 junior possibles. We have been doing juniors practice all week, which consists of passing, tackling, falling, dribbling but mainly sprints up and down the pitch[363].

And on Friday the 13th there were house runs again and I did worse this time and came 8th. I hope I won't drop any lower than that.

Lionel who is a member of the Youth Travel Bureau has sent a message saying that he has got tickets to go to Paris for the international – don't faint but read on. They are 75/- from London or 71/- from Southampton. The train leaves on 3rd April at 18.35 and Southampton at 20.11 (Friday evening). It arrives back on Sunday morning at 9.30 in Southampton and at Waterloo at 11.37 - which gives us a day in Paris, as well as seeing the game. J thought maybe we could all go to see the game or maybe only Dad and us, for we think it would be a very rewarding way of spending some of our post office savings; after all what is it for if it is not to spend, and this would not be a waste. And if Dad came you could catch the train at Waterloo.

Now I know what your reaction will be, surely you boys won't want to go off when we have just come home; but after all we would go on a Friday evening and come back on Sunday morning only a day and a bit later; also I am sure you would like to see the game and spend a day in Paris; also the Melvilles went to Switzerland with the YTB and say it is very good. So what do you think about it? It would be wonderful fun. The sooner we decide the more likely we will be able to get tickets, which Lionel can arrange. [...Schedules of travel repeated in list form.]

Last night there was a subscription concert. It was 'The Opera Players'[364] They were every good and the tenor Kenneth Macdonald had a very fine voice, and the base was a wonderful actor; he was really very funny. The plot of the first was very funny. They both lasted for about an hour; in fact they were both very good. In the first there was hardly any scenery at all but quite a lot in the second one. Jennifer Vyvyan who is coming next concert is I think the soprano we heard in the Albert Hall.

---

[362] Jeb had been running wild at Gresham's. Logie and Jo lacked the time to exercise him on a lead and did not like to lock him up indoors, so he was given to friends in the country to be looked after in their large home. Unfortunately he started running off again. He did not harry stock at first, but farmers presumed he did, partly because of his size; but in due course, he did start chasing animals, and in the end had to be put down.

[363] Known as 'short sprints' or '25 running', this was an excellent form of training.

[364] See programme in Visual Essay#

The conjuror who was supposed to be coming in the middle of the week had had flu so we had a film instead –To catch a Thief with Cary Grant and Grace Kelly. It was a very good film about diamond smuggling in Nice and Montecarlo; it was in colour with wonderful scenery with car chases along the coast. It is lovely to think we will be by the Med and in the mountains in the summer[365].

J   22 Feb 1959

The big pump or scare at the moment[366] is that in about one hour's time I will be reading the lesson in Chapel. It is a passage from Ecclesiastes. The HM goes over it with us in chapel and it is very difficult to read slowly and loudly. I will probably lapse into an inaudible gabble after one verse.

Began training for the Ten with a run of 11 miles or so over the fells to Dent.... Rugger, fives as usual... Music, singing...

In German we're doing Schiller's Jungfrau and Rilke and in French we've done our essay on Ruy Blas.

Nothing in particular, not much spare time and the week rushing by..

We had a talk on the Army illustrated with 2 live Saracen armoured cars with full equipment who came up from the royal Armoured Corps[367]. The chap I spoke to was much like these other Army people but obviously a good chap, The Hon Capt Allenby, from Eton – which was evident from his voice. And apparently he passed bottom into Sandhurst. He was ADC to Harding or Foot in Cyprus, I forget which. Dad met him. Commanding a troop of armoured cars did sounds rather gay.

Next week it is civics and the Chelham (?) Opera Group...

S   22 Feb 59

I am glad you think the International is a good idea; I hope you will be able to say yes soon as the seats may be running out. What a pity Uncle Robin and Helen are coming that weekend, but if we did go we would be back by lunchtime easily; also if Jamie is going to France anyhow, it would save him a journey and I could come back with Lionel if Dad decides not to go. But I am sure he would really enjoy it, especially as it is bound to be a very good game.

Yesterday was one of the big days of the term because it was the Ampleforth running match and for the first time it was here. The course starts on the far side of the rugger pitch on Buskholme, then up to Pepperpot round Akay Wood, over the bridge to the golf course then along the top of Frostrow, then down after 1 ½ miles by road to New

---

[365] A family trip to S. Jean de Luz, San Sebastian and the Pyrenees was being planned
[366] I do not recall the slang word 'pump'.
[367] Saracen armoured cars were widely used in the British Army in the 1950s and 1960s

Bridge, and finally back to Millthrop Bridge along the fields. It is 4 ½ miles altogether, 1 1/3 road, 1/3 track and the rest fell or field. The Ampleforth chaps are very serious, and all have black track suits and special shoes that can only be worn once. There were 8 from each school and at the start they all went ahead, and by the golf course they had one chap 80 yds ahead, but by the finish we had 1st, 4th, 5th, 6th, 8th and 9th and they had 2nd, 3rd, 7th and 10th. So we won, and the chap who won it for us is in Winder House and is only 15 ½ , which is quite fantastic.

On Sunday 6 of us went out onto Holme Fell and had lunch beside a stream by Charlies Pinnacle. Then we ran around and had chases along the side of the steep hill by Combe Scar [very steep]. There we saw people laying a trail with chalk, it was Head of School Fuchs; then half a mile on came two people from Powell House just walking along the trail and wiping it out which was a silly thing to do but annoying in that half an hour later Fuchs [Powell House himself] found out and saw us and accused us of destroying his trail. We denied this but I don't think he believed what we said, as if we did not have anything better to do than to destroy his trail.

After this we went to Dent and had tea of fizzy pop and chocolate, and then went back and played a game on Tweedledum and Tweedledee which you probably know[368]. The game was that each side (3 aside) has to guard a jersey on one of the hills, while capturing the other side's jersey from on top of the other hill. The hills are about 100 yds apart and the game is very energetic. In fact it is only a fight and a good way of letting off steam.

Jamie read on Sunday, I thought very well; it was nice and clear and easy to listen to. He reads this week in the mornings in Powell Hall and he never starts to go up onto the platform until after the hymn or psalm has ended. Most other readers go up well before the end, and both today and yesterday I thought he had forgotten or was day-dreaming, but he had not.

Last fortnight I came 13th out of 23 [in form order] – not very high but not very low either.

We won both school matches today though Boyd the captain broke his collar bone on Saturday.

Thank you for your letter, Daddy. Probably very good reasoning[369] especially as Uncle Robin and Aunt Helen will be at home.

J   1st March 1959

Thank you for the letter and the card. Cezanne's Lac d'Annecy is awfully nice. Thanks also for forwarding the card about the Junior Hunt Ball. I had heard that Sarah Andrews[370] might be doing something about that, but I didn't know it was actually coming off.

---

[368] A pair of grassy knolls just outside Sedbergh
[369] Arguments from my father objecting to the trip to Paris as proposed by Sandy
[370] Another member of our gang of friends in Rye

It's a great pity the HM won't let me come back late next term. Although a full fortnight in France is a good thing it would be better if it could be longer. It's all very well saying one can learn French at school but one can learn it quicker and better in France... spoiling the ship for a penny worth of tar... It's the way people of good but not A1 top brains get their exams is by learning a language abroad to the extent that they can... I know it's expensive, and I realize the whole thing is very difficult and I don't like to say all that, but I can't help seeing the importance of it.

Enclosed is the form for the State scholarship for next term...

All going well. Fives and squash competitions.... Then Mile in three weeks. I'm not in particularly good training for it. Yesterday I did a 12-13 mile run, a shortened 'Black Force' over Calf and along to the back ridge of the Howgills, then down to the Lune. The cloud was right down to Fell gate, but I managed not to get lost... It was cold and windy in the wet cloud up on top and I was glad to run, which is something.

Lots of musical practice – in house music... In orchestra Mozart's Jupiter symphony is going excellently and is good fun to play in.

With watercolour I'm getting the feel of things much more and cutting out the niggly little things which I tend towards..

My Goethe essay on Iphigenia auf Tauris was a 'genuine worthwhile piece of work' from Jack Hammer, which is better than just the usual 'B, Quite good' which isn't much reward for blood, sweat and tears. I've got a giant essay on Victor Hugo, man and poet, for Friday.

Greedy list: a picture again, a Monet, Vlaminck or Cezanne. For a book, the Impressionists, as sister volume to The Moderns. A new squash racquet. Mine won't be restringable again they say in the shop. A subscription to Paris Match for a bit. Any kind of gramophone record token – or a book token would be very nice.

Last night we had a bad opera from the Chelham group, The HM was very disappointed. There were one or two good moments but on the whole it was very amateur and unconvincing. We had a civics on the modern red-brick university. He was good but he hasn't convinced me or anyone else that they are really a splendid substitute for Oxbridge.

Half term gone, days getting longer – and the rest.

S   March 1st

About Patrick[371] it all depends how long he stays for, but I should think about in the middle of the period when Jamie is away would be best, but it would be nice to have him for a few days any time.

Talking of plans, what a simply wonderful idea to try for tickets for West Side Story; it will be wonderful if we can get them. Unfortunately Lionel and I cannot have a day in London after Jamie has gone to France,

---

[371] Patrick Mills, cousin a couple of years younger than Sandy, brother of Janet

because he is going on the school Corps party to Germany for 10 days, which is a party of about 30 going around seeing the camps, tank training, towns etc. About which Jamie and I decided last term we would not want to waste most of the hols with the corps as I will be at Corps camp next hols.

The ten training has started and we have all written out our time tables so we know exactly what we are to do each day; it is great fun making it out so as to build up to a peak with road runs, fell runs, stamina runs and short runs carefully arranged. I started on Friday by simply doing Winder, and was pleased with myself as I did it in 29 minutes from House to House, as it was my first run of training. Today we are going to Kirby Longsdale /sic/ which is quite a long way but not as far if we go over the side of Holme Fell.

This year's ten mile entry will be easily a record; there are 32 people going in for it from this House alone. In all there will be easily a hundred. So we (the House) are having trials; these are timed, one to Cautley, one to Danny, from which an order will be made of runners in the house. If I run really badly in those trials I will find myself at the back of a queue of 32 people at the start of the ten itself which virtually means, unless one sprints, being last at Green Hill. So the answer to this is that I must run well in the trials, which is easier said than done.

Last night there was an opera group that came to the school. I suppose that as we get the best of everything in the way of music here, with people like Leon Goosens, Royal Liverpool Phil, Dennis Matthews the pianist and Dennis Brain before he was killed, that our judgement of good class music is pretty high - but these people were very bad. They were not a patch on the people who came 2 weeks ago – I did not realise how good they were until I saw these people. Not one of them could sing, the tenor and 2nd soprano could act a bit, the bass could not even get as low as Daddy's high notes and he had a terribly weak voice.; and the first soprano cracked on her high notes. The second piece, Doctor Miracle by Bizet was much better than the first, 'Policeman's Serenade'.

On Sunday we went nearly to Kirby Lonsdale just past Casterton, where we met some of the school girls. One of them knew Jamie from when he was at the Sykes. We talked to 5 of them for about an hour and consequently they were late for their opera practice and we found ourselves 9 miles out at 4 o'clock with tea at 5.45, and we had to bath and change. It was awful running back and we had to run along beside the railway on the track beside the sleepers; but we got back in time for tea.

Next week is field day and the film of St Joan which we saw in London.

J   8th March 1959 [Sunday]
Thank you for being so quick in returning the state scholarship form. I've been considering the problem about going to France and I think you are probably right about it. I think form the 12th to the 27th is all right really but can I ask for peace in the morning at home and retire upstairs in our

room as a firm rule with a few exceptions of course, for a couple of hours every day. I think that with some really concentrated reading of modern French and learning of idioms I should get myself into full swing for when I go abroad.

Everything is going well, school competitions etc and I have come through two more rounds in the squash. Beat Hart House by 63 points in fives. We should win against Winder tomorrow and get a place in the final.

The ten is on the 24th. Please can I have written permission to enter for it, I have had the doc's, and for Sandy's too please sometime next week.

In the Cautley trials... Groups went off every 5 minutes. We did a 5-minute mile on the first bit, which finished me for the fell run. Took 33.15 to Cautley yesterday, I came about half way up the list. Danny trial – nearly 8 miles - is next week.... Perhaps my age will make up for size and weight. Dear is coming up next week and should be able to see two very exhausted grandchildren flop down Danny hill. Sandy did very well in the Cautley trial. We (those in authority) are very pleased with him. He came third in the whole house including the guys who came 20th and 5th in last year's race. However, I fear 4 miles may be his distance rather than ten but it may not be, one never knows[372].

By the way, I need a new passport completely. How do I go about it? I can get a photograph here from Mr Lowis the chemist.

Thank you for the gorgeous tin of shortbread. You'd think that with all the exercise I'd have lost weight. I lost 5 pounds over the Xmas holidays and have put on 6 in 7 weeks.

The cook and most of the maids have gone[373] so we're down to washing up and laying tables and things.

We've been having furious practices at everything. I've been conducting the House Shout[374]. I've been going through it all with the HM and it's very difficult indeed. [I learnt a lot about music from those sessions].

French essays for the Wakefield prize– on Vigny's Servitude et grandeur militaire, and also on Victor Hugo's poetry – which is my best hope for doing well but I doubt whether it will be good enough to pull me out of bad de Vigny answers[375].

Last night we had the film of St Joan which we saw at the Odeon Kensington some time ago, do you remember. It was still good on second seeing but nothing really great. Liverpool Philharmonic are sending up 14 guys to give a concert this evening. 4 of them are coming in to House Tea which should be interesting.

---

[372] On the contrary, Sandy excelled in the ten mile race.

[373] Not clear why

[374]Nickname for the unison singing (of two songs) in inter-house competition for a cup

[375] Victor Hugo pulled me through and I won the prize – see letter of 28 March.

S   8 March

Thank you for your letter and for the shortbreads which are lovely. It was very 'd' of you to send them, they are just the thing to have at the moment when we are supposed not to be eating chocolate and very rich things.

On Friday night we had the doctor's exam and we were all very nervous; and having had various things done to us we had to jump up and down onto a chair 12 times and then have our hearts and breathing tested. But as the doctor says himself half the people that are tested are so nervous of failing that he can't really tell. But I passed and so did Jamie; four of the 32 failed, leaving 28 which is probably an all time record. The whole school has 142 entries on Wednesday, but this will probably boil down to 110 or 115.

The first trial was yesterday. It was to Cautley and there was such a wind against us it was a gale all the way from Siberia to Sedbergh; and it came roaring down the Rawthey valley, so as we ran along the side of the hill it was dead against us. We started at Lupton house in groups of 4 or 6, and had our times taken at the far end and an order worked out with our starting times taken into account. I took 31.28 mins which is very slow had there not been a gale; but to my surprise I was told I was second fastest in the house. We were not supposed to know our places but one of the prefects who did not know that told me. I have come to the real conclusion that 3-4 miles is my best distance for I know that I cannot beat the people I beat yesterday over 10 miles. But there is a Danny trial sometime next week and I will find out if this is correct; but anyhow yesterday's run will put me up the house starting list a bit.

It is now Monday and yesterday Lionel another chap and I went with pack lunches fell training. The bitter East wind was still blowing and we ran to Cautley along the ten course; then we went up to Uldale force behind Baugh Fell. We ran hard to it and had lunch there. Then it started to rain then hail and it was very cold. We ran down the hill and then walked back to Cautley then turned round from Cautley to Hebblethwaite gill and down the gill and back. When we got back the rest of the house was doing divinity prep and so we just sat in the baths with a bottle of ginger beer and book each: very civilized! Today I will have a rest.

Then in the evening there was a concert by members of the Royal Liv Phil, conducted by a man called Fritz Speigl. It was titled 'an entertainment of lighthearted, comic, curious as well as serious music. They really were good. The first thing was an overture with excepts from 48 famous works, like Beethoven's 4, 5 or 6 and Water Music, Fingal's Cave etc. We had to write down as many as we recognised. It was very hard. because just as you thought you knew it, the music had moved onto the next one. Then there were some small singing pieces, funny ones, with a soprano and bass and they could both sing, especially Celia van Malles who had a lovely voice. Then there was ballet music, opera, solos for violin and oboe, Eine Kleine

Nachtmusik and the last piece was a Concerto for Two Tuning Forks and orchestra. They played the tuning forks wonderfully on the side of a double bass.

St Joan (film) was on Saturday night. Having been doing the play by Shaw, to see someone turn Shaw's Joan into a Hollywood beauty star with no outstanding characteristics was awful for it knocks all the main points of Shaw out.

I am now 9st 5 and 5' 8 ½" from the weigh in on Friday. I have got a Chemistry book and will send it before the weekend. Apparently the exam is in 2 parts now but the syllabus and types of questions are all roughly the same.

I hope you had a good time in the Middle East. Will you be having your nose operation or is it "all better now".

I am going down town now and will get Sally a postcard,

J   15 March 1959 [Sunday]
[a brief thank you note for birthday presents.]

Thank you very much for the book, cake and the print. It sounds like the lion, the witch and the wardrobe.

I would love to have that print framed of Vlaminck's I think it is one of his very best. with the splendid sky, cold colours and movement. With that, my Marquet of Naples, my Monet and Cezanne I have a very pleasant gallery now[376].

The Phrase and Quotation Dictionary is a thing I'm always looking for and is going to be a great blessing with my essay work – and also fascinating to plunge through. Am going to try to look out some useful latin and greek tags. No essay on art would be complete without Horace's 'ars est celare artem'.[377]

The cake looks wonderful – I say looks because yesterday after an 8-mile run I did not feel like cake.

I had a good week and a lovely birthday...

S   no date [15 March 59]

I hope you got the parcel of the Chemistry book and Sal got the postcard. It was the very best of a bad Jacksons collection.

There is a concert by Jennifer Vyvan tonight. It's a subscription one. She was the person we saw singing the Messia /sic/ in the Albert Hall. The programme was not so very good but she sang Mozart's Allelulia for an encore. She had a lovely voice and this was easily the best of the whole programme.

---

[376] I had them all until a very recent house move.
[377] 'Art is to conceal art'; Ovid (from Ars Amatoria), not Horace.

Tuesday was Field Day, and we were doing infantry training with the rest of the corps. We were in an operation against 3 platoons who were trying to defend their colonel who we had to capture. Our platoon didn't even see the enemy from 12 till 3.00 but finally we found them and had a very good battle and caught their colonel and tied him up with rifle slings. Then we were at Danny and had to march all the way back and about a mile out of town we joined up with the rest of the corps and some town policemen and marched back to school down the Main street; most of the town came out and little children ran alongside, It was very funny and anyone would have thought we were coming back from 5 years in Cyprus.

Today Jamie and I are going out with Mrs North who is an old friend of Dear; she is picking us up after Morning chapel

The weather has been lovely except yesterday. On Friday it was an extra half. We went up to Lilymere and mucked about beside the lake. We hardly went any distance because of the Danny trial the next day.

On the day it was very wet and muddy and again we started off in groups of 3 – 6. I did 64 to Danny and 29.25 to Cautley – which was faster than my Cautley trial. When it was worked out, I came 2nd again. I only hope I do as well in the Ten as I did in the trials.

We went out with two Mrs Norths, mother and daughter; the daughter, aged about 50 was nice but old Mrs North was terribly nice. We had lunch when we got there and after lunch we walked and had tea. They have a nice house full of antiques, beautiful silver, Japanese cabinets and vases etc. They showed us the Treasure map of Lilymere which they found in a letter which was written in the 1600s. They sent this to the British Museum who said the paper was of the 1600s but the writing probably not; but apparently they looked for the treasure with all sorts of experts but could find none, and now think they looked in the wrong direction. My theory is that there must be something, not just a practical joke which would have been pointless..

I hope you had a good time in the M/East; hope the centre of the universe comes to spend a day in little Old Rye; it would be great fun if you would need thousands of servants, but I can't imagine what one would do with him in the daytime,

I am glad Sally liked the postcard.

S   Sunday 23rd March 59 [22nd March]

Thank you for the lovely letters and for the Ten Shillings for our journey. I hope the removing is getting on o.k. I think it would be much nicer to go down to Westwick on the Friday afternoon instead of the following morning but I expect it will depend on how much you have to do in the office. How awful of Anne suddenly to decide to go, will you get someone else or a daily. I think a daily is miles better.

On Thursday there was the 10 mile. We had 2 good runners, one who came 3rd last year and another who is on the running team. It snowed before lunch and then we went out to 10 mile lane and saw them after 6 mins. The start was fantastically fast and our 4th runner who was 2nd reserve for the running team fainted at Thrush Gill but after a bit he went on and caught up 20 places. There were 85 runners. Then after everyone had passed us at 10 Mile Lane we went on to Muddy slide and saw the first 10 to get there. Johnston from Hart was 1st there and Scott who was best last year was second. Then we ran back but as we were going across somebody's land a gardener sent us right back so we had to sprint for about a mile and arrived back 2 mins before the finish. Johnston won in 1 hr 15, which was terrific as none thought he had a hope. He is also on the First XV and the First XI, which is a jolly good effort. Our No 2 runner came 5th and our No 1 came 15th.... There was a furious snow storm half way round for about ½ hour. It was a terrific race.

The 10 Mile concert was absolutely terrific. All the things in it were good, especially the Toy Symphony with the HM playing a cooker whistle, Mr Ward on a child's drum (which he hit too hard and his drumstick went through the drum on both sides), Mr Foster on a triangle, Mr Bishop who played brilliantly with a bird whistle (it sounded just like 2 chaps in the Crazy Gang who whistled) and Mr Marriott played a baby's rattle and Mr Madge on a policeman's whistle affair. It was very funny. And the masters' quartet was very funny. Jamie played a super solo in the 'Orpheus in the Underworld'; everybody stopped playing completely while he played; it was a very tricky bit with fast runs and high notes. Then all the runners came up in order and they sang the verses and we sang the chorus. The Three mile was on Friday, we had 4th, 5th, 10th, 11th, 15th, 23rd and 41st; the winner did a very good time, 20 secs over the record.

There is a yard soccer competition I am in Team 2. There are 10 teams, and 2 groups of American comps...

We drew against Jamie's team yesterday which are called the 'B-Lzeebubs'.

Have just been for a walk; tickling fish, we caught and killed an eel of 12 inches.

J   Saturday, 28 March 1959

Sorry this is in pencil, am writing in bed for a day recovering from a heavy cold of a nasty kind which has been hanging on for a long time. And having a relaxing time too.

There is quite a lot on hand on all fronts.

First of all the Ten. Sandy did A1 splendidly. He was the success in the house, only beaten by Moffatt who came 5th. To give you an idea of the speed and standard, I was placed 70th dead in a time of 1.27.3. With that time last year I would have been 52nd, and the year before 15th! Sandy's time would normally make him 3rd or so, and it really was a superb feat of running. It was great to see him up at the front on the stage, pleased as Punch.

The conditions except for Baugh Fell were good and I had an enjoyable day. And not hurrying, because I knew that competing out of training could be bad.[378] I got to Cautley about 90th but by the time I got to Danny I had moved up to 66th, having crossed Baugh Fell 3 ½ mins quicker than I had done in the trial. My lack of training started to tell on the road when my calves turned into lead, and several people overtook me and then there was a final sprint of 7 people together in a group. The concert was fun, everyone very gay; the music immaculate – lacking zip in Pomp and Circ but Jupiter was first rate. Our wind Quintet went off ok too; and 123 people on the stage was a huge squash.

I managed to win the Wakefield French prize, mainly on the strength of my huge Victor Hugo essay. On the de Vigny Serviteur I got an AB and an A- coming second. But I was top by a mile with a straight A on the V. H. Now I must have a bash at the German – Romeo and Julia auf dem Dorfe, Kleber's .

Reaching the big climax in practice for the House Shout now.

Thankyou to Sally for her nice Easter card..

Last night we had in chapel behind a huge curtain in front of the choir stalls the last scene of Sayers' Man Born to be King. As a whole it was very effective but it lacked something in a few places.

Then we had a long half holiday – with all sorts of sports including Cumberland wrestling, yard hockey and an evening of Scottish dancing, which was great fun and very good exercise. In the walking race I was a judge hidden behind a hedge watching out for people running.

This morning spent 4 lessons and a half doing an essay on Rilke's poems.

S   No date - ?late March 59

Thank you for the letter and parcel. This is my second day up today. I got up at lunch time yesterday. I have been in the house sickroom by myself. The rest are in the san and I am in the sickroom because I presume the san is full. Anyhow I have had a jolly good time except for when I first went in when I felt ghastly. I have been reading and writing. I have read five penguin thrillers and three comic plays by Shaw. I have also got my diary up to date. Yesterday it was raining so hard that they didn't play Juniors but had the Ampleforth trial instead. So as I was still in the house I missed it; but I will therefore go into the second trial I think which is in two weeks time, which consists of the first 20 of the first trial and those

---

[378] I had been off-exercise for some time on account of further knee damage

that couldn't run. This will give me more time to get back into training then than if the trial had been on Tuesday.

How awful about Penny. Dear must be completely knocked out. She said she wanted Sid and I to find another. And I am writing today to tell her what I have done.

Summer term 1959

J   3 May 1959 [Sunday]

The holidays seem to have flown past... There's no doubt that despite having worked fairly hard in France I feel very well recuperated and ready for well pretty well everything. This is so much a better term than Easter in all ways. I think it's going to be great fun too.

Thank you very very much for taking us to West Side Story. It really was huge fun. I've been listening to the record practically non stop since we got back which is also first class. I can see that it means nothing to someone who hasn't seen the show for there's a lot of this rather odd ballet almost-music. But when one has seen it, it is quite different. The hero Tony on the record is considerably better I think and the rest are just as good as the actual thing, Anita for instance.

The term has just about got under way... My study wasn't very dismantled and I had it completely habitable before tea the day of arriving. The Vlaminck goes very nicely with the others and is very much admired.

Yesterday I went up to classify on the range – so that someone else can have the pleasure of 400 rounds or something. Alan Ladd would not have been proud of it but it was fairly straight and I got an 8" group at 200 which would do for potting off a standing dustbin.

I've been playing cricket in the house on league games and I hope to open the bowling on the House team if there's a gap – but I'm not playing on Littleside. As I said I just can't spend every afternoon from 2.15 to 6.30 or 4.30 to 6.30, according to the day of the week, on the cricket field. It just wouldn't be practical at all, so I'm playing school tennis[379] and going hard for a lot of standards in the sports..

I'm in charge of house swimming again and we have got some not bad swimmers on the whole. There is also the inter-house drill comp and I'm in charge of our squad – only four weeks for that.

---

[379] I gave up school level cricket in my second last year, being only a marginal candidate for Littleside and played tennis instead. I enjoyed practicing serving and playing the ball up and down the tram lines for length and accuracy. I played in a number of Tennis VI matches; and, as our letters show, I played quite often in my last summer with Sandy.

The Wakefield German comes up this term, on 20th May in fact, which means getting to know one book backwards, And the Woodwind prize comes round again which means lots of hard practice. I'm playing in an octet on Speech Day (Schubert I think) and as usual have a full plate in front of me and looking forward to it all....

S   7 May 59 [Thursday]

Here I am on Thursday morning writing this three quarters of an hour before early morning prep while all around are asleep. The tennis racquet still has not arrived; but thank you very much for the lardy cake which is delicious and in very good condition. And thank you so much for the telegram. It is so nice to get one, and for your two letters. The owl is terrific and it stands above my belt on a shelf staring down at me. I am sure the raquet *[sic]* will arrive soon; it sounds terrific and it makes every day wonderful because I think the racquet will arrive during it.

The holidays were terrific, especially Wednesday evening and West Side Story. I enjoyed it terrifically and it was terribly 'd' of you to take us to see it. The journey was uneventful. We played 2 ½ hours playing bridge, not for money, which was fun.

I have played lots of tennis and on Saturday had coaching from Mr Alban, the master in charge, who was a blue at either Oxford or Cambridge. He got my serve a lot better, and I hope to play with him again today.

It is now just after breakfast and the tennis raquet has not come so I will put this in the post to let you know before the weekend that I am here in one piece. From what you said the raquet should have gone off last Saturday. If it has not arrived by Monday I will telephone you but I expect it will arrive soon and it certainly is worth waiting for.

J   10 May 1959

...Took my umbrella - the wooden shaft was broken or cracked, so the umbrella could not open and stay open properly - to the woodwork shop in the art school to see what they could do about it. The problem with binding is that the slide thing would not fit over the binding. I'll try having it done with marine glue or something which is meant to be stronger than wood itself. If it can't take the strain do you think it would be a good idea to get another one but with a metal shaft.

I haven't played cricket but I've played tennis three or four times but never well. My serving has come on and my forehand is sometimes reasonable but I seem to have lost control on the whole. Sandy is playing considerably better and at the moment it seems that Sandy, a chap called Snodgrass and myself are in the running for the last place on the team.

Am looking up the theory of throwing the weight and discus and trying to teach myself a few things -which will help with coaching too.

Not playing cricket I have more time in the afternoons to do things, reading and work and fit in things like music too. In the house we have got a little jazz group going and it is really quite good. We're very fortunate in having this guy Nelson who is No 2 in the National Youth Orchestra as a trumpeter but he also has a great love and understanding for jazz. Clarinet, trumpet and piano with bull fiddle and the drums added.

In the middle of the week we had the London Illustrated News reporter, or rather photographer here. It is a good thing for propaganda if they put in the right photos, but it was rather a farce.

A scene from the ten was faked up at Cautley, a rugger practice, river bathing etc. – things for all seasons and scenes like school prefects in informal discussion with the HM in his study – which has never happened before. The man took 150 photos of everything, orchestras, chemistry labs, a typical study – completely untypical in fact. It's one of these double page things ... and should be appearing in a few weeks time. Could you buy a copy because it would be a nice thing to keep and I don't know what will happen here when 500 people or so troop in to buy a copy from Jacksons.

I look forward to hearing about the reception with the Shahinshah.

S   10 May [Sunday]

Thank you very very much for the lovely raquet which arrived on Friday and could not be a better present, It is a lovely one and I have played tennis nearly every day this term and a lot of school tennis; I am getting my backhands a lot better mainly because I am playing with a thick handle borrowing a raquet with one until the new one came. The old one is here as well but I wanted to get used to the thicker handle instead of a squash bat handle like my old one. While I remember, tell Sally that the chocs were very good and I will send her a postcard before Wednesday at the latest

The London Illustrated chap was here. It was very amusing. He came on Wednesday and took photos of all sorts of things, including some people out at Cautley and one of the Corps advance infantry charging out of a smoke screen and of us fly-tying; he took one of all of us doing this and then a close up of a chap tying a fly; the chap was carefully arranged in his chair with the best fly in the room in his vice and he was supposed to be putting the finishing touches to it; and then his desk was piled up with peacock feather and birds wings and all sorts of carefully unorganised fly tying junk. Then the chap who was about to take the photo saw a pair of Benson and Hedges tins on the desk and quickly took those away muttering about advertising. The whole thing was very amusing. You must look at the copies when it comes out and buy one or some more as Dear

235

and Uncle Rab will like them. I think it comes out at the beginning of June or in June.

Last Sunday we went out to past Cautley with pack lunches but they were not worth having. Thye consisted of 5 plain biscuits and 4 half sandwiches and nothing else but we bought chocolate, squashed flies and orange squash. We found more fishing pools and tried to catch trout by scaring them under rocks where they hide. Then you try to catch them. When you touch them they don't usually move; but I get such a shock that I jump so quickly that they go. One of us felt one and quickly put his hands round it; he could not see it, but then there was a swish and off went a 2 ft to 3 ft eel, a wopper. It only went about ten yards so he took my knife and stabbed it right through the head and it thrashed around so naturally he took his hand away and it went off to die somewhere; we couldn't find it.

I have only played one game of cricket this term but I took three wickets and only made 2 runs. If I am going to play one game a week I can borrow some boots off someone who has just bought some new ones and will be lucky if he plays more than 1 game this term; so I will not buy myself [any] as it will save quite a bit.

For the last three months we have been planning to go to Switzerland for 10 days in the winter.... We plan to go with the Youth Travel Bureau with whom Lionel and his two brothers went last year. ... the dates are from the 1ˢᵗ to the 13ᵗʰ . It would mean missing New Year at Holt. [More details given and references to what the Melvilles did the previous year...] What do you think about it? It is very cheap; it would be terrific fun and an opportunity to go with 7 chaps from here cheaply is an opportunity I probably would never get again.

We have just had a terrific sermon, about the best I have ever heard, from a chap who has a church in Leeds where they help and keep people who have no houses, jobs or money. Everyone thought it was wonderful and there were films to be shown afterwards about his work. No one was planning to go, but after the sermon everyone went

J   17 May 1959 [Sunday]

...Jolly d the Shah of Persia asking you to go to Persia with Dad on one of his trips. That really would be something. I think he might extend the invitation a little bit so that S and I could come too and be guests of the Centre of the Universe too.

I'm starting investigations about Canada fairly properly. Please what is Uncle Paddy's address and also cousin Dick Weaver's? I wrote to the Canadian immigration office to find out the form about various things but they were very cagey and stated also that if I was only going for six months I'm a visitor and a visitor is not allowed to accept remunerative employment. How they check up on that I don't know but a) they were pretty clear about it and b) I'm sure if I went 'on pleasure' and got into the

DEW line through Uncle Paddy it would be possible. The DEW line at $400 a month is still in action at the moment because a friend of Bobby Hamer (in our house here) is going for 2 months this summer, aged only 17 ½ . Am hoping to get a passage which Hamer knows about on the Something Terminal line which ships bauxite for aluminium – but it is a circular route and one can't go direct to Canada so it would take longer. Also the St Lawrence is of course frozen in January so If Mr Hamer can't get me a place on one of his boats it'll be via Jamaica to Vancouver.

Meanwhile things are pushing along pretty well here. Been playing tennis with varying degrees of success, still jousting with Sandy and one other for the last place on the team. We've had some very nice weather for it.

Played one game of cricket. Bowled a few maidens but didn't take any wickets. Batting (it was a house practice game) I made 45 for out 3 times.

On the work front things have been fairly mixed but not too bad. I did my best French prose and my French unseen and essay have been fairly decent. My German proses etc haven't been quite so good. We have the German Wakefield prize the day after tomorrow on Kleber's Romeo and Julia auf dem Dorfe. This time everything is answered in the exam, no set essay – and I've got a couple of days of learning quotes to do.

We had a civics from John Arden, a OS, the playwright and Angry Young Man. He had a beard, the longest hair I think I've ever seen and an Indian actress wife. He spoke to us in corduroy bags, sloppy jacket and a thick woollen tie with a knot 1 ½ inches square. He spoke quite well, having some good theories and some obviously rather impractical ones and was pretty stimulating. What the public wanted he thought was a simple straightforward play which all classes would understand, with something to say, not like TSE's first plays. He was very insistent about this understandability, but apparently his own plays are quite unintelligible. He's dead keen on Bernard Myles' Shakespear stage theory and is meant to be one of our leading young writers.

On Saturday we had an excellent, first rate lecture recital from Gerald Moore the accompanist. He was most amusing with a style of humour like Victor Borge's and played superbly. He played quite a lot of the Erlkonig which was tremendous, He's accompanying Fischer Dieskau on television singing that on Thursday apparently. He showed how the same music played 5 times can sound quite differently and one would not have known it was the same music.

So the life of gaiety and song sweeps on. Oh yes, apparently S did not have a good report at all at the weekend The HM had had a talk with him and I should think from the tone in which he, the HM, was speaking, seriousness will be instilled.

S   May 17th

Thank you for your letter and how nice meeting the Shah and his asking you to go with Dad in January.

The weather here has been lovely for about ten days with hot sun every day, then we had two half hour thunderstorms and I have never seen it rain so hard in all my life. I Hope I enclose a photo of me in the ten; the chap over my left shoulder is Sir Vivian Fuchs's son Head of School who came in in the twenties. It is not very good but a fun photo to have.

I would like very much to have the binoculars here at school and I would be very careful with them.

Every day this week I have played school tennis, which is fun and also Mr Alban is a very good coach, at least he has taught me a lot.

Today we are going to Uldale Force where we have been before. It is about 7 miles out and as it is so hot we have been very diplomatic and got the HM to offer us a lift out to 5 miles; this was of course a major victory in the history of the struggle for freedom etc. Actually it is very 'd' of him to take us!.

The HM dropped us off at Rawthey bridge and we went up to the fall and bathed in the pool for a bit, then climbed around behind the falls and sunbathed, and then came back over the fells; you have to climb very steeply for about a mile then you run down the side of Baugh Fell for about 2 miles, all down hill, with shirts off and right into the Cross Keys where we bought lots of drink and drank it beside the river.

I am glad you think Switzerland is a good idea. One point to save money is, do you think I could borrow skis from Aunty K as YTB will send them over very easily. I can hardly wait to go to France these hols; Talking of France there is a chap here hiking across France and Germany and Austria , he wonders whether we have any old kilts at home that he could wear for the holiday[380], but I think the only ones of my size are J's and mine.

I Played cricket with the house team on Monday and scored 13 including two 4s of a 1ˢ XI bowler. Otherwise I have played tennis.

We are having Chemistry papers now and last fortnight I came higher than ever before in Chemistry, but awfully in Physics; but yesterday I did a very good practical test. The HM got a bit narked about last fortnight's physics but I will make sure that if I fail my exams it will not be for lack of work this term,

J   24 May 1959 [Sunday]

I have written to Cousin Dick[381] asking if he can give me any advice, and am very interested to hear what he's going to have to say. Another difficulty

---

[380] To wear a kilt was good for hitching lifts

[381] My mother's second cousin Dr Dick Weaver and his wife Kay lived in Hamilton, Ontario. I duly stayed with them for a few weeks on first arrival in Canada in March 1960.

has come up. Before any boat can give me a passage I have to join the Seamen's Union. Very sensible from their point of view, but I don't see how one goes about it. Can Dad find out an address?

How fascinating about Taptoe and the rabbit... maybe it will bring out the hunting sense in him. Rather wizard that you are setting up as a riding instructress.[382] I presume these are just small agreements but I'm sure you should be giving paid lessons. The more expensive it is to be taught by Mrs Lockhart, the more people will come and trust their terrible daughters and wild ponies to your charge

Another week with a lot of tennis. S is on fine form and when he and I beat the first pair 6-4 and the second pair 6- [figure illeg.] they put him on the Six. He seems to have had a wonderful time yesterday in the match away at Kendal. No doubt he'll be telling you all about it.

With the aid of a weight two pounds overweight my weight-throwing is becoming more consistent, but still short of a winning distance. But there's time yet.

The Drill Comp is 10 days away and I'm turning from harshness to kindness as the time approaches. They're quite good but not winners.

Then there's work and a formidable amount of it too. I've been having some better results in French. I had an A- for an essay which had few mistakes in it and have had A - - for English essays on French literature. My German essays and proses are not so good though the unseens aren't too bad.

The whole idea of consolidating on 12 authors the whole sweep of the literature of a country in one year's work seems pretty mad, if you ask me, but there it is...

In this lovely weather river bathing and quiet walking on the fells is advocated, but with the amount of work on it just is not possible and the orchestra requires practice too which fills in a couple of hours of the day. By slow degrees we are getting closer to Speech Day and that time of term which things start picking up hectically.

S   24 May

I am glad Dad likes the tie. The weather here is still quite lovely, with day after day of blue sky. I hope you are sending the binoculars which I would like very much to have here.

Tennis has been lovely all week and yesterday I was in a six to play against a men's club in Kendal.

It was the best match ever. It really was wonderful, as people who had been on it last year had said including those who had played on the rugger XV. We went by taxi. The driver said on arrival 'I don't think I am going to the right people, I am supposed to take a 'cricket side'. We told him we

---

[382] My mother was well qualified to do so after her advanced training in Germany.

were the right people. He said, ok then, how many of you are there? We said 6. He said, 6, well that makes one in front and four behind. It was not till later that he realised 1 + 4 = 5 not 6.

On arrival we were shown round their superb modern pavilion cum pub only 3 weeks in use. The courts were behind the cricket ground and bowling green. There was a cricket match going on and in the league they were allowed one professional per side; and theirs was an Indian who had played for India who got top score and took six wickets. They only had two courts so two pairs played while one watched tennis and cricket and drank. It was a boiling hot day. We played the third pair first and won. This guy Stone was a terribly nice chap and great fun. At tea we met them all, real old Kendal men. One of them looked like Vivian Fuchs, terribly distinguished, a British knight out for his annual game of tennis. They were terribly nice and had real north country accents and spent their time gardening, looking after families and playing tennis. One chap talking about GCE said he only took three but he wasn't very clever. One of us asked him if it was three O levels. He said yes but it got him into university. Then added 'O no it was A levels'. Their accent made it all difficult to follow sometimes.

After tea we lost to their first pair who weren't terribly good but got every ball back to our base line. Their second pair were very good net players and beat all our pairs. We had a drink then they had to go; and we talked to the barman and got onto rugger. He knew Uncle Logie and told us what a wonderful man Dear Man was, and he started to stand us a drink and we had great difficulty getting away to our taxi.

Today was the best day of term. It was a scorching hot day. Mr Durran said he wanted to go to the Lakes and after Chapel took us to the Langdale pikes. When we got below the pikes we bought some beer and pop in a pot and cooled it in an ice cold stream. At the tarn half way up we stopped and ate our lunch and drank our drinks and watched people climbing seriously on a rock face. We went up a gulley which was not dangerous and the view from the top was lovely; we could see all the big mountains and Windermere and the sea. We ran down the easy side and bathed in the tarn which was crystal clear and then back to the car. On the way back we stopped for a pint of orange on the way. It really was wonderful fun.

I hope your operation will be all right Dad and you will be out soon.

Drill Cup is next week and I have to start cleaning things. Also I am playing tennis every day now.

J   31 May 1959

Dear Daddy,

I hope everything is comfortable after your operation. From the name of it, it sounds an ok place and I see from the Times that Jack Hawkins is raising money for it at the moment.

...The usual gay round of entertainment was limited this week to a lecture on Rhodesia and Nyasaland from someone as old as Livingstone who spoke with his eyes closed which made it very hard for the audience to concentrate. He obviously knew a lot about the subject but a lot of people used a lot of the lecture to catch up on lost sleep.

We had one excitement this week when the house tutor Mr Durran was all but electrocuted. It was just after the prefects had gone to bed when the most hair-raising screams ending in a choking cough came from somewhere. From the acoustics it seems as though it was in the yard and Matthew and I thought that a maid was being murdered or something and that it was out of our domain[383]. Just then Jake (Mr Durran) tottered in through the door and went to Matthew's cube, gasping for the HM and a Bronze[384]. Matthew then got me out and dashed off to get the HM. White as a sheet Jake was groaning on the floor of his room having tottered back and collapsed there. So I applied artificial aspiration to five or six minutes till the Dr appeared,

Apparently he had just mended, as he thought, his electric fire, had it on his knees and plugged it in. Then to see if it was going evenly on the bar he reached back for his light switch and then the smoke went up. He couldn't put it down or let it go, and blacked out. 'Thought this was it. Thought I was dead.' It must have been a quite frightening experience but he recovered ok very quickly

Had the usual round of tennis this week – some rather long sessions, but not as long as staying on a cricket field for three hours. They are nice people who play and that's always a pleasant thing, and we don't seem to have any of those serious rather greasy tennis types.

Have been throwing the weight consistently at about 38 feet, which should get me to the final with a bit of luck. Unfortunately we have no one on the staff who can provide expert coaching which might help me to yet better results.

Today I've been reading the lessons in chapel which is a mixture of rather fun and rather frightening. More the latter today because I have 15 long verses of Exodus that don't say very much and are full of repetitions.

All the time I have plenty of work to do – essays, appreciations, proses the lot... And it's been a lot of hard work especially in German.

We nearly had an explosion in class this week when Tom Boyd, captain of the XV, one of our scholarship four who had been in a huff all the tutorial, I don't know why, got up as soon as Jack Hammer said we could go, stumped to the door and proclaimed loudly 'There's a whole damned evening wasted'.

---

[383] The maids, on strictest instructions, came and went through a separate yard and entrance to the house from the boys. They worked in the kitchens and only came to the boys' side to do cleaning in school hours.
[384] Someone with life-saving qualifications

Jack H[385] who is a conscientious master if any one is, and who had given an hour and a half of his evening giving us an extra tutorial was naturally furious. After a couple of minutes raging at each other, we the other three managed to haul Tom Boyd out in a silent peeve and tried to explain to Jack for we thought he would never give us any more and very valuable tutorials again. All came out well in the end though.

There's the Drill comp on Tuesday and everyone is cleaning, pressing, polishing madly. Then music for the Concert and instrumental competitions.

Another excitement has just cropped up. The mill at Millthrop Bridge burnt down in the last two hours. Unfortunately I was reading the lesson or else I would have been fire fighting to save the house down there. All the Sedbergh Fire brigade and Kendal fire brigade turned out – some men in pyjamas still. All the house Pyrenes were carted down there and the house attached to the mill was saved with squads of boys taking out all the furniture. Must have been huge fun. It's under control now but it will give us one thing to look at on our Sunday afternoon walk which is usually so boring.

Thus the term pushes on and we move in to the all-hecticest period of June

S   3 June [Wednesday]

The binoculars are really lovely ones. I am writing to Granny and Grandfather again.

The weather has gone back to normal. Have played tennis everyday for exercise. Played some very good doubles with Mr Alban. Yesterday there was a match against Stonyhurst. They take tennis much more seriously than we do and have a professional coach who coaches the whole school. Some of them were nice, two were awful; but they were good tennis players. We lost every match as second pair, but our first pair won all their games.

Next matches are against the OS and Rossall - which is at Rossall, so I must try and get on that one.

The HM has ordered us to have a guardian angel watching over us when we go to Switzerland if we go to Switzerland - who could be a master or a prefect – to make sure we don't get on the wrong train or get drunk. What it has to do with him I can't imagine. What we do in the holidays is our own business. He says we are not just a party of friends but 9 boys representing Sedbergh School and we must have a guardian angel. Personally I think it would be better fun and better for us to be without one. Anyhow Mr Melville is writing to you and to the HM. I think we are quite responsible and will certainly not get drunk etc, and if we are not sensible it is a very good way of teaching us.

---

[385] Jack Hammer

Thank you for your letter, Dad. I would quite like to go into the Guards, especially for 2 years, but it would be nice to know more facts about it.

Yesterday was Drill Cup and we have been pressing and polishing everything for the last few days like mad. We came 2nd by 4 marks out of 100, which is jolly good for Jamie[386]. The Marshall of the RAF is coming on Speech day, will give out prizes and inspect the guard of honour. He is arriving on the cricket pitch by the gym by helicopter..

After drill cup we went out tickling fish. We found some lovely pools. I caught one about 6 ins, not very big, and between the three of us we caught 4, 2 over 9 ins. It was great fun and we will go again when we can.

J   7 June 1959 [Sunday]

I'm glad everything has gone so well with the recovery from your nose operation. Jolly nice too to be home for 10 days. That's just about what I could do with for a pre-exam period. This term is pretty conc. stuff as the Modern side would put it. It's nice there's a good kennels place for Taptoe, that'll be very useful and save having to impose him on anyone.

We haven't had any heat for a long while here, and have just had 2 days thorough rain. Jackson's down town are quite hopelessly inefficient about my brolly for on Tuesday they say it'll be here on Thursday and on Thursday, come again on Monday; then on Monday, we'll have it for certain by Friday. But so it goes on with everything at that place because they have a complete monopoly. At least the wind and rain is more inducive to work than days when one feels it is a sin not to be outside doing something.

The week has gone at a normal sort of pace. We had the Drill comp on Tuesday and came 2nd - 2nd to a squad of veterans just about, who had an RSM and seven sergeants in their ranks and a squad of only 24 compared to our 32. The inspecting officer was pleased with our turn out and it all seemed to be quite good. Mr Durran, another master in the corps, left watching certain that we would win. We were second a long way ahead of 3rd and only 1 pt behind 1st. The whole thing was a worthwhile job but it's also good to have it over with. Now cleaning behind the brasses needn't be quite so concentrated.

We had a French oral exam for the S levels. It's only out of 30 – out of 390 – but it can still make up for those extra marks dropped elsewhere. I think it went pretty well. After reading the passage he began 'Have you lived in France?' which was rewarding if not comforting. Then I just about led the conversation on the subjects I had checked up on, even down to getting him to ask me about the psychology of a book I'd been reading and the author's philosophy of life. I think it went down fairly well. The next thing

---

[386] I commanded the squad. See my letter of 7 June below.

on the list is the German. That's going to need much more work to read up on my interests.

... The next big commitment coming up is the Kingfisher Usual old problems but greater by far and usual road paved with good intentions – at least I hope not. We're trying to get it bigger and better and going to a new printing firm. I'm trying James Gilbert rugby footballs, Hardy's fishing and all kinds of things [for advertisements]. It has to thrive on advertisements and we have an average circulation of only about 30. Our plan is to print 100 or so and send out complementary copies with a letter to old boys.

Our house team is looking pretty good [cricket] and that comes up next week now. Although of course only 11 bods will play we have a lot of fielding practice for the whole house – not one member excluded – and those are good fun. In putting the weight I've got a pamphlet on the modernest American method and am putting that into practice. Mechanically and theoretically it is clearly the best method, which means I don't have to chop and change styles now, which is a good thing..

We have practice for Speech day orchestra. Chief of Air Staff Sir Dermot Boyle is coming down by helicopter, landing on the cricket field in his Whirlwind 55 and inspecting a guard of honour before going to the speeches.

Meanwhile Racine, Lamartine and Hebbel. I still like French romantic literature although most of the form suffers from 'mal du mois'.[387] Next weekend is fun when one doesn't go out, watching thousands of parents gurgling Speech day tea, very little work and heaps of free time.

S   7 June 59

I hope, Dad you are fully recovered from the operations and that the days away from the office don't count as leave.

It is Speech Day on Saturday and lots of arrangements are being made for Sir D Boyle... I think the Illustrated News is coming out soon and both J and I have ordered one.

As I sit here in the Head's chair I have by my elbow LBL carved deeply into the table which is rather fun.

Yesterday I was not able to go fishing, but the others went and they caught one ten and a half inch and one ten inch trout. This is by tickling with a coarse handkerchief so that when we get a hold round a fish it does not slip through our fingers.

But I was playing in a tennis match, another one against a men's club; and they were of a much higher class of people. (They had 2 jags to start off

---

[387] Intensive study of literature, particularly of the European romantic movement, in my last years helped me find a way to understand and express better such philosophical ponderings or religious feelings as I had. My interest in music and European art contributed to this too.

with), but they weren't really quite as nice as the other ones. We started at half past two and when it came on to rain we played squash till tea, Then we went back on to the grass courts. We lost to the first and third pair, but had a good battle with the second pair and finally beat them 8-6.

In chapel they are going to move the back wall back again to enlarge the seating. It is needed, and by the time the bill comes in for it, we will have left. They are going to put in some loudspeakers half way down for the back to hear the organ better. It is a good idea but I think it is bound to change the atmosphere slightly.

The HM will not let us go to Switzerland unless we have a chap over 21 with us. I think he is being unnecessarily fussy but I think he will write to you.

Oh dear me It is Thursday and I forgot all about this letter thinking I had posted it. Yesterday 6 of us took a short cut on a run and got caught and thought we were in for a beating. At 5 o'clock the person who had caught us called for us and told us to put on games clothes and then to go up Winder by the front face, so he could see us. This we did in 40 mins, which is very fast but it was an awful bore

I have an hour's chemistry with Mr Mawby after work with some others; and am also doing Latin with 3 others in reading prep once a week and chemistry.

J   c. mid-June 58

Sorry my letter is so late, No excuse except complete busyness over the weekend. It has been a superb weekend in all ways and a good break before the final three weeks of grindstoning which are coming up now.

Friday was drenched in thunderstorms but then we had two clear hot days. The only trouble with the heat is that General Somebody is having the annual inspection of the Corps and I expect the troops will be fainting down the line.

My Speech-day weekend job was car parking which was rather fun. It involved quite a lot of organisation which got itself done somehow, then things are fun actually doing the car parks. One sees the parents, visitors and the cars and is generally in the middle of Speech day, greeting good mornings everywhere, this and that and the weather all over the place. I must have spoken to as many visitors as the HM. All rather fun.

The HM, although he does speak pretty well, made a few boshes like a spooned 'hole in heart' coming out as 'heart in the hole operation', and spoilt a speech by Vignoles about Brendan Bracken by repeating it all. The trouble is that he so much reads the thing that he forgot to cut it out. Apparently some of the parents are getting fed up with some of the same jokes about money – he ought perhaps to have a five-year cycle for his jokes.

The governors during the speeches sitting up on the dais were, with some exceptions, a wonderful collection of old cronies, Gen Sir John Shea, aged 90+ was the liveliest of them – a wonderful old bird. I don't think so much of Lord Peel though. However on the whole it was a very enjoyable affair.

Cricket in the afternoon. Our house team, with 3 1ˢᵗ XIers, 4 seconds and 2 thirds, gave an excellent display of quick fielding – got them out for 54 and 5 for 15 having got 150 before. Speech day cricket is always very gay with the crowds round the pitches. And then in the middle of it, at 4.20 the Air Marshall's helicopter hopped back from the rugger field and he left whirring round the field waving through the open door.

On Sunday I was sitting bang in the middle of the parents and visitors letting fly with all the chants and hymns they did not know. They may want their sons brought up in the most Christian ways but on the whole from the part they seemed to take in the service there seemed to be little fervour or even interest. The bishop of Glasgow preached and praught well.

Then Sandy and I went out with Ruth – a huge lunch with shandy all over the place and then off into action. We looked for cats – apparently there are 20 wild ones about – in a barn. Armed with Indian cutlasses we must have looked like a local dramatic club practising their pirate parts before they get into costumes. Then we went off rough shooting with a 12 bore and a .22 rifle. We had a wonderful 2 hours stalking, chasing and letting off rounds generally though we never hit anything. We popped at hares, crows, woodpigeon, also with the .22 at Lapwings and starlings and we stalked a deer through the thick undergrowth of a wood which was huge fun.

We allowed 40 minutes to get back and arrived just as the masters were going into chapel having done the last 11 miles[388] in 13 minutes. Not half stepping on the gas and with the Jag's wide snow tyres we screeched at every bend with the motor whining at high revs. We were obviously going to miss the start of chapel and would stop saying that Sandy was feeling sick.

Now things change. General inspection and then three weeks to day the first exams – French literature - horrible, horrible, horrible.

Apart from all that I had 3 fillings in Kendal and have 3 more to come which he said, and I agree, would be better to have done in the holidays. I don't want to have to keep coming over to Kendal. He was a nice man and quite efficient and he gave me the new high speed drill (300,000 revs per minute – max speed is 450,000) – when the only thing people feel is the coldness of the water. I felt the heat of the drill – anyway it's better than the old slow drills... He says I clean my teeth badly and brush too hard – and it's not just enough to go at them with a brush often.

---

[388] Down the winding road from Kirby Stephen to Sedbergh

S   14 June, Sunday; and finished on Tuesday 16th

Sorry my last letter was so late.

Today we are going out with Ruth, with lots of shooting I hope.

Yesterday was speech Day. Sir D Boyle came in with everyone assembled in front of Powell House; he came in over Frostrow, circled round and made a lovely landing on a 1 ft square white dot on the cricket field. The whole town had turned out to watch from by the church. He inspected the guard of honour and the band which was very smart.

Mr Vignoles the new Chairman of the Governors made a speech, mostly about Brendan Bracken; the HM made one but not as good as last year. Sir Boyle gave a very good speech; he is a tall broad man with a slanting forehead, great big bushy eyebrows ad weather beaten face and silver grey hair and from his speech seemed very able. It is nice to know there is such an able person at the very top of the air force. That was the impression he gave; anyhow his speech was the best.

Our 1st XI beat the OS, Sykes made 49. Sir V and Lady Fuchs were here during the match; he really is a splendid looking person. At 4.30 Sir D and Lady Boyle took off again, this time from the rugger pitch and flew round the middle of the ground waving goodbye.

On Sunday we went to Ruth in her wonderful new car, after a very long sermon. We went straight to Keisley stopping for drinks in a pub. Then we went off with old cutlasses to try to kill some of the 50 cats that live in the barn and eat the farmer's eggs and ducks, lamb etc., but they were away up on the barn top. We had a lovely lunch of chicken pie, fruit salad and cream washed down with gallons of shandy of varying content. Then we went shooting with a .22 and 12 bore and saw lots of game. Jamie put up lots of partridge but had the .22 at the time. I shot at a hare but had a dud bullet or so I thought but when I opened the gun there was nothing inside. They must have ejected themselves. We also found a deer and got within 75 yds of it but wouldn't have been able to fire at it with a .22 for fear of only wounding it; anyhow they're probably someone's deer.

Then without realizing it the time had gone and we rushed off to be in chapel at 7. We left Keisley hill at 6.15 and first we were held up by sheep outside Appleby golf course; were at Kirby Lonsdale in 18 mins and got outside the chapel with one minute to spare – and because of driving so fast I was feeling a trifle sick [ha! ha!] but lasted the service out.

Today is general inspection which is a bit of a bore but quite fun doing the drill ceremony

J   22 June 1959 [Monday]

Thank you very much for the letter and the postcard. I like very much Paul Klee's 'They're biting' card.

As for plans for next holidays, they're all excellent in their ways and yet may have their snags. I don't mind travelling down on a Bank holiday

Monday and sitting on my suitcase all the way; that would not make a difference. I think it would be nicer however if we both went to Bemersyde at the end of the hols for say 3 days, going up as you say on the 15th – but that only gives us a short time at home after we return from France. There's no doubt we want to be at home as long as possible and for as much as possible of the hols – and although I'd very much like to go to Ireland it is another few days off the holidays at home , and there's the expense as well..

This MacIsray person[389] sounds very gay – just the sort of person to have around in a small war or revolution.

...In tennis I came crashing back into form – for a bit – and seem to be getting more consistent. The only person I could replace in the team is Sandy and although it would be a close thing who gets on the next match I think he is better and safer. I twice won a game serving aces to one side although often double faults to the other. It wasn't that I was hitting the ball very fast, but they were swinging hard and I seem to have mesmerized the opposition.

I've been swimming quite a bit, and throwing things a lot....

Nose to the grindstone now. A fortnight to go and then the first exam - the whole of French literature in toto. The exams go on fairly quickly once they start. Sandy is working hard too and the general atmosphere is what one would expect a fortnight before exams looming everywhere.

S   25 June [Thursday]

Thank you for allowing us to make the Switzerland trip provided we get everything properly under control before the end of term.

The big news here is that Mr Melville has offered to come and take the party and to stay in a hotel near the youth hostel. Also Mr Melville is coming up next Sunday and is getting all of us to meet in the Bull. He is going to arrange everything and has written to various people already. It is very good of him; I expect he will be writing to you. [...one whole page of planning detail and related matters – timings, passports, Mr Melville very good skier, etc].

Exams start with Physics practical at 8.40 am on Monday 6th, then Physics I and Chem I on Thursday and Friday. Essays are on the 17th; and between the 6th and the 17th there are 16 exam papers all together.

Sports start next week for which I will have to train but I can't quite think when I can, what with all the work and prep I have got to do through the days including reading prep because it is too dark in the cube at night to read.

Hurrah! there are 8 people leaving this term and I am 3rd head so I am 3rd or 4th in line to get a study next term. If they keep me down to be 1st

---

[389] Wartime colleague of my father's in Italy

head and all my friends go into studies I don't know what I'll do, but it seems unlikely.

Next summer there are millions of people leaving and if I stayed till the winter I would be 18.8 and 3rd in the house, e.g. 2nd prefect. I seem to have had bad luck with my placing in the house; still if I get a study next term I will be happy.

J   28th June 59 [Sunday]

... re comments on bad handwriting

...Haven't done very much except general revision. We're thinking more about sports now as we're almost into July.

Ruth is taking us on out on Sat or Sun which is just the job.

I'll give you an exam preview – 10 papers and the General Paper in each language. total marks 390, pass mark varies according to the year and can be anything between 180 and 200

Marks	Subject	French	German	Hours
120	Literature Divided:	Tues 7th	Sat 11th	3
60	Appreciation			
60	Essays			
50	2 Proses	Tues 7th	Thurs 16th	1 ½
20	Dictation	Thurs 9th	Thurs 16th	
120	2 Unseens	Mon 12th	Fri 10th	2
50	Essay	Wed 15th	Tues 14th	1 ½

I hope that is clear. It only remains to get on with it and hope for the right questions.

Field day next week will be a good break. We're going up near Kendal somewhere – or between Kendal and Windermere. There are rumours of it being inter-school, but I doubt them. Anyway it's all very serious and Sgt Lockhart has been drilling his platoon at tactical withdrawals at high speed over rough country.

There's been a lot of rain – and I've played a lot of squash as a good way to keep fit....

Then we have instrumental competitions and a French recitation prize. And the rain has helped work by getting rid of the close weather and hay fever – good for lots of revision.

S   29 June [Monday]

I will enclose an exam time table of mine which start in 8 days time. The term really has gone fast. We break up one month from today, and camp breaks up on 5th August. I can't wait to get to Dover on the 20th. Will we drive all the 20th and get to Saint Jean on the 21st? I Hope our staying place will be near the sea.

This last week I have done nothing interesting, just work. I did 2 brilliant French proses which Jamie went over for me, getting top and 3rd top marks, but Mr Gairdner most unusually did not take the marks in - which was a chiz, but shows that crime does not pay

Dear sent me some chocs for getting on the Tennis VI but unfortunately I was off it last week; but I hope to get on again for Rossall

Today a friend and I went with the Melvilles to Windermere and back. We said we were going out with them, but we spent the day by ourselves. In the morning we had fish and chips and apple pie in a café and took a boat and rowed about on the lake; We tested each other on physics and chemistry from our all our notes which we had brought with us. It was good fun. We spent from 1 to 3 on the lake and then called on your friends who sent you their love and insisted on our staying for tea. And their son was wandering around eating chocolates; he showed us his new sports car with all the latest gadgets. We had a super tea. Mr was ill in bed unfortunately but they were very nice. We could not stay too long. We had to go after tea and wandered around Windermere or Bowness I forget which it is and met the Melvilles at 5.45 and got back in time for Chapel. What are the people in Bowness called? Can you tell me quickly so I can write them a letter.

Exams

Mon 6	Physics	Practical
Wed 8	Chemistry	Practical
Thurs 9	Physics I	
Fri 10	Chemistry	
Sat 11	Eng Lang II	Composition
Mon 13	French	composition
	French	Story
	English Lit	Henry V
Tues 14	Elem Maths	
	Eng Lit	St Joan
	Physics II	
Wed 15	Latin	comp
	French	Dictation
	Eng Lang I	
	French	Unprepared
Fri 17	Maths II	
	Latin II	Unprepared

Nearly all are 2 hours, except dictation and the practicals which are 2 ½ hours. I will be kept busy all week. The moment one subject is over another ones is there.

Thank you for the form which arrived today. The HM still doesn't want us to go and certainly will not allow young Melville and friend so we will have to find 2 more people. Jolly good about ski clothes, if I can get them; also maybe Dear has some skis – apparently they have to be very small these days and not much taller than your head.

Ruth has offered to take us out again next Sunday which is nice.

S   7 July [Tuesday]

Thank you very much for the letter and the 10/- which will become very useful and did yesterday during an away match. I do hope you go to Gigi; it is so wonderful especially Maurice Chevalier singing 'I'm glad I'm not young any more;' I hear that in cheap cinemas the audience burst out clapping and shouting, but I don't suppose that is Shaftesbury Avenue form.

We have the physics exam and will know the result the same day. I will not even open a book today because I am going on the Six to Rossall, as is Jamie; we were playing 3rd pair together which is great fun. We left at 6.45 and drove straight to Rossall (2 hours) in a bus, with the first eleven. The bus was awful, especially in the evening when it was hot coming back. Rossall were in quarantine for chicken pox, so we were left by ourselves for 2 hours in the morning. We went down to the sea, which is only about 100 yards away from the school buildings and cricket field; and you can see the Blackpool Tower from there. We walked along the front to the first playground and refreshed ourselves there and walked along the sea shore. Lunch was at 1 and we had it only with Sedbergh boys. We started tennis at 2.30 and lost our match; all our teams lost. It is not that the other side seem any better but they seem to get the points. We played till nearly 6. There were no gaps between the netting and the main Blackpool Road which was rather off putting. On the way back we stopped in Lancaster for fish and chipps /sic/ and arrived back in time for prayers and another big meal of sausage, spuds, beans and strawberries and cream. Very good..

I expect I will arrive in London about 12 but it would be best to have the appointment[390] till a lot later to make sure.

I would like to go to David's[391] next hols after France. What with camp I don't want to miss all of July at home. Also would it be better for J and I to spend 2 days or so with Dear at the beginning of the hols? I would love to have a day on the Tweed.

---

[390] With a medical specialist for a check after closure, many years earlier, of a spina bifida
[391] Cousin David Mure, the farmer in Kent – p.202, fn 395 above#

Today we had the practical from 8.30 till 11. We have to do one question then choose one more. I got the answer to the first one right, which was plotting of light through prisms to find the refractive index of glass; and I got a nice graph with the right answer. And I also got a nice graph for Question 2.

I still have to tell you about our field day at bridging camp but I'd better finish [squeezed in to bottom of page].

J   Wednesday 8ᵗʰ July

Thank you very much for the 2 letters and for the 10/-. The 10/- came beautifully timed.

The sun seems to be wonderful all over the country. It first blazed on Saturday here and we all got very red playing tennis. I had a splendid day and went with the Tennis VI to Rossall as 7ᵗʰ man and substitute (and as subs-captain at that). S and I were third pair together which was good fun. Sandy's rather funny playing tennis. He enjoys it very much obviously but I think that from 2 o'clock till 5.30 he smiled only once; he looks worried and earnest even after a good shot or game won. We didn't do terribly well, losing to all their pairs .We got better however as we played a better pair and did match up to their second pair. The sun was scorching and the court as hard as could be, with a white light kind of tarmac surface and by the end the old plates of meat were pretty worn out.

I've been playing tennis a lot and 100% better than earlier in the term. I think I've got more confidence and am beginning to move about the court better now.

Been swimming a bit and the breaststroke competitions are under way. Also the relay which hasn't been swum yet. I don't think SH will do very well. House cricket is doing very well. In the final we got Sedgwick out for 154 and are 97 for 4 ourselves with plenty of time at our disposal.

Of course the thing at the moment are the terrible exams. The worst is over – French literature and the worst of the slogging revision work gone with it thank heavens. The exam I rather mucked up in the timing. Out of three hours I was rather slow to get going on the appreciation and left myself only 1 hour for the two essays, which was utterly stupid since I did not have time to do very much of the second one. French prose and dictée next and they are not so bad. On the whole exams are a good season, if one may call it that. No set work, long long-breaks peaceful hall for revisions and a general atmosphere of work, tension and relief if you know what I mean.

How gorgeous going to see Gigi, Someone has a record in the house and it sounds huge fun. Looking forward to the holidays. Time is whizzing along now

PS As for Canada, Daddy, could you possibly ask this person or anyone who could help, if there are any shipping lines going to Halifax in January. This business of working one's passage isn't very easy. I've tried a couple of firms but with them it seems to be out of the question.

S   14 July

Thank you very very much for all the lovely food; there is enough to last a time and is delicious. It was rather like unpacking a box of chocolates in front of Jeb with all the people standing around and watching my every move.

I hope you had a nice birthday. Hope you got our telegram and little thing and hope it is the right size..

The physics practical was a piece of cake. The chemistry I did badly in; I only hope that the chemistry theory that I did well enough on Friday will pull my marks up - one has to get a certain per cent on both papers added together. Chemistry is now finished and results come first week in September; and there is no good in me having a post mortem on the paper. Physics 1 was a reasonable paper. Yesterday morning was the essay on various things, I did a short story about the football pools. I thought it rather an amusing story! but I don't know what the examiner will think. Tomorrow morning we have French comp and story

On Field Day we went to the army bridging camp near Lancaster and arrived in the pouring rain.. We had lunch with the regulars, that is to say it is a TA camp. We went down and did a bit of bridge building, a heavy girder bridge, the same principle as the Bailey. We had to do it with cranes which are terrific machines. The trick is to lift up the bridge to go 15 ft in the air. The whole thing was about 80 ft long and we could not hold it and it came down fairly fast but everyone got well clear. In the later afternoon we built a bridge out of rafts which was good fun then we drove motor launches up and down the Lune; then we went back and had a mug of strong army tea with sweetened condensed milk for the third time.

We had the film of Henry V on Thursday night, which is quite good, nothing terrific. I know Henry quite well now and can recite quite a lot. I presume you have a copy of Henry at home, so read Chorus to Act IV, first 9 lines and my yesterday's inspiration called instead of 'Near Agincourt', 'Near Piccadilly'.

Now entertain conjectures for a time
When creeping smog and pouring rain
Fill the wide streets of the capital.
From coffee bar to coffee bar through the night
The blaze of either duke box rudely sounds
That the smooth hep cats almost receive
The secret rhythm of each other's shoes

Advert answers advert and by their neon lights
Each night club sees the others sawdid/*sic*/ sights.

Brilliant don't you think; I don't, but it's not bad for inspiration if it can be called that. Yesterday there was another tennis match – v East Lancs. They were the men of the First Team of a club called East Lancs. I was playing with the school secretary [of Tennis] a pal of Jamie's who is the 3rd best player. We lost the match all together, but our pair won more games than any other pair. Still it was great fun playing them because they were good players and nice chaps. But we will have four of the same six here next year..

The HM thinks I am leaving next summer, at least he told me I was. I have no hope of being anywhere near a prefect by that term although I would be 3rd in the house in the winter but that is impossible. Maybe you could write to him about the matter, then we could talk about it

Has Mr Melville written to you?

Thank you again for the food parcel. I will go and eat some now.

J   15 July 1959 [Sunday]

...The worst has now passed by, last pair of exams coming up tomorrow. Although they are hard ones requiring huge concentration they need more the culminating work of a year than last minute revision. Here are [evidently enclosed, but now missing]] a couple more papers. I'm afraid my A level essay standard is higher than my S level relatively, if you see what I mean, i.e the extra scholarship, thought, content and arrangement is lacking. However I wasn't stuck for material and idioms. The trouble with one man marking all the stuff from one school is that he's bound to get all the same idioms churned up at him, all Jack Hammer's pet phrases and Horsy G's brilliant notes varied and badly linked together.

The general paper I thought was a stinker. I loathe such papers. But I did at least get three essays written though I had to close down early on Damon Runyon. I chose that when stuck for a third question after the other two – perhaps not a terribly happy choice of author, let alone question. Last year I did the appreciation and when I think of it, it must have been one of my more unfortunate strokes of madness.... I challenge you to make a good answer to part h). By the time I had laboured over the word 'phoney' in my mind for 20 minutes it sounded well so 'phoney!' that it nearly drove me mad.

We have sports and swimming sports and the Kingfisher all charging up at a high pace. In the sports one guy who came second last year [in the weight] and came 2nd in the discus is just short of the record of 45' odd. I regret that I remain still at about 40', sometimes more, often less which, although it has been won with 39. 38 and even 37' before now, will be no use this year. I must keep bashing. In the discus, I'm not doing so bad - if you'll excuse a Yorkshirism. I throw it 95 feet or so which keeps me up with two or three others. More hard practice needed.

In the swimming I managed to get to the final of the breaststroke.[392] I expect to come 4th by a long chalk, but on the way I've beaten two or three chaps who have got their school swimming colours for the breaststroke. The record is 39.3. It was near to being broken by one boy who did 39.6 and the next who does 40.0. I do 42 dead (two meanings of the word) with a bit of luck.

Oh yes, all's fine for going up to Bemersyde to stay with Dear – she will meet me at Melrose on Tuesday morning. What I don't know actually is what length of time I stay. The dentist appointment isn't the day I come down is it? When do you suggest I should come down south? Day or night, late or early, it's all the same to me (an Alexandrine with a bit of poetic licence there)

Only a fortnight to go now...

J   19 July 1959

As for the Benenden Tennis Tournament, what you have done is absolutely perfect – just the job. I think it would be fun to go to the dance but we can work that out in the holidays.

Everything is going splendidly exams are over at last. Three hours on end for three or four days tend to squash the brain a bit – what with all the revision in between.

We finished with the German prose and Dictation. The prose was of the characteristic AS level type. I kept on thinking of all the words in French. The German dictation, as was the French one, was pretty easy. Looking through the paper afterwards I couldn't find any mistakes thought that probably means there will be one or two.

For this last fortnight the work has been absolutely the kind I like. With French we are reading a play and doing our holiday work which is nice, a sort of thesis, 3-book minimum synopsis and appreciation from one author. We've got three authors to get done by December – Mauriac (the one I'm on to now), Duhamel and St Exupery. I like reading French so I enjoy that. In German I'm reading Minna von Barnheim (Lessing) and some modern reading, Bochart's short stories.

Sports are the real interest at the moment. I must say I'm looking forward to the last ten days, they should be fun. Saturday was the first. My organisation job is the Senior hurdles – which has a round every single day

---

[392] I did well at swimming in my last year - in breaststroke. I had practised a lot, being in charge of house swimming. There was less competition in the breaststroke because the top swimmers concentrated on crawl and backstroke. In the competitions, I came second in the final right behind the winner who was challenging the school record.

– that's fun too charging around singing out names, listing times and generally being officious!

There were the relays and I am second fastest in the house in the 220 (about 25.3), and run second. We came second, but one team was actually ahead of us but then dropped the baton at a changeover and we zoomed into second place. In junior relays we had a winning team, which was good. In the weight I am lying third as yet. In the 100 yds I won my heat (in 11.1) on a wet and slaggy track, but a dozen were faster. In the half mile I came third in my heat with a standard, catching up 5 places in the last 220.

The Wind competitions are on Tuesday. I think the standard will be higher than last year. And the French recitation prize, for which the subjects are La Fontaine's Le Chene et le Roseau, which is fairly long, and a sonnet.

Off with Ruth today and Jimmy[393] will be there, which is nice.; and the Kingfisher will be topping everything in the final push – and then packing.

Oh yes, a funny coincidence. The scene: a smoky bar in a restaurant in Bonn. The chief of Canadian Aluminium in Europe meets a compatriot. In the course of the conversation, 'I've got a boy at Sedbergh.' 'Oh yes, I hear that a boy there, James BL has got a job fixed up on the Dew Line' A small world for the famous. Who on earth it was I don't know[394]. Anyway as far as I know I haven't got a job fixed up there. Odd

S   19 July 59

Jolly good about the tennis tournament and very amusing about the private tennis competition.

I was in the final 6 last week against the masters, who we beat easily. I hope we will play some tennis in Spain and the Pyrenees. Also can you swim in Pyrenees streams and are there trout? I hope we can find a little hotel with a tennis court and trout stream? How long do we stay in Saint Jean for?

We have finished the exams. I won't bore you with an account of them but bring you the papers.

Now we are doing nothing but sports training and tennis nearly every afternoon. I got a standard in the half, coming 3rd in my heat; and on Wednesday will try to get a Mile standard. I have entered this one for I know I can't get a quarter standard which is very fast. I missed a weight standard by 4, then 5 inches then a no-throw. Then there is the discus on Friday which I have been throwing well and have got a few over the qualifying distance for the final last week in practice – but not far over and I

---

[393] Ruth's husband Major Jimmy Rose
[394] The Head of ALCAN in Europe was Bobby Hamer's father; but the name of his (apparently Canadian) interlocuteur was unknown.

don't suppose I will throw well on the day. Since yesterday I haven't even opened a work book of any kind – it is glorious.

Ruth took us out today as her car broke down last week, which should be fun, especially as Jimmy is here.

Later: We had a great time and a super lunch of roast duck and had target shooting competitions in the afternoon. The local doctor was there who is nice and his wife is rather queer but nice.

I did the Mile in 5 mins 12, which gets me a standard, and came 3rd in my heat but sadly only 2 get into the final.

Glad you like my parody of Henry.

Will I be meeting Daddy in London? On the 5th I believe you said something about going to the RAC club lunch time. If he is not there, I will go to Lyons.

We leave at 6 in the morning on Tuesday. Tonight there is a film of the Bolshoi Ballet.

I hope you go to the White City, it sounds enormous fun. [Tattoo perhaps?]

Address at camp:
Beckingham Camp
Beckingham
Lincs

J   26 July 1959 [Sunday]

... Glad the filter[395] is what you want and I do hope it fits. I'm sure it can be easily changed if not, actually we got it through the proper Agfa people so it should be ok.

As for Bemersyde, I think I'll probably come down on Thursday if that's ok. This has been a splendid week in all ways.

Sports have taken place and although I didn't really get anywhere they were tremendous fun. In the weight I mucked it up – which I could have won without thinking. I was leading at the end of the second round, then in the third round I gave a bung that went straight level and did not rise an inch – I almost threw it downwards instead of upwards at 45-50 degrees. What was maddening was that I gave it a tremendous shove and even at a 5 degree angle it went 40ft. Two people pipped it and I came third.

In the discus I also mucked it up and with a series of bad throws failed to qualify for the final, with 85 ft. Afterwards, doffed in scarves, long trousers etc I took the perishing thing and threw it three times, never less than 93 or 94 feet.

---

[395] A joint present from us both for my mother on her birthday, 11th July. I recall that the holder was black, of Bakelite material, and used with filter cartridges.

To my surprise I got to the semi final of the 100 and the Quarter in 57.6 my best time; and I longjumped 18ft, the standard being 16'9" So in all I got 12 standard points which was satisfactory.

Thinking of sports I can't remember if I told you about my breaststroke race. In the end I actually managed to come second, just behind the school No 1 and beating 2 and 3 in 0.9 of a second under the record. The winner was 0.4 under the record.[396] In total in the sports the House came 3rd which was a good effort I think....

Work has virtually finished now for the term. The HM was wondering whether it would be worthwhile, if only for practice, having a go at the Hasting Scholarship in French at Oxford [Queen's]. Jack Hammer is indif and says Cambridge is the real thing. I've yet got to ask Bertie Mills. I'll be clearer about things by the time I come back.

I'm afraid I was only 2nd in the Woodwind competition. At least I beat all the junior types who in the strings are winning competitions. I should be able to tell you later where I came in the Varin French medal.

Last night we had an orgy and dined in Mr Durran's rooms (he was away in Cambridge); - but not your baked bean eggs and bacon type orgy. We had asparagus soup followed by crab shrimps, prawns and oysters for hors d'oeuvre, then salmon and salad for fish, 2 chickens cold, potato salad and a huge fruit salad of raspberries, strawberries, cherries and cream, cheese and coffee. All for 6/- each, washed down with cider cup. It was a tremendous evening with toasts, speeches, gaiety and song. Three hours of it. And a lot we got free from the Matron and Moffat's mother.[397]

Packing in full swing; trunks got down this morning so I'd better get on with it. I've got the Kingfisher to do, and my study to tidy and papers to sort out – reams of them for next term's work.

S will get a study hooray at last! – and the last day of five years dawns with a huge thunderstorm and amazing heavy rain.

PS Won the Varin Medal[398] – which makes up a bit for the Langwill Woodwind.

S   3 August 1959, Beckingham Camp (in pencil)

Thank you for your letter. Sorry I have not written. We have a very full day, but after yesterday's rest I am feeling fine.

---

[396] The winner was fellow clarinettist, A.M. Jackson (Winder House).

[397] A rare, and for us rather sophisticated, end of term celebratory-cum-leavers' dinner.

[398] For French recitation; the competition took place, I recall, on a very hot summer's afternoon, reciting two poems in front of two or three masters in the MLVI classroom.

Yesterday we went into Lincoln city which is a nice town. We went to a restaurant, saw a film and did a little roller skating, which is quite easy after so much skating practice.

At camp we have a film every night. The first was a western and very good, the last one was one of the worst I have ever seen, with Marlon Brando as a GI.

Today we had 3 inspections and a march past.

We get up at 6.45 each day, and we go out, 2 platoons, and each has to have a base unknown to the other platoon and then sends out patrols. I am a patrol leader. These patrols have to find the enemy and, without fighting anyone, then return. After only 1 hours rest and a drink platoons go forward again, this time to attack each other, and it goes on till the end of the day. Great fun.

Tell Dad I will meet him at 1.15. Although all my clothes are dreadful from having been wrapped up in my kit bag I will not turn up in anything too awful.

See you Wed, hooray!

Chapter 6: September 1959 to July 1960

J   22 September 59 [Tuesday]

... I can't thank you enough for all the time you have given us and all the many many things have given for us and done for us which made the holidays so superb. It's funny to think that my last school hols are gone by now but I look back now not only on ten years of wonderful school days but ten years of even more wonderful school holidays.

Thank you for taking us both to Gigi. I'm so sorry Dad couldn't come and see it too – with Maurice Chevalier and Leslie Carroll it would be impossible not to like it because they're so very very charming.

But best of all in the holidays was the trip to the Pyrenees..., Well, now sunny France is far away. Going through Wigan and Warrington yesterday I've never seen anything more North English, superb in its way; everything grey, cold and dank with a kind of misty fog. I can see well how people can long for it, for there's something most exciting about it.

Here everything has gone off with a tremendous bang.

I did get my two S levels but haven't seen my marks for it yet. I'll get the detail in due course. My French language was apparently ok but French literature wasn't so good. Nobody is wasting time here – it's straight into German and French preps – several of each already lined up.

We pushed off on a training run yesterday doing strenuous PT, first on top of Winder then on Windy Gap and then a third go on Higher Winder and then loosening up on the rugger pitch when we got down. I won't say I'm not tired though.

I have no new appointments but am going to be senior cadet – and am Orderly Officer the first parade of term so I'd better get polishing the old brasses[399].

Have moved into my study with a new and rather simpler line in decoration. The troops believe in stuffing the studies full and cramming every spare inch of wallpaper etc. I have just a couple of pictures, and no overhead light, just two low lamps which are on one switch. A bit of orl-right!

The old hundred year old trunk is not much the worse for wear for its journey but I haven't quite decided whether it'll be takeable home.

---

[399] CCF became more enjoyable in the last year. I had always enjoyed the cowboys and Indians aspect of field days, crawling through the bracken to hunt down the enemy, or carrying bren guns and waving rattles to represent their noise; and enjoyed the sniping in the range. I did not mind the routines, and the week's camp on Loch Earn was fun - where I joined the engineers, building floating pontoons and mucking about in the water every day. I finished up as Senior Cadet for my last term and enjoyed the job – apart from panics over getting the General Inspection parade right.

Thinking of sending things, yes please there's the butter and my watch I forgot.

Off into the new term

S   c. 22 September 59

Hope you got my first half letter I posted just to let you know I am still in one piece. The trouble is I cannot remember what I told you so I will probably tell you many things again.

I have just seen the O level marks; the pass mark was not given but I did average in French, badly in Physics, fairly badly in English language, well in English lit, well in chemistry, awfully in Latin and top of our form in Maths with 72 & 80 out of 100 (2 papers). I still have my copy of the French trans which is exactly the same as the one I sent in but more untidy and not looked over for careless mistakes (I don't suppose I corrected them all). I hope you will like to see it.

Photos have not come out yet from A & N stores[400], but I expect they will come soon

We had our first pottery lesson but did nothing as we have just been shown the theory of things and Mr Madge my biology master (and Hart House housemaster) gave us an exhibition on the mechanical wheel. He is very good and it really is absolutely fascinating watching a vase taking shape from a lump of clay. Next week I will do some modelling from clay and if it is any good I will get it fired in the furness [sic] then coloured and glazed. The week after I will have a try on the wheel.

With biology I presume I am staying till the summer, is this correct[?] If so I take AO level in biology. (There is no O level but it is always taken after 1 year here and is between O and A level, Also I can take additional Maths O level and Government O level if I want.

Yesterday I played house rugger. I played wing forward opposite Jamie. Also I played a good game of squash against Lionel. Have you heard anything from his parents about Switzerland?

Hope you are quite all right now, Mum, thank you for your letter.

Thank you again for a lovely hols

This term we have to read 1 Russian and 1 American 19th century serious novel

S   no date –c. 27 September 59

Here I am sitting in a study[401]. It is going to be very nice I think but has not yet got over our moving in. I have an excellent photo 10 x 12 of Dear Man about 35 years old, also your picture of the man with the glove. Then

---

[400] Army and Navy Stores, Victoria
[401] After 3 years and a term to wait

we have one lovely oil print of a Dutch fishing village which we framed with another of the old frames in the cellar and glass in the other which no one else has found. I am about to frame a print of the Haywain by Constable. We also have the bull fight poster and two posters of winter sports. The carpet is fine.

Thank you for the wonderful hols, they were really terrific fun, especially France and Spain.

The O level results were good this term, 1 of my friends got 7 and one 6 like me and Robertson. My study mate got 4 which was bad luck and the worst was 2. I am taking government as one of my ops[402] and at the end of the year one can take an O level in British government & constitution which I can take if I want. The biology master is very good I think, but we have only had one lesson.

I hope you are going to send a photo of yourself as I have one of Sally and one of Dad but none of you. Also you said if you really hate that cigarette box you can send it to me as a pencil box as it would make a rather super one.

I am in Lower Sixth Modern and have Mr Braham as form master and Mr Mawby for Chemistry; we do Biology and Chemistry nearly all the time with some Physics, with a few periods of Current affairs, English and options.

Yesterday I had my film back and I am sending you the best photos. 2 bullfight ones were underexposed, the mountain scenes were rather misty but I will send the best six.

J   28 September 59 [Monday]

...Thanks very much for the letter and parcel. I was wondering what had happened to the second garter with a flash. The watch is going beautifully and it a great help to have one – although not being used to it I went through a very active knocking about rugger practice with it on!

How lovely that you'll be coming up at the end of October. That's absolutely wizard. I'm looking forward to it already immensely. I think, if that's all right by you, that Sunday would be the better day because we have longer to see you and there could easily be an away match for 1sts or 2nd whichever I am on. However I will check this in a PS.

I'm glad the dinner party was a success. This is splendid about Mr Wisner's offer[403]. Yes I'd very much like him to try it if it would be possible – a chance to be snapped up and not to be missed. I will delay sending off a batch of letters to sundry shipping firms that I've just written. It would be

---

[402] Options, i.e. optional subjects
[403] Frank Wisner, an American colleague of my father's from Washington days and good family friend who offered to try to find a contact in the shipping world who might be able to arrange for me to work a passage to the Eastern Seaboard.

very nice if he could do anything or even suggest anything through Niarchos. The Yank in the house, who is awfully nice, has met Mr Wisner's son. I don't know how but it's rather an odd coincidence. His name is Hillyer D Young, if the name means anything to you and he wants to go into the Central Intelligence or whatever it is.

Everything in full swing here... wonderful September days with pitches perfect, blue skies mists and everything. In rugger only practice and trials so far and the back row of the scrum is very much undecided. There is last year's lock and then five others contesting for the wing forwards. Hoards of training and having passed through the blisters stage we are getting a bit fitter[404]. Wing forward is pretty killing in these fast games on dry pitches but it's all huge fun and there are all the nicest people on Bigside.

That's taken up most of my exercise but I've had a little bit of squash bets with Sandy and Lionel Melville – playing for a 6d bar of chocolate. Junior fives to coach and they're going to be good. I made a mark in the shooting range, getting the two best groups in the Empire Test (with a .22) – which was rather surprising but gives a bit of backing to the Senior Cadet!

As Senior Cadet, am taking the Corps parade and doing the guard of honour for some visiting General. All good fun with a swagger stick but taking him around I have to answer his probing questions about things about which I know no more than him. So far my duties involve little except a whole lot of administration and organisation in the way of sending, collecting things and seeing people and so on – more and more chances per week to forget something!

Things in full flow and there'll be more when Jack Hammer gets back from Moscow.

Here is an important question re Hastings scholarships to Queen's Oxford. Mr Gairdner thinks that as it will affect my term's work only a little that it's worth taking it, mainly because it is based on French and would be valuable practice. It takes place in November three weeks before the Cambridge ones. I could also have an interview with Worcester Coll, the HM thinks. What do you think? The HM is also waiting for a letter from the Master of St John's and also a one from the man at Clare – both of which are being pursued. It remains for me to work, work, work!

S   No date [c. 28 September 59]

---

[404] I recall training runs up Winder for the whole of Bigside early in the winter term. I was fast going up, but very slow coming down. Then there were many 25-yard short sprints sessions for fitness as well as practising on the fields and using a scrum machine.

Thank you for the parcel of left behinds and the picture of you and Sally. It is a very nice one. The photos from Army and Navy haven't come yet but probably they will tomorrow.

I am going to take one film here and then send the camera away which Mr Lowis[405] says will take about three weeks but I think it would be nice to take some photos of here and friends in the next 2 months.

Thank you for your letter which came this morning. Sorry you are ill, how awful for you but what a good thing Dear has come down which was jolly 'd' of here. Hilda was asking yesterday where Dear was. She said she was always 'up yonder' (Bemersyde) or 'down there', pointing to the south. She said she was hoping for a letter from her but she knew that Dear would write in her own good time. I talked for hours with her. It is very nice and rather hard to get away. I told her about Rab's appointment; she was very pleased and said she'd tell Sid but no one else. She obviously loves to hear of the family.

It is wonderful if you can come up here but I doubt if Dr Harley will let you drive all that way with Sally if you are in a convalescing state; it is a wonderful ride however and I hope you can make it. When does Dad go to Africa?

I agree that it is a bit of a waste of time doing Physics but if I was in General Sixth I would do only Bio and no chemistry, but in the Lower Sixth modern we have the choice of Physics, Chem or Bio or Physics, Chem and Maths.

I am glad that Dad is writing to Mr Braithwaite, I would like to more about the various colleges.

A good friend in another house lives 4 miles away from Hugo and is a good friend of his and is trying to persuade Hugo to go to Cirencester as Hugo does not know what to do. Julian his brother, the Oxford cox, has been thrown out which is bad luck; I am very surprised they throw out their winning teams. I am going to get in touch with Hugo who incidentally is leaving in Summer Term 60 having taken his O levels last term. I would love to see him again.

Have you heard anything from the Melvilles?

Have just had a long talk with two chaps who leave the term before me about Agricultural colleges.... what courses they offer, what you can attend, sports played, etc....

The biology we are doing is very interesting. We are starting on small insects and animals, which I thought sounded rather dull but is fascinating. We do a lot of microscope work and I hope I will be able to do some in the Christmas hols if there is any time and certainly in the Easter hols. If anyone wants a little item to put on my greedy list my glass [slides] for putting things on under are all broken

---

[405] The chemist in the town, and father of Simon Lowis in School House

I agree that it seems ages since we saw Gigi, but it is wonderful that you are coming up. I have just finished the apples and pairs [*sic*]; they were lovely. There is a school squash comp this term which I hope to go in for.

J   October 4th 59 [Sunday]

Thankyou for the letter – and the butter which arrived in something near liquid form but has regained strength in the grub locker. It's awfully good butter - very creamy too and nicer than ordinary New Zealand. I'm sorry to hear that you've been ill and in bed again – it's very bad luck, especially with that nasty bug. Even in its mild form I know it.

Have booked rooms at the Bull with the man who does everything from polishing the door knobs and I'll go in again and check that he really has written it down.

Yes, I'll carry on writing to shipping firms, and then to some of the Canadian companies

Here we've been scorched to our deaths – am longing for rain. Midges, gnats, sweltering heat and trying to pretend its winter for rugger. Rugger coming to a close soon. Wing forward position still undecided on the 1sts – between Hodgson and myself playing in every game possible. The captain says he's going to give us both a game on the team and see how it goes before the School matches start. I think we must be fitter than most others on the field. Hodgson played on the 1st team against the Assassins a week ago and I played opposite him for the Assassins. Then we both played against the 2nds. Then on Saturday I captained the second XV and we won against Lytham School 23-6. It was good fun but in tremendous heat and on a pitch which was dry as a bone.

Have played a bit of squash but I have blisters - in fact everyone has blisters from the hard ground at rugger. Squash has not been sparkling and I'm going to try to get a few lessons from our new PT man who is also the cricket coach (reckoned by MCC to be the second best school cricket coach in the country) [?J. Coates, I think]. With that venerable institution Ernie (Dear will remember him) now gone, he is producing a revolution, a bloodless one, in the PT world. We do circuit training and physical games, all very modern and up to date. They are meant to be an 'ancillary to rugger' and I think they are very effective.

Everything is pushing along on the work front, but in this heat – after games – no easy job. In German it is Emilia Galon which is quite humorous; Keller, of which the humour has so far eluded me and an essay on Stierkampf. In French, Victor Hugo's poetry – which I did for the Wakefield.

The HM has sent for the entrance forms for the Hastings as a prelim manoeuvre and has now lined up exams for the next century for me. In December it's the St John's group and my order of preferences for colleges is St John's (Lupton Hebblethwaite) Christs (Otway) and Emma – all colleges with strong Sedbergh connections the HM says. He says Clare is starting to swing away from public schools and not worth pursuing as well as the other three. If all goes wrong there are entrances and schools in March and if those collapse he will trying bullying and pulling strings everywhere..

Music continues playing with one of the music piano staff duets, and orchestra is good fun except that I've got a stinking solo in Borodin Prince Igor dances.

Last night we had a mock election – amusing and instructive, some humorous barracking and some good character parts, Heber Percy as an Empire Loyalist very properly, Unionists, communists, the lot....

S has a very nasty boil on his forehead and is rather under the weather from it – he's getting constant injections. Otherwise everything is splendid and this afternoon I'm going out for a bike ride on Dear's old bike!

S   n.d. [4 October 59]

Hope you are all going over to the Rugby Match[406]; it is a pity it was not held last year when we had such a good team. Anyhow, we should win.

Are you taking Hugo out?[407]

What time will you arrive? Will it be on Saturday?

I hope you are better and having a nice rest when you do get up. I have a large boil on my forehead and spot on my chin both ousing /sic/ in puss and so I have to have penicillin injections twice daily and am off exercise. I am on light ex unchanged this is the first day off any ex since I came here, which is 3 years 1 term and a bit, a pity to spoil the record but probably a good thing to have penicillin.

Thank you for your letters and the butter which came yesterday; also thank you for the photos. I will enclose 2 negs of Sally and Jamie so you can get them printed how you want. It has been wonderful fun taking photos and I am very lucky my first film has come out so well, as you say I am longing to take more photos.

Today is a glorious day and all of us except Lionel and I are going to Hells Gill behind Baugh Fell with Mr Durran. Lionel has a headache and a very hoarse and sore throat because of shouting so loud at the mock election last night. This was in Room 15. It was redone about a year ago and is made into a permanent lecture hall - exam room etc. It seats only about 300 but it is a very comfy and lovely room. There were four speakers, Conserv, Labour, Lib and Communist, and everyone started shouting 'don't evade the question' but he said it was like Suez and Cyprus.

[In pencil]. My boil has got a lot worse and I am in the school san having injections every 3 hours (4 times a day). But it is not really that bad and I am getting better.

---

[406] The first fixture against the Rugby School XV for many years if not ever
[407] Sandy's friend from the Dragons Hugo Rowbotham was at Rugby School.

They all spoke in turn and then we asked questions to them all. They were very good and all of them knew their stuff except the Comm. who could not answer Hungary properly. [Long complicated joke story retold...]

I agree that there is plenty of time to get [identify] an agricultural college but one hadsto put down for places before one goes and we don't want to make a mistake.

I hear from Lionel that his Pa and Ma are in Switzerland and will look for a place for a winter hol which is cheap.

Provided I am fully recovered by then, see you on the 31ª.

J   11ᵗʰ October 1959 [Sunday]

... [A para mostly about my poor writing, and difficulty reading back my own lesson notes....]

Well, the exams I take are 10 November in Oxford and 7 December in Cambridge; so there it all is, looming up ahead. IMPORTANT Please can you send to me (or the HM) my birth certificate or copy thereof. I've just filled in my entry form for the Hastings Schol [scholarship] exam and the HM would like to get them off as soon as possible. As for Oxford I will write to Granny and Grandfather and ask if I can stay with them for those three days.

I'm glad the x-ray has shown everything to be ok and that you are all right for coming up here at the end of the month. Isn't there such a thing as a literary medical magazine in which to write your Kafkaesque article[408]. Thinking of dreamlike worlds I wonder if Adams[409] ever got 'Experiment with Time which has been on order for 6 weeks now. They said they'd keep it for me.

I was lucky enough to play on the 1ª XV against the West of Scotland Colts whom we beat by 10-0. We played on Riverside which has more grass so the ground was nice. I was playing blind side wing forward, a position I haven't had before. The sun made it very hot and it was also very low making it difficult to see the ball sometimes as fifth man in the line out. It was only a training match for the first really, and I doubt I'll stay on the team.

Still playing quite a lot of rugger despite the drought. They are watering Riverside pitches with fire hoses and pump it up from the river. As the HM says, the surest way to bring on rain.

Getting fit slowly. Played a bit of squash too but one doesn't feel up to much after Bertie Mills training sessions.

In the Corps I'm now acting RSM with an RSM's baldrick and hat. General Dunbar appears on Wednesday. The guard who are to do it are

---

[408] This was about the hallucinatory side-effects of a drug my mother was taking as part of treatment for depression.

[409] Stationers and booksellers in Rye

most of them the same people who were there for Air Vice Marshal CAS[410] and they are rather hot stuff with their drill.

In the house a few of us are trying to persuade the HM to allow us to play some jazz. His principle is that he allows it in houses but not amongst people from various houses. I think he is frightened of jazz groups becoming a poor gathering of idlers who want an excuse to get rowdy. If that is so, it seems to me that he has failed in his teaching us what is worthwhile. But it remains to be seen.

Time whistles on pretty fast. More and more tutorials and always expected to have more and more done in our spare time. The tutorials are much needed. So what with one thing and another everything is pretty busy...

S   October 12th 59

Thank you for your letter. I do not think I would like to read a book about penicillin at the moment as I felt like a pin cushion a few days ago but I am out of the san now and better. Is Dear still with you and when does she come up?

Unfortunately it is raining now so the drou[gh]t has finished. Casterton went home 1 day ago because of no water and we were all hoping to break up though it seemed unlikely; we thought we would spend 5/- on travel and spend 3 days in the Lakes – actually we would never break up for lack of water.

The Melvilles are in Switzerland, and are being v helpful indeed. They will save us quite a bit of money as they can lend both ski trousers and skis and ski socks, balaclava, etc.. When they get back to London Mrs Melville will be writing to you.

I have had the photo of the street and church in [illeg.][411] done again. I think it is quite good. I took two photos of Jamie playing on the 1st. I hope they come out. I hope you will bring the photos up with the viewer when you come. Talking of coming up I don't see why we <u>should</u> take the yank out, but as he is such a good chap it would be nice but he is a year behind J and a year in front of me, but no matter, I think it would be nice to take Lionel out also; it would be a nice gesture to his parents as they are being so good about Switzerland

If you see either a map of London restaurants or a map of Chelsea or something similar could you send it as there is now after a bit of reorganising a piece of dirty wall 2' x 1 ½ ' and so far I have nothing really nice to cover it.

Last night there was a lecture by Mr Evetts FRS It was really an account of his adventures while cotton growing in Zulu land in the 20s. He was very

---

[410] Chief of Air Staff
[411] Gabas, or a nearby town, where we stayed on holiday in the western Pyrenees

269

good and exciting but terribly funny, a real true Englishman who had just fought in the first world war and had had many good adventures. He told them splendidly.

The Sunday that you come up, the service is in the parish church which makes it a lot longer which is a pity.

On Friday there was an extra half and we went up the Lune. We found a field miles from anywhere with 3 bullocks in and tried to practice bullfighting, but they did not come within 5 yards so it was not much good.

I have played basketball in the gym four times. It is just starting as a game for amusement; it is quite good fun; we play 4 a side and have made nets; proper ones are coming.

We must hurry up with our driving in the hols as we are slow compared with others. Two people of my age and term have past their test and have a licence. Lionel takes his next hols. All of those people drove around on minor roads then bigger ones and have had a few lessons and passed first time. We must get L plates.

Another lovely day today and we are playing rugger every day now. I am starting on my English; it is the Life of Dorian Gray by Oscar Wilde. Another thing we have to do for English is give a 40 minute talk. Mine might be this term or next, and I can't make up my mind what to talk on.

See you in 2 weeks. Sally is coming I presume but not Taptoe

S   No date – [Monday 19 October 59]

Thank you for the letter and for the photo. I think it has been done terribly well. I am very pleased with it. Thank you for getting it done.

I hope you are quite all right now. The house must seem very empty without Dad or Dear. Has Taptoe gone yet for his months kennels? I hope they manage to make him obedient; they will have a very hard job; at the end he will probably obey them a bit but not us. However it is worth a try.

Have you got or has Dad sent for the Essex college prospectus; I should love to see it; have been getting the Cirencester one to look at and compare. It is coming from one of the 3 chaps here going to Cirencester.

Dear has just come and we saw her for a couple of minutes but she was in a hurry to get up north.

We were going to climb Helvellyn today but Mr Durran has too much work, He says he will take us to Helvellyn or the Langdale Pikes next week which is v. nice of him.

On Wednesday a general came and we did a battle which was great fun. It was done in a wood and we had to capture an enemy tank. There were six men guarding it. We were allowed to capture it by any means. We were allowed to fight the enemy hand to hand and to take their ammunition etc. Another chap and I were pulling away the tank (a wooden one) and when we pulled it set off a booby trap explosion under our feet, which was quite a shock. The whole thing was very realistic I thought. Great fun.

You know you asked for a greedy list. The thing I would really like would be that Peter Sellers record, the long playing one, when he takes off many people. It is an absolute scream. It is called The Best of Sellers'.

What a jolly good idea about asking Hugo out. He would love to go out to tea with you.

Today is the match against Dorward's XV and it is pouring with rain but the pitches are still very hard. However the match today will probably get us off a house run.

I have to send this off now as I have to do some forms which need filling in quam cellerime (how many 'l's in that?); and I have to finish my Physics prep which I will do first. This morning I burnt my finger on some nitric acid but not badly thank goodness.

I was working out a route for top of Ben Nevis, Scafell, Snowdon so we thought of Ruth driving and I am sure we could do it in under 20 hours; and if you find anyone willing to take us I'm sure it would be terrific fun. The bet is to be on top of all three by foot and car only.

Sorry my letter writing is so feeble. Will write a long one next week.

J   October 22nd 1959
More chat about pens and handwriting...

Thank you very much for your last letters. It always seems two because there is Sandy's as well. It is very pleasing that all your photographing is going so well. It seems the best idea that you and S should have a dark room and do your own developing and printing. I think the one of Sandy's of you with the old Pic du Midi d'Ossau as background is awfully effective[412].

I've done quite a lot since I last wrote. I'm afraid I don't think I am going to get on the 1st XV as the team seems fairly settled now, which is about time as the Rugby match is a week from today. However I get a full complement of rugger and play all games available. I very nearly played for the A.F. Dorward's XV amongst the 4 or 5 internationals but the man I was going to substitute turned up after all. Last week I was 16th man for the firsts and did touch flagging. You get the best view of the game but the trouble is that now and then you forget you are touch flagging, and at one try I was nearly fifty yards away when the man who scored knocked down the corner post. Luckily I was looking very closely and thought he went into touch first. Luckily, so did he.

Had a good match on the 2nds on Saturday against Barnard Castle School. Most enjoyable, Did a lot of tackling and scored one try but nearly gave the match away by a bad penalty kick from which the other side nearly scored. It was a very gay trip altogether and the people were awfully nice;

---

[412] See Visual Essay

and amongst other things we watched a rugger international on television in the afternoon.

School squash competition coming up again, and there is stiff competition, With one friend, who claims he is the West Nigerian Junior Champ – but has actually never been south of London, we are playing for a penny a point over three games – a chance to win 1/6d.

Thankyou for sending the entrance forms. These exams seem to be creeping up terribly fast. Under three weeks till the one in Oxford. There remains a huge amount for me to do because we are getting all the ordinary work as well as revision to do – essays, appreciations, the lot. And although I went quite a long way with my Latin some extra Latin is going to be needed and by no means easy.

Dear came up through Sedbergh. I missed her through a tutorial which was a pity but Sandy saw her. Apart from playing the clarinet with Mr Brooker, the music master who plays the piano, my time for general things has been cut down.

J   Sunday 25ᵗʰ October 1959

... As for Tuesday[413] am going to be 16ᵗʰ man and touch judge and won't be playing unless someone falls ill between now and then – so I will be running up and down the pitch waving the flag , and there may not be very much time afterwards to see you– so it might not be very interesting for you to come up – and anyway we'll be seeing you the following weekend at Sedbergh. So, it will be lovely if you will be there, but not tragic if you aren't. If plans change in any way (e.g. I don't come at all after all, or I am playing in the actual team) I will send you a telegram at Granny's on Monday or even Tuesday. Maybe someone will break a leg climbing out of a train or something..

Yesterday we went to Blackpool – not to see the lights but to play a 2ⁿᵈ XV match v. Arnold School, one of those which is called a Public Secondary School – a mixture of a second class public school and a local secondary school, half boarders, half day-boys.

We arrived in the morning and Sid Braithwaite drove us along the Golden Mile and generally showed us the sights of Blackpool (where he was stationed aged 17 in the 1ˢᵗ World War!). It was raining and the sea was rather wild and stormy and very fine in fact and the place was almost deserted. It is about the end of the season but the rain has hurried it on.

As for the actual match we won very luckily 8-3 in the very last minute, they having had a penalty goal three minutes before that when scores were level – right under the posts which was somehow miraculously missed. This cheered us up and we got the vital try. We had a most

---

[413] The date of the 1ˢᵗ XV Away rugger fixture at Rugby – my father as an Old Rugbeian, former captain of their 1ˢᵗ XV, and a former master there, was especially interested.

enjoyable trip altogether with rowdy singing on the bus, fish and chips in Lancaster and so on. The only bad thing was that after an early lunch we had a whole hour and a half being shown round their school without ever being able to have a quiet sit down. Our dogs were worn out before we stood on the field.

Lots of French work at the moment. I'm getting a great interest and enjoyment in Balzac and a fairish dislike of German essays – but otherwise work

S   Monday 26 October 59

[More ideas for tackling the Scafell, Snowdon, Ben Nevis circuit challenge by car and on foot ....Assume Ruth drives at an average of 42 mph... maybe 18 ½ hours in all... etc etc.]

Thinking of running there were house runs on Friday; the chap who came equal with me in the ten came 1st. I was ½ minute behind at 3rd in 25 ½ minutes which is better than my last year's Ten training run.

I have heard from the Melvilles. I expect you have. [More plans and thoughts...St Anton ideas...]

Did you say something about getting someone to look at my vertebra in London; when if so will this be?

If you have time can you please buy 5/- of bangers (fireworks) this is one shilling from each of us which I will give you when you come up. It does not matter but it would be kinder for Jamie if he did not know as 3/4 will be for the others here. We will keep them for the very end of term and would be appreciated by all if you could get them! We will let them off on the last night or morning to save questions of any prefects. Our inspiration was the learning of the theory of booby traps in the corps.

I hear form Jamie that he will be with you tomorrow in Rugby as a 16th man, which is jolly good.

Another thing for the greedy list is a five year diary like the one I gave Jamie. He has kept every single day and will soon be starting on the third layer. So I think I could keep one up. Incidentally I have a long account of our wonderful holiday in France which I wrote at the beginning of term.

Will finish this in Long Break after Physics prep on Monday.

Have just finished the practical which was the preparation of Sulphuric Aluminium Phosphate; it is very complicated and we leave the crystals to evaporate till next week.

Matthew, Head of House, tell me that if I want to come in the first 10 in the ten I have to start thinking about it before December and definitely go back reasonably fit next term - as apparently if you can get your average fitness to x you peak at x + y; therefore the higher x is, the higher y is. Anyway I will have to do a little training after skiing.

Otherwise it is the usual round... Not much else to add...

S   2ⁿᵈ Nov

Thank you very much for a wonderful weekend. I hope you enjoyed it and it was lovely seeing you and Sally. Hope you had a good journey and your tyre is ok.

I will talk to the HM about a specialist in London when you have fixed a date and will send for some prospectuses.

It is raining today and it is 3-1 on House runs.

J   Wednesday 4 Nov 59

Dear Mummy,

Thankyou very much indeed for a wonderful weekend. It really was huge fun and I think the way we spent it without zooming around was just the thing. Altogether it was perfect and peaceful, I hope that you and Sally are settled and can relax after all your travelling up north. I must say I think that Sally, all things considered, was on jolly good form after having been on the move from home such a time.

A full week and good old Sedbergh weather since you left, drifting rains and mist or else cold and very clear air. The heating is now on around the school and we have a fire in the common room, so living quarters are on the whole not so cold.

On Monday we had house runs in the pouring rain.[414] Melville had [had], and presumably enjoyed by George, an argument with Cass Matthew about sprinting up the hill at the end. He refused to take part in a final sprint race with the others and got beaten for same. So his rebel spirit is flying somewhat high at the moment

On Thursday we had Field Day and the exercise and battle field were original in choice this time. Instead of Holme Fell or Frostrow we fought up over Winder, Crook, Higher Winder and Calf. My platoon consisted of boys in their second term of Corps who were new to Field Day. This is a great asset in one way in that they are quicker and keener than the old salts. We had a splendid three-pronged attack on an arms dump on the top of Crook – and took a lot of prisoners (a difficult thing to do in a mock battle) and exterminated the rest of a platoon. This was considered easily the best organised and executed attack of the day by higher authority which was a bit of a boost for the Senior Cadet - me. We were also the only platoon capable of going into action when we came into attack an arms dump on Windy Gap. At all but 2,000 feet it sure was windy. The damp grass was freezing with the wind blowing like long streams of icicles. We had to do all the re-grouping and cleaning of rifles etc, up there too. It was all good fun

---

[414] Colin led the front of the senior pack while I took the rear. I can see him now, bouncing ahead into the mist and rain, and then coming back to see how we slackers were getting on in the rear, and then disappearing once more into the gloaming to his post at the front.

and pretty exhausting, and I haven't been up on there on those heights yet this term, let alone with Corps boots and rifle and haversack etc.

This afternoon we played 2nds v the 3rds and beat them pretty thoroughly. The ground was wet and cold and it took some time before the game got hot. Such a day always brings a rather half-hearted start and it's all rather cold-blooded.

The main thing of course is work, coming into the peak period now. The trouble is I seem to have got a rather heavy sinus with a cold, a perpetual snuffle at the back of the nose and a rather heavy eye. It doesn't help getting on with the work. In French I'm doing modern and late 19th century painters as a talking subject for interview/ oral – and might be quite a good bet for a general paper too. There's something rather enjoyable about preparing a subject like that for an exam and getting it all down in black and white, sections and main points etc..

I don't think the HM has come up with any new things since you spoke at the weekend. He is still going to have a word with Blair Cunningham, an Hon Fellow of St Catherine's – and no doubt I'll have to go and sip tea with Blair-C.

All the rest you know. I suspect there's a library book or two which we shoved in the boot of the car. I did not check carefully enough but I can't see anything missing yet. If I need one, here I'll borrow a book from someone else – and Sandy could always take it back if it turns out that I did leave one in the car.

Thankyou very much again for the so short but so enjoyable weekend. It was wonderful to see you and Sally. Please give my love to Dear too.

S   No date,   [c. 4 November 59]
Letter to JMBL at Government House Lagos

Hope you are having an enjoyable trip.

Mummy was up here on Sunday with Sally. She arrived rather worn out after the journey when she left the ring you gave her in a pub and thought she had lost it; however she has it now; then she had a puncture and found that the spare tyre had a puncture too; so it was a long journey.

Sally was in terrific form on Saturday.

Winki Young the tame yank came out with us to breakfast. He is a splendid chap and told us why he came to Sedbergh. He wanted a typical British public school, decided Eton was not typical and he wanted nicer country, so it was Sedbergh, Glenalmond and Loretto and he was told they were all equal but Sedbergh was the most typically British and the toughest, so he came here.

We went to Kirby Lonsdale for a delicious lunch and then a walk on Barbon Fell. Jamie drove (very well) and we then locked all doors and windows when we went for our walk. On returning we saw that the key was in the car; all doors were locked and we could not get in. A man came up and got a screw driver and poked it under the rubber of the little front window and pushed across the handle and opened it and then opened the door. So now we can burgle any Morris we want. We had tea in Dent and played dominoes with some very local locals, who were drinking beer at 4 'clock.

Lionel came to dinner in the Bull and we had a very amusing time. It was fairly certain that the Melville parents are going skiing and if we go they have a place in the Tyrol I think and it sounds terrific fun. The Melvilles were arranging it all.

Mr Durran who is unfortunately leaving this term which is a great pity because he is made for Sedbergh, took 6 of us in his car to Hawes Water in the Lakes, a vast lake sunk deep into the hills rather like the lake at Gabas [Pyrenees holiday spot]. It was boiling hot when we arrived. We ate our lunch in the car and then climbed up the surrounding hills to a tarn 200 yds by 200 yds surrounded by vast crags on 3 sides with a perilous looking ridge running round the top in a 'U'. We walked along it having climbed up; actually it was quite safe; then we came down a long scree. There was a glorious view from the top of the lakes and Windermere and the big lake mountains.

I am writing to 3 or 4 Agricultural colleges for prospectuses. Major Pym advised two of them; and I am sure as I can be without a year at David's that I want to go to one. Most of them require 5 O levels and 1 year's work on a farm before. Mum says you are going to see Major Pym sometime. I Hope I can talk to him some time too as there was no opportunity when we were there last hols with Mum and Sally.

Are you coming up here if you have time after Africa I Hope you will be able to make it. Jamie is on the 2nd XV not 1st XV and has a match on the 21st at Lancaster.

Hope you have a good journey back.

S   8th Nov 59 [Sunday]

Dear Mummy,

Thank you for your letter. How ghastly Monday morning must have been when Sally was sick. I Hope she gets better soon; I hope you are having a nice time and rest at Bemersyde. I Hope you got Lionel's letter. I told him not to but he insisted on sending Sally something.

His parents were up this weekend and I went out with them for tea and dinner after a game of rugger, and we played seven a side and the refs watch stopped and we played for an hour and a quarter which is very long indeed.

Talking of rugger I played the best game I have ever played, at Full Back, yesterday; It was terrific fun I am enjoying the rugger more and more now; and wish I was good enough for inter school teams as they must be even more fun.

Carrying on about the Melvilles, there were Mr and Mrs and an Uncle and Aunt (not Dad's friend). Uncle Melville is a Scots Colonel, and knows Uncle Rob well. We had tea in the White Hart and then went in convoy in 2 Vokses [VWs presumably] to Kirby Lonsdale. Incidentally we were having tea in the White Hart when the police came in to tell us to lock up the cars and remove keys and not to accept a lift from anyone as there was a murderer coming from Newcastle to Blackpool through Sedbergh, most exciting.

In Kirby Lonsdale Lionel and Nigel (his younger brother) and I played billiards while the others boozed. We had an excellent dinner in the Royal Hotel. They are all amusing people.

They decided on Austria because it is cheaper. Mrs Melville has booked but is still waiting for a reply for pension etc. in St Anton, 4,500 ft in the Arlberg. The Melvilles say it is better to hire skis over there. Although there is a slight risk with it, it is much cheaper; but they say hire boots over here. They say they hire them at Lilywhites but this is probably unnecessary as there will be plenty of other places; advised are Lilywhites, Moss Bros, Jackson and Weir, Simpsons. My shoe size is 8 ½. All rather expen. The Melvilles say it is not worth hiring them over there and he gets a reduction on the whole ticket thing. I have some photos of St Anton it looks a jolly 'd' place. As to ski trousers and skis, the Melvilles say they cannot supply them but I think I am right in saying that yours were being altered for me. The Melvilles will probably be writing to you soon.

Field Day was on Tuesday. We did an exercise pretending that the Winder Calf Cautley fells were in the sea and the fells an island. It was not very good but fun all the same, as Field Days always are. And for once we had enough blanks so it was quite amusing, and I was a scout which is fun.

We do pottery in the afternoon once a week for 1 ½ hours. We have been making hand made pots so far and start on modelling next week. I have spent two afternoons on the wheel which is quite fascinating.

J left for Oxford yesterday morning with Matthew.

Peter Ketin the concert pianist is coming next week to give a recital; and I think there is a film on Friday. And what a bore because of endless practice a House concert for the 3rd Year running at the end of term. The house will be almost dry of good ideas – but it is always fun in the end.

By the way have you got the £3 from the Melvilles yet so I can put it into the post office (I have seven pounds there already which will make it 10 for the Swiss money. Thinking of money, remember that Dad has got £14 worth of trumpet. [IN agreement with the school and parents, Sandy had by now given up playing an instrument].

Thank you for your last letter received this morning

Today it is snowy here but it had thawed by lunch time; there was corps in the afternoon and our platoon was practising a 'feu de joie' which is when you make a hollow square and then starting at one corner you fire one by one all the way round as fast as possible. It is harder than it seems and makes a terrific noise. It is supposed to be part of the CCF Tatoo for the 100ᵗʰ anniversary of the CCF in Britain.

I fell coming down Winder on Friday and cut my leg and went immediately to Matron as it was deep. But after 3 days it has not started to heel and it looks as though it is going septic. Matron put on some cream last night and it is not worse, so it might be getting better.

Is Dad coming up for the weekend sometime?

J   15 November 1959 [Sunday]

I'm terribly sorry I haven't written for so long. I owe you a huge lot of letters as it were. Well, I've certainly been having a full and enjoyable time since I last wrote.

As for Oxford first.

We went down on Monday morning and got down there by six-ish. On the way we had a two-hour wait at the inevitable Bletchley. It really was at its blotchiest. When we walked around the place it was getting dark and drizzling rain and the atmosphere was dank and cold, I reckon I'm only just getting over my walkabout there now. The train at Bletchley was full of northern school boys presumably come to take the same exams. They all seemed to be working hard at mechanics. The scene in the Bletchley station with all these northerners sipping their Bletchley teas was quite something. There were four of us from Sedbergh, all from different faculties and we went to Queen's College to get to know the general form. Apparently the HM did not know or was not asked if anyone was not staying under the College's wing so it took some time to fix things with the steward who had booked rooms and wasn't very pleased. Apart from that there was a taxi waiting to take me on to Belbroughton Road and although he was getting jolly good money for sitting and waiting he too was far from pleased.

It was lovely to be staying with Granny and Grandfather although I suppose I wasn't there much of the time. Their goodly Mrs Maine or however she spells herself is clearly a tremendous asset. The breakfasts she produced for me were a schoolboy's dream. After porridge and before toast and fruit every morning she dished up two fried eggs, a huge whole round of fried bread, three sausages or three rashers of bacon and fried potatoes. I couldn't complain of starting the day hungry. The routine for the day was that I began breakfast before Granny and Grandfather and left to get a bus at a quarter to nine. I always, urged on by Granny, gave myself much too much time and had half an hour every day before the exam. It was actually a very pleasant way of starting the day with a twenty minute brisk walk in the morning sun.

After the morning exam we all trooped along to the Forum and dance hall and rather poor restaurant – at one time rather good apparently but the cost of 3/6 made me expect little and be little disappointed. Good school lunches eaten perhaps with more relish and less water. After that we would have 40 minutes in which to do anything we liked. In three lunch breaks as it were we managed to see most of what one should see in Oxford. Oxford was definitely at one of it loveliest seasons. Every night there was a hard frost and then crisp mornings and wintry sun.

After the afternoon exam with the same procedure we had tea with Old Sedberghians twice and went to a flick once. The flick was 'I'm all right Jack' with Peter Sellers, Terry Thomas and the rest. It was very good fun indeed. On Tuesday the three other Sedberghians came round to dinner at Belbroughton Road before we went to see the film of Moliere's 'Bourgeois Gentilhomme'. The evening was a success in all ways. I think Granny and Grandfather enjoyed having the three who were all terribly nice people and we discussed all kinds of things.

The exams were differently organised from Mr Hammer's oeuvres d'art. There was no 'start writing now' and 'stop writing now' and "The exam will end at 12.31; I have added a minute for interruption when the secretary came in." In a very civilized way we just sauntered in when the door was opened and casually putting our coats down and finishing our conversation we settled down. A don might try and make an announcement above the hubbub which would eventually get through and perhaps seven or eig t minutes later a suitably solemn atmosphere would reign.

Whatever the exam one always had three hours (I don't think this will be so at Cantab) and of course one could leave when one wanted, go out if one pleased, smoke, chew sweets and so on with no invigilator. Three hours later the secretary would come in and that was the sign to start finishing. Some people would start getting up, handing papers in and begin chatting, even looking over the shoulder of their pal who might be hurriedly trying to finish. One could go on writing for as much as seven or eight minutes again, and perhaps about ten minutes after the official end the last boy would have wandered out.

Then we went out to see this film that was made by the top French acting company and it really was tremendous fun. We chose to go to that rather than to Oxford Univ German Society's Faust which the other boys wouldn't have benefited from or enjoyed much probably. One can hardly do greater credit to the film than in the fact that Colin Matthew and Christopher Wood, both historians and 'Cliotics' par excellence, went to see it a second time. If the Frogs only knew the little but great honour that was thus being done to them they would have been very pleased!

Otherwise I had on the whole a peaceful time with early bed, etc. and plenty of relaxing.

On the way back we wound our homeward way up through Birmingham and Crewe and Kendal. Not terribly exciting towns. We had some time in Birmingham and walked around there. I think that of all the towns I know that would come at the bottom of the list of where I would wish to live. It was cold and filthy and draughty. Windy would be too polite a word but it managed to blow Wood's umbrella inside out. The station itself was sordid and was full of wogs and more wogs.

Now I'm back in the fray and a whirlpool of activity. I was away all Saturday in Ampleforth.

Rugger I've had two splendid games from the point of view of outcome – won by a firm 3-0 against Rossall though territorially speaking it was a huge victory. The tackling on both sides seemed to work like a steam roller and we managed to stay on their 25 most of the game but never scored...

The match last Saturday was away at Ampleforth and that was very good fun in all ways. They are more like us than any other school we play and are mostly boys from the south and highly civilized which is a change from the philistine though worthy barbarians that we meet sometimes. The school itself is in a lovely position on the side of a hill, much surrounded by woods and trees in their gold and reds of autumn overlooking a nice valley. They like us are miles away from anywhere. The game we won 24-6, their 5 being penalty points. We scored seven tries... They played our First XV on Tuesday and the outcome was a bloodbath 0-0. I got my 2nd XV colours (socks) on Saturday last.

Yesterday we went with Jake Durran rock climbing up in Langdale. We started on a small crag going up it and roping down – abseilen business which is a very painful method of coming down because basically all your weight is taken on your shoulder. It took a bit of time even on that small crag to get confidence and not cling to the rock too much. We also practised slipping on a rope and dangling in the air to see what it felt like. Then the three of us went properly up a crag called Scout crag about 250' high, roped up properly together. I don't mind the actual climbing with the feeling of firmness which the rope gives – though there were one or two very tricky spots – but the worst in my opinion is the perching on a tiny ledge overlooking space taking in rope as a chap comes up from below. I don't think I'll take up rock climbing as a hobby though I've learnt the rudiments and wouldn't mind doing one or two easy climbs perhaps but not more.

We were rather late returning and it was dark by the time we came down the fell – and we got back to Sedbergh in 55 minutes. This doesn't sound like anything special unless you know what the car was like. We went there fast, taking an hour and a quarter, and even then I thought the bottom of the crate might fall out any moment. We got back shaken but in one piece a couple of minutes before Chapel. What with Ruth and things I seem to have a knack of doing that.

Now I'm back to the round of daily work, tutuorials and proses on all sides. There's a concert and a film - Carlton Brown of the FO - this week. I'm looking forward to finding out the secrets of Daddy's trade.

As for the exams at Oxford, the two trouble sticklers were the General Paper and the French literature. The General Paper was not like any I had practised at all and began with two questions for comprehension, logical thinking, deduction conclusions etc. I spent rather too long trying to worry them out I'm afraid and didn't give myself enough time for the two essays.

In the French literature the appreciation gave me trouble in that, as rarely happens, I couldn't understand it fully. I got hold of the wrong end of the stick I thin, but I don't think it was too bad. I stuck accurately to the two 40 minutes allotted to me for the literature paper but didn't really get round either properly. For such a short time it really is a matter of shaking the sack and getting down to a minimum of material. As for the language papers I think they went rather better. There was a very nebulous teutonic prose to put into German which wasn't too bad and a rather more tricky one which at first sight was easier. The unseens were comprehensible in all cases. There were 4 to do in 7 hours and I think I made some quite good versions. All in all the language was about what I expected for standard - and I learnt that I've got to have a vocabulary as large and fluent as possible. The literature and general papers were good experience – and I can see that in literature there's a lot to be done in 6 questions in 3 hours at St John's. But all in all it's been a tremendous help having had these exams. I think I'll be able to feel less nervous and more at home as it were at Cambridge.

The days are moving forward fast, only a month to go. I do hope Daddy that you will be able to come up this week, that would be wonderful.

A separate note on a day at Rugby School for JMBL (who was there as a boy at the turn of the 1930s and as a master in 1937-39)

One of the most enjoyable things of this term, which I haven't told Daddy about yet, was my trip to Rugby... It was a pity I wasn't playing though I nearly had to when someone hurt themselves in the gym there. We travelled by train - bus would not have been much fun. We had tea on the train being let in like a lot of apes after everyone else had been served their 'afternoon tea' – and just about cleaned out the kitchen. When we got to Rugby our first port of call was the Stodge where we had a three course meal and coffee, in highly civilized fashion both teams together. I asked about ODs there, but there were none on their team, Mr Broxton and so on. They were terribly nice people and it was great fun being with them. They were certainly very 'couth' and some of our more barbaric members found them not a little amusing. They have a certain air of sophistication and almost boredom, which I would say was purely superficial. Most noticeable was this affection of boredom, of being 'shagged'. We got the

CHAPTER 6

impression that it was just not on to be enthusiastic about anything.[415] They seemed to affect to be interested only in the next house dance. I listened to various comedy records with them and their sense of humour would be termed 'senior-dayroomish'. They were the few I met in Kilbracken. A certain Skinner, next year's captain of the XV who seemed to have cousins and 4 brothers at the school etc, – maybe you know the name – and there was Cuthbertson, captain of cricket and schools racquet champion and so forth; and the Head of House who was a great nephew of Odgers - and they were all very nice. One of them was doing a copy and if one is to judge by that the general standard of writing of English of a senior prefect in the school I would not put any higher than ours. I saw Mr Broxton who was in great form and I had a message from him inviting me to come to take tea with him the next morning after 'Distribution' – unfortunately I could not go because we had gym then.

S   No date [c. 15 November 59]

What an awful photo – v. funny [no clues]

I hope you had a good time in Lagos, Dad; thank you for your letter. I realized on Friday morning that Dad would be flying back from Africa and Mummy driving south with Sally in fog all on Friday 13th. However, I expect all is well.

The weekend you come up Dad, there is a concert and a film (Carlton Brown of the FO) which we could watch together. Jamie is playing in the 2nd XV in Lancaster, and the 1st XV has a match here.

As said there is a house concert which is a bore except for the dress rehearsal and the thing itself. Lionel, Robertson and a few others are doing a short skit on the bar fight that comes in all westerns; this will make rehearsing more fun. The problem as always is clothes. It would be jolly d if you could come up with a pair of jeans (Dad, when you come), one coloured cotton shirt, 1 black cowboy hat and the holster and gun belt we have at home. That would be v. kind.

My leg went septic (on the knee) though healed quickly and no injections thank goodness

Thursday was an off day and we all went to Combe Scar. The snow was quite thick up above Sedbergh and I took your camera and finished off the film in it which I get tomorrow with photos of Lionel and others. I gave the camera to Mr Lowis who said he remembered Dad buying it for your wedding and said it was a very good camera. He then said he would have to send it away and it might cost quite a lot but with such a good camera it was worth it.

---

[415] I recall the visit well. I stayed in Kilbracken House (in the sick bay) and I remember being amazed that the boys came down to breakfast sleepy-eyed in their dressing gowns.

Did I tell you that basketball is now played fairly often in free time. It is quite a good game. We play it in the gym but have not got proper hoops yet, which the school is buying. We played on Saturday night and it is very energetic if one plays hard.

We lost our first match the week before to Rossall – awful , 10-6; yesterday there was a match against Ampleforth which we won 11-6 with two lovely tries.

How jolly jolly 'd' of you about Switzerland; it sounds wonderful fun. I am looking forward to it like anything. I quite agree with you about going up to London on the 21ˢ or around there, good idea. We have an invitation this morning from the Binghams for a dance, 8-12 on the 18ᵗʰ. We will reply yes and cancel if anything goes wrong.

I think my Christmas greedy list is mainly things for my study and a Peter Sellers novel and I would love a compass; also I need a strap for my wrist watch as this one is split. Otherwise I have no real ideas as the moment, and I always prefer a surprise, but I hope this is a help.

Oh dear, I have done two bad biology essays but one good biology test.

S   No date, mid November 59?

Forgive me for the red ink. I have none other left in the study.

Thank you for your letter and the telephone call. It's all a most terrible and sad business but I feel that in our case the least said about it the better.

I would very much doubt if Auntie Jo would want to come up so soon, and to drive all that way; but as you say. But if she does not come for any reason, what do you think is the best thing? She might actually want to.

I have had an offer from Beilby. What he suggests is that he drives Kim and I and the luggage to Holt and then he stops the night there and starts off next morning. Please tell Aunty Jo that he, Beilers, would like to do that. It is perhaps a bit far out of the way and perhaps we better go straight to London? ... further ideas for start of the hols.

J   Late November 59   [Sunday 22ⁿᵈ November]

...Thankyou very much for the letters, the telegram and the 'celebration money'. It really was rather exciting and I'm terribly relieved – so was the HM! I'm very sorry I couldn't pull off anything in the way of an award but there it is. I've now got this other chance to give the better of my best – so this next fortnight it's one hundred per cent concentration.

What exactly the £12 is for I'm not sure. I suppose it's a kind of rebate if that's the right word for the entrance exam costs and expenses etc.

I'm sad and yet pleased to say that I was the only Sedberghian to get a place or anything of the four of us who went down there – and one of them was one of our three State scholars of last term's exams. All three of them have another go at other places, Matthew at Christchurch and Wood is also trying for the John's group.

I must say it really is rather nice to be able to work for a Scholarship Exam having in mind that I've got a place at Queen's – a kind of all or nothing effect has a spurring on capacity.

I'm coming down the last lap now... and work is starting to take a revision form which greatly relieves the pressure. Over this weekend I have an English French and German essay, of which I have a tigsy suspicion someone will fall by the wayside a bit.

Everything including school years coming into the last lap now. Sets rugger has almost finished. 1sts have one more match but we have now completed our 2nd XV matches. Sadly we did not bring a culminating victory but in fact lost rather heavily 22-0 against Lancaster Grammar School who had been having a good season against other schools' 1st XVs. It was a tremendous ding dong battle and we were rather discouraged by having a penalty taken from the middle of the pitch leading to a runaway try when one of our centres fumbled the ball. We had 70% of the ball from line out s and scrums but the backs (with 2 substitutes) were on very sad form and never looked like penetrating the opposition who came up so far that we ended up doing nothing except going backwards.

We had quite a bit of time in Lancaster afterwards and several of us went to see the film Mon Oncle with Jacques Tati – most enjoyable and more fun than the school film for the term which we had on Friday called Lucky Jim with Ian Carmichael- Terry Thomas gang again. Good as usual.

House matches Tuesday week, then down to Cambridge and after that virtually no rugger for me. I don't know what to suggest for when Daddy comes up. It is also possible that I may be going to Loretto as 16th man – but unless they want a wing forward I will choose not to go, because it means 2 days away from school, a long bus journey and only a slim chance of playing.

There were two things you said you would see about when you came back from Africa, Dad. One was about the possibility of a passage to work on one of Niarchos' boats through Mr Wisner if he would be so kind. Is that possibility getting any nearer? – because I will have to get going soon to find out about possibilities from shipping lines about the country soon. I suppose end of March would be the time to go. I'm busy writing off at the moment to firms in Canada (quite an expensive business too!) trying to find out the form. And that comes to the second thing – on Mr Ignatieff and his being able to help me on the question of 'visitors not being allowed to accept remunerative employment'. It obviously is possible [to find a way around that] because we hear of British students doing such things as I hope to do – but I don't want to get caught out somehow.

The other thing about the hols is that we had an offer to stay with General and Mrs Hobbs with the rest of the Rye gang who are prepared to suffer us for Saturday and Sunday 2nd and 3rd January – after a dance on the

Friday night, not New Year's Eve[416]. I think it depends on how long we are going to be at Holt[417]; anyway there is plenty of time yet.

On Thursday we had a first rate piano concert from a certain Peter Katin (who broadcasted on Friday night). A tremendous technician and virtuoso but perhaps not so full of music as some people we have had. He played Mozart, Beethoven and Chopin in fact the lot. That ends our gay round of entertainment. Bashing on for another fortnight. I do hope very much Dad can come up

S   No date, [22 November 1959]

We have just been making our own sandwiches as there is a shortage of people in the kitchen. Mr Durran is coming with us and has been hacking away at frozen meat. It is not a very appetizing lunch, consisting of one meat and two [illeg. mingey?] sandwiches, + egg and apple. We are going in two cars – Mr Durran and Mr and Mrs [illeg] (the assistant house tutor) in another car with 3 other boys. We then go one car south (us) and one car north of Wild Boar fell and we go over Wild Boar fell and ride back in the other car. We plan to meet in the middle – which is unlikely; however it is a very good idea.

Sorry you can't come up this weekend, especially to celebrate Jamie's place at Queen's which is terrific.

I have here beside me the prospectuses of Essex college, Cirencester and Harper Adams Shropshire. The fees of all are approximately £300 a year for 3 10-week terms. Surprisingly Cirencester is the cheapest. From the prospectuses I would like to put down for Essex and Cirencester or preferably both and very soon for there are no places left for 1960 already so I would like to hurry up; the boys here are down already. If I put down I could easily withdraw; 2 chaps here who are down have not yet got the required O levels. I will talk to the HM about entry for both; you have to put down then I think you go for an interview. The Essex one is 230 persons if you get a grant (means test mainly) from local county people and £430 if not this is 130 more than most others. So if I was to go there I would have to have a grant, otherwise I might as well go somewhere else.

Cirencester. £300 a year; NDA after 2 years, you have to do an exam after one year, 200 acres, modern science equipment, farm, buildings also forestry land. 'Bicycles are encouraged, motor bikes not allowed' - good instructions. It sounds very good fun from the prospectus, and not just a place for The Hon Theodore Pinkington Fosselthwaite to go after Eton because he can't get into university. But if all the people like Major Pym say

---

[416] General Hobbs (father of Sarah) commanded the Colchester, garrison and the family lived in rather grand circumstances.
[417] To stay with Uncle Logie and family at Howson's, Gresham's School. See Visual Essay.

it is rotten then there is little point in going. But the main thing is I think to put down for it.

So much for colleges.

There was Peter Katin on Thursday. He was brilliant. I really enjoyed his Moonlight Solomonater as Victor Borge calls it. They got the wrong film; they sent Lucky Jim instead of Carlton Brown; a pity I was longing for it again. However it was quite fun, amusing anyhow, but no belly laughs as in CB.

I have a thing about Austria here. The Melvilles are not going to St Anton but to a pension in Kitzbuhel.... [Long passage giving details of expected arrangements, change from St Anton to Kitzbuehl etc; costs ; then about the need for a holiday job at United Dairies (staying with the Melvilles) to earn pocket money for the trip etc...]. Anyway I am determined that we shall do it; it will make the holiday in Kitzbuhel more fun.

You will be thinking that I can't do it in the Christmas hols as it will leave only a week and it is Jamie's last holiday before Canada and Queens. This is a pity as it would be better to spend the week in London before. But in the Easter hols J will not be here so it would be fun to do a week's work or just over with Lionel in London as the price has gone up. I'm sure you will agree to this. We can work out when next hols. People say in London you can get 6-10 pounds a week. Lionel is telling his parents of this who, he says, are bound to approve.

Kitzbuhel sounds wonderful with thousands of runs and good slopes for beginners and many lifts. Also it is supposed to be a very gay place with many entertainments. I wish I could send you these photos and pamphlets about it.

House runs today. I was third again in the pack. House matches are next week starting Tuesday 24th. We have a bye, so we will be playing someone on the 5th of December, but if there is a draw in the first round this will be postponed. So if you wanted to come up on the 5th and 6th we could send a quick telegram. [Further details of possible train arrangements...]

Thank you for sending the clothes and thank you for your letter this morning; jolly good about the enlarger would be fun to use it.

S   28 Nov 59

Thank you for your letter. So glad you agree to working in the Easter hols with Lionel. I should get at least five pounds to go skiing with. I quite agree with you about the garden path and skiing. First it was a youth hostel, then a small hotel and then Kitzbuehl[418]; the place there is a bed and breakfast pension with lunch and supper (probably dinner), vouchers which

---

[418] Sandy's spelling of the name varies

is supposed to be cheap. I told Lionel about the expense and said it must work out at under 50; he said his parents agreed to this.

The initial cost seems to cover all except insurance and pocket money. As you say, Kitzbuehl sounds so wonderful that pocket money will fly. The Melvilles say that ski boots must be hired as soon as possible but I don't see why I should not hire them in London on the 21st.

The weather has been better. We had an extra half on Friday which was a glorious frosty blue sky day. We went to Lilymere and in the woods there and marshes where there are many pigeons, pheasants and duck. It is a glorious place. We had great fun there.

Last night Mr Hetherington came to talk in civics – he is the editor of the Manchester Guardian – sorry Guardian. He looked as thick as a lunatic but he was obviously very swift. He spoke of newspapers generally with reference to their motives and morals. He had some amazing stories about all today's papers (papers of that very day) and commented on front page headings, sub headings and photos. He was extremely interesting. He had a pile of news sheets he had cut out of the paper the night before. The pile was only a fifth of the original; some of it had been discarded by the sub editors – at the end he left it so it was a free for all. I got one chunk of the pink white newspaper with lots of news with one interesting thing about a tin of haggis which someone thought was stewed steak, also Mrs [name illeg.]and political news. I will bring it home; it is rather fun.

Yesterday I played for a team made up from our house and Hart to play against the Bradford boys team. About five of them played for clubs near Bradford; the rest had only played once or twice and their age varied from 15 to 19 at a guess. They were a terribly nice lot of chaps with a great sense of humour. Jokes were going round all the time. All the same they played pretty rough rugger. I was full back again where I have played for the last two weeks in house games. I enjoy playing a lot at full back. We won quite easily and they scored a goal. It was right in the corner, and the ref told us after that it was not a try but they had to score once; and we thought they had not a hope of converting it from there, but the chap got it right over the middle with a lovely kick. Once when we were on their line, the leader of their forwards shouted 'come on, bunch it'. And when the ball was thrown in by their side one chap jumped at and punched it back into touch. He thought he had heard punch not bunch.

I talked to the HM about agricultural colleges yesterday. He says he does not know enough about them but thinks that I should see Major Pym and then put down before the new year two or preferably one college. He agrees that it would be safer to put down soon; I will get the information about putting names down before the end of term.

We will catch the early train at the end of term.

J   Nov 29 1959

Thankyou for your letters. I am very sorry indeed Dad can't come up but the cost certainly is ludicrous and it just doesn't make it worth it. There wouldn't have been any rugger for him to see either now. Sorry about the card with the measurements, I do hope it hasn't upset things sending it so late...

Everything is going along wonderfully here. We've had lots of house rugger and some final chopping block work on Bigside. In the practice games the 2nd XV has had 90% of the ball in the line outs and about 70% of the scrums. The weight of the scrums are about equal but we have a very good hooker and a very good jumper. Mr Mills was getting very annoyed with the 1st XV and we had to change to other forms of practice.... I've played more squash and fives... and School squash comp. I've just had two days being Captain of Football [i.e. rugger], sticking up notices and seeing the Head groundsman, etc - rather fun. At house rugger SH has a chance of winning the pot... and I think we should get into the final anyway. I will have to keep up training down at Cambridge!

A week to go till I go to Cambridge. I have got the cheque for £12 'meritous award'. Shall I cash it and use it for expenses? That would seem to be the most sensible. I've got my French literature fairly tied up now and am bashing into the German. I'm getting up quite a lot about French artists and modern art from various sources and on the language line I'm learning fair copies and essays by heart.... In the last 6 days including today I've had 9 tutorials.

On Friday there was an extra half and three of us went bicycling over Barbondale again. At the very top of the pass with the light gone at about five o'clock we met our assistant house tutor and his wife plunging over the fells in anoracs and boots. We directed them to Dent giving them of our supplies of chocolate and sweets and toffees that we'd bought to keep us going. They were pretty lucky to meet anyone at all on the fell at that time of day and they might have wandered off anywhere. Having biked the eight miles back just in time for tea we were greeted after tea with a call for a rescue party.

A small boy from Powell House with a bad foot hadn't wanted to go down Cautley spout (steep and screes) and was last heard of heading back for Calf and Sedbergh that way over the top. At 7.30 we went with torches and Verey lights up Cautley valley having driven up there and plunged through the rain sending up flares here and there. With the excitement of trotting over the black marshes and scrambling up the crags, we went on for a couple of hours. The crags round the spout lit up by green or red lights were like a dream. The most wonderful thing of that kind I've seen. Niagara lit up at night wouldn't be a patch on it. Jagged rocks, the thundering falls in spate, black crags outlined against the sky, dead trees growing in the rocks of the ravine and the whole thing lit up from the light which itself was out of sight in the gulch. I must attempt to paint, wash or draw it though I could never do it justice.

Anyway we came back to school and the other party about half an hour after we came back came back with the boy. This was about 10.30. He had been sitting between Calf and Cautley spout fairly unperturbed and thought the Vereys were fireworks.

Apparently he has always been slightly 'cuckoo' or what you will. Had the other party come back with no news the whole school would have been put into action or at least quite   a lot of it.

I missed through doing that an apparently awfully good lecture by the editor of the Manchester Guardian.

I met and had a long talk with the HM of Uppingham, Mr Lloyd, whom you know, Was he a tutor at Rugby or a boy there or something?. I thought he was very nice and he seemed to have rather better ideas about boys and punishments etc than one headmaster I know. My complaint with the HM is that there is far too much 'Why did you push the French master into the swimming pool'. Either he was a very unnatural boy or else I don't know what. Anyway enuff said, as Molesworth would say.

Have you seen the London Illustrated of this week. A pretty mixed bag of photographs. They need interpreting to quite an extent and with a few exceptions very bad actual technique I would have thought – overexposure, light wrong etc. The best one is the realistic corps attack (with school buildings through the smoke!) on a German position (having the drains up).

A fortnight and five days to go Hooray. Time accelerates; last tradesmen's orders, last laundry, last German prose for Jack and so on.

S   no date [probably Tuesday 6 December 59]

Sorry to hear that you are still ill with a cold. I hope it gets better soon. As you will be in London next week instead of this will you be there when we arrive?

The school exams start next week Thursday and early morning prep has finished already thank goodness. Yesterday there were house matches. We played Evans; neither team played very well but it was terribly exciting. I do wish I had been playing and I will have left by next Christmas I feel I am really missing something essential but there is Juniors (House 2nd XV) next term which we should win on paper. I shall be playing full back for them as I have played there on all house games and against the house team. It is a pity that we have such a good team my year; half of my whole set are on their house team.

Tomorrow is Sunday and if it is raining we are going up Whernside which is snow covered. There were house runs again this week and I was 2nd in our pack. I still cannot beat the chap who was equal with me in the ten.

289

What a day yesterday was. Mr Durran offered to take us up Helvellyn and we missed reading prep through having to make our own pack lunches. We started late because Mr Durran had communion after chapel (Church of Scotland), and we went off in the three year old Land Rover he bought last week. It is very nice and just the thing for him. There were five of us and him and room for more in the car. When we arrived at Helvellyn, we ate our pack lunch at the bottom and after climbing about half way we ran into thick cloud with visibility down to about thirty yards. Nearer the top the snow was a foot deep and the visibility nearly nothing.. Mr Durran knew the mountain very well and we went along Striding edge which as I expect you know is not dangerous normally. There are big drops down snow-covered slopes either side. The ridge itself is 2 to 3 yards wide rock covered with slush. We climbed the ridge, about 200 yds, very slowly and then scrambled up to the top.

Coming back the temperature suddenly dropped and the slush started to freeze. Mr Durran did not know the other way down well enough and we might have got lost; so we went down very, very slowly and had to keep going as it was four o'clock and starting to get dark. I have never been colder in my life – with shorts on and snowing and howling wind and particularly slush and ice. The ridges went on and on and, as the visibility was down to 15 yds, we did not know where the end was. It was getting worse but we came to the end of the ridge and walked down to the car. Mr Durran said he was very ashamed to take us with the chance of the snow freezing but it was a jolly good experience and lucky he knew it so well.

Thank you for your letter and the hospital things which I will not lose. If the train is not more than half an hour late we will have lunch at Lyons before going to the hospital.

On Saturday there was a subscription concert, which was an intimate opera. They did three plays. The first was very boring and not funny or good music. The second was the old story about two Victorians on a desert island. It was jolly good. The third was a new opera by Antony Hopkins called 'Hands across the sky'. It was first performed at the Cheltenham Festival this year[419]. It was very good, especially one song called 'I love Squig' which was really a skit on a modern musical song, a sort of Chelsea chorus girl. It was very clever and funny.

I have just played my first round of fives in the house fives competition; only about 15-20 people play fives in the house now and as I haven't played for about a year I was reluctant to enter. However I just won my first round – but will be beaten next round.

I am interested to see in the papers that the Yanks have got TV in Egypt which you were saying is v. v. important. Sir Caspar John Admiral in the navy came to speak to civics on Friday night. He was very clear indeed as to what he said. Stating very simple facts about world affairs and leading up to

[419] Said to be the world's first science fiction-themed operetta

what sort of navy we should have in the future. Questioned on Suez he said it was a political blunder the politicians had made and called upon the services to get them out of it. This is supposed to be unrepeatable in public.

Thinking of unrepeatable things, quite often people ask, not boys but masters, Mr Melville etc, what you, Dad, do in the Foreign Office. I usually say I have no idea what you do, which makes me look silly – so please will you give me an answer which I can use; which will make it far simpler.[420]

The camera is not back from the lab in London yet or wherever it is and Lowis do not know whether it will be here by the end of term. Shall I ask them to forward it to Rye if it comes in the hols or shall we leave it till next term

S   No date [Sunday 13th December 1959]

So glad you are coming up to London on the 17th then we can all go back together; hope it is ok if you come up by car. Where will you be for lunch in case we arrive early. Thank you for your answer about the FO it will do fine in reserve for anyone who asks in the near future.

Oh dear there have been exams this week and although I guess I did a good biology paper I did a bad physics one I think. The English paper question one is too hard for us as we have done nothing about poetry, but it is quite interesting. I will enclose ir if I can find it, but the study is rather a mess at the moment with house concert things including 11 pistols, four of them [word illeg.]. We collected eight of them from masters yesterday. Also the famous Spanish poster has been called upon by Mrs Thornely for decorating the dining room with a Spanish air; the black man[421] is a splendid matador and there are castanets, swords, hats etc round the room as well as the decorations and holly. It is all very jolly.

Today we have the Christmas lunch also the dress rehearsal tonight.

We are having terrific fun practising. The scene has all the typical things of a western bar; we have our pistols now and spend most of the day in drawing matches, practising drawing them from the holster, two chaps facing each other, hands away from the body etc. It is all very prep-schoolish but terrific fun and that is what matters. Assuming the audience has the same sense of humour as we do I think it will be very funny. Last year I thought it would not be funny. The whole skit builds up into a duel which another chap and I do. We start at opposite sides of the stage coming across and then drawing. The chances are ten to one chance that he will drop the gun or get it stuck but others say it is worth risking; so I

---

[420] My father was a Director of SIS. He described himself in general conversation as a senior FO official based in London who travelled often to the areas where he had responsibility.

[421] The Black Man was a fine jet black statue, about 18" high, of a naked athlete of Ancient Greece, in a starting blocks position. Many years previously he had been a house trophy awarded to the victor ludorum but no longer competed for. He was by tradition dressed up at the end of the Christmas Term, each year in different, sometimes very elaborate, apparel.

only hope it goes ok. Our fight is well practised too. It has to be as there are four people in it and the piano player also joins in. It really is terrific fun acting it; more fun than any other act I can think of.

Jamie seems to have had a very good time. Jolly nice to go home in the term time. His general paper is fascinating.

The camera has not come. Shall I get Mr Lowis to leave it till next term do you think?

Jolly 'd' about the ski trousers. I also hear that the Melvilles can lend me some skis which will help a lot. Wonderful to think we will be home in 4 days and in Kitzbuhel in two weeks. I better post this now so you get it tomorrow.

See you in four days then.

J   Last letter from school: 'Tuesday, School House, Sedbergh' [The date was 15ᵗʰ December; term ended on Thursday 17th]

Thankyou for the letter at Cambridge which was very nice to get in the middle of battle as it were. ... I think I'll just begin with the end - about my return last night which I do hope hasn't worried you

Having stayed the night with the Sykes I thought it would be rude to come in, as Des and I did, at 12 o'clock and then leave at 7.00 am so I took the lunch time train. The trouble was all made by the fog. Had we not been an hour late I could have rung up the HM in time and told him exactly where I was and when I would be in. Except for standing from Preston to Carnforth watching a good lady's pram and parcels and maddeningly slow travel because of the fog, the journey was fine. Maybe what annoyed me, and others in the House, was the fact that the HM seemed to get more worried about my getting lost on the incalculable British Railway system than about a small boy getting lost on the fells. There were reports of quavering panic – but maybe that's an unjust. Anyway it's all blown over now.

To go back to the beginning Liverpool Street was overrun with scholarship candidates and there was a special train full of them standing down the corridors. I met Michael Evers at the station and a couple of other Rugbeians whom I'd met before in November.

There was a surfeit here of suede coats, creased cavalry twill trousers fitting like drainpipes, Robin Hood hats with shaving brushes in them perched nauseatingly over the top of oily heads and such an array of shoes that they would belong in a fantastic dream. That shows the effect on a public schoolboy of giving him his freedom and then setting him to compete among his fellows; the cigarette machines were all emptied and the bars crowded. I escaped from all that with the science fiction 'Experiment Quartermass' which was really rather good.

My rooms were F5 3rd court which sounds rather splendid. The boy I was with was Colin Campbell the Head Boy of Gillingham Grammar School. He was a bloke of pretty high brain power and terribly conscientious. My great memory of him will always be 'Did'jer turn the gas off?' Wonderful but boring, he had a knack of knowing exactly which lights I had left on and anything I had forgotten to do, where the Divinity lecture room was, how much gas cost per hour – and a great deal of French and German. He had been awarded a scholarship out of several hundred people to go to a German family for three months. We had some very interesting talks together, particularly on the subject of advantages and disadvantages of public school v. grammar school educational systems. We sat and talked and drank coffee – he bought in a pint of milk daily – and the last couple of days we revised.

As for the exams, yea yea! nay nay! Difficult to say. Unseens in French and German weren't too bad except for the second German one – a piece of Grillparzer in verse. The proses were as ever tricky and my vocab in German wasn't wide enough to cope thoroughly whereas in the French with some stupid blank minded exceptions, things were better. In the German essay I wrote on tradition and renewal in art which was maybe a bit involved for subject matter; in French I managed to hold forth on heaven helps those who help themselves. The literature paper was fair in French and worse than fair in German. The main 'specs' for which we had prepared at school did not turn up. In the German Lit instead of the usual 15 questions there were only 7, of which three I knew nothing of at all, so my choice was limited. The good thing about the paper was that for the first time I managed to answer all six questions in the three hours - which was pretty good for me. I hope the material didn't suffer because of that

In both orals I managed to hold forth fairly fluently if not accurately in German as in French. In French I managed to get on to the painters about whom I knew something and the oral was pretty ok altogether. The Frenchman was a funny shy little bloke with a nasal accent which was hard to interpret. In the French oral I was taken by four people but in German by only one, the lady professor. As for interviews there was only this one talk with a don which was mainly to put me straight as to where the exam rooms were and so on. It was from him that I got the valuable information that Emma had a fake roman portico – which I managed to churn out later. ... To take it all in all, some was easier than expected and some a bit harder

Altogether I had an excellent week and it was tremendous fun..

Amongst the 350 candidates at John's there were several Sedberghians and we went to see a highly exciting but not very good film about the FBI. There was a news flick of the longer variety about the varsity match and Christopher Wood and I (Hastings schol companion at Oxford too) thought we'd give a cheer at the announcement Oxford won by 9-3 - which was received with caustic indifference and shifty looks from surrounding undergraduates.

293

And I don't think even Sandy or Lionel Melville would have been able to complain about the food – which is something.

On Friday I had a morning exam and went up to London at midday. Getting as far away as possible from exams was wonderful and I spent 70 blissful minutes in the cartoon world. Them I met up with Rosie and Desmond Sykes and went to eat in a little place which Desmond frequents, an Italian restaurant. It was seeing Rosie off at Charing X that Dad and I had our surprising and pleasant if short encounter. Desmond and I went to a cinema and armed with fish and chips and iced milk from one of those milk machines sang our way back in his car to Sawbridgeworth.

In the morning, a goodly change from French and German prose, we chopped logs, then walked round the village. Several friends of his were coming round and we sat and chatted and drank coffee in a very Sykesean way in a summer house with an electric fire, radio, lights, wicker chairs etc. It was all very pleasant. One boy is the Junior Javelin champion and has been with the AAA to Paris and Rome and throws the discus and all kinds of athletic things. I left the Sykes to do the longest tube journey ever done 4/2d worth.

Mad rush back here... orchestra rehearsals, squash competitions and house match final yesterday. We lost 5-8, a very, very great pity. All honours went to us I think. We led all the way until 3 minutes from the end when they scored a breakaway try. Territorially the match was played on their 25 and their first score was very lucky. I'll tell you all about it later, but I must break away. The house concert should be fun and the school concert very good.

I've just got a letter this morning saying I've got a trial with the Sussex Schoolboys at Brighton College (report 1.45) on Monday 21ˢᵗ December. I have to confirm by return post that I will be able to do so. I am doing so. Is that ok?

Well, thus comes to an end my last letter as a schoolboy. The happiest days of your life they say. They certainly have been wonderful, wonderful days. I hope and think I have profited much from the many experiences that have come to me and have learnt many a lesson without having to pay too dearly for it. This term has been the most superb finish to five, ten years. I now, for the first time in my life, realize that I have no house or home so to speak at Sedbergh. It's a glorious place and I'm very grateful indeed for your giving me these splendid days.

I leave so to speak with tears and cheers and am looking forward like anything to the coming days.

Spring Term 1960
All Letters from here onwards are Sandy's[422]

3 February 60 [Wednesday]

I hear from the HM that Kim will have to take common Entrance at the end of term or whenever it is. (I will look in my brown book). It is at school on 22nd Feb. I hear that Kim does not even know but he arrives a week before which is going to be very hard for him.

Got your letter. Sorry you did not get my letter. I hope Matron remembered to post it and it will have arrived on Monday. How ghastly that greasy little Turk sounded; just what I would have expected a Turk to say; though nice that one of them was pleasant.

On Sunday I went and saw Mrs Williams at Lilymere. I went with a guy called Huxley who is a really good guy absolutely strait [*sic*]. We walked all around the grounds. It is a lovely place getting quite a good amount of game. Then I went to Mrs Williams who said that the four month pup was very nice but that some other people wanted it as well. However she said there was a possibility she might be able to buy it for Dear. Does Dear definitely not want a dog (as opposed to a bitch)? Important

Hope J passes his driving test. Shall I send for a provisional licence? 3 out of my 6 closest friends have already passed their tests.

I hope that you hear from Swan soon. And what about the LEA Grant to Essex College? Have you heard anything from Mr Braithwaite yet?

We have started the House Unison; we are singing 'The Linden Tree' by Schubert and 'Now for Vengeance' sung by Doctor Bartoli in Figaro - I think it is Figaro because he comes into the song which is full of rousing stuff etc.

Thank you for your letter this morning and for the cheque, I have already paid out of the Post Office so I will put this back into it. How very annoying about Jamie's scholarship the Trevelyan; silly of someone not to tell you.[423]

It is raining very hard and has been for the last two days so I expect there will be house runs today, and having had flu I am so unfit.

The food which has been wonderful [so far this term] with buns or fruit every [day] for tea and no more just egg on a plate or sausage on a plate but both together and we haven't seen biscuits and cheese or soup this term as

---

[422] I was at home in Rye until the end of February when I left for Hamburg to await arrival of the Niarchos cargo vessel on which I was to have a passage to Baie Comeau on the St Lawrence River.

[423] Odd that I was not encouraged to enter the competition for Trevelyan scholarships. No one from School House was, I think, although a number were from other houses.

a main course; but in the last four days it has suddenly gone back to what it was last term.

PS I Hope you have not completely forgotten to send the other half of my pocket money as no doubt I will be running short soon.

19 February 1960 [Friday]

Thank you so much for the letter and the photos, which are jolly good I think, especially the one of the apple tree. Did you take it at f8 and $1/125^{th}$ like it said on the back? I would have thought this would have been much to[o] fast and I took my skating ones yesterday at f8 and an 80th.

I hope they will be ok. On Friday night it snowed and on Saturday I went out with Mr Moore and 3 others to climb Whernside and behind it. We went in his Sunbeam, Talbot, a lovely car[424]. It was very cold and the tarns on top were frozen hard but we had no skates as we were training. The trouble is that I have not trained since and there is the final trial on Saturday but as I can't get on the team anyway I can't bring myself to go training instead of skating although I do run to the skating tarns. And tomorrow when we get to Lilymere I am going to run there and back instead of the bus.

On Sunday it snowed very hard (a blizzard) and we had arranged to skate on Baugh Fell with pack lunches but the HM said we couldn't go (quite right too) as there was such a strong blizzard. During lunch it suddenly cleared and as we had lost 2 hours the HM kindly offered to drive us to the bottom of Baugh Fell and also to pick us up before tea.. This we did although it took us an hour to reach the tarn because of the thick snow. It was quite lovely on top and the snow, or most of it, had been blown off the ice. My skates are very nice indeed but my ankles are so weak that I sometimes wear a crepe bandage to support them. The HM drove us back with Richard in the car sucking Smarties. In case you don't know there is another child on the way, due I am told in early July. The HM was in good spirit, he always seems to be when preforming non strictly headmasterly duties.

There was 20 degrees of frost yesterday and Tuesday. Yesterday we went skating with Mr Moore. We always seem to get the masters but nobody else asks Mr Moore but he is normally delighted to go and says No if he doesn't [can't]. We went to a big tarn just past the Moorcock. It was lovely up there and I took 10 photos to finish off a film. I am getting them printed very small and will get the best ones enlarged. I am the only one of my group to have a camera so any good photos are wanted by all of them and they said they are paying more than the prints to make up for the negs

---

[424] Sandy was greatly taken by the Sunbeam Talbot, and when he first had a car of his own in Cirencester days, he bought one, a very old and battered one.

and film costs. I have another film and will probably finish it before long if the fine weather lasts.

Thank you for your suggestions re biographies. I think I will want The Duke when I have finished Monty which is fascinating.

Jolly d for Jamie going on Niarchos's cargo beat especially if going to the West Indies. If he goes from Hanover[425] on the 15th that means he will be crossing the channel the day before on his birthday; I haven't an idea of what I will give him but sufficient unto the day is the evil thereof (if that's what I mean).

Today I collected the eagle I made in pottery last term which has been slipped, painted and glazed and also fired twice in the kiln, so it's a miracle that it has survived all this. The beautiful hemispherical flower vase I made has cracked in the kiln through bubbles or grit or bad section or something; but I will try to make another; although the principals are so easy it is very hard to make one worth firing.

Yes we have the HM's permission to stay on another day to climb the peaks.

Hooray this weekend is half term and among other things Lionel and I get the gramophone for the rest of the term. I am not so sure this is really a good thing as one has people singing, eating, drinking, fighting and semi-jiving, tapping feet, slapping hands etc, etc, as the place where people let off stream is always in one of the gramophone studies and it is not easy to throw people out.

We have 1½ hrs physics practical to-morrow which is always good fun.

24 Feb 60 [by postmark – Wednesday]

We didn't get any skating on Lilymere which was a pity but the house yard was very good, the best it has ever been according to the HM. There has been lots of snow, six inches or more on the playing fields and much more on the fells. On Thursday I went training for the trial but it started to rain. But on Friday it froze and there was wonderful sledging but no skating. Some of the drifts on Frostrow were very deep indeed and we had great fun roaring through them which was for a short time about the most energetic thing I have ever done. On Western [place name illeg] there was a deep snow[-]covered hole in which a chap from the house got stuck and had to be pulled out. It might have been unpleasant if he had been by himself (we always go round together).

Yesterday there was still a lot of snow... the trial course goes over Frostrow and it was very slippy. It was the first trial and there are 8 chaps on the team but I came = 9th.

Today we are going up on Bakers [?] fell to try to catch some horses by running them down in the snow but I don't expect we shall catch any.

---

[425] It was Hamburg.

I hope I enclose the medical certificate you sent last term also a photo of J in house concert, not a very good one, taken by Mr Durran. He wrote to all of us at the beginning of term, mine arrived at home if you remember. He has replied since to some of our replies and doesn't seem to be doing much that is his cup of tea; a great pity he left.[426]

Very glad you hope to stay the night; it would be silly not to as I will hardly see you on Tuesday except in the late afternoon... on Wednesday maybe we can have lunch and then watch the 3.

This story will interest Jamie as he knew the people. Today Whitman was upstairs and saw small Aitken tipping the contents of a pint water bottle into a fire bucket; the kettle was from Slater's locker (who is in the very bottom of the junior dayroom). Aitken sniffed the bottle and said 'is that gin' then Slater told him to shut up, and Aitken replied that he had tipped it away by mistake; whereupon Slater got somewhat angry. Whitman could not really believe this but thought he looked cross enough. So he went five minutes later and smelled the fire bucket which was stinking of gin. Slater was seen to empty the fire bucket into the bath later on. Staggering story don't you think, very funny.

Today I took some 3 mile training with a prefect. As we were coming up to Millthrop bridge, after two hundred yards there we had been running very slowly. I was taking the back of the first half and the last chap suddenly yelled and collapsed on the side of the road. This was five yards in front of some old ladies who proceeded to slang me (because I was beside him) for trying to kill him and 'ruin a poor little boy' – most embarrassing. Actually he had stomach cramp and was quite ok after a bit but the old ladies weren't convinced.

Glad David is looking forward to having me. I am looking forward very much to going; in form (biology) we are doing soil structures, fertilizers and many aspects of root crop and corn farming. It is very interesting.

The gramophone is now right beside me and we are relatively peaceful; and it is very nice – and so is everything right now.

I thought that Matthew had gone[427] already. The new head of house Lewis is very good; he hasn't persuaded Lionel to run in the ten yet but almost. Lionel did not run in any of the trials.

How is Kim and his CE? Is he coming up here with Dear? That would be very nice.

I think I shall take my driving test at the end of the next hols; lots of people here took it in the hols after their birthday. Then I could help you drive down south at the end of the term or to Bemersyde and then south.

Have written to Dear and to Granny and Grandfather. We had to write an Ode to snow' in English and I put my version in my letter to Granny as I

---

[426] He took a Mathematics post at Winchester.
[427] On a gap year world tour; I forget where exactly he went, although in mid-1960 we met up for a couple of days in Northern Ontario.

thought it would amuse her. I really enjoy writing English now, I mean essays and poetry, though Ode to Snow is such a soppy thing to write about.

Too wet to play rugger etc... fields flooded; so we have done little but run. We have also played quite a lot of basketball now the new equipment has come (£40 from Lilywhites. We play four a side with no touches so one can play off the sides as well. This virtually means that the ball is in play until a goal is scored and it is very energetic...

We started off on Monday the first exercise of the term with a house run. The skiing must have made me reasonably fit which was just as well because I would have felt ghastly if I had still been breathing out turkey, Christmas puds, apricot brandy and Austrian gateaux. However I just came first by about that third of brandy butter I refused on Christmas day.

Today for the first time the sun came out and it was lovely especially up on Calf where I went in the afternoon; it is also much colder so maybe we will get some skating soon. The CIGS[428] was supposed to have been coming for the inspection next term but can't come so we are now having someone who is much more important than CIGS, but I can't imagine who it is. So we are already preparing for the parade at which after the inspection we do a military tattoo which is rather fun.

There is a flu epidemic going around the school and I have got a terrible cold though no flu. Lionel has caught it and is in the san. Thinking of Lionel he does not know if he is going to run in the ten but like me is running in the trial which I think is being postponed till next week.

Will you be coming up for the ten mile? It would be awfully nice if you do.

What is J going to do and if he goes abroad, tell him I will right /sic/ to him sometime but the weather and my cold make me too cheesed off to write now.

I had a great shock yesterday and no doubt you will too, because on going down to Lowis to get the camera cleaned and shutter mended I got a bill for £3/19/-, although he said his estimate was about £2. It was sent to Zeiss works[429]. The trouble is I have after paying pounds to the Melvilles, Christmas and last term's developing etc etc, I only have a two pounds dead in the Post Bank. So now I have 0 pounds and 5/- in the post office. But the camera looks in lovely condition – and so it jolly well should for such a price.

[in pencil]   I don't suppose this will have reached you last week as I am still in bed with flu and also a boil on my face, so this will be late. I am much better today and have no headache. I had J's letter to cheer me up

---

[428] Chief of the Imperial General Staff
[429] The camera, a 1940s Zeiss of high quality, was a gift, or possibly long term loan, from my mother.

this morning and I will write when I have sent this. I don't know how long it will be before Matron sends this.

PS   You might like to know that at the moment I am listening to that beautiful German song

> You are so wunderbar
> I wonder who you are

which sounds too funny for words.

2 March 60 [Wednesday]

Good that you will be able to stay here; only 3 weeks now. When is Dad going to the Middle East?

Some of the photos of the skating re quite good and some on Wild Boar fell. I have written the exposure down on a piece of paper and have now written it down on the back of the photos. I am going to try some inside ones on this film. I have taken 2 hundred watt bulbs so I can cut down on the time exposure. I find it is fascinating also expensive – but except for drink I have not bought anything at the grubber this term.

Jolly good that the County Grant can be given at all four colleges. I would prefer Cirencester myself as i) the head is a good chap with a good reputation, ii) it deals in farm management (I don't count hens and poultry as farming, iii) most likely place to make useful connections because it has a good reputation iv) there are some nice chaps from here going there, and v) I presume all grants are the same so it will be cheaper going to Cirencester. Essex seem rather better situated between Norfolk and Kent but the Cotswolds are lovely, what I remember of them.

There was a film on Saturday which was the only one of term and caused an awful row among the boys and consisted of a documentary film of an opera at Glyndebourne which is not the thing to replace the thriller or musical we were expecting. But it wasn't as bad as everyone expected, though of course one can't admit this.

There is film we must see next hols, we have a record here. It is called Five Pennies – Danny Kaye and Satch who are terrific and also Benny Goodman and Glen Miller; the music sounds wonderful.

There was a special parade on Thursday for the Queen. The band were wonderful, playing brass band swing [Glen Miller?].

There was a juniors game yesterday; we won 16-3 but I forgot to tell you that we lost the one before so we are not in the final. The 3 scored against us was a penalty so I had nothing scored against me[430]; also I did little except kick and a few runs, but it was a good game.

We have started ten mile training yesterday. I went round to Danny in 75 which is 15 minutes too slow but I walked most of the way across Baugh

---

[430] The reference to 'the one before' must have been to a senior house match - in which Sandy was evidently playing as full back.

Fell then ran up and along most of Frostrow afterwards. Mr Morris training is very varied - from long 12 mile runs to short 6 mile runs with ¼ mile sprints and only one flat out run a week.. His theory is that after a few weeks' bad training people are completely exhausted by the time of the ten mile. day. So we are doing his special training – I hope he is right.

We had a conjuror last night, probably the first ever and it was a unique experience. Everyone agreed that it was the worst display ever seen anywhere. He spent three quarters of an hour cracking the feeblest jokes you have ever heard, feeble puns and jokes which everyone had known for almost ten years, then kiddies stories and silly songs and chanting babyish magic spells. He then hauled one unfortunate wretch up on to the stage to wave his hands in the air and say the magic word. And of course it didn't work, so the poor chap had to keep on spouting it. The tricks were card tricks and pieces of string and handkerchiefs. He would have been lucky if he had fooled Sally. The whole thing was appalling - and the chap had only had two weeks notice as the proper conjuror who was going to come had died. He got the head of School and a pre called Kenmure (who J will know) and treating them as 8 years olds proceeded to make complete fools of them with magic words. They took it very well.

Here are the hospital card, and J's photos. I will send this now.

Mrs Williams[431] is still in the air about the puppies. [Dear wanted to buy one]

No date, March 59

Thank you for the three letters last week and the two checks [cheques]. The camera looks as good as new. Yesterday I went up on to Holme Fell and in the Dee valley with the camera taking some photos of various friends and the countryside and the fells etc.. I will want to have photos of all the fells around with various chaps in the foreground so I am taking a film of strictly the best views and chaps in front which I will like later on. I tried one from the top of Holme Fell facing the sunlight of the sun with a chap as silhouette in front; it will be rather good if I exposed it correctly, which I doubt[432].

The last three days have been quite lovely with mist hanging in the valleys in the morning then wonderful blue skies. Today the HM is dumping us at Rawthey Bridge and we are going up Wild Boar Fell and down into the start of the Eden valley which I have only seen but never been to. I will tell you all about it when we have done it.

Four of us would like to stay here an extra day and go round the Three Peaks from House to house. It is almost exactly 50 miles and hills like Ingleborough are quite steep. So we will start at 6 (if we do it) in the

---

[431] Of Lilymere House
[432] See Visual Essay

morning with breakfast at Dent at seven which we will order before starting on the twelve crow fly miles to Pen-y-Ghent about 15. We think it is a terrific idea. I hope you do, I am sure you will. Then we will catch the nine, not the seven o'clock train the next day and arrive home almost dead; actually we will be fighting fit as we will be able to sleep on the train.

We have made many inquiries but not got very far yet about work in London. We think the 4th Monday is a good starting day. We have yet to get a reply from United Dairies who are our best bet. Anyhow we will get something.

We went up Wild Boar on Sunday which was a lovely day with an east wind so that it was extremely cold on top. We ate our very good pack lunches on the lee side about 10 yards from the top. If you remember it is a table top mountain, then ran along the top about a mile to the cairn. It was very cold and when we got to the Cross Keys we were exhausted and went in for a pot of tea and their special apple pie. Just as we had started we heard the familiar voice of Mr Bennett, who Jamie will know well, and he came in next door and wanted a full tea. So we quickly shut the communicating door and sat down again. But the trouble was that we had to run home in time for tea and he had a car. And we had to go through his room to get out and pay. But in the end we left the money on the table and opened the French window and ran back. The whole thing was rather amusing.

What bad luck on Kim being late; awful to have to take CE at such short notice. Also I agree it is a bit tough having to go to a strange Frog school boarding. I would think it tough even if he could speak French.

This term we have had to read two auto or biographies for English one of a man alive after the Great War, on 19th century or earlier. I am reading Monty's memoirs for the late one; partly because I think only think, that he is coming here next term for inspection. It is very interesting. Although says he is blindly big headed he must have been a very great man; about the finest of the last war – at least that is what I gathered from his book. I don't know what to read for a nineteenth or earlier one – suggestions?

I wish the queen's baby would be born quickly so we can have an extra half or day off or something. There is a glorious rumour going around that we will get from 9 in the morning to 9 in the evening free and we'll all have packed lunches and teas. Of course it is possible but improbable - as Robertson myself and one other started it; of course this is very babyish but we had great fun to see how fast it goes around, especially if you add 'no one is supposed to know'. Very prep school but good fun when someone says 'have you heard that'.

Yesterday I went on the weekly Ampleforth training run which I qualify for with 19 others. It was very fast indeed with some 440 yd timed sprints. Some of those running were very good and everyone seemed much less exhausted and to have taken much less effort than I. I am not looking forward to the next trial, the last one, on the 18, 19th and 20th, but I will go round it just to see how good everyone is for the ten, although I think there is an awful lot of difference between 4½ miles and ten, I will then have some idea of how fast the really good runners go – we have none in the house.[433]

Today it snowed. I hope it lasts so we can get some skating and sledging. The HM suggested that Dear and Kim come up hear [*sic*] which would be fun but I don't know what you think about it.

Summer Term 1960

1 May 60 [Sunday – term started 29th April]

Thank you for a lovely evening in London on Thursday. West Side Story was tremendous. It is a funny thought that I have finished my school holidays; they have all been happy and terrific fun, and I am sure not many people can say this with truth. I suppose I have many more holidays to go, but not back from school, except Cirencester in a sense.

I entirely think it would be a waste of time going to Essex, so does the HM, so all is well.

Had an uneventful journey up here and lots of holidays things to talk about.

We had a terrific row about studies when some senior guys decided they wanted ours. So we quickly moved in and have everything up and did a whole day's job before tea so when we were queried we were finished decorating etc - and so we are still here. We have the best study and a gramophone so we are all set for a wonderful term.

Last night I played tennis with Lionel on the house court which usually takes a month before it is in use..

Good news is that on Friday 9th the Shutterbug is making good in the Abbey [434]so the house is getting a bus to go to the lakes. Breakfast at 8 and leave at 9. Four of us are getting off at Windermere where we intend to sail before lunch etc. Very 'd' of them to get married in my last term; he can't be such a bad chap after all.

We have a new form master. He is very young. He takes us for Physics and seems quite good. A new school rule is that whenever boys leave school with parents etc they are advised to wear Sunday clothes. Good thing!

---

[433] Sandy did superbly well in the Ten–Mile race in March 1960, coming 10th in 1.17.10, which would have been a winning time in some years, and was second best in School House. Sadly, no letter exists reporting the day.
[434] The wedding of Princess Margaret to Tony Armstrong Jones (Lord Snowdon)

Hope Sally enjoys her school.

We had an amusing journey up to London with Jeannie and Alison[435]. Jeannie is really very amusing indeed.

I will write more later. It really was a glorious holidays.

8 May 60 [Friday]

I had a lovely birthday. Thank you very much for the presents last hols and now.

The [golf] lessons seem to have got me through a barrier and it was good fun, especially the round with the pro; and the soft bag was a wonderful buy. So now, with the Rye tie, I am really well equipped.

Granny and Grandfather sent me a very nice photo album; it is a lovely big black one, and really jolly 'd'; also Uncle Robin sent a pound and Aunty K a ten bob which was jolly 'd' of them

This has been a terrific week. On Friday we went to Windermere.. Left at 9, after breakfast, no early morning prep; 12 of us got off at Bowness with the intention of hiring a sailing boat. When we got there the silly old man, actually I can't blame him, would not lend us a boat at first; but after much persuasion that we were all expert sailors he said he would. So he gave us a cabin cruiser about 25 or 26 ft long and another 20 ft decked yacht, two of them. Seeing the size of them we were rather put out as there were only three of us who could sail. So we three took one each and set off. It was much easier than sailing the Firefly and very sedate and slow. We could have sailed all the way to Ambleside with the wind. We turned into the wind every now and then to make it more interesting. We lunched on board and went ashore for a drink in Ambleside. On the way back the wind dropped and the larger boat was very slow. It cost us 6/9 each which was jolly good really.

In the evening there was the film The Mouse that Roared with Peter Sellers. It is the one J was telling us about, about a little country that was unlikely to survive so they got the Americans to occupy them.

Do you think you could send the bullfighting slides and do you know anyone who might have a good book on the subject; because it is all very complicated and skilful and the kill is only a small part.

The tennis is very good fun but I played two bad games with Mr Alban which was silly of me, in fact it might cost me my place in the first match. I practised by myself and with Lionel for 2 ½ hours in the afternoon and went every evening.

On Tuesday we shall be climbing Ingleborough.

In Biology as far as I can see Mr Madge the biology master has no intention of finishing the AO level syllabus; we have not even started on

---

[435] Alison and Jeannie (Kathron) Sturrock, two of the three daughters of Jan, my mother's close friend in Benenden School days, and good family friends

Botany at all. The syllabus was not completed last year and half the form failed! But I have a book of exam papers and will start on all questions asked more than once between 55 and 58. Mr Madge spends a lot of time doing things that are on the A syllabus so we wont have to bother about them next year. Not very helpful because 2 others and myself are leaving this term and getting rather fed up with him.

A vast and most delicious cake arrived on Friday; it is scrumptious Thank you very much and Jill I presume, and Sally perhaps and maybe even Taptoe?

I am eating 6 4-penny oranges a week to try and keep healthy and spotless. Food not so good as last term,

Thank you again for the lovely hols and presents.

Postcard 10 May [60]

Sorry I didn't realise all the trouble that I caused you from Mr Cooke. I hope it will be a last and final fling before becoming 18. I wrote to Mr Cooke and the secretary on Thursday[436]. I also wrote to Carolyn[437] about the tennis; which I want to do. What about the running?

When a parcel arrived for Dad at the weekend, it is from Jamie and I.

19th May ?60

[... long passage on techniques and problems of photography, and on his and MEBL's efforts. S was very thrilled with the last batch he had taken...]

There is a competition here on Speech Day 11th June for photos taken by Sedberghians; the subject is to be called 'Play'. Might those ones of Sally be interpreted as 'play'. Do you think any are good enough for the Observer competition?

I am glad that Dad liked the Nuit St George [sic]. I did not know if it was a good one but the shopkeeper said it was generally acknowledged as fairly 'd'.

[re End of term arrangements...]

... Thank you for the barbecue invitation. Sounds 'd'. What are we doing next hols? Will we be able to spend a weekend with Dowcs and go fishing; and will I be able to go for a few days chez Lionel who is having a dance and is inviting Winki the Yank, the very best of a Yank; terribly nice and has so much money he does not know what to do with it. He took us to Barbon hill climb in the Aston Martin. His family have 4 cars plus one

---

[436] Possibly with reference to a complaint from a member of the Rye Golf Club about unsuitable behaviour, or dress, of Sandy and friends on the course

[437] Carolyn (Bunny) Fisher, one of our gang of friends in Rye; later made her name, when Bunny Campione, in the 'Collectibles' world at Sothebys and on The Antiques Roadshow

pick up. Do you remember that he had a map of Europe and asked where he should go for his hols. He took our advice and went to Tel Aviv, Jerusalem and toured the Holy Land too.

Paris was very expensive, he said, I spent 100 dollars in a night there. This was a big joke Cairo, Athens, Paris, Madrid. He is going to Lionel's dance before he returns to the USA. Broad[438] and Hux are also going.

That reminds me can you book me a driving test for the week after the beginning of the hol. Tuesday 2nd August in Hastings. I suggest 10.30. Do you agree with this? I will race on Monday and should have recovered enough by Tuesday. On second thoughts maybe it would be better to go for 2.30.

Plans for the last night of term; the best plan so far is a barbecue at our private bathing place. Most people to show they have left school go out and get drunk just outside Sedbergh and stagger back and are probably sick in their studies. We will have only mild drink and bangers.[439]

I am getting a big kick out of life here. Although I have played some bad tennis fours and there is only one person who is left from last year's team and Winki is on[440] without doubt. I have played some good singles, but that is not what they want. However I am the house authority on the discus and can throw it a few feet further than anyone else. Unfortunately this is because they are so bad, but it is still nice.

Plans for weekend outings to Windermere and Barbon Hill climb with parents of friends...

What about the motor bike? Do you think it would be a good idea if I got I near the beginning of the holidays. Do you think an advert in the Sussex local paper is a good idea? What price should I be counting on?[441]

27th [May 60]

Went out with the Melvilles. We went to lunch in Kirby Lonsdale and then river bathed in the afternoon on the Lune. It was a boiling hot day and lovely in; we all bathed and ducked and draked and generally fooled around enjoying ourselves. They are all such fun as a family with an unceasing capacity for enjoyment, you really must meet then sometime. Mrs Melville is bang up your street. She is the same sort of person as Mrs Hoare[442] in many ways

---

[438] John Broadbent
[439] Sadly, this plan led to complications – see footnote at end of the Letters
[440] i.e. on the Tennis VI
[441] I suspect that Sandy was cleverly angling for a car here, counting on the probability that my mother would be horrified at the thought of him riding around the Kentish lanes on a motor bike. It had that effect anyway; see letter of 2 June.
[442] Elizabeth, mother of Carolyn (see fn 419 above#) was a close friend of my mother's - a cheerful, artistic and larger than life figure.

Lionel's fifteen year old brother, and a friend of his, was there too; we debated, discussed, argued and laughed away the whole day through. We went out again after chapel for dinner. Oh dear, there we go again, three meals out but no-one knows yet.

More plans for going out with Melvilles, and Winki too, and holiday getting together... ·

Will write again on Wednesday

2 June 60 [Thursday]

I think it is a simply terrific idea to get an old car or van. Very exciting; also a very good idea to do a couple of weeks at Bryants as well [local garage]. But what possible use could I be to them to start with; they wouldn't let me mend some one's car. And what about Dear's money I do hope you will write to her.

We meant to go deer stalking but couldn't make it because of a leave. But yesterday Lionel, another guy and Beilby, who is the only decent prefect and a splendid chap, went up to try to find them. After about an hour and a half we came to the big valley where they are said to be (only one guy in the house at the moment has seen them). This valley is about one mile across and divides off into two valleys at the top with streams coming down each and meeting. None of us had been there before and it really is the most lovely place around. It is not plain like the Howgills and Winder but heather and rock and streams with lush grass.[443] We sat on the edge of the valley looking down. We could only see part of it because of outcrops and hills all over it. I had my binoculars but we saw nothing. So we went down about 200 yds into the valley and stopped again and I was looking down the valley when suddenly I saw in the middle of the bino three vast brown red sheep lying down just how a sheep doesn't lie down. It was terribly exciting sitting on one side of the valley and everything in complete peace then suddenly there were the deer in the binos. I can't describe how exciting it was.

It took a long time to get down to the stream at the junction; they were about 200 yds above it. We started to go up but after about 30 yds the rock was eroded and it was a flat stream after that. We sat watching them carefully and they had not seen us. But the way we had come down, the wind was behind and one of them suddenly put its head up and seemed to smell us and then the others did and they started walking away up the hill and then they ran.. When they had gone we stood up and about 2 mins later we saw another lot of 9 including 2 lovely stags. The deer are not the park deer but bigger and more majestic. To get to them we had to do a 2 mile detour to come up at them against the wind and over the hill. We did this but they were half a mile up the valley when we crept over the rise; they

---

[443] Probably over Dent and Deepdale#

must have seen us or seen the ones we made run away. There was another herd of 5 at the head of the valley, all up where the streams started. It was lovely watching them.

Today we are going up with pack lunches and binoculars to try to shoot them with the 2 or 3 cameras we have. I think camera shooting them would be just as much fun as killing them with a gun. They were so lovely yesterday, I wouldn't have shot them even with a gun.

We have just had the drill cup and we have been practising like mad, harder than any other year. I spent hours cleaning my equipment and the silly man only glanced at me. He asked other people things; he told someone that they had middle aged spread and they looked a mess. He also told Broadbent that the screw sights of his rifle were up; but Broadbent did not know how to put them down. We came 3rd, a feeble effort after all our practice

What do you think of the idea that you give me a cross channel cheapest ticket so I can hitch hike down from Calais with this chap Beilby and stay with his grandfather's place for two weeks. His grandmother asks him every year and insists he brings a friend because she says she cannot entertain him. So he asked me for 2 weeks. Last year he spent £5 + £15 railway return. I said I would love to go but would not be able to go if the journey cost more than £5 return. He says he would like to hitch hike down. Last year he hiked down while his friend went by train. He went by eating bread and lettuce and cheese and sleeping in fields. He reckons we could get down for about £3 for food and the channel as an extra. His grandmother gives him all meals and a car and petrol. His father says he will lend him a car if the cross channel ferry is not more than £15. The car is a small Austin and does 40 mpg making petrol about £8 if coupons can be found.. His Dad would pay this instead of the train fare.

Do you think

a) the whole thing is just not on;

b) ok for 2 weeks if hiking + channel ferry, making £10 in all;

c) I am bats to think I can spend 2 weeks in France on £10;

d) ok if in car and bike;

e) not ok either way.

I know and am grateful that you have just spent £50 on my going to Austria and now are about to spend masses more on a car; so if you think this is the tiniest bit extravagant you must say so. I would like to go and you may think the chance is not to be missed of being able to go for so little money as £10. Please consider carefully, and will Dad please write and let me know what you think.

I was thrown off the tennis team for the Stonyhurst match for my bad play at the beginning of the term. All the other matches are after speech day and I am playing 100% better now so I should jolly well get back on.

Biology AO level is July 7th, not long really.

Hope I enclose a driving form. Today I made a little owl and have painted it. It is very solid but if it comes out of the kiln ok I will send it to Sally for her mantelpiece.

Am writing to Grandfather.

9 June 60 [Thursday]

Thank you for your letter and the photos of the bullfight. I really must have the book for my talk as it has photos of all the passes and I will hand it around.

I had a tremendous weekend. On Saturday, 5 of us went to the Barbon Hill Climb. Henderson and Beilby, a prefect, and I went on bikes as it is our last term and we are allowed bikes. Had a pack lunch, went in to the pits, the starting place. Apparently the event has grown enormously. 2,000 spectators, a big social occasion. Lots of Aston Martins. Classes for all sorts of different cars, old Bentleys, Vauxhalls, pre war cars etc . There was one 9-litre car; the noise was fantastic. Most of the drivers were men of 40 up having to wear crash helmets and goggles over RAF handle bar moustaches [sketch]. Then of course there was the cool school of young men wearing cavalry twills and silk shirts and turned up noses, who said they thought it silly to wear crash helmets. After ice cream we rode over to Dent over High Barbon which was quite hard work and then back to Sedbergh having bought something to drink in Dent.

On Sunday I went out with the Huxleys. Broadbent came as well. We got in to his Humber, the Aston would not have got us all in, and went to have breakfast in Barbon. We had a jolly good meal, then telephoned Windermere for a yacht but they were all fully booked. Then went after chapel to Windermere to the Low Wood hotel, which is the water ski place and met there some friends of the Huxleys.; they had a beautiful small and glam 19 year old daughter, Caroline. and very spoilt by her parents but a very nice person indeed; we had a picnic lunch at their caravan on the shore and then three of us and Caroline went out in their speed boat, a very powerful one,

Caroline went skiing with us in the boat; then we all tried but could not get properly up. Although there were quite a lot of other people water skiing no one told us how to start. Caroline was quite good but didn't know how to tell us how to do it.

In the evening the three of us were beaten for taking three people out at once (one son and 2 others). We were told that the rule is 2 people for 1 meal or 1 person for tea. We had never heard of this before, and all of us had done it before. [For instance] I went with the Melvilles to Windermere, four of us, making 5 in all.

When one gets to 18 or 17.11 and like the others should have been a prefect last term at least in any other house, one gets rather angry at being beaten unfairly by the Head of house who still regards one on a level with

309

junior day room commoners because we are not prefects. It is easy to take the knocks of [= as] a little guy in the house when one knows that some day one will be a big guy. But it is not so easy when one reaches a stage when one knows one should be a big guy but never will be. It is like the story of the outside cat who remained an outside cat. However this is only a minor point in a very very happy existence and I am lucky enough to say that it is the first and only regret in my life.

Actually if I was a pre I would not be having such a terrific time so maybe it is a good thing really, and it only gets us down when we are beaten which I hope is only once. One of the prefects is completely different to the rest and not a seniority snob or a power bug. In fact he is a jolly 'd' guy and gets more respect from any of us than all the others put together, but he isn't a bit of a popularity bug either. He organises the House discus throwing and training and so consequently I have quite a lot to do with both of these things

[... a para re photography and technical questions of aperture and speed ...]

Do you think that you can send me a packet of those penicillin pills the doc gave me. I am having some more spots coming up again and I am having an anti-spot campaign with eating fruit, etc. But if I go to the san they give me penicillin injections every 3 hours which I do not like.

I got your letter this morning. What a terrific idea about the car. I rather agree with the point that a motor bike has little protection. What about Dear's money?

No date [12 June 60]

Jolly d about the trumpet money[444]. [I expect I will be in need of some by the end of term. What do you mean by 'Put the rest in the bank'? Do you mean the Post Office, or do you think I should put the £10 in the Bank?

Yesterday was Speech Day and unfortunately it was raining and we didn't have a chance of going out anywhere by ourselves. It is raining again now after an early morning bathe on Sunday. This is the second Sunday I have early morning bathed; it is quite a good idea every now and then because you get up an hour or so before breakfast to do things.

Yesterday there were more visitors than ever, well over one thousand people in Powell Hall and as usual there was a ghastly squash. The HM spoke, a list of the benefits of the public school with many rather irrelevant but quite funny jokes. Then Lord Monkton spoke very well but all these sort of people do; then The HM told us that Sedbergh gives most for the amount of money of any school in the country (hear, hear, clap , clap) and no regret that the fees are going up 50 pounds (silence). After speeches and

---

[444] Sold to the School when Sandy gave up lessons

before the service I had to park cars in the pouring rain but it was ok once we had reached our saturation point, and in chapel we got the most comfortable seats.

The concert in the morning was brilliant, quite the best thing that I have ever seen here. It was the Batsman's bride. It had some very good songs. Each song was a skit on something else written the same way. There was a dance to swing, and the fat bowler singing on Handle Allelulia Allelulia chorus to the words of How's that. The village umpire had the most marvellous song in a crackly rustic voice; there was quite a bit of Gilbert and S and a Strauss Waltz and many others. It was so good that all of us who went on Friday went again on Saturday.

As it has rained such a lot we have not been river bathing yet; because it is too suspicious to go out in the rain with mask, flippers etc.

[Plan for a secret midnight exit the next day from the house, armed with coffee and food, to go deer stalking with a camera on Holme Fell...] Winks the tame yank who is Henderson's best friend, is coming with us tomorrow night.

Dear came here yesterday and took Kim and I out. We watched Kim play cricket (he took seven wickets) and then went to Cautley and then to tea in the White Hart; the salmon and strawberries were delicious. We discussed Scotland it sounded great fun to me [a trip by Kim, I think], including the Tattoo and Ben Nevis. I think the starting day is 1ˢᵗ September.

Thank Dad for his letter to the HM; it was a help to me - the letter more than the HM - but I have a copy of this year's syllabus. The paper is divided into three: man, plants, animals. We have done all Man, 90% of animals but no plants at all – under three weeks and we have not yet started! The starting [word illeg.] for plants go on the end of next week or the beginning of the week after next

How very sad about Aunt Pat; I do hope she will be OK. Dear says she is going out quite soon. Jolly good that J has got a job.

I have not forgotten Sally's birthday. I have made the present – it needs touching up (pottery I think).

We have just been fencing, Lionel, Henderson and I; they have all the proper equipment but nobody uses it.

no date [probably 19 June 60]

Thank you for the letter and the enlargement of Sally.

Deer are out, fish hunting is IN! - because it is fantastically hot, even too hot to climb the hills. Saturday was an off day, and Sunday we went bathing and went to our private pool for the day. We took underwater things, masks etc and lo and behold what do you think we saw - fish of 2 ½ to3 lbs – two sea trout under the rocks and some smaller ones upstream. So long as one keeps under water and comes up behind them they take little notice,

311

so we have made a 3 ft stick with a [double spinner] hook stuck into the end, and wrist strap of elastic like this [sketch]. We will have a guard but if anyone comes we are either fishing for eels, or if the possibility were that one had a fish one could always let go. Am dying to try this out and have great hopes. I am sure Hilda would cook a fish for us.

As you can see in one of the photos there is a water's meet, a big salmon pool, 25 yards upstream, but we must learn to walk before we can run.

About the running on Bank Holiday[445] I will either do it with absolute full training or not at all, but the training will be difficult, I would need three weeks before the tennis competitions. Timetable:

Saturday 16 to 23   School Sports
Sunday   2nd last day   Mum comes Tuesday   to Holt
Thursday   travel
Friday   tennis

So you can see it would be difficult to keep up the training and be fit but I could probably manage it, I am sure I would if it were not my last term.

I am sorry to hear that you have to go in for an operation. Hope you can get into the Westminster this time.

I agree with what you say about France this time, but I would love to go to the Highlands, to take photos, climb, fish, shoot. Do ask Dear if she can get us seats for the Edinburgh Festival too. I am sure Kim has not seen it.

Good grief, speaking of Kim I forgot to tell you that he has just won a minor scholarship. Congratulations all round. Really fantastic! He is on Panters Cricket but still on Colts B. He is playing very well and it will not be long before he is recognised[446]. Talking of cricket, I had a good game and made 32 in 15 mins and it gave me much pleasure.

Back to holidays I should like to work at Bryant's garage straight after Lionel's dance (6th). Would come back on the Sunday and could start on the Monday morning. Two weeks would go to the weekend of the 22nd; then to Scotland and back in time for when J gets back. If J gets to Liverpool or Glasgow I could meet him and travel down with him.

Hooray it's speech day in a few days' time.

In Biology we have not spent one minute on anything that is in the O level syllabus. We have been broadening our outlook. All preps as well have been non-O level, tho' it gets us pretty mad.

Had a nice letter from Grandfather.

24 June 60

Last night Saturday night was beautifully clear so the four of us decided to go up to Holme Fell. At 1.00 [a.m.] Lionel went out of the cubes and waited for 5 mins; at 1.05 Winkie went out, at 1.10 Henderson and at 1. 15

---

[445] For a race with the local (Rye or Hastings) Harriers
[446] Kim was on the 1st XI for two years.

I went. Then we changed in our studies and left the house by the library. We drank coffee in a thermos and cheese and mint cake in the bottom of the garden. By a complicated route we reached the bottom of Home Fell. At 2.30 the first faint lights of dawn appeared over Baugh Fell. The sky was completely clear except for very small parts of the horizon. The dawn came in the most wonderful colour producing the most fantastic silhouettes. It was so lovely that we did not even go running after the deer but sat and watched the dawn. I might have some good ones [photos] but I didn't really know what to take it at (whether to expose for the light or the dark. The sun's rays themselves then came across the fells first on the very high tops and gradually falling. As the sky was absolutely clear the sun was very strong and hot. Dawn on a clear day on Holme Fell is one of the loveliest things I have seen.

We came back and trotted past the house and into the swimming pool for an early morning bathe. No one saw us or took any notice; so so far all is ok. I think we have been lucky.

I did not sleep for two seconds last night so this morning we took pack lunches out and slept and sunbathed by the river; but just after two o'clock a water bailiff came along and told us to clear off. We said we had been there for a year now, but he still insisted so we had to go. This is a great pity because of the privacy we will miss; it will be hard to find another place so private. We tried catching fish; there were two big ones there but we couldn't. Alan Barnes of my form told me all about it; apparently the best thing to use is a snare of copper wire around the fish's tail. He is fantastic himself; he goes out in the day, catches them and hides them and collects them at night and goes over to Kendal to sell them at 5 or 6/- a lb to the Fl...[name illeg.] or the Queen's Head. Last summer two of them sold 200 lbs and got 50 pounds, 25 pounds each. It is no tall story as he takes people out with him and comes back from Kendal with 3 or 4 pounds; it should be interesting

I am doing my bullfight talk tomorrow. I sent to the Spanish tourist office and they sent me 12 slides of bullfighting; none were as good as yours (of the kill) which looks splendid in big projection on a screen. I have my foss all written out, I will talk for 20 mins then slides for 15 mins, then 5 mins questions. It should be rather fun now I have the slides.

The general inspection is on Friday with a tattoo in which I am in a platoon attack. The idea of our attack is just to produce big bangs and smoke (we advance through a smoke screen).

I am still not on the tennis six. There are eight of us all within striking distance but only six places. But on Tuesday the tennis master Dave Alban and his wife took the eight of us out, after tennis, to the Lune. We bathed and then had tea and sandwiches, cakes, strawberries and ice cream. Jolly 'd' of him wasn't it.

So glad you have a bed in hospital. So much better to go now than after the hols.

We had haircutting today; my hair has been cut quite well but terribly short, so that I am bald two inches round my ears and all the way up the back.

You will just have had your operation when you get this, so I hope all is well. I expect you will be feeling a little groggy I do hope you will be well enough to come up on Sunday the 24th.

3 July 60 – envelope addressed to MEBL at Westminster Hospital

How wonderful that the operation was so successful. I hope you are having a good convalescence or rest or whatever you call it.

On Saturday I played in the tennis match v the OS; most of them were very good chaps although two of them a little OS-y if you know what I mean, constantly recalling the good old days; 'wasn't it funny when old...' all through tea. The older the OS get the more magnified their pleasant memories become and any unpleasant ones are forgotten until schools sounds 'perfect bliss, the best days of your life, you only have it once young man so make the best of it' etc etc. They aren't far wrong but like the chap in Salad Days' I prefer to add 'so far'. Anyhow they wore a pretty heavy collection of tightly stretched OS sweaters, very simple hearty and pleasant. We had to stop at six when they had a date with the White Hart. It was unfinished and no one worked out who was winning but it seemed to me that they won more sets than us (they had one jolly good pair).

I gave my talk on Saturday morning. The slides were very good and the whole thing was a success. I had two books and diagrams of basic passes. I talked for 20 mins then with slides for 15 and questions were still being fired when the bell went (wasn't it a pity Johansen was knocked out, the thought of a bell reminded me[447]). I could answer all the questions because no one else knew a thing about it except what I had told them, so I was quite safe. I will return the book tomorrow.

Sports training is growing fast. I am doing most of the house training. This is because Beilby is the prefect i/c sports, so I do all discus and such training. No other prefect would even ask my opinion let alone let me do anything.

Sorry about the red biro; I left mine downstairs and have had to borrow one of Winkie's who sleeps in the next cube.

Back to sports again. I will have to do some serious training for the Rye Race! Right at the moment I am wearing my Halo because we all have exams and life has therefore temporarily cooled off.

We have been congregational practices every other day in preparation for the BBC who are here; we also have a full run through off the service and a congregational practice taken by a BBC man. I am expecting to have a microphone right beside me (I am beside a pillar) so if you hear a

---

[447] Presumably some celebrated boxing championship event

crackling noise you will know that it is me eating my potato crisps!. I hope you will get it on the tape.

What plans for the end of term? What day and when will you be arriving?

Please will Dad send me the cheque some time so I can deduct £2 for the end of the term.

It is now rest day, Saturday. I am sending one scrufy [words illeg., looks like *painted fat owl*] for Sally's mantelpiece with the library book.

No date – [probably Monday 11 July 1960, letter to both parents at home]

Thank you for your letter. I posted the parcel this morning so I hope it gets to you soon.

The service yesterday was really rather interesting; to someone in the congregation there was not a sign of broadcasting inside or outside the chapel except 5 mins when the choir, I don't know why, didn't have aerials or anything; the complete lack of equipment was most impressive

During the service I had a transistor set I borrowed and a neighbour and I listened to the lessons and sermon coming over a fraction of a second after the person read it. At one stage my neighbour nudged me to turn it down as it was getting so loud so I gave the volume a quick flick but the wrong way; so half a dozen words seemed to blare out around the chapel; actually it was not very loud; a few people directly in front of us turned round, but no one of consequence – for as said I am under a pillar, and no on of consequence is under a pillar. Did you hear it? Was the singing good? What did you think of the sermon addressed to me?

Do you think you could send me the funniest thing - a Kummerbandt or isn't it a German name – I mean one of those things you wear with a kilt instead of a waistcoat. It is a kilt evening dress isn't it? You see that, like Horse Herbie, a Story goes with it. The story was simply the dos and don'ts and cons the pros. Someone saying that it was a bore to wear a waistcoat or pullover, so a kummerband would do instead; and wondered whether one would be allowed to wear one? But no one will ask. No one would even notice a kummerband if you had your jacket done up most of the time. I remember that Dad had a dark red one; but any colour will do.

The Biology exam is on Thursday so I am not writing a long letter. We still have much of the syllabus to do. I don't know why we don't take O level instead of OA level which is a year in advance; it would be a bird in hand instead of two in a bush.

I will write to you again at Lyndhurst[448] after the exam.

---

[448] Home of the Melville family in the New Forest

20ᵗʰ July 60   To JMBL in Africa – [Term ended 26 July]

I am sure you must be having an exciting time in the Congo. From what you said yourself I thought that you were in Leopoldville on the day of the fight there, but Mummy who rang on Saturday night says you weren't.

Mummy rang up about Kirsty – a terrible thing to happen[449]. Also Mummy does not sound too well and I don't think she will be going to Holt; and I presume that Aunty Jo will not be coming up here now, so I don't know how we are going home; no doubt something will turn up, but I think it is necessary for me to go home as quickly as possible and I will do that.

On Sunday evening we had it all planned to drive out for dinner in Kirby L[onsdale], but as two leavers got sacked a couple of days ago (with only a week to go) we thought that discretion was needed; also Sid wasn't very keen to hire us a car. But we went out on Sunday morning instead.

I am having to take three school exams, physics, and chemistry and an English essay – which is a nice one because one can't swat.

Sports started on Friday. I put my weight standard and won my half mile heat. But the next half mile was before the discus qualifiers, so it was either to try to get into the half final or try the discus. And as I knew I could not come 1ˢᵗ 2ⁿᵈ or 3ʳᵈ in the half because there are some marvellous runners, I tried for the discus; I threw 8 ft over the second qualifier – which won't mean a thing to you but is good enough to get me into the final. Today is the mile, but I doubt if I'll get a place in the final as there are at least for people capable of breaking the record....

I hear that Dear has offered one hundred pounds for a car. That is a wonderfully generous of her; that amount should get a very d car especially with second hand prices shooting down because of the date of the old car tests announced yesterday[450]

Have just rung Mummy up, she sounded much better. Kim and I are going to Holt.

Mummy says she has a car for me – a '46 van – terrific![451]

I have just seen that I am in a reasonable mile heat cheer cheers

---

[449] 10 year old Kirsty, daughter of Logie and Joe, died on the way to hospital after being hit by a car after getting off a bus directly outside the Gresham School gates.

[450] Newly introduced MOTs

[451] A post-script for a leaver. Sandy's last term ended in a sorry story. He and his gang of friends had crept out of the house for a midnight feast, using Sandy's car which had pre-positioned near the Dee. They had a riverside barbecue with fizzy pop and bottles of beer all laid in in advance. Unknown to them, however, there had been a head count in the house when another leaver was spotted returning from having a drink in the town. No action was taken on the morning of leaving school, but Thornely wrote to Sandy a week later asking for an explanation. Sandy, who had been the organiser of the jaunt, accepted the blame; and as a result was told not to re-appear at the school for five years. It was an unlucky blow, and one Sandy resented for a long time afterwards.

APPENDICES

Appendix I
A short comparison with life at School House in the early 1980s

Dugald Bruce Lockhart, SH 1981-86, (Jamie's elder son) compared the picture of life at School House in the 1950s which emerges from the letters with his recollections of house life in the first half of the 1980s.

In no special order, one first reaction was how well read I was and the sheer number of books I read. He did not think he read one book a term outside school work. He was also impressed by my knowledge of and interest in music – 'we never took that kind of an interest. I remember the subscription concerts but they were more about getting out of the house on a Sunday!' Dugald was in the choir too 'but this was generally frowned upon by others and definitely not cool!'

He was interested to see how long it took for me to get the vital jam delivery and the bible which also took ages to get to me: 'I don't think I had much in the way of deliveries of course, because you were overseas, but I remember bringing loads of chocolate and dried onion soup which one mixed with yoghourt - a dip Flip invented in Austria, I think.' The Grubber, he added, was called the same when he was there.

Dugald noted that we had breakfast, or rather were woken, earlier than they were in his day: 'We had the same chanting of the time from the stairs, but from 7.30 until ten to eight; we had to run around and knock on every door shouting 'five minutes to breakfast' before ten to eight and if we were late we had to do 'maps'. A propos, you called the dorms cubes but this we didn't.

Nor did he remember having a 'bootroom' test on songs etc. The fagging, however, was very similar: 'I got a fiver a term from Robin Savage who went on to work for British Aerospace.'

Dugald did, however, 'remember us always hogging the radiators to warm our bums. It seemed from your letters to snow much more in those days, and we never ice skated on Lilymere - Bruce Loch yes. And snowball fights against Sedgwick – yes, we did that too but often would team up with Sedgwick and fight against Hart House. And we were softer than you, and played yard cricket with tennis balls - never a hard ball!'

Dugald pointed out that in our time we seemed to spend (as did many others by our accounts) quite a few days per term in the san - I remember only twice I think being in sick bay but it was at the house - I never went to the san proper.' There were no flu epidemics at school in the 1980s; but Dugald had a very similar experience of having a plaster put on a fracture in A & E in Lancaster – with long, long waits. Water on the knee seemed to be a common illness, especially among tall people with weak legs.

On games and sports, he remarked on 'your rather modest comment on your bowling one term - 3 for 47 is actually very decent! I bowled leg breaks and fast for the house and opened for the first eleven but never scored more than 37 - against Giggleswick I think...'

And he was amazed by the tale of toughness at Sedbergh implicit in the account of Bromley's accident and drowning in the river – 'amazing they made you do those feats in such weather (we also never saw the Rawthey in such a spate - 6ft waves etc!) and thought you wrote in a rather adult way about the event.'

Dugald's general impression was that our generation was apparently 'much more interested in books and culture, and were definitely more grown up than we were, unless you were putting on a good show for the folks!' He was also impressed by my bird watching skills – and 'never saw a tree creeper or bull finch'.

Reviewing accounts of my middle and later years at School House, Dugald had some comments on food. In his time, 'fruit salad, as a Sunday second course, was an unpopular dish. On Tuesdays and Thursdays there were meat dishes – stew and shepherd's pie usually; Friday was fish of course and Wednesday was something fancy like sweet and sour pork balls.' House tap water was rusty and had to be run clean ; and in the early 1980s there was a new lay out of bathrooms altogether. There were six baths downstairs; and the upstairs bath rooms had been converted in to day rooms. 'Showers in the downstairs bathroom, in an extension behind the booter-bathroom and library, were not used – and were considered fleb. We still sat 3 in a bath – comfy to get into - to get warm, not to wash, with mud and dirt at the bottom.'

There were no fortnight orders; and Dugald did not recall a system of merits and distinctions. His recollection was that an Asterisk in the School's termly Brown Books marked school colours? He remembered seeing the inscription inside a desk top of 'Im Schweisse unser Angesichts' in the Modern Language VI classroom.

In Dugald's days fagging was brought to an end; and there was no caning then.

In the dorms, first year boys (only) had to stand by their wash-basins for inspection after washing. He remembered early days of shaving; 'it was cool to have stubble, which could be encouraged by dry scraping with (borrowed) razors. A beard was cool.' As in the 1950s, no scarves (and no gloves of course) were worn until you could wear colours (house or school).

There was no ice rink in the yard but a slide from the gate to the main House door, made by stamping down ice, crushing and walking and then sliding it. There were no extra halves in winter terms. Temperatures were in Celcius; in Dugald's day; Fahrenheit was unknown.

Summer term was much longer in the 1950s. It finished around 6/7 July; the other terms were about the same length, the upshot being in Dugald's days they had a longer summer holiday. Dugald was also given a fly tin as a present at Sedbergh – by me.

There was no house orchestra in Dugald's day. Nor was there a 'Kingfisher' house magazine. But a sailing club at Killington had been founded by then.

There was a phase of inter-cube ragging at ends of term - Junior Dayroom plus prefects and one or two other seniors attacked Middle Dayroom. Dugald got into trouble once for being part of the party although a prefect and was demoted.

On studies at School House, Dugald turned down a single study. It was more fun with company but with each creating his own space. 'Low lighting was the thing – desk lamp, heavy drapes and posters on the wall (mostly to disguise old dirt and damage).'

To his recollection, pubs were near enough yet far enough. He remembered once drinking 4 pints of beer in the Sun at Dent. The Danson room was open 3 times a week, after prep, for 6th formers. Beer was permitted, maximum of 1½ pints, but the Head of School had to be present. In Dugald's day there was a practice in School House of 'House lunches on the private side with the Blackwells. The usual form from the wife of a housemaster was 'Ma' - and sometimes 'Maz'.

Dugald experienced little in the way of day visits from relatives and family friends and exeats. 'They could be confusing anyway and sometimes one did not want the routine of a weekend disturbed by going out in cars for meals. You preferred to carry on. It was upsetting, to be out with parents (not only ones own) because it made one think if home and another possible life. You arrived back in the house with a strange feeling. After being dropped off, all very suddenly, at the top of the house yard – you were in limbo. Unpleasant; you did not want to engage. It then took an hour or so to get over it and get back into the routine of school – so your thought was 'why go through all that?"

Appendix II
What happened to us after Sedbergh School

Jamie

Before going up to St John's College, Cambridge I took a 'gap' eight months in Canada; I worked in the winter in a law office in Hamilton, Ontario, then in the summer I migrated to Northern Ontario and worked first on Roads and Bridges as a labourer; then at two hotels, near North Bay and then on Manitoulin Island, as a general hand and a bell hop. I spent a few weeks as assistant to a piano and organ restorer and a three week holiday in the bush with my Uncle Paddy, his two sons and a friend, camping and fishing with canoes, dropped off at a specific mileage on the cross Canada railroad, far from any habitation.

At St John's I read French and German for Tripos Part I and then switched to economics, partly out of reluctance to engage with Middle High German and mediaeval French. My happiest memories of German are of being taught by two wonderful scholars, Dr J.P Stern and his wife Sheila. Economics intrigued me, and I was soon deeply interested in the economics of less developed countries. My enthusiasm for the subject must have rescued me from a third.

At this point I tried to find work in the developing world, wasting a lot of time looking for a job in Francophone Africa where, in short, Anglo-Saxons were not welcome. The upshot was that I did a year as a trainee in the Credit Lyonnais in Paris where I learnt quite a lot about banking, and brought my French to complete fluency. In the autumn of 1964 I then started as a junior officer with Kleinwort Benson, merchant bankers in the City, for three very enjoyable years at the bottom of the banking ladder. In 1966 I got engaged to Flip, whom I had met at a British Embassy dance held on a bâteau-mouche in Paris in December 1963. I resolved to try again to get into the field of developing countries, and duly obtained – through the Overseas Development Ministry – a three-year contract on the eight-man staff of the Central Planning Office of the Government of Fiji to help write the country's first Five-Year Plan ahead of Independence in 1971. Flip and I were married in February 1967 and went out to Fiji by boat that July – a glorious delayed honeymoon.

They were halcyon days, with a wonderful home life (two sons born there) and many good friends. In the Planning Office I specialised in public finances, the transport sector and the flow of funds in the economy. I was offered further employment with or through the Overseas Development Ministry, but decided I was not trained or cut out by temperament for a career as a professional economist. After a short further spell in banking, as an assistant manager at First National City Bank of New York (later

Citibank), in Fiji, its first branch in the South Pacific, and then in the bank's London office, I found the opening I wanted and joined the Foreign Office via a late entrant scheme at the end of 1972.

Apart from duty in London, I served in Nicosia as Press and Information Officer from 1975 to 1979, in Vienna as First Secretary from 1981 to 1985 and then as a counsellor in Lagos, Nigeria in 1985 to 1988 and, finally, as a political counsellor in Bonn from 1992-1995. It was an immensely enjoyable career, and each posting, in its different way, challenging professionally and exciting personally. I then took retirement in 1996 in order to try something different while fit and ready to experiment.

The following year I went to run a small charitable trust in London, through which I was able to develop pump-priming initiatives in the field of international peace and security. I designed and established a forum for Greek and Turkish dialogue, bringing in the Royal United Services Institute in London as a neutral umbrella organization and the International Peace Research Institute of Oslo (PRIO) in a mediation role. This forum, which came to act in a public advocacy role and as a private back-channel for contacts between the two countries, comprised former senior diplomats, former and current politicians (including at different times four former foreign ministers), military figures and leading academics and working journalists from both countries. With support from the governments of Norway, Britain, Greece and Turkey, the forum (formed at a time of near-breakdown of relations across the Aegean) tackled bilateral questions and some issues relating to Cyprus between 1997 and 2004.

During this period of semi-retirement, I embarked on a series of historical writings focused on nineteenth-century travel in Africa. I transcribed, edited and published in three volumes, the collected travel diaries of Hugh Clapperton, Commander RN (1788–1827), across the Sahara and in West Africa in the 1820s; I wrote several articles on Clapperton, and published research, guided by different academics, on other early journeys of exploration in pre-colonial West Africa, including the Lander Brothers' remarkable Niger journey of 1830. I also wrote a biography of Clapperton in *A Sailor in the Sahara* (IB Tauris, 2007).

Since 1996 I have lived (with my late wife, Flip, who died in 2013) near the coast of north-east Suffolk, where I have held a number of exhibitions of watercolour paintings and regularly sailed and raced my Loch Long, a fifty-year-old, twenty-one-foot classic keel boat, on the estuary at Aldeburgh. I have also written histories of the Loch Long Association and of the class at Aldeburgh for their (75th and 50th respectively) jubilee year in 2012. More recently I have been engaged, with social anthropologist Alan Macfarlane in writings about our respective upbringing and schooling based on family documents and letters home from the Dragon and Sedbergh Schools.

Sandy

From Sedbergh, Sandy went to Cirencester Agricultural College, where he spent three immensely happy years in Bledisloe Lodge and made many good friends. After Cirencester he and Chris Gosling went on a Gap Year journey around the world together - the trip lasted from 1963 to 1965. Sandy left England first and made his way to Southern Rhodesia where he managed for its South African owner a maize farm with 60 staff. But he had met two girls on the boat out to South Africa, one being Tessa Pressland, his future wife, and when Chris Gosling arrived all four set off to travel the length of Africa, climbing Mount Kilimanjaro and travelling up the Nile on a paddle steamer through Sudan, and then via Ethiopia into Aden. They then all went to the Far East and worked and travelled in Australia for another year.

Sandy returned to England by way of South America with Tess, and went to work as a pupil on the farm of our mother's cousin, David Mure, at Pluckley in Kent. The following year he and Tess were married and in 1967, with some modest family help and a large agricultural mortgage, they bought Upper Boycourt Farm, a small cottage surrounded by forty acres of fine land on the weald of Kent, and fourteen Guernsey cows. They arrived at the farm on 25 March 1968 and set about working extremely hard to build the farm into a viable business and to turn the cottage into a large and attractive family home where he lived for forty years.

'The farm', as it was simply known in our family, was also a second home for Flip and me through the twenty years when we lived abroad, and there Sandy and Tess acted as guardians when our sons went, with his children of the same age, to Dulwich College Prep School at nearby Cranbrook.

In the 1980s Sandy took an interest in politics – an interest forged in the milking parlour, where year in year out he listened to Radio 4 for three hours in the morning and three in the evening while attending his cows. He told me that, without recognizing quite how it had happened, he had found himself at home with current political and social affairs and familiar with arguments on both sides of any issue. He duly entered local politics through his connection with the Weald of Kent Preservation Society's rail committee. He accepted chairmanship of the committee and campaigned successfully against the proposed route of the Channel Tunnel rail link which would have damaged much of his beloved countryside. This connection led to him joining the Conservatives. In 1989 he became a county councillor, soon becoming Conservative group leader, and in 1997 leader of the Kent County Council after the defeat of a loose Labour-Liberal Democrat coalition.

The rise of Sandy's political career coincided with a (reluctant) decision to sell his dairy herd (with gross returns under increasing pressure from the European milk quota system). He invested instead in apple orchards at nearby Charing on the edge of the North Downs, buying and renting land to build up a viable farm, on some 300 acres, employing a manager and numerous employees with a large amount of equipment, cold stores, a large packing station and seasonal pickers from Romania.

By 1997 Sandy, who had started out as a critic of local authorities, quickly became one of their greatest defenders. As leader of England's most populous county, with an annual budget of £1bn, 45,000 employees and European politicians beating a path to his door, he was described by the Guardian as 'probably the most powerful Tory in Britain'. During Sandy's leadership, Kent was the first county council to negotiate agreements with central government, pioneering a system that is now part of the local government scene. Sandy became vice-chairman of the Local Government Association for two years and then its chairman from 2004 to 2007, overturning a long period of Labour control, His struggle to make the voice of local authorities heard transcended party politics.

Awarded an OBE in 1995 and knighted in 2003, Sandy became a figure of considerable influence in the Conservative Party and a close adviser to successive leaderships. At the turn of the decade he was operating on a national scale. In conservative politics, he acted not only as chairman of Maidstone East constituency, but also as first vice-chairman, then chairman of the Conservatives' group of south-eastern counties. He was created Baron Bruce Lockhart of the Weald in 2006 and greatly enjoyed the few occasions on which he was able to attend the House of Lords before he suddenly fell ill the following summer.

Sandy stood down from the LGA in July 2007 to become chairman of English Heritage, where he battled hard in the annual spending review, securing a reversal of English Heritage's real-term cash decline for the first time in ten years. It gave him pleasure to be able to get out to inspect or to join in the opening of English Heritage's facilities around the country, but it was not to be for long. Sadly, on 14 august 2008 he died of cancer which he had been fighting bravely since the previous summer.

Among a wide range of charitable interests and commitments, Sandy particularly enjoyed being on the board of trustees of Leeds Castle. He was delighted to be made an Honorary Freeman of the City of Canterbury – and the boy who struggled to get his five 'O' levels at Sedbergh was tickled pink to receive honorary doctorates from the University of Kent and the University of Greenwich.

VISUAL ESSAY

Photographs of home and school life
taken between 1954 and 1960

Ten milers at Green Hill:
Jamie 1959   Sandy 1960

Settlebeck 1955

Millthrop bridge, 1955

Des Sykes, 1955

Uldale Force,

Dear Man and Jamie, Duets at Bemersyde, 1955

Dear at Bemersyde, 1955

Tying casts, Bemersyde 1955

Tennis: Sandy, Jamie and Kirsten, Aldeburgh 1956

Jeb Sulhamstead Fellad, Crufts Sup winner 1955

Sandy, off to school, April 1956

Jamie and MEBL, Dartmouth 1956

Jamie and JMBL, Dartmouth 1956
Myles Moffat, 1955

Rawthey by Riverside, calm pools

Rawthey in spate

School House photograph 1956

Jamie and Sandy c. 1957

MEBL and Jamie, Sedbergh 1957

Jamie and Sandy, Aldeburgh 1956

RAC Country Club, Epsom, 1957 – after haircuts

Ruth Rose, Bem
ersyde,1957

Sandy fishing the Tweed at St Boswell's

Grandfather, Campbell Hone, and Sally
Belbroughton Road, Oxford1957

Granny, Maud Hone, and Sally, Oxford, 1957

Expedition with Jake Durran, Winter 1956
Wilding-Jones, Garbett, Robertson, Whitman, Sandy

School House Jazz band, House concert, 1958

School House jazz band, House Concert 1958

MEBL and Robin Hone, Linlithgow, 1957

Ushers at Wedding of Uncle Robin Hone and Helen Cadell
In centre of five boys in kilts: Jock Stein (Sedgwick House, cousin of
Helen),; to his left, Sandy, Jamie

Jamie, 1958, with blue house colours scarf

Westwick, Rye
Sandy in background, JMBL and Sally
J and S's room at top of gable, with a sea view

Freiburg im Breisgau, dancing party, Easter holidays 1958

MEBL, Pic du Midi d'Orsay, Pyrenees, 1958

Tennis, St Jean de Luz, 1958

Tennis at Rye, 1959
Peter Brodrick, Rob Christie, Jamie
Rosie Bayley, Sarah Hobbs, S
arah Andrews
Sandy

School House swing band
House concert, 1959

Green Hill, Ten Mile race, 1959
Jamie and Simon Lowis

Le Rochecorbon, Tours, 1959

School House photograph, Summer term 1959

Sandy, Wilding Jones, Huxley, Broadbent on Pen y Gent, Summer 1958

Wilding Jones, Sandy, Huxley, Broadbent, Pen-y-Gent

Lionel Melville and Sandy, Sunday dress

Bielers Bielby 1959

John Broadbent, 1969
note double sided blue house scarf worn as a turban for warmth

Holme Fell waiting for dawn, March 1959

Dawn from Holme Fell, 1959

Barbon Expedition,
Lune valley meadow after lunch; Sandy and Beilby

Broadbent and Huxley – listening to music

Barbondale, 1960 photo by Jake Durran (his new Landrover)
Lewis, Bendle, Bielby, Melville, Sandy, Broadbent, Huxley

Barbon hill climb

Sandy's caption: 'Broadbent watching the races'

Huxley, Dentdale

Lionel Melville and Sandy 1959

Summer 1959, expedition with Jake Durran (who took the photo)
L to R: Huxley, Robertson, Sandy, Wilding Jones, Broadbent

Andy Robertson

Picnic by the Lune en route to Barbon Races
Sandy, Beilby, Henderson in tidy cricket clothes

L to R: Watson, Sandy, Melville on Baugh Fell

Three Peaks from Sedbergh on foot in one day; atop Ingleborough:
Sandy, Fawcett, Huxley, Berry, Broadbent

Jake Durran's car
Huxley, Robertson, Sandy, Wilding Jones, Broadbent

Drinking from Stream,
Pen – y Ghent, 1959

Watson, and Elvis 1959

Sandy, on Cautley section of Ten Mile race, 1960

Sandy finishing in 10th place in 1 hr 17 mins
in the Ten Mile race 1960

Jamie and Sandy at Rye – Sandy taller for first time

Cousin Kim, A. K. Bruce Lockhart, School House 1960-65,
and Jamie, Rye Harbour, January 1960

Family gathering for Hogmanay at Gresham's, Holt 1961
J at Cambridge, S at Cirencester
Back row: Malcolm, Kim, Jenny, Jamie, Sandy, Karen, Rhu
Middle: Rab, JMBL, Logie
Front row: Jo holding Kirsty, Freda, Dear, MEBL, Pip

A collection of sketches made at Sedbergh
by my grandfather, J. H. Bruce Lockhart, Headmaster of the Sedbergh
School and housemaster of School House, 1936 – 1954.
The drawings were culled from his sketch books by my grandmother,
Mona Bruce Lockhart, in the early 1960s.

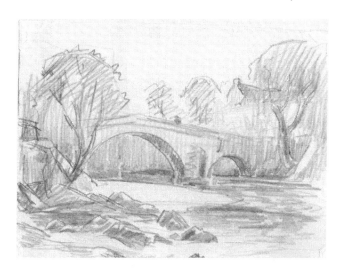

Millthrop Bridge downstream over the shingle bank

Rawthey in snow

Lilymere, second boathouse

Lune viaduct and pool

Watersmeet, the Rawthey and the Lune

School Chapel

361

Printed in Great Britain
by Amazon

35226829R00217